DEATH BLOW TO JIM CROW

The John Hope Franklin

Series in African American

History and Culture

WALDO E. MARTIN JR.

AND PATRICIA SULLIVAN,

EDITORS

DEATH BLOW TO JIM CROW

*The National Negro Congress
and the Rise of Militant Civil Rights*

ERIK S. GELLMAN

The University of

North Carolina Press

Chapel Hill

© 2012
The University of
North Carolina Press
All rights reserved
Manufactured in
the United States
of America

Designed by
Jacquline Johnson
Set in Minion
by Tseng Information
Systems, Inc.

The paper in this book meets the guidelines for permanence
and durability of the Committee on Production Guidelines
for Book Longevity of the Council on Library Resources.

The University of North Carolina Press has been a member
of the Green Press Initiative since 2003.

Library of Congress Cataloging-in-Publication Data
Gellman, Erik S.
Death blow to Jim Crow : the National Negro Congress and the
rise of militant civil rights / Erik S. Gellman.
p. cm. — (The John Hope Franklin series in African American
history and culture)
Includes bibliographical references and index.
ISBN 978-0-8078-3531-9 (cloth : alk. paper)
1. National Negro Congress (U.S.)—History. 2. Southern Negro
Youth Congress—History. 3. African Americans—Segregation—
History—20th century. 4. African Americans—Civil rights—
History—20th century. 5. Race discrimination—United
States—History—20th century. 6. Civil rights movements—
United States—History—20th century. 7. African Americans—
History—1877–1964. 8. United States—Race relations—History—
20th century. I. Title.
E185.61.G278 2012
323.1196′073—dc23   2011022145

16 15 14 13 12   5 4 3 2 1

Contents

Illustrations

Acknowledgments

This project began through conversations with Hilmar Jensen at Bates College. Hilmar's soft-spoken intellect convinced me to study history, and his scholarship on John P. Davis led me to focus on the National Negro Congress. In graduate school, my Northwestern committee—Mike Sherry, Martha Biondi, and chair Nancy MacLean—provided invaluable insights and encouragement. Mike Sherry's "so what?" question still rings in my ears, and his careful reading of my work helped tremendously. Martha Biondi's commitment to struggles for justice and deep knowledge of African American history forced me to rethink how to be a historian, as well as sharpened my analysis. Her support and advice during the revision process have proven essential. Nancy MacLean became everything I had hoped for and more as an intellectual mentor, and her critique of numerous drafts of this work helped immeasurably. In addition, she nudged me to become involved in Chicago history projects, civil rights litigation, and local unions, all of which have informed my academic work. I am proud to continue to seek her mentorship even if she insists on treating me as a colleague.

In addition to my formal committee, a number of professors and fellow students at Northwestern critiqued chapters, outlines, proposals, and other fragments of ideas that went into this book. Thanks especially to Darlene Clark Hine, who has offered me expert advice and comments on all aspects of my scholarship and teaching. I also value the friendly advice and conversation with Lane Fenrich, Jon Glassman, Mike Kramer, Kate Masur, Susan Pearson, and Will Reno. But it's really your colleagues who have the opportunity and burden to watch you struggle, thrive, and, on occasion, embarrass yourself. Michael Allen, Justin Behrend, Kate De Luna, Greg Downs, Abram and Kristen Van Engen, Brett Gadsden, Alex Gourse, Neil Kodesh, Jenny Mann, Jana Measells, Gayle Rogers, and David Sellers Smith all made life at Northwestern vibrant and memorable. Each of them had an impact on this book. In addition to these colleagues, a few others went beyond the call. Guy Ortolano made several trips to the Tamiment Library to look at photographs. Ronnie Grinberg read innumerable drafts and provided essential feedback. Debs Cane gave blunt advice, sometimes with a cackle, and had to live with me during some of the rough writing stages. Jarod Roll did so as well, which may explain why he moved across the Atlantic Ocean. Since then, in writing scholarship together, Jarod has become a true collaborator and has read and critiqued every page of this book.

Over the past decade, I have come to understand why Nelson Algren embraced Chicago as "this particular patch" and defined it as "never a lovely so real." My own embrace of Chicago stems from finding excellent sparring partners and colleagues across the city over the years. Leon Fink, Adam Green, and Jim Grossman have provided essential insight into African American and labor history through formal and informal conversations over these years, and I look forward to continuing collaborative work with each of them. The participants in the Newberry Labor History Seminar have never been at a loss for debate, both in session and at the bar afterward. My colleagues at the Chicago Center for Working-Class Studies—especially Carrie Breitbach, Bob Bruno, Winifred Curran, Jeff Helgeson (now in Texas), Jack Metzgar, and Liesl Orenic—pushed me to become more invested in Chicago's neighborhoods and have shown me how to make ideas matter in public forums. I have also found Chicagoans who have committed their livelihoods to struggles for justice and who have flattered me by allowing me to labor with them. Bill Dempsey of UFCW; Elce Redmond of South Austin Coalition; Susan Hurley of Jobs with Justice; James Thindwa of Chicago ACTS; Mike Pitula of LVEJO; Alexis Canalos, Jessica Lawlor, and Carrie Sallgren of UNITE-HERE represent just a few of the many activists and organizers who have taught me more about protest politics than I could ever teach them.

Most of all, however, 430 South Michigan has become my center of gravity in Chicago since 2006. My colleagues and students at Roosevelt University have exceeded my high expectations for a school founded and run on the basis of social justice. Leon Stein and Susan Weininger welcomed me into Roosevelt's community. Celeste Chamberlain, Chris Chulos, Sandra Frink, Fabricio Prado, and Margaret Rung have made the Department of History a congenial place. My philosopher neighbors, Stuart Warner and Zarko Min-

kov, have also made the department a lively intellectual home. I have bene-
fited from the insights and friendship of Jeff Edwards, Stephanie Farmer,
Michael Ensdorf, June Lapidus, Mike Maly, and Sam Rosenberg. I look forward to further Drake Center coordination with Al Bennett, Kim Ruffin,
Jacqueline Trussell, and Joel Okafur. My faculty mentor, Ellen O'Brien, has
gone well beyond her job description, mixing sage advice with witty remarks.
My colleagues at the Mansfield Institute, especially Heather Dalmage, Nona
Burney, Steven Meyers, and Nancy Michaels, have made service work feel not
at all like work. Retired professors never seem to leave Roosevelt, which has
allowed me to seek out the mentorship of Charles V. Hamilton, Jack Metzgar,
and Christopher Reed. Roosevelt also harbors historians outside of the history department, including the always-engaging Brad Hunt and Carl Zimring
down the street at the Evelyn T. Stone College of Professional Studies, and I
am especially thankful for the support from the historian who also happens
to be the Dean of Arts and Sciences, Lynn Weiner.

This book, though, became a reality through the patience and amenability
of a number of archivists and librarians across the country. Thank you to
Joellen ElBashir at the Moorland-Spingarn at Howard University in Wash-
ington, D.C.; Tab Lewis at the National Archives in Washington, D.C.; Jennie
Levine at the University of Maryland; William LeFevre at the Walter P. Reuther
Library at Wayne State University in Detroit; Michael Flug and Beverly Taylor at the Vivian Harsh collection at the Carter G. Woodson branch of the
Chicago Public Library; Les and Linn Orear at the Illinois Labor Historical
Society in Chicago; Stephen McShane at Calumet Regional Archives in Gary;
the reading room staff from the Chicago Historical Museum; Gene Vrana at
the International Longshore and Warehouse Union Archive in San Francisco;
Sue Englander and Lauren McCoy of the Martin Luther King Papers project
for their help with research in the special collections at Stanford University
in Palo Alto; Catherine Powell at the Labor Archives and Research Center
at San Francisco State University; Erika Gottfried and Gail Malgreen at the
Tamiment Library at New York University; Tracy Drummond at the Georgia State University's Southern Labor Archives in Atlanta; and Stan Piet at
the Glenn L. Martin Maryland Aviation Museum. I also appreciate the assistance of research staff members at the Library of Virginia in Richmond; Virginia Union University in Richmond; the Bancroft Library at the University of
California in Berkeley; the Beinecke Library at Yale University in New Haven;
the Schomburg Center for Research in Black Culture at the New York Public
Library; the South Caroliniana Library at the University of South Carolina in

Columbia; the Robert W. Woodruff Library at Emory University in Atlanta; the Southern California Library for Social Studies and Research in Los Angeles; and the Southern Historical Collection of the Wilson Library at the University of North Carolina in Chapel Hill. The most important acknowledgment, however, goes to Northwestern's Victoria Zahrobsky, who managed to obtain rare books, microfilm, and other key sources from around the world, which saved me from even more research trips.

This book has gone through revisions that made it much stronger, thanks to Chuck Grench at the University of North Carolina Press, his assistant Rachel Surles, and associate managing editor Paula Wald. Michael Honey provided an incredibly thorough report of this project at two different stages. Each report highlighted overarching themes as well as particular details and offered a clear blueprint for revision. I also want to thank the anonymous author of an early reader report who challenged me to rethink key aspects of my argument, especially in the chapters concerning Chicago and Washington, D.C. Finally, the incredibly detailed and thoughtful critique of Waldo Martin sharpened both the analysis and the context of my arguments, which carried me to the finish line. In addition to these readers, I benefited from conversations about the National Negro Congress with Joe Allen, Eric Arnesen, Bruce Baker, Timuel Black, John Breihan, Peter Cole, Cindy Hahamovitch, Toby Higbie, Will Jones, Alex Morrow, Scott Nelson, Kim Phillips, Lisa Phillips, Ian Roxborough-Smith, Danny Schulman, Tom Sugrue, Kerry Taylor, and Jim Wolfinger. Simon Balto and Lauren Lowe, both former students, edited the entire manuscript with great care, and Elisa Caref read and indexed it. I have labored to implement their suggestions, and only now can I fully appreciate why so many historians claim that any remaining errors belong only to the author.

I cannot overstate the generosity and wisdom of Thelma (Dale) Perkins in discussing the National Negro Congress. In May 2003, Mrs. Perkins allowed me to visit her in Chapel Hill for an entire week. The resulting conversations about her experiences provided a window into the NNC that other sources did not offer. I also want to thank a handful of others for similarly invaluable conversations: Esther Cooper and James Jackson, Ishmael Flory, Margaret Goss Taylor Burroughs, Leslie Orear, and Thomas Fleming.

Friends have come and gone from Chicago over the past decade while I stayed put. Sara Bryant, Scott LaPierre, John Pham, and Tania Ralli defined my early Chicago experience. Dan Gleason, Anna Fenton-Hathaway, Joanne Diaz, Jason Reblando, Nat Small, and Stefanie Bator are among the many people who give shape to my life in the city now. But no person has become more important to me than Liz McCabe. Her kindness, patience, and ability to distract me make everything so much better. Thank you, Liz, for making innumerable small and large contributions in helping me bring this book to fruition.

My family has sustained me with inspiration and encouragement. My grandmother Elizabeth Gellman, from a Jewish working-class South Carolina family, never ceased to amaze me with her artistic talents and wit. And her husband from Niagara Falls, Jack Gellman, showed me compassion through action and taught me the importance of a casual wink and smile. I have had great support from my extended family in western New York. All of the Zaretskys—Deborah, Allen, Ben, Josh, and Michael—have inspired me by their own examples. The Gellmans, especially Sonia and Hannah, have always cheered me on and made the effort to stay close. My Danish family— Dorthe, Gunn, Bent, and Mormor—have given me warmth and joy from afar and have welcomed me in Denmark with open arms. But most of all, I thank my father, George, who proofread every line of the manuscript; my mother, Bodil; and my brother, Ken. Your generosity and unwavering support made all of this possible.

Introduction

In May 1935, a dozen top black intellectuals and civil rights advocates, in collaboration with a handful of white allies, came together at Howard University to take "a candid inventory of the position of the Negro in our national economic crisis." John Preston Davis, a Harvard-trained black intellectual and leading critic of the New Deal, introduced the three days of discussions by saying, "The first word is mine. But the last word is yours." Despite the passage of a wide array of New Deal reforms, more than 4 million out of 12 million African Americans remained in poverty. "Looking fifty years into the future," Davis portended, "nothing is presented for the Negro except maintenance of his inferior status by government fiat." To reverse this dire prediction, Davis called for a radical restructuring of American values. He believed a mass movement needed to coalesce that would force the government to shift emphasis from "private property to protection of human beings." While other speakers differed on strategy, all agreed with the urgency of Davis's remarks. T. Arnold Hill of the National Urban League declared that "if the present trend continues," black workers would enter a state of "economic peonage, every bit as devastating as plantation slavery." If, however, African Americans "maintained a faith" of organizing black workers, "sufficient strength can be gathered" to then join "forces of white labor to halt . . . a future of permanent relief." Drawing on his ten years of experience organizing the Brotherhood of Sleeping Car Porters (BSCP), Asa Philip Randolph also advocated for a labor approach to economic uplift. Black workers "not only must organize themselves," he said, "but what is as important, they must pay the price in suffering, sacrifice, and struggle" because only "economic power" would bring about the larger goal of "industrial and political democracy." The conference produced so much alarm that a group of its participants vowed to make it more than a talkfest; they held over in Washington to devise a new organization, which they named the National Negro Congress (NNC).[1]

This book tells the story of how the NNC and its independent youth affiliate, the Southern Negro Youth Congress (SNYC), demanded and attempted to enact a "second emancipation" for African Americans between 1936 and 1947. Although the NNC and the SNYC began as separate organizations, this study treats them as a single activist network since the two groups overlapped in members and shared common objectives. At its peak, this network boasted over seventy-five NNC and SNYC councils across the nation. This study explains how the NNC became the black vanguard of the Popular Front, a coalition broadly defined as interracial, labor-based alliances of radicals and liberals in America who united to expand New Deal reforms and beat back what they saw as an alarming growth of fascism, both at home and abroad.[2] Moreover, the chapters that follow explain how NNC members acted within this Popular Front coalition to help launch the first successful industrial labor movement in the United States and remake urban politics and culture in America. This study delineates how the NNC fostered and tried to sustain these strategic alliances, which crossed class, gender, and racial lines to generate the most militant interracial freedom movement since Reconstruction. Moreover, it addresses an unsettled question in modern American history: how, in the crucible of depression and war, did African Americans and their allies find ways to mortally weaken Jim Crow, if not deal it the "death blow" they had hoped for?

By focusing on the NNC, I put a black-led network at the center of a narrative usually dominated by white unionists, New Dealers, Communists, and other antifascist leaders. Historians of the Great Depression and the Second World War have chosen these subjects because they left more immediately obvious legacies. During this period, labor unions rose from the ashes of previous defeats to become a political force in the lives of American workers for the next several decades.[3] White ethnics formed coalitions to demand relief, employment, and security.[4] In fighting the Second World War, America destroyed fascist dictatorships abroad. After the war, the United States became a world power, reconverting its political economy in an increasingly Cold War climate.[5] All of these dramatic transformations have been documented by historians, but analysis of African American civil rights across this tumultuous era as a dominant theme of American history remains less explored.[6]

The Cold War largely banished the NNC's legacy from popular memory.

Indeed, McCarthyism's victims became guarded and activists were reluctant to discuss their experiences or preserve the record of their activism during the Depression era.[7] By the 1960s, this silence began to lift. Scholars who were influenced by the black-led mass movement of their day began to look back to the 1930s and 1940s and piece together what they saw as a significant "prelude" to the movement that emerged later.[8] Encouraged by these pioneering studies, a larger group of post–Cold War revisionist historians placed African Americans within the narratives of the burgeoning industrial labor movement, the New Deal, and the Communist Party orbit. Some addressed how black and white workers interacted within labor unions and industries.[9] Others looked more closely at how activists fought to expand the New Deal's democratic reach.[10] A third group has shown that liberals worked alongside Communists to organize workers into unions, foster new forms of working-class culture, and fight for racial justice.[11] The cumulative work of these scholars has made it possible to comprehend what Jacqueline Dowd Hall has termed the "decisive first phase" of "the long civil rights movement."[12]

Yet because no one has examined the era's most militant civil rights federation, the NNC, the black-led Popular Front chapter of the movement remains obscure.[13] Since the demise of the NNC in 1947 and the SNYC soon thereafter, these two organizations have been given only cursory mention in books about the labor movement, civil rights, and radicalism. In addition, scholars have evoked the name of the NNC as a hand grenade in debates about the Communist Party's role in black freedom movements, as well as those concerning interracial versus black nationalist strategies for racial advancement.[14] While all of these studies informed this one, I argue that we need to understand the NNC through the mind-set of its core group of activists, who crossed lines of class and race within labor, government, and urban communities. Following this network of people through the twists and turns of the New Deal, Second World War, and postwar reconversion illuminates how the NNC helped challenge the dire predictions of economic peonage and second-class citizenship for African Americans made by the black intellectuals at the Howard University conference in 1935. Just as important, the process shows how the NNC struggled, stumbled, regrouped, and battled again to contribute to a decade of shifting economic, political, and cultural transformations, from the local neighborhood to the international stage.

The NNC challenged the underpinnings of Jim Crow by engaging in a variety of militant forms of activism. To be sure, the militant tactics employed by the NNC—including pickets, boycotts, and marches—were not new. The

Knights of Labor, International Workers of the World, and other labor unions had endorsed confrontational tactics, albeit often segregated by race and without successful results. Moreover, the NNC looked back to the first emancipation of the 1860s to recover the history of black resistance movements so that it could then apply these strategies to its contemporary struggle against Jim Crow. In the decade prior to the NNC's formation, African Americans witnessed the rise of Marcus Garvey's movement, which mobilized thousands of blacks for marches and parades sponsored by the United Negro Improvement Association. Yet since the NNC sought to eschew black separatism, it often downplayed this particular model of militant protest even as its members, including some who had been in the Garvey movement, took tactical lessons from it. And just before the NNC's formation, Communists and Socialists organized the unemployed and hungry in local campaigns at which people demonstrated in large numbers. Thus, the NNC did not invent militant forms of resistance, but its leaders combined several strands of protest movements from African American history, the labor movement, and radical political parties into a black-led, interracial, mass movement that catalyzed both labor unions and black advancement organizations to see these tactics as necessary and employ them across urban America.[15]

To apply these tactics on a mass scale, the NNC had to organize people and organizations into a broad alliance. The NNC's core network, consisting of a few hundred dedicated activists, connected isolated pockets of antiracist resistance and coordinated them into a national movement. Local councils brought together racial, labor, cultural, and religious institutions, whose members represented hundreds of thousands of African Americans, and these larger coalitions pressured unions, New Deal agencies, and other institutions to provide equal access for blacks. The NNC tackled a range of issues in different localities, which included fair employment, protection from extralegal violence, evenhanded distribution of New Deal benefits, and sanitary living conditions. Its activists saw these forms of discrimination as symptomatic of the larger problem of racialized laissez-faire American capitalism, which had bolstered the federal government's retreat from protecting the rights of its citizens.

The NNC differed from previous national civil rights groups because it confounded class and racial boundaries. The NNC, according to A. Philip Randolph, would set "a great precedent on the part of Negro workers" and "their sympathetic allies" by "destroying all of the poisonous seeds of jim-crowism."[16] Its leaders breached lines of middle-class respectability by persuading African American communities to embrace boycotts, strikes, and marches. These tactics required members to use the streets as spaces of negotiation, breaking from other black leaders who met privately with welfare capitalists they hoped to persuade. Its members anticipated that these public tactics would foster new forms of community among African Americans. Then, from a position of power generated through unity, the NNC hoped to ally blacks with labor campaigns for economic justice. This process allowed NNC leaders to avoid what they saw as an either/or trap of integration or nationalism. The NNC's activist-intellectuals agreed that race in America was less a moral issue than a material one and less a southern problem than a national one. In short, the NNC saw the working class as having the potential power to force U.S. institutions to protect human rights above property rights. This conception of industrial democracy was the NNC's American Creed.

Because white Americans had planted so many "poisonous seeds," the NNC's mission "to express the struggle of the Negro on all fronts" caused recurrent problems for its activists.[17] As radical reformers, NNC members had to appeal to African Americans, labor movement leaders, political party members, and government officials, while simultaneously pushing their own militant antiracist agenda. As the political context shifted, the NNC increasingly looked to the Communist Party and the left wing of the CIO (Congress of Industrial Organizations) for support. I argue that although the NNC used these allies to enable much of its activism, these ties also tragically hampered associations with other New Deal and urban African American constituencies. Meanwhile, conservative employers and government forces like the Dies Committee, a congressional committee headed by Martin Dies Jr. of Texas that investigated "un-American activities," exploited tensions within this Popular Front coalition to sap the NNC's strength. This book explores the contradictory beliefs that NNC members held and the tough decisions they made about how to sustain their movement. Rather than condemning or applauding the NNC for its decisions, I examine how it sought to hold its coalition together without losing its militant antiracist vision.

This book is the first study of the NNC but is not intended to be the last. It does not explore the activities of all seventy-five of its councils across the country, but rather it analyzes five regions where the NNC and the SNYC, during particular chronological periods, had significant influence.[18] Examining local contexts parallels the NNC's own priorities. Unlike the National Association for the Advancement of Colored People (NAACP), the NNC functioned as an organization of organizations and required its members to work within broader coalitions like labor unions, churches, and civic groups. This strategy entrenched NNC advocates in community organizing, while simultaneously putting them in the larger NNC network to demolish Jim Crow in all of its forms. This study flows then from the local to the national and even international, rather than from the top leadership to the local councils. That said, this book does not attempt to list and discuss the histories of every local organization that allied with the NNC. While the NNC ultimately desired to represent hundreds of organizations whose cumulative membership numbered millions of Americans—and it demonstrated this broad reach on particular occasions through national conferences and mass mobilizations—in reality the NNC consisted of a core group of members who did the bulk of the planning and organizing on a day-to-day basis. This study traces the history of this core network and places it within the wider context of the labor movement, political parties, government bodies, and other organizations only when the NNC became active collaborators (or enemies) with these other groups.

My exploration of the NNC begins where it held its inaugural 1936 conference—Chicago. Following the conference, black industrial workers (until then largely excluded from unions and forced to be strikebreakers to obtain industrial jobs) joined the new CIO's steel and packinghouse unions in large numbers. NNC leaders in Chicago, I argue, convinced workers to join these unions, which then became their "strategic grip" to initiate working-class and antiracist protests.[19] The narrative next moves south to Richmond, Virginia, and the creation of an offshoot of the NNC, the Southern Negro Youth Congress. In the former confederate capital, SNYC members allied with black tobacco workers to form an independent black-led union movement "in defiance of custom and tradition."[20] The chapter explains how young black southerners allied with older black workers to change the "Virginia Way" of race relations, but also how unions, politicians, and southern liberals thwarted the aggressive challenge of the SNYC by 1940. The third chapter focuses on activism against racial violence in the nation's capital. The local council in Washington, D.C., crusaded against lynching and police brutality as two similar forms of what it termed "domestic fascism." To obtain physical protection for African Americans, NNC activists amassed political pressure to win gains in economic security as well.

After an interlude that explains the dramatic split of the NNC at its 1940 Washington, D.C., convention, the concluding chapters examine the NNC during the Second World War and after. These chapters explain how new wartime circumstances proved enervating in some ways but also offered new opportunities for the NNC in New York City. During the war, a remarkable group of black women "held down the fort" and transformed the NNC back into a fighting organization. Last, the narrative travels 700 miles south to Columbia, South Carolina. This chapter examines how SNYC membership in the postwar era grew in the Palmetto State due to the application by its leaders of novel forms of activism based on an international yet grassroots politics, as well as the SNYC's open challenge to Jim Crow in the South, which foreshadowed the southern mass movements on the horizon.

Together these chapters explain how the NNC reoriented American protest politics in an attempt to realize its postwar motto: "Death Blow to Jim Crow." Its members opened new sectors of employment to black workers, demonstrated against extralegal violence, and resurrected a proud African American culture based upon the history of the Civil War and the Reconstruction era. While accomplishing these tasks, the NNC always stressed interracial brotherhood and pushed for larger multiethnic coalitions of workers to address civil rights. In a pervasive environment of racism, these contacts across the color line turned some white workers into allies for African American rights, and even staunch racists had to contend with a direct challenge to their views for the first time in a half century. This movement did not imagine race relations as an intellectual dilemma or a seedbed for the next generation. Its activists remade the American labor movement into one that wielded powerful demands against industrialists, white supremacists, and the state as never before, positioning civil rights as an urgent necessity.

Let Us Build the National Negro Congress

During the half century before the formation of the National Negro Congress (NNC), the federal government developed a Jim Crow society based on a national ideology of white supremacy. Between the demise of Reconstruction in the 1870s and the turn of the century, southern governments disfranchised southern blacks and poor whites, barred them from all but the most exploitative employment opportunities, and denied them protection under the law. For example, only 28 of 604 Supreme Court cases concerning the Fourteenth Amendment between 1868 and 1911 dealt with the civil rights of African Americans. During this period, courts used the Fourteenth Amendment to protect corporate interests rather than enforcing its original intent of protecting U.S. citizenship rights. Yet during the 1910s and 1920s, industrial job openings, persistent racial terrorism, and a decline in cotton prices led to a northward migration of 1.5 million blacks. These blacks gained the franchise by moving out of the South, subsequently becoming a significant block of voters in northern cities. They also realized, however, that other forms of Jim Crow discrimination in housing, jobs, and civil liberties existed above the Mason-Dixon Line.[1]

The onset of the Great Depression made the federal government potentially receptive to the demands of African Americans. In May 1932, presidential candidate Franklin Delano Roosevelt called for "bold, persistent experimentation," because "the millions who are in want will not stand idly by silently forever while the things to satisfy their needs are within easy reach."[2] Americans took Roosevelt seriously and after the election made new demands on the federal government for reform. "At the heart of the New Deal," historian Richard Hofstadter surmised, "was not a philosophy but a temperament."[3] Roosevelt left the experimentation open to interpretation, inspiring interest groups to organize and push for reform within the New Deal's broker state.[4]

African Americans, however, had few large-scale organizations in the early 1930s to make claims on the state. During the previous two decades, black social service agencies in northern cities had focused more on accommodating the hundreds of thousands of newcomers than on organizing them into a politically potent constituency. With the onset of the Depression, economic hardship undermined many of these race-based institutions, leaving a void in professional leadership. The NAACP, for example, had "tracked a steady upward path during the 1920s," historian Patricia Sullivan explained, but two years later "was perched on the edge of bankruptcy" because it "was dependent upon a segment of the population hardest hit by the collapse." Meanwhile, the National Urban League confirmed through research studies an alarming level of unemployment among black workers, but the league lacked the forces or method to reduce the trend since its job placement division and funding from white employers dried up with the economic crisis. These organizations would regroup later in the 1930s, but often with a new set of politics and protest strategies. The NAACP debated strategies for working-class and economic advancement at its 1933 Amenia conference, which showed the organization's openness, at least rhetorically, to new approaches. But meanwhile, black nationalists, Communists, Socialists, and others filled some of this void by orating on street corners and marching against spreading hunger and homelessness. With space for new leadership and respite from migration, the Depression created the potential for fostering new forms of protest politics in black urban communities.[5]

One group that had already experimented with these new forms of protest was the Brotherhood of Sleeping Car Porters (BSCP). In 1925, A. Philip Randolph, a Florida-born minister's son and prominent black Socialist in New York City, took on the role as BSCP president. The BSCP had to fight not only against the Pullman Company and the American Federation of Labor (AFL) for recognition, but also against black public opinion. According to Randolph, in the 1920s unions "had become anathema in the eyes of the Negro generally, because of the feeling that Negro workers were discriminated against by white labor unions." Black clergy and other civic leaders took money and other patronage from white employers and saw an alliance with management, not workers, as a route to place blacks into job openings. Randolph and other porters fought this mentality in the late 1920s, but like other African American groups, the onset of the Depression decimated the membership of the BSCP, which dropped from about 7,000 in the late 1920s to only 771 by 1932. Thereafter, the BSCP, bolstered during the New Deal when the National Mediation Board awarded it exclusive bargaining rights for Pullman porters, began to reverse the momentum of decline. As a result, the BSCP successful pressured the AFL's Executive Council to grant the union a charter in 1935. The union was still far from securing a union contract from the Pullman Company, but its years of activism had opened the minds of many African Americans to the possibility of unions as a means of racial advancement.[6]

Meanwhile, the largest generation of college-educated black youth came of age in the 1930s. The enrollment of African Americans in colleges increased sharply in the 1920s as welfare capitalists redoubled their philanthropic efforts. Although Langston Hughes, after visiting several campuses in 1932, called these black students the "Cowards from the Colleges" for their social conservatism, students at Howard, Virginia Union, and Fisk soon thereafter became politically active.[7] At Fisk, Ishmael Flory and Lyonel Flourant created a student group called the Denmark Vesey Forum. In December 1933, they protested the lynching of Cordie Cheek, a young black man who had lived only a block from campus. As a result of their activism, Fisk administrators expelled Flory and pressured Flourant to transfer. Both of these student leaders later became active NNC and Southern Negro Youth Congress (SNYC) leaders, making a choice to use their education for militant activism rather than to become part of what W. E. B. Du Bois and others had previously defined as a "talented tenth" of educated blacks who should uplift the race through respectable behavior and professional pursuits.[8] Though not as militant as Flory and Flourant, the vast majority of black students graduated in the 1930s without job prospects, making them a talented yet restless tenth open to new forms of protest politics. And this tenth began to cooperate with young white college students who found themselves in a similar predicament. Aubrey Williams, the white director of the New Deal's National Youth Administration, reported in 1935 that as many as 8 million Americans between the ages of sixteen and twenty-five were "wholly unoccupied."[9]

Another important development during the early 1930s was the new visibility of "Reds" in urban black neighborhoods. The Communist Party (CP) responded to the crisis of the Depression by organizing Unemployed Councils, which staged interracial demonstrations at relief stations to demand unbiased government assistance. Within black neighborhoods, the CP formed tenant organizations that reversed evictions and exposed abhorrent living conditions. The CP, however, would not have made such inroads into black communities were it not for the party's response to the arrest of nine young African American men on March 25, 1931, just outside of Scottsboro, Alabama. On that day, the "Scottsboro Boys" were charged with raping two white women aboard a freight train. The International Labor Defense, formed in 1925 as the legal arm of the CP, convinced the defendants' mothers to allow its lawyers to serve as defense counsel. The mass marches and meetings, financial appeals, and press accounts of the trials would eventually save the defendants from execution and convince many African Americans of the sincerity of the party's fight against racial injustice. As Revels Cayton, the NNC's executive secretary after the war, explained about these early 1930s activities, "It was through the Communist Party that I first found my way to contribute to the struggle of working peoples everywhere."[10]

The CP's official change of policy to the Popular Front strategy of broad antifascist coalitions in 1935 created even more possibilities for interracial militant protest. During the early 1930s, blacks witnessed Communists and Socialists fighting each other almost as much as they struggled for the rights of workers. Throughout 1935, internal reports of the CP showed that a faction of the Socialists, led by Norman Thomas, began to call for united action and to break away from the "old guard" Socialist Party members. The threat of fascism, both at home and abroad, had sounded an alarm to many activists in both radical parties to ally rather than bicker, and these conversations became public when Norman Thomas and Earl Browder met in front of an audience of 20,000 at Madison Square Garden in November 1935. While both leaders still criticized each other, Thomas said that Socialists and Communists needed to "learn to get along" now before they had to do so in a "concentration camp here in America." Just one year before, the New York Times reported, "fists and chairs flew in the Garden . . . at a joint rally against fascism." This time, however, the crowd sang the "International" and "Solidarity Forever."[11]

To young black leaders like John P. Davis, the shift to an antifascist Popular Front alliance became an opportunity to expand the energy of the coalitions that had formed around the Scottsboro case. As the CP admitted, the League for the Struggle of Negro Rights had failed to develop a broad base in black urban communities. Instead, CP leaders noted, Davis's Joint Committee on

National Recovery (JCNR) in Washington represented a model for a larger coalition of groups to work for racial advancement.

To bring forth this new Popular Front model, many leftist activists and intellectuals looked to Davis. Born in 1905, John Preston Davis was the third child of striving middle-class parents who had recently settled their family in Washington, D.C., when the father, William Davis, took a federal civil service clerkship position. Davis attended Dunbar High School, the elite school for blacks in Washington, where he showed his academic potential, winning a scholarship to Bates College in Maine. At Bates, he developed a talent for elocution and became one of the stars of its debate team, which traveled to national and European competitions. Aspiring to become a fiction writer, Davis moved to New York and became part of the Harlem Renaissance. In the late 1920s, Davis completed a master's degree in literature at Harvard, took a job at Fisk University, and then returned to Harvard for a law degree. In the midst of his second stint in Cambridge, Davis became less interested in his coursework than in the political upheaval resulting from the onset of the Great Depression. Davis left Harvard and obtained a job working for the Capital News Service, a Republican Party–funded press that targeted black voters. To Davis, this job represented a paycheck during hard times that could support his creative writing aspirations on the side, but the job put him into an awkward position. Republican Party leaders, fretting over the possibility of losing black votes to Franklin Roosevelt, assigned Davis to stump for Herbert Hoover. The Republican Party retained the majority of the black voters in the election, but Herbert Hoover lost, and Davis faced press accusations that Republicans had paid him to publish propaganda reports for a black readership. Returning to Harvard, Davis increasingly gravitated to courses taught by Professor Felix Frankfurter, who had a reputation for defending minority rights (he would become a Roosevelt appointee to the Supreme Court in 1939). He also began to work with the radical attorneys of the International Labor Defense who had taken up the Scottsboro case. Davis graduated from Harvard and returned to the political and cultural circles in Washington, D.C., with a new understanding of the potential of Roosevelt's New Deal in relation to black Americans. When he attended the June 1933 hearings of the National Recovery Administration on a whim, what he saw in the hearing room shocked him: not a single African American group was represented. Davis knew this spelled disaster for black workers because the hearings sought to establish wage codes for all major industries.[12]

Davis reacted to the lack of black representation by improvising. He formed a group called the Negro Industrial League (NIL), declared himself and his black Harvard colleague Robert Weaver its leaders, and requested that the NIL be allowed to testify on behalf of black workers at the hearings. Taken aback, the National Recovery Administration panel granted the request, and Davis and Weaver followed through by presenting an array of damning statistical data about occupational, regional, and "historical" wage differentials that were intended to keep blacks in economic servitude. Davis argued that the current status of black workers would thwart economic recovery because blacks needed decent wages to obtain buying power as consumers. The NIL received plaudits in black newspapers and the apprehensive assistance of Walter White of the NAACP. White saw Davis's work as important for black economic advancement as well as a strategy to fend off younger critics in the NAACP who demanded that the organization deal with the dire economic situation. Over the next year, Davis and Weaver testified on hearings for textiles, timber, coal, and other job classifications. They won some wage gains, but lost others due to duplicity among liberal New Deal Democrats who placated their southern white supremacist colleagues by keeping black workers dependent. After Weaver left to take a position teaching at a black college, Davis continued without him by fostering an alliance between the NAACP, the Elks, the BSCP, and twenty other organizations. To signify and amplify the organization's wider scope, he changed the name of the Negro Industrial League to the Joint Committee on National Recovery. The widened scope, however, did not necessarily come with consistent financing. Davis and his wife, Marguerite De Mond, who worked as a secretary for the Association for the Study of Negro Life and History, personally financed much of the JCNR's efforts, including a series of data collection trips across the South. On these trips, Davis was often accompanied by Charles Hamilton Houston, who would become the architect of the NAACP's legal strategy against segregation. As they traveled through impoverished southern communities, the level of economic degradation and exploitation of black workers outraged both men and invigorated their lobbying efforts in Washington. By 1935, the JCNR had become a national coalition of civil rights forces well before the development of the Popular Front. Davis, not yet thirty years old, had emerged as a strong critic of the New Deal's racially biased policies, had become a respected expert on African American workers among unionists, and had established a reputation as a civil rights leader in Washington and across the nation.[13]

By 1935, all sides were marveling at Davis's intelligence and energy as a writer and organizer of protest, but none claimed him as their own. A prominent "Negro Socialist" and NAACP leader told black Communist Ben Davis, "We don't trust that fellow John P. Davis. You communists don't trust him and we don't. Last year he was with the Republican Party, what next?" Socialists and Communists, as well as Republicans and Democrats, eventually came under the NNC tent subsequently pitched by Davis with similar levels of disquiet. The independence and energy of Davis signaled the possibility that a black-led Popular Front had potential to represent a coalition much broader than a CP shift in strategy. The NNC might just be able to bring these political factions together with other New Deal reform and labor groups to fight for the rights of African Americans and expand American democracy.[14]

Within the working class at large in the early 1930s, an increasingly vocal minority in the labor movement began to call for organizing industrial workers. The impact of the Depression had decimated the AFL; by 1931, on average more than 7,000 dues-paying members quit the organization every week. John L. Lewis of the United Mine Workers and a few other maverick labor leaders looked for new methods to advance workers' interests. In previous negotiations with coal operators, Lewis had rarely succeeded because company owners cited the lower wages they could pay to unorganized workers. Thus, during the early stages of the New Deal, Lewis and his trade union allies tirelessly lobbied President Roosevelt to protect workers. Roosevelt in turn assigned New York senator Robert Wagner to draft the legislation. Wagner, with the support of Lewis and a few other union leaders, fought back numerous attempts to amend and remove the all-important 7(a) clause, which protected the right of workers to organize, and shepherded it through Congress and then the Senate. On June 16, 1933, American workers achieved an important victory when President Roosevelt signed the National Recovery Act into law with the disputed section intact. Still, Lewis became increasingly frustrated over the next two years, as the AFL failed to take full advantage of this new right. "When unions neglect to organize the unorganized," Lewis concluded, "they pay the penalty for their own neglect." Coming to a head at the 1935 convention, the Lewis wing of the AFL proposed a minority resolution to organize along "industrial lines." The ensuing debate became heated: the AFL voted against the resolution; delegates cursed each other on the convention floor; and, as a finale, Lewis punched William Hutcheson of the Carpenters Union in the jaw. Following Lewis's punch, a "motley group of idealists, hardboiled career labor organizers, liberals, fanatics, [and] Communists" formed the Committee for Industrial Organization. Soon thereafter, they formally split from the AFL and renamed themselves the Congress of Industrial Organizations (CIO).[15]

Meanwhile, African American intellectuals, activists, and workers had become invigorated with new approaches to combat unprecedented levels of poverty. As Davis pointed out through his testimony at hearings and in numerous articles in black newspapers and journals, New Deal legislation omitted the largest sections of black labor and allowed for race-based differences in wages, giving African Americans a raw deal rather than a New Deal. The experience of lobbying in Washington from 1933 to 1935, and some small victories that ensued in removing race-based differentials in wage codes, convinced Davis of the need to unify black organizations on a larger scale to fight for access to the New Deal. "I am convinced that we face a revolution [and] that the black man will be the spearhead of this revolution whether he likes it or not—whether you like it or not," Davis wrote excitedly to his longtime friend and intellectual combatant Ralph Bunche.[16] Both men, however, knew that conditions for revolution would not alone make a civil rights movement.

In 1935, they began to put ideas into a plan of action by organizing the conference at Howard University. Entitled "The Position of the Negro in Our National Economic Crisis," the conference included a broad political spectrum of participants, including intellectual and scholar W. E. B. Du Bois, A. Philip Randolph, Howard professor Emmett Dorsey, and government administrators like Howard Myers of the New Deal's National Recovery Administration. The differences in opinion among the participants ranged from intraracial cooperative movements, to faith in the New Deal, to a rejection of capitalism as a means to solve the economic problems of African Americans in the 1930s. Despite their strategic differences, all agreed on the need to emphasize class and race in order to advance African American interests. Out of these conversations came an idea to focus on the working class and unify African Americans through a coalition that they named the National Negro Congress.[17]

This meeting proved serendipitous. Both Norman Thomas of the Socialist Party and James Ford of the Communist Party attended this conference and agreed to work together on domestic civil rights issues. In addition, conference participants noted that a few maverick unions that had organized black workers alongside whites previously within the AFL—especially miners under John L. Lewis and clothing workers under Sidney Hillman—had stormed out of the AFL's annual meeting in disgust when it voted against organizing industrial workers.[18] With these circumstances in mind, the group of black intellectuals in Washington founded the NNC. Thereafter, its organizers issued a pamphlet listing its goals, "Let Us Build a National Negro Congress," which featured the visage of Frederick Douglass on the cover. On the local level, the NNC formed sponsoring committees in several cities and prepared for its inaugural national conference in Chicago, to take place in February 1936.[19]

CHAPTER ONE

Labor's Triumph and the "Black Magna Carta" in the Chicago Region, 1936–1939

At 9:30 P.M. on a cold December night in 1936, employees at Wilson & Bennett Company in Chicago stopped working inside the metal barrel factory. They decided that night that they had had enough of wages that ranged from sixteen to twenty-five cents an hour. "This is a sit down," they shouted, and then they quickly drew up a placard that read, "SEND THE CIO." The Congress of Industrial Organizations soon thereafter answered their call in the person of Eleanor Rye. Over the past year, Rye had become a stalwart organizer for the Labor Committee of the National Negro Congress (NNC) and then an official organizer for the Steel Workers Organizing Committee (SWOC). With the workers locked in the factory, Rye slipped through a police line, scaled a fifteen-foot-high fence, and sneaked into the plant. She entered with union cards that read "SWOC." Workers inside almost threw her out because they thought she represented a company union rather than the CIO. Rye calmly explained that SWOC was affiliated with the CIO and that she and others in it had organized thousands of steelworkers in the Chicago region since the summer. Jubilant that the CIO had indeed arrived, the workers immediately signed cards for membership. So began a grueling three-month strike. Black and white together (the plant workforce was 70 percent black), they held out and claimed victory that April. They won raises in wages, a forty-hour week, overtime pay, and—especially important for the black workers—a strict seniority clause that promoted by merit and time of employment rather than by race. Previously, a report had called this plant "one of the worst sweat shops north of the Mason and Dixon line," but now it became, according to the national union, "one of the strongest steel lodges in the Midwest."[1]

Just one year earlier, a successful strike of these 1,000 male and female, white and black, factory employees would have been thought impossible. Something had noticeably transformed the culture of labor organizing in Chicago. St. Clair Drake and Horace Cayton, black sociologists in Chicago, noted a change in protest politics in their landmark study, *Black Metropolis*. "By 1938," they wrote, "it had become respectable to support a demonstration or a boycott in the struggle for Negro rights."[2] Often out of necessity during the Great Depression, white ethnics in Chicago began to deal with African Americans in ways that challenged their previous notions of the color line in the urban North. These new configurations would even convince the often-cynical writer Richard Wright to conclude in the late 1930s: "The differences between black folk and white folk are not blood or color, and the ties that bind us are deeper than the ties that separate us." He, like other blacks and whites in the vanguard of this shift, declared, "We are with the new tide. . . . Men are moving! And we shall be with them."[3]

This chapter explains how, during the last years of the Great Depression, a determined group of African Americans in the NNC helped create the first bona fide industrial unions in America. For African Americans, this process of unionization within steel and meatpacking plants involved battles over leadership, politics, and culture within their communities and new interracial alliances outside of them. Previously, the majority of the region's black workers ceded the reins of leadership to middle-class professionals, who met with middle- and upper-class whites to obtain the spoils of welfare capitalism and municipal machine politics. During the Great Depression, however, new militant forms of protest, often led by working-class unionists, became the primary means of racial advancement, as blacks in Chicago completed a shift from the Republican Party to the "New Deal" Democratic Party. Other studies have made cogent claims for how individual unions and political leaders helped bring about these changes in terms of civil and labor rights in the Chicago and Northwest Indiana region, but this study views that change from the perspective of the newly inaugurated NNC. By examining the development of the NNC—its first conference and the follow-up steelworkers meeting and the activities and influence of its Chicago Council members—this chapter seeks to chart how it contributed to the region's racial landscape and also why it failed to sustain its labor-based civil rights movement.[4]

The NNC's agenda was much more expansive than simply changing leadership models or helping unions. By getting workers into new industrial unions on the ground floor, NNC organizers hoped to make African Americans the "strategic grip" of them. This achievement, they believed, would in turn provide an unprecedented amount of power for blacks to force white Chicagoans to treat them with respect as workers and citizens. Some individual blacks came to the CIO on their own, and others shunned boycotts, strikes, and marches, but all had to contend with the NNC vision because it challenged previous beliefs in talented-tenth professionalism, black nationalism, and labor unions. Using their activities among steelworkers as a base, NNC activists led this transformation. While the immediate aim was to organize industrial workers, John P. Davis, the head of the NNC, thought this movement had the potential to "write a Magna Carta for black labor."[5] This metaphor fit the situation in Chicago well. Chicago's African American vanguard did author a new set of power relations, but, like the original Magna Carta of 1215, implementation was another matter.

▨ ▨ ▨ Before the creation of the NNC, Chicago's Urban League and NAACP branch represented the most respected organizations for black racial advancement. But during the early Depression years, both organizations fell into dire straits. Based as it was on donations from the black community and white philanthropists, the Urban League's operating budget disappeared in 1930, and the organization subsequently went into debt and had to struggle for its very existence for the next four years. When the Urban League asked board members to contribute "service" to the organization, the staff realized by the anemic response that most board members had only given "the prestige of their names." A. L. Foster, the Chicago Urban League's head, largely carried on alone. Once considered the "citadel" of "respected" leadership, the failure of both parallel black institutions (black-run banks, insurance companies, and businesses) and white welfare paternalism (corporate and industrial employers) exposed the league as lacking resources and too conciliatory to deal with widespread poverty and unemployment.[6]

The NAACP's similar problems led it to draft a less patrician leader, Arthur Clement MacNeal. Black Chicagoans knew MacNeal as one of the masterminds behind the 1929 Don't Spend Your Money Where You Can't Work Campaign, a grassroots amalgam of liberals and Garveyites who endorsed boycotts and picket lines in front of chain stores. This campaign highlighted race and took to the streets, diverging from previous NAACP and Urban

League strategies that had involved polite discussions for the placement of blacks into employment fields. As coeditor of the *Chicago Whip* newspaper, MacNeal wrote fiery editorials about the jobs campaign, to the point that his politics lost him so much white advertising revenue that the paper became financially insolvent in 1932. Yet MacNeal and others won hundreds of job for African Americans (they claimed as many as 3,000) in Black-Belt chain stores, and the idea spread across the country to other cities whose African American populations had expanded significantly through the Great Migration of the previous decade. "The *Whip* [boycott] was successful," the Urban League's A. L. Foster admitted. "This was pressure not education. The Chicago Urban League was not getting the big job done."[7]

MacNeal needed a new job after the *Whip* folded, and the local NAACP needed a new president who had the energy to claim it from the dustbin of 1920s-style parallel institution politics.[8] With many black institutions bankrupted, the branch focused on employment for African Americans in reforestation projects and other early government jobs in the New Deal. After the passage of the National Industrial Recovery Act in 1933, the branch scrambled to get in touch with employers who they predicted would fire their black employees rather than pay them government-stipulated wages. The campaign met "some success and many failures," but it was not due to a lack of the branch's efforts. Outside of economic empowerment, the Chicago branch ensured the desegregation of all Chicago beaches (the cause of the city's 1919 riot) and demanded the equal treatment of black customers, who complained that department stores did not allow them to try on items like shoes and hats.[9]

Unfortunately, tensions between the NAACP's national office in New York and the branch leaders in Chicago grew with the branch's militancy. The national office canceled plans to hold antilynching rallies in Chicago and fumed over a campaign that targeted Julius Rosenwald's Sears department store for its second-class treatment of black customers and its refusal to hire skilled black workers. These campaigns, the New York office claimed, compromised the NAACP's national lobbying strategy and threatened its financial donations from white philanthropists. The Chicago branch not only fumed over the constant need to justify its work to the New York headquarters but also tried to renegotiate financial arrangements that siphoned more than half of the money raised in Chicago to New York.[10] In addition, W. E. B. Du Bois's surprising 1934 pronouncements calling for an emphasis on black financial power over integration caused an uproar in the Chicago branch. Although MacNeal's previous experience with the *Whip* campaign had black nationalist strains that might have overlapped with the new stance of Du Bois, MacNeal's subsequent experiences had transformed him into an ardent "whole hog" integrationist. MacNeal led the so-called Chicago revolt against Du Bois. Roy Wilkins of the national office was taken aback by MacNeal's harsh dismissal of Du Bois, but he nonetheless seemed pleased to have MacNeal's militancy dispel the rumors that he or Walter White had conspired to force Du Bois to resign in 1934. For once, New York and Chicago seemed to be on the same page, but the militancy of the Chicago branch nonetheless continued to worry the national office.[11]

For the next three years, the Chicago branch leaders challenged the national NAACP to develop new strategies that foreshadowed the rise of the NNC in Chicago. The "technique of bridging the talented tenth and the masses is available," MacNeal explained, because the Depression opened up new modes of cross-class alliances. "Gaining supporters for a program from white people is clear," MacNeal wrote, but "failure to start . . . this new clear-cut and aggressive program" out of fear of losing white liberal support "would be fatal." MacNeal wanted to continue to work with whites, forcing them to become allies and partners, but no longer truckle to them. The summer before the NNC's February 1936 convention in Chicago, the NAACP branch's education committee hosted a speaking engagement for John P. Davis, then working as the head of the Joint Committee on National Recovery in Washington. At the Wabash YMCA, Davis mentioned the upcoming NNC formation, and the branch's audience welcomed the idea.[12]

More than any other organization in the black community, the Brotherhood of Sleeping Car Porters (BSCP) promoted unionism, which provided a base for the NNC's advocacy of organized labor. Since 1925, BSCP organizers like Milton P. Webster had been fighting an uphill battle to win over Chicago's blacks for the union cause rather than continue the "patronage politics" of the Pullman Company (headquartered in Chicago) and the Republican Party machine, which rewarded blacks with jobs and donations to their community institutions in return for their unquestioned loyalty to the company and political machine. During these early days of organizing, Robert Abbott, editor of the *Chicago Defender*, the editors of the *Chicago Whip*, black clergy like Archibald Carey Sr., and professionals like banker Jesse Binga sided with the company. But with the help of the Ida B. Wells Club and other women's groups, as well as attorney and former minister Charles Burton, the union and its citizens' committee began to turn the tide by 1927. An aborted strike the following year and the onset of the Great Depression thereafter hurt the

BSCP membership, but the union had effectively won over a significant group of Chicago's black community leaders. These backers included Junius Austin, a former Garveyite supporter from Pittsburgh who opened the Pilgrim Baptist Church in Chicago; Thelma McWorter, industrial secretary of the South Side YWCA; and Neva Ryan, who attempted to organize domestic workers. To many black middle-class Chicagoans, models of individual uplift of the 1920s now seemed inadequate to address the problems of the economic crisis. In 1933, the BSCP had only 250 of the 1,150 Chicago members it had had in 1928, but due to black community support and the onset of the New Deal, the porters in the union weathered the storm, and by 1935 the union topped 1,000 members once again. BSCP leader A. Philip Randolph, backed by a host of Chicagoans, had, according to historian Beth Bates, been "laying the foundation for a coalition of activists that would use the labor movement to make claims for full civil rights," and now many of its members and supporters looked to join the coming NNC to win recognition for their union and make their struggle into a national battle for civil rights.[13]

During the early Depression years, it also became a common occurrence on Chicago's South Side to "run, quick and find the Reds!" Upon his arrival in Chicago in 1931, Horace Cayton witnessed Communists "three abreast, forming a long uninterrupted line," as they marched through the streets of the South Side. Impressed by their "serious and determined" countenances, despite the "poverty of their dress," he followed them to an apartment building where a family faced eviction. Black Communists with many others marching in tow confronted the police and refused to leave until they put all of the family's furniture back into the apartment. During one moment similar to the one Cayton witnessed, police opened fire and killed three African Americans in the ensuing melee—10,000 people attended the funeral. The following year, James Ford, a dark-skinned black man, spoke at the forum in Washington Park as the candidate of the Communist Party (CP) for vice president in front of thousands of onlookers. "Every time a black Communist appeared on the platform, or his picture appeared in the newspaper," Drake and Cayton wrote in Black Metropolis, "Negroes were proud." Hard times had given the Communists a new life as the party increasingly abandoned sectarianism on the ground in order to deal with the hunger, unemployment, and housing issues of local people. And while African American membership increased by the hundreds, many thousands more began grudgingly to respect CP activities and noticed how black Communists became leaders in the Unemployment Councils and interacted with whites on a level of equality. At the national level, black Chicagoans closely followed the CP campaigns on be-half of Angelo Herndon and the Scottsboro defendants. Meanwhile, a cadre of black leftists like John Gray, Henry Johnson, Edward Strong, and Eleanor Rye came from these networks, increasingly collaborated with members of the NAACP and BSCP by the mid-1930s, and eagerly planned for the NNC's first conference in Chicago, which was to take place in February 1936.[14]

▨ ▨ ▨ On a bitterly cold February weekend, 750 delegates from twenty-eight states traveled to Chicago's South Side Bronzeville neighborhood to regis-ter their names at the Eighth Regiment Armory for the first conclave of the NNC. Inside the armory, banners read "Jobs and Adequate Relief for a Million Negro Destitute Families" and "Black America Demands an End to Lynching, Mob Violence."[15] Outside, thousands huddled around loudspeakers to hear the speeches of what the *Chicago Defender* termed "IKN's"—"Internationally Known Negroes." Top black intellectuals, churchmen, labor leaders, and art-ists—including Ralph Bunche of Howard University, the Reverend Adam Clayton Powell Jr., James W. Ford of the CP, Lester Granger of the National Urban League, Roy Wilkins of the NAACP, Langston Hughes, Richard Wright, and Arna Bontemps—debated during sessions on unions, youth, churches, businesses, war and fascism, the role of women, and interracial relations. As one delegate remarked, "I have never seen so many 'big shots' together in my life." Nevertheless, he concluded, "these big men were unassuming and mingled . . . with the rest of us in perfect harmony. There seemed to be no big I's and little U's [because] everyone was bent on getting something worth-while done."[16] This combination of people, the African American *New York Age* reported, "offered the most complete cross section of Negro life in the United States ever gathered under one roof." Although this last comment may have exaggerated the regional, class, and professional variety at the NNC, it also evinced just how novel this type of gathering was in 1936.[17]

The NNC convention in Chicago proved unique because its participants not only talked about working-class blacks but also looked to them for leader-ship. Unlike the conferences of the NAACP, or previous attempts to unify black protest organizations like the Negro Sanhedrin—an earlier attempt to unify black organizations into one powerful movement, which met in Chi-cago in February 1924—or even the 1935 Howard University gathering, the NNC opened its sessions to the public, and working-class laborers, artists, and other spectators participated in the deliberations.[18] Delegates like Frank X. Martel of Detroit, sent as a personal representative of John L. Lewis and the insurgent CIO, attended the conference to speak about black industrial workers. Meanwhile the NNC's president, A. Philip Randolph, wrote a fiery speech that defined "the problems of the Negro people [as] the problems of the workers, for practically 99 per cent of Negro people win their bread by selling their labor power." Randolph himself had to miss the meeting at the last moment due to illness, but fellow BSCP leader Charles Burton read his labor-centered speech.[19] A *Chicago Defender* reporter took special interest in how the "'Labor Leaders' showed more organization and spirit than any other group" at the sessions, and that "one thing can be said for the Congress, the delegates actually worked." With four official sessions involving black workers and many more conversations that occurred in the halls of the Armory, in eateries like the Belmont Grill, and in the streets of the Bronzeville neighborhood, it seemed like the delegates had rediscovered black workers as a first priority. Underneath a photo of one of these lively debates, a reporter summarized their questions: "Should Race labor organize? Are the opportunities of the Race greater outside the organized ranks? Should Race labor affiliate itself with the American Federation of Labor? Would not a separate union of all Race craftsmen be better?" Many of the resolutions passed at the gathering— including an endorsement of the BSCP, criticism of company unions and the exclusionary policies of the American Federation of Labor (AFL), and a call for a nationwide drive to organize industrial workers—indicate how the delegates settled these questions. The NNC continued to fight for inclusion into the AFL, dismissed company unions as paternalistic, and saw the CIO as an undefined yet exciting opportunity.[20]

Black artists sidled up alongside the labor delegates at the Congress. Chicago migrant Richard Wright chaired the "Negro Culture and History" panel, which featured writers Arna Bontemps and Langston Hughes and artists Augusta Savage and Frederick Douglass Allen. The presentation by Wright, entitled "The Role of the Negro Artist and Writer in the Changing Social Order," indicated how these artists sought to place themselves into social movements to ameliorate dire Depression-era conditions. They agreed that "in the past Negro institutions have exploited Negro artists and writers" and that "Negro cultural workers have generally been neglected and suppressed" by both white and black elites. The Depression had caused them to work "at almost starvation levels," and, like their labor brethren, they saw a writer's union as a means to solve their poverty and combat "caricature and subservient roles" in white culture. They hoped that the NNC would sponsor Negro culture magazines, conferences, and exhibits to depict deeper forms of

Jay Jackson, "Will It Help Him?" *Chicago Defender*, February 22, 1936.
Courtesy of the *Chicago Defender*.

black culture, and, alongside the Federal Writers' Project, put them to work. By viewing themselves at the NNC conference as "cultural workers" in the struggle for a "new Bill of Rights for the Negro people," these artists realized, in the words of Wright, that "they are not alone."[21]

Despite the unity forged at the conference, others criticized the newfound NNC in ways that revealed how it differed from previous efforts. The NNC meeting, one reporter concluded, "provided a powerful impetus toward racial unity, while at the same time stirred up more bitter controversy than any gathering of Negroes."[22] On the first day, a rumor spread that members of the notorious Red Squad branch of the Chicago Police Department would seize the Eighth Regiment Armory, its scheduled venue. Amid this uncertainty, Mayor Ed Kelly of Chicago and Robert Abbott, the editor of the *Chicago Defender*, backed out as speakers at the last moment.[23] Moreover, a couple of church leaders, having attended many of the sessions, stormed out of the Congress, labeling it "atheistic."[24] A few reporters, especially Kelly Miller for the *New York Age*, leveled criticism at the NNC for being too "leftward." Miller called the NNC "revolutionary," implying that Randolph, who had "an avowed leftist tendency," and James W. Ford, a Communist leader, concocted the NNC as a conspiratorial plot. As proof, Miller explained that the Congress "failed to denounce Communism" and therefore must "be rated a lamentable failure." Yet Miller's real ire stemmed from the fact that "outstanding leaders of thought and opinion, whose combined wisdom have guided the paths of the race so far . . . were not consulted."[25] In essence, Miller was uncomfortable with the threat posed to the established black leadership by the NNC's militant and working-class focus. Miller, like other established race leaders, feared the NNC's appeal more than its weakness. As one delegate from Virginia complained of these so-called leaders, "to gain or retain a place in the limelight they resort to a measure unworthy of a high school pupil."[26] In fact, those in attendance would have embraced Miller's comment about the "revolutionary" nature of the NNC. One African American reporter called out these "Walter Winchells . . . of the Negro press," who "failed to attend" but nevertheless denounced the gathering as "pitifully futile" and a "waste of time."[27] Expressions of "universal unrest" and new direction for racial advancement, the NNC's defenders concluded, made the conference remarkable, not lamentable.

Many of the pundits who criticized the NNC also labeled it as Communist. This label infuriated the NNC's president, A. Philip Randolph, and gave him cause to write a sharp rebuttal to charges of Communist "domination." Coming from Randolph, a Socialist who had criticized many of the partisan shifts of Communists during the previous decade, the statement's stinging tone carried legitimacy. "Since when," he asked black Americans, "can Negroes, the victims of the . . . Ku Klux Klan and Negro-phobists, North and South, afford to raise the 'red scare' bogey?" The NNC represented all political faiths, he explained, including Communists, a "legitimate political party" whose members "need make no apology for it." Calling red-baiting a "regular indoor sport" that aimed to "condemn those who aggressively fight for human and race rights," Randolph turned to religion, the bedrock of black life and traditional "respectable" leaders. "Jesus Christ and his followers" were "nailed to the cross" and "persecuted as Communists." Just as the Pharisees and Scribes charged that Christ "stirreth up the people," Randolph wrote, U.S. Dixiecrats and conservatives sought to stem "the swelling tide of discontent." His powerful editorial, which was printed in several black newspapers, ended with a militant challenge: "If we Negroes are so yellow, so cringing . . . and childish to permit the 'red label' to halt our march toward the true status of men [then] God help us!"[28]

Editorials by Randolph and other black journalists reconfigured the terms of debate over whether the NNC was "red." A. M. Fields, for example, wrote an article for the *Chicago Defender* titled: "Red Scare at Race Congress Proves to Be a Colossal Joke." Letters also poured in from readers defending the Congress. Lester Granger, looking back on the "worst winter in fifty years," which welcomed the delegates to Chicago, believed that "all the Communists in America and Russia could not have inveighed the great majority of those delegates into that trip last winter unless there was something far deeper than inspired propaganda driving them." As another observer succinctly put it, "The new ship is in safe hands."[29]

Internal records of the U.S. CP support Randolph's interpretation that the party did not control the NNC. While members of the party helped distribute leaflets, raised a modest sum of money to help organize the conference in Chicago, and did other "spade work," black CP leaders did not "want mechanical control" of the NNC. Instead, they believed that "proletarian elements" should lead the NNC and that CP support should "embarrass bourgeoisie leaders with our diligence, our loyalty . . . our willingness to meet them more than half-way on any issue." As participants in the Congress, CP leaders would reap the benefits of a larger struggle by not attempting to control the movement. In fact, even if the top black Communists had wanted to control the NNC, they lacked the power to do so in 1936. The Popular Front and broader alliances may have changed the outlook of American CP members and allowed them to work alongside liberals, but Chicago district reports found "no struggles" developing among Communists in African American neighborhoods for "some time." The CP organizer blamed the "poor attendance at meetings" about issues such as economic relief and labor organizing on "very loose organization" and a "lack of understanding" of "united front tactics." If top Communists in the "Negro Division" of the party placed emphasis on the NNC, it was because they were desperate to have an impact. They came to the NNC's executive meetings as participants, not as members of a powerful and domineering organization.[30]

After the heated debates over the NNC had abated in the black press, many African Americans in Chicago saw the potential for a unified and militant black movement. When the *Chicago Defender* asked four black Chicagoans what they thought of the NNC, all of them responded with enthusiasm. One of them, a mailman named Rufus Jordan, summarized it best by expressing support but withholding judgment. "If the Congress follows through," Jordan claimed, "we may have a new deal for the race from the American government."[31]

▧ ▧ ▧ While a New Deal for blacks may not have seemed imminent, the passage of the Wagner Act the previous July had reaffirmed the right of workers to organize unions. The act stipulated that the government would protect collective bargaining rights and punish employer interference or coercion through a National Labor Relations Board, which inspired a new interest in the industrial labor movement. The NNC convention crowded out other news on the pages of the *Defender*, but a small article titled "Jim Crow Practices Assailed by Miners" in late February indicated the source of much of this new labor energy. The United Mine Workers of America (UMW), headed by John L. Lewis, who led the revolt against the AFL, renounced "narrow" and racist craft unionism at the AFL's Thirty-fourth Annual Convention in Washington, the same month as the NNC conference in Chicago.[32]

Despite this secessionist union movement, local black leaders and workers did not jump at the chance to join the newly founded CIO. When Roy Wilkins asked A. C. MacNeal for his opinion, to be included in an NAACP report on the NNC Chicago conference, he praised John P. Davis for his "fine organizing ability" and expressed his belief that the NNC's program "should give the Board of Directors . . . some ideas that should become part of the Association's program if it is to expand." Perhaps channeling his own frustration at wanting a militant program but lacking the resources to implement it, MacNeal explained that "the program of the Congress is generally what the Negro wants but I doubt if the Congress has the machinery or personnel to accomplish it without the energy and financial backing of the Communists." MacNeal's sponsorship of the NNC at the local level and his positive opinions of John P. Davis helped convince Wilkins to align the national NAACP with this new "organization of organizations" on particular issues. But the following year, MacNeal resigned his position with the NAACP and instead sought to advocate his approach through the Chicago Council of Negro Organizations (CCNO).[33]

The CCNO sought to bring more traditional black leaders together for joint action, but NNC members in Chicago saw it as an attempt to "steal their thunder."[34] The CCNO had the endorsement of MacNeal and BSCP Chicago head Milton P. Webster, which was especially frustrating to the NNC. The group had an air of "respectability" within Chicago's South Side community and espoused a more traditional uplift policy that did not endorse an economic justice platform that included industrial unions.[35] As Webster made clear to the Chicago NNC members, any union activism not related to their own enervated the BSCP's own strength. Charles Burton and Randolph of the BSCP and NNC leadership obviously endorsed the opposite viewpoint. But the irony of the hard-fought battle of the BSCP to gain respect among Chicago's African American leaders was that by 1936 some of them had become conservative in protecting their brand of unionism against new approaches to organizing workers. Webster, for example, had worked for a decade on obtaining respectability for the BSCP in Chicago, first losing his porter job and then his sinecure within the Republican machine for stubbornly backing the union.[36]

The NNC responded to the CCNO threat by seeking a compromise. Aware of the hesitancy on the part of the CCNO liberal black leaders to coordinate with new industrial unions, Charles Burton, the BSCP Citizen's Committee leader and newly elected Chicago NNC head, outlined an agenda that did not mention the CIO. The NNC would launch campaigns around public utilities jobs, police brutality, laundry and domestic worker unions, and "bona fide" unions for stockyard laborers. From Washington, John P. Davis agreed with Burton's approach and urged Chicago members to work toward a merger with the CCNO. While this did not happen officially, overlapping members and a sympathetic A. L. Foster of the Urban League helped smooth over tensions. To the NNC council, concerted action remained the most important outcome, and if the CCNO wanted to take credit, so be it.[37]

Yet even those NNC activists who saw the CIO as a potential vehicle for a movement empathized with those who feared joining any labor union with whites. Leonidas McDonald, an organizer for AFL Local 87 of the Amalgamated Meat Cutters, felt that "the National Negro Congress has begun to close the door of mistrust that Negro workers as a whole has for organized labor," but added, "Is the Negro justified in this mistrust? I will say that they are justified in a sense." However, McDonald saw in the NNC the potential to bring labor and black activists together and avert further economic disaster. In a speech before the Chicago Federation of Labor in March, he evoked the recent takeover by the Nazi party in Germany as a "fresh lesson before us," that a "split working class" will lead to "concentration camps." McDonald "commissioned" white labor leaders "with a great task . . . to fight in your own local . . . against jim-crowism.[38] This stand of white workers, in turn, would reverse the indifference that black workers and community leaders felt toward unions.

Immediate action seemed necessary because black steelworkers faced an increasingly harsh and exploitative work environment during the 1930s. Interviews conducted under the supervision of Claude Barnett, the 1919 founder of the Associated Negro Press, which provided articles to its black member newspapers, provided a rare glimpse into the lives of black steelworkers in Gary, Indiana, a city that until the Second World War had produced one eighth of the world's steel. This survey of 450 black steelworkers revealed stories of racial discrimination and humiliation that demanded immediate attention. A worker from Oklahoma, for example, had lived in Gary for the previous fourteen years. Employed by Carnegie-Illinois Steel in 1932, he first worked as a pack feeder in the hot mill and then moved to a skilled job as an operator of a roller. However, in 1935 the company introduced new machinery in his department and gave a white man his job to operate it. Without any acknowledgment of his seniority, the company transferred him back to the status of a common laborer. As another worker who had come to Gary from Georgia fourteen years prior explained, many blacks who obtained skilled work in the steel mills after the 1919 strike were demoted during the Depression years. A third worker claimed that "Negroes must stand back and watch white men, often without experience, come in to these better paying jobs," and, even more humiliating, the company ordered these same black workers to train new white recruits to do their jobs. In short, the status of black steelworkers eroded during the 1930s as they became shut out by hiring freezes and relegated to the hottest, dirtiest, and most dangerous jobs that "no white man would keep."[39]

These conditions, however, did not mean black workers would necessarily embrace a new interracial labor movement. In fact, Barnett attained sponsorship for his survey of the Gary "situation" from John Stephens, manager of industrial relations at Carnegie-Illinois Steel. Both men believed that African Americans, if given the right incentives and education by steel companies and black institutions, would shun the new union movement. "There is no question in my mind," Barnett wrote to Stephens, "that a program of urging colored men to give allegiance to the company representation plan" would allow black workers to "follow their traditional instincts of remaining dependably loyal." While it would be easy to dismiss this statement as Barnett's attempt to secure funding for the study and assuage the concerns of the company, the interviews of workers also reveal their ambivalence toward unionization. At least 200 black strikebreakers helped destroy the steel strike of 1919 in the region, and while other unskilled black workers honored the picket lines, white steelworkers associated blacks with scabs. The degeneration of this early union campaign in 1922, many steelworkers believed, was the result of racial fissures. Even the Communists doubted whether such a struggle among steelworkers was possible. In the spring of 1935, steel organizers in the CP reported little progress nationally and remarked that "Chicago still remains the weakest link." All of this evidence added up to black workers having few reasons to trust white steelworkers. White workers had not objected when a few plants had recently segregated their washrooms, nor had they argued with foremen who hired new white ethnics to replace skilled black workers. Thus, African American responses to the CIO ranged from the "best thing for the colored worker" to "can't do any worse," to "undecided," to "skeptical."[40]

To many black intellectuals, African Americans' ambivalence toward the nascent labor movement evoked their history from before the Civil War. W. E. B. Du Bois's 1935 *Black Reconstruction*, heavily influenced by the Depression years, depicted African Americans as "workers" similarly hesitant on the eve of the Civil War. He concluded: "What the Negro did was to wait, look and listen and try to see where his interest lay."[41] While black workers remained undecided in 1936, the NNC saw the opportunity to foment something akin to what Du Bois had termed the "General Strike" of slaves that had occurred during and after the Civil War. NNC leaders depicted black workers in the New Deal era as veritable slaves. The NNC's Labor Committee, for example, issued a pamphlet that called upon all black steelworkers to "join hands with our white brothers and sisters" to "liberate us from the shackles of company union slavery."[42] Adding to the symbolic significance, students from Hampton University in Virginia brought a gavel "inlaid with wood taken from the hulk of the last slave ship that ever touched the shores of the continental United States" to open the Chicago NNC conference. The image of this symbolic gavel, as Richard Wright and many other commentators noted, resonated during the speech of NNC president A. Philip Randolph, who demanded a "New Bill of Rights for the Negro." Like past slave rebels—Gabriel Prosser, Denmark Vesey, Nat Turner—evoked by Randolph and other NNC leaders, they hoped to act as catalysts for the organization of black workers.[43] Moreover, they saw new industrial unions as akin to the Union army—something to hitch their star to and turn into a freedom movement.

The NNC sought to cross-pollinate its labor approach by highlighting the history of the black working class through cultural means in Chicago. In April 1936, for example, the NNC's Fine Arts Committee in Chicago sponsored a symposium honoring Arna Bontemps, the author of *Black Thunder*, a historical novel that described Gabriel Prosser's 1800 slave conspiracy in Virginia. Held at the Abraham Lincoln Center, a public community center built by the Unitarian Church in 1905, the symposium featured a wide representation of African American leaders—reporter and aspiring poet Frank Marshall Davis, Vivian Harsh of the Hall Library, Thyra Edwards of the NNC, and a representative of the Association for the Study of Negro Life and History, an organization created by historian Carter G. Woodson in Chicago two decades earlier.[44] The South Side Writers Group, another development that came out of the NNC conference, also feted Bontemps for the publication of *Black Thunder*. For Richard Wright, the leading force in the new writers' group, Bontemps's work "filled a yawning gap" for "competent" black novels. Margaret Walker, a poet and writer from Chicago, recalled that this novel "came closest in feeling and philosophy" to the militant strain of black historical memory that these writers sought to recover in the 1930s. Just as important, "well known Negro artists" held an accompanying exhibit to the NNC's literary symposium.[45] Like Bontemps and other African American writers, visual artists like Bernard Goss, Margaret Taylor Goss, and Charles White increasingly sought to depict black historical events in ways that reclaimed past generations of African Americans as active rather than passive historical participants and as central to American history rather than peripheral.

Richard Wright, writing on behalf of the NNC for *Illinois Labor Notes*, studied Chicago to better contextualize the current moment in African American history. He thought blacks in the city had become "ensnared . . . in a tangle of problems which admit no easy solution." African Americans, unlike during the previous century, now faced a "bewildering set of circumstances that obstructed a clear vision," but through the "aid of facts" as "discussed in the National Negro Congress," activists would chart a course to "building a better future" in this new modern context. In Chicago, blacks faced "hysterical opposition" from whites in Hyde Park and Kenwood when they tried to move into these neighborhoods. Meanwhile, Wright observed, the "streets of the 'Black Belt' on Chicago's South Side are filled with people who have nothing to do." These horrid conditions, Wright and other NNC members believed, revealed a state of emergency akin to war. "The fall of the gavel [at the NNC conference]," they concluded, "was heard in the four corners of the Union—sounding the alarm for the struggle of Negro people for freedom."[46]

▨ ▨ ▨ Despite the risks involved in backing the new drive for industrial unions, the NNC endorsed it in the belief that justice came from economic power. After the NNC convention, John P. Davis persuaded renegade CIO leaders to coordinate with the NNC to get African American workers into this larger coalition. Concerted action, Davis argued, was needed to avoid the disastrous racial splintering that had occurred during the strike wave in 1919. In June, Davis cornered Van Bittner, a CIO leader, at the Hollenden Hotel in Cleveland and gave him the hard sell. They discussed the plans of the recently founded SWOC, especially in relation to the 85,000 African American workers in the industry. SWOC, headed by trusted lieutenants of John L. Lewis from the UMW, represented the CIO's first attempt to organize industrial workers. As a result of this conversation and other nonofficial negotiations, Davis convinced Bittner to appoint him to make a "careful survey of Negro trade unionists in the Great Lakes area." Based on this survey, Davis then recommended three organizers who were within the NNC fold in Chicago and Northwest Indiana: Henry Johnson, Eleanor Rye, and Leonidas McDonald. According to their agreement, SWOC would pay Johnson and McDonald as organizers, and the NNC would pay Rye's salary if the union would reimburse her expenses. By the month's end, Davis had obtained seven NNC organizers, had begun drafting a SWOC-endorsed pamphlet as well as an article to appear in the first issue of the steel union's newspaper, and had obtained permission to participate in all closed meetings of steelworkers.[47]

Davis did not recommend these three African Americans just because of their NNC affiliation. Any cooperation with SWOC depended on the success of these organizers, he reasoned, and "the men at the helm of steel organization want action from us and not promises." He described Johnson as a man of "better than average formal school training." In fact, Johnson, the Texas-born son of an Industrial Workers of the World organizer, had attended classes at City College and Columbia in New York City, held a plasterers' union card, had previously organized sharecroppers in Alabama, and then had worked for the International Workers Order (an offshoot of the CP) in New York, before being transferred to Chicago in 1934. In Chicago, Johnson continued to promote unionism among black workers and began a Defense Committee for Civil Rights that promoted black history, art, and culture. In just the six weeks since the NNC founding conference, Johnson already had contacted over 600 area organizations. The NNC provided him with a newfound level of respectability and a national network to extend "broad influence among Negroes." Davis called him a "hard worker [and] good speaker," who possessed "ample physical courage." Like Johnson, Leonidas McDonald showed promise because of his previous experience. He had grown up in Chicago and joined Garvey's Universal Negro Improvement Association in the 1920s (which Davis did not mention to SWOC officials because of its black nationalist philosophy). He became a representative of the Chicago Federation of Labor as a member of the Amalgamated Meat Cutters, and yet he expressed an eagerness to break with AFL methods and organize interracial industrial unions. Last, Eleanor Rye held a position with the Furriers Union, was a "leading spirit in the Women's Auxiliary of the Chicago Local of the [BSCP]," and as a woman would "be able to reach Negro steel workers in key departments," presumably through their wives, "with even greater ease than most men."[48]

Since they would concentrate on steel, these organizers saw the entire region as their domain, as steel plants stretched from South Chicago all the way into the Indiana Harbor and Gary across the state line. They planned to operate far south of Chicago's Bronzeville neighborhood, which provided the added benefit of not having to compete with the CCNO for leadership, as well as being able to draw from the significant cadre of activists from Indiana who had attended the NNC conference. During those February sessions, Stanley Cotton, Walter Mackerl, and George Kimbley of the American Steel, Tin, and Plate Metal Company worked with the industrial labor section, and Jacob Reddix, a Roosevelt School teacher in Gary and head of a consumers' cooperative organization, became a national vice president of the NNC.[49] Solidarity between these men had developed over the past decade. Mackerl and Kimbley had attended meetings and rallies of the local Universal Negro Improvement Association in the 1920s. In the early 1930s, they admired actions of the CP's Unemployed Councils and lived in the same building as a local black Communist named Jesse Reese. They played cards together and talked about the conditions in Gary and the region. As historian Ruth Needleman noted, "Most conversations led back to the steel mill and the prospects of a

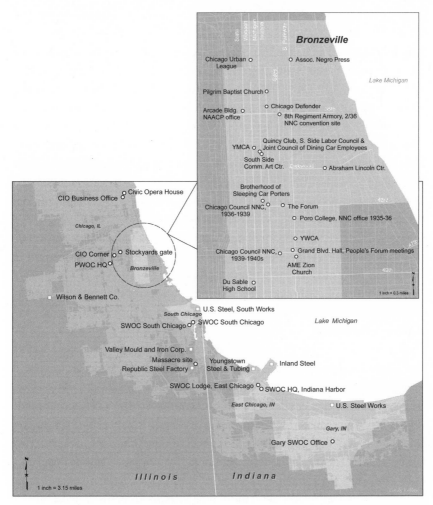

The world of the NNC in the Chicago area, 1936–1940. The NNC's activity in the Chicago region stretched from the South Side's Bronzeville neighborhood to the steel and packinghouse factories to the west and south to the Indiana Harbor and Gary. Map by Emily Kelley.

union." While they made local plans, outside help from NNC organizers bolstered their efforts as well as legitimized their thinking about a new movement on a national scale.[50]

The three NNC/SWOC deputies—Johnson, McDonald, and Rye—felt somewhat liberated because the Calumet region was much less crowded than Chicago's stable of so-called race leaders. The slow progress in Chicago, they believed, stemmed from too many black professionals whose empty rhetoric compromised action. Aside from the CCNO, the BSCP leaders in Chicago had an attitude, according to Johnson, of "don't try to agitate me." Rye described Charles Burton, the head of the Chicago NNC Council, as "almost impossible to work with" and as "solely depending on Mr. Johnson" for raising money. When Johnson "came into the office there was nothing here to work with, no chairs, not even a pencil or paper with which to write a letter." Soon after this incident, Rye raised money for supplies and got the office up and running. Thereafter, much of the money the organizers received from SWOC, Johnson told Davis, had been voluntarily given to the Chicago NNC Council with little tangible result. "The way the Congress [in Chicago] is being conducted," Johnson joked, "I consider it $208 that could just as well be spent in one of the cabarets on 48th Street." While these complaints should be taken as a sign of internal frustration with melding together the different strands within the NNC's black-led Popular Front, NNC steel organizers had more freedom to operate in places like Gary, Indiana Harbor, the far South Side of Chicago, and East Chicago. Although this constituted a formidable amount of additional territory to cover, the tangible goal of organizing steel, funded by the CIO, became inviting to organizers.[51]

Nonetheless, the small group of progressive Indiana steelworkers hardly represented the majority opinion of 8,000 black steelworkers in Gary and another 5,000 in the Indiana Harbor.[52] McDonald, for example, spoke at an Indiana Harbor church in August whose minister had received generous donations from "Mr. Block" at Indiana Steel. After his speech, this minister told his workers that "unless it was the will of God" for steelworkers to get "more than 47 [cents] an hour . . . and better working conditions," McDonald's campaign would "fail." Also, James Hart of the UMW, assigned to the SWOC drive in Gary, red-baited more than organized. A frustrated Johnson complained that Hart "makes lengthy reports in the field organizers meetings," while he, Johnson, "turns in four [union membership] cards to his one." Johnson heard that Hart took many opportunities "to direct slanderous remarks at me" for being "red" but that Johnson had many "valuable friends in Gary" (like Mackerl, Kimbley, and Cotton), and thus refused to fall "into the idiot's trap." Although Johnson was tempted to slander Hart in revenge, he would instead say publicly, at least, "what Marc Anthony said of Brutus, 'Mr. Hart is an honorable man.'"[53]

The passion of these deputized SWOC organizers showed in the relentless organizing that they undertook during the summer and fall of 1936. It was so relentless, in fact, that Johnson and others wrote fewer progress reports because of the long days and nights in the field. However, these sporadic reports, when pieced together, show the determination of these NNC workers to get blacks into SWOC. In Gary, they held meetings three days each week, two times a day (to correspond with the steelworkers' shifts); in South Chicago they held two weekly meetings at a SWOC office at 9233 Houston Avenue; and in the Indiana Harbor, McDonald led meetings four days a week in a building on Pennsylvania Avenue. By September, Johnson reported "very slow progress" in South Chicago but that "Mac" (McDonald) and Eleanor Rye had made considerable progress in the Indiana Harbor. The previous Saturday night, they held an open-air meeting attended by "about three hundred people" that featured McDonald as a speaker and the Repertory Theatre Group, which connected the labor campaign to the NNC's cultural work. The actors performed a scene from *Waiting for Lefty*, Clifford Odets's famous play about the organization of a taxicab union, which depicted skeptical workers who eventually were won over to the "unite and fight" strategy of new unionism. They did not need to "wait for lefty" to lead them, the workers declared, but could organize themselves to "tear down the slaughter house of their own lives" and "let freedom really ring." Reporting on the performance, Johnson noted it was "enthusiastically received" and netted "roughly 70 Negroes" for the union on the spot.[54]

Aside from mass meetings, these organizers took great care in their day-to-day work to become part of steelworkers' lives. Hank Johnson, described by his contemporaries as an "ace" organizer, believed that a union only gained strength through personal contacts. By living in the community, Johnson gained the trust of the network of Gary organizers already intent on building the union. He then hired them as "volunteer organizers to whom I give . . . ten cards, and they are recruiting Negroes into the Union." Naming Cotton, Reese, Mackerl, Kimbley, and Ivory and Katherine Wright as the "six most active" of his fifteen-person team, Johnson boasted that they had recruited hundreds into the union. Meanwhile, Eleanor Rye worked on convincing the wives of steelworkers. Organizing women's auxiliaries alongside Helena Wilson, the women's auxiliary president of the BSCP, and white SWOC staffer Minneola Ingersol, Rye visited steelworkers' households, where the workers wives' conversed with less hesitation about the new union.[55]

Eleanor Rye also handled the propaganda and education campaign. Johnson complained that Rye had a "misplaced emphasis" on mass meetings and did not concentrate enough on the tough day-to-day interactions that made staunch union members. While Rye had less experience organizing workers than Johnson, she nonetheless played a vital role for swoc and the nnc in 1936.[56] Rye admitted some of her early errors and that she had "learn[ed] a lot these last two months." Yet Johnson hardly appreciated all of the roles Rye played for the nnc and swoc. Expected to do the office work for the Chicago nnc Council and field work for swoc, help McDonald in the Indiana Harbor, and attend to her family, Rye performed admirably. "I'm having a hell of a time with domestic affairs," she wrote to John P. Davis. "I don't seem to find time to clean, wash . . . etc." Meanwhile she fretted over her husband, who despite illness had to "continue working, coughing, losing weight, [making him] tired to death." While other prominent black Chicago women paid her compliments, Rye burned out by the fall of 1936. In one letter to Davis, an overworked Rye concluded: "Goddam this lousy world."[57]

Despite her frustration, Rye made a huge difference in tying the gains of swoc to the nnc. She mobilized people to attend mass meetings at places like the Metropolitan Community Church in Bronzeville, where Van Bittner, one of swoc's top white officials, Horace Cayton, the African American sociologist, A. L. Foster of the Chicago Urban League, and Thelma McWorter, the ywca industrial secretary, spoke from the pulpit alongside Hank Johnson. In these "enlightening talks," all the speakers "defined the difference between industrial and craft organization of labor," in order to convince African Americans that this union movement would include them rather than perpetuate job discrimination.[58] By late August, Rye was bringing union women into the public eye with regular meetings in the swoc lodges, by convincing leaders like the bscp's Helena Wilson to speak about the benefits of a union to other black women, not least of which was the creation of social services like a nursery for much-needed temporary child care for women who worked full time to support the family budget.[59] Although Johnson and Rye criticized one another, they actually complemented each other very well. Rye handled larger mobilizing events and press coverage and increasingly also worked behind the scenes with McDonald, playing an especially crucial role in fostering a community of swoc women. Rye also cultivated relationships with certain *Chicago Defender* reporters to discuss the plans for the steel drive. "We have been able to get practically everything in the *Defender* we want," she wrote at the end of August. "Waters and Lochard," she confided, "have been very nice to me. Morris Lewis too, I get Carte Blanche down there." Other journalists, like George McCray and Frank Marshall Davis, became nnc members, and their pioneering work in the field of black labor journalism convinced Chicagoans to support the nnc's civil rights and labor goals.[60]

Meanwhile, Johnson worked relentlessly at factory gates and on street corners as well as inside churches and barbershops to persuade workers within South Chicago and Indiana steel communities to join swoc.[61] Their cumulative work, one reporter claimed, brought steelworkers together in the Chicago region faster than in any other area and "advanced race relations at least ten years."[62]

▨ ▨ ▨ While the NNC triumvirate helped a network of black steelworkers to coalesce, it remained crucial for the workers themselves to participate in events, convince other workers in their departments to join, and become their own swoc leaders. Johnson and McDonald lived among the workers but did not work alongside them in the steel mills. Instead, they deputized a group of local organizers, who became vice presidents and stewards of local swoc lodges. Stanley Cotton became the vice president of his tin mill Lodge 1066, Mackerl was described as an "inside guard" for his local, and Jesse Reese, who became a vice president of a tin mill lodge in Youngstown, Ohio, impressed his peers by walking a picket line for seventy-two straight hours during a strike.[63] It was these steelworkers who sustained the union; the NNC activity would not have succeeded without them.

Looking at one such self-made leader, Joe Cook, reveals the process by which local activists became dedicated to the NNC and how the movement in the Chicago region progressed. Born in a rural town outside Winston-Salem, North Carolina, around the turn of the century, Cook worked in his family's tobacco fields from a young age. Both of his parents had been slaves, and after the Civil War they managed to escape sharecropping by purchasing a few acres of land. As a young man, Cook decided to migrate to Wilkesboro, North Carolina, during the First World War to find his own job. It was in this environment that Cook experienced the backbreaking and humiliating urban labor to which African Americans were relegated. He took a job in a leather tannery in the Vats Building, hauling hundred-pound bags of lime and emptying them into tubs. This process produced constant clouds of lime dust, which filled Cook's nostrils, ears, and lungs. Working ten hours a day, six days a week, he earned only twelve dollars a month.[64]

Cook had two other experiences in North Carolina that shaped his understanding of labor. First, he decided to attend the North Wilkesboro Baptist Church. He left the church in disgust, however, when the Reverend Philip Thomas praised his boss during the sermon for contributing one hundred dollars to the church's building fund. Not long after, a foreman at the tannery where he worked approached Cook about buying war bonds. Cook declined the offer, saying that he hardly made enough money to eat and pay rent. The foreman fired him on the spot.[65]

Not unlike other black laborers during this period, Cook migrated in steps from the South to the North. He worked for "plantation pay" in West Virginia coal mines as a mule driver until he found work at the Sharpesville, Pennsylvania, Valley Mould plant in 1919. During the strike wave of that year, Cook watched the tensions brew between organized labor and management and convinced other blacks in his plant to join the strike wave in steel. "Joe got us all to stick together," black steelworker Clarence Mabe remembered. "We stayed out for about three months—it was mighty rough on people to go without pay for that long but no one scabbed." The story disproves the notion that all African American workers acted as strikebreakers in 1919. Yet the strike still failed, due partly to the union's resistance to organizing African American workers and partly to the importation of black strikebreakers. Cook blamed the craft unionism of the AFL for dividing union members by skill and therefore by race. He and his fellow black workers concluded that the union's lack of support killed the strike.[66]

Cook's organizing skill became vital to everyday survival with the onset of the Great Depression. When in 1926 the Valley Mould Company announced the opening of a South Chicago plant, Cook and four others "got into a car and took off for Chicago." At forty cents an hour, the pay remained low, but matters became unbearable when the Depression caused layoffs and cuts in hours. At best, these black workers received two days of work per week, and Cook established a relief committee to pool resources and "help people survive." In short, before the formation of the NNC, Cook had already become a veteran labor organizer.[67]

The NNC, however, became a key resource that expanded and legitimized Cook's understanding of labor and protest. Cook missed the inaugural NNC convention in Chicago during the winter of 1936 but attended a Pittsburgh NNC/SWOC conference of 165 black steelworker delegates on February 7, 1937. Black professionals and church leaders, according to one account, "joined together at Elk's Rest with Negro men of steel ... in a solemn resolve to unionize the Negro steel workers as a decisive step toward economic emancipation of their people." Philip Murray, chairman of the Steel Workers Committee, confirmed this resolve. During his speech, the audience "turned to applause, to stamping of feet, and finally to a rising vote of thanks" as he concluded by declaring, "Economic liberty can only come through a strong union." Other speakers included A. Philip Randolph, who reminded workers that "organization is the basis of power," and Bishop W. J. Walls of Chicago, a key early NNC sponsor. Representing thirty-five churches in his diocese, Walls asked steelworkers to challenge their clergy back home to live up to Christian ideals. "You men," he said, "go down the aisle on Sunday and say to that preacher 'If you want to eat my bread, the time has come when my minister must stand by my toils and my struggle to put bread and meat in my children's mouths, and if you don't do that we don't want your gospel because it is not Christ's.'" This potent combination of clergy, labor leaders, and professionals brought a new sense of urgency and respectability to the steel drive. Cook and his wife, Rose, returned to Indiana and dove in to full-time activist work in the community and among steelworkers. They no longer felt alone but rather part of a national NNC and SWOC network of black laborers.[68]

Since the Pittsburgh conference, Johnson reported, follow-up meetings "[grew] like mushrooms." Cook concurred. He reported that "we sure are making progress with the Negro," after a meeting in Gary drew 350 workers, the "largest meeting of its kind held in that city." Meanwhile, McDonald reported on a mass meeting in the Indiana Harbor where the Reverend L. R. Mitchell publicly eschewed the $750 offered by steel companies and instead backed the CIO because they "will unlock the door to better living for all people." Cook kept connected to these developments and the NNC's Chicago organizers by participating in the Negro Labor Relations Committee. This committee was established as a division of the NNC council and held meetings at the "People's Forum" in Bronzeville, which brought white union organizers into the black community. For example, Nicholas Fontecchio, an Italian American SWOC organizer, discussed "the CIO and the Negro Worker" at the Forum; his talk focused on leaving preconceived notions of racial identity behind in favor of working-class unity as Americans. With more than half of all Calumet steelworkers organized by early 1937, comprising 115 new SWOC lodges, these efforts had produced a full-scale union movement.[69]

In May 1937, after helping Johnson, Rye, and others win strikes at Wilson & Bennett Company and set up lodges in a half dozen other South Chicago locations, Cook took his union local out on strike against Valley Mould.[70] The strike was precipitated by the firing of three men at the plant for union activities. When Cook approached this foreman about safety conditions, the foreman burst out against "damn niggers." He looked forward to their early deaths because then "there'll be no more niggers hired at this plant." Having heard this remark, Clarence Mabe recalled that Cook courageously retorted, "Man you will live to regret what you just said—I promise I'll make sure of that." Despite employer intimidation, including the organization of an independent union to compete with SWOC for members, the strikers held out through July. With Cook out on the picket lines and his wife directing the strike kitchen, the members of the new interracial Local 1029 of SWOC elected Cook as president, the first African American to achieve such a distinction in the Midwest district.[71]

In the midst of the strike, Cook attended a march near Republic Steel on Memorial Day in solidarity with SWOC's strike against "Little Steel." In a field in South Chicago, he witnessed firsthand what would become known as the Memorial Day Massacre. On Sunday, May 30, 1937, approximately 5,000 people assembled for a picnic and demonstration in the open fields adjacent to Republic Steel. More than half of Republic's 8,000 black workers in Chicago had become SWOC members and walked out. Other black workers honored the strike, while about two dozen decided to continue working and stayed put. Concerned about these workers giving African American loyalty to the union a "black eye," union members like Cook and Jesse Reese picketed overtime to show the union loyalty of African Americans. Another black union brother from Indiana Harbor, Lee Tisdale, a furnace worker for Youngstown Sheet and Tube, joined the march. Suddenly, police began to fire on the protestors, killing ten. Tisdale died of infected bullet wounds because he was kept in a jail cell for days before being hospitalized. Tisdale's widow claimed that "he was shot in the back," but the police claimed to have been "attacked" by the strikers, and their story initially won out in the mainstream press. Cook and other black steelworkers, furious, channeled their anger by becoming stalwart unionists. "Some suggested we get our guns," a SWOC member recalled. "Joe listened to the men for a time. Then he picked up a picket sign and said, 'Men, this is our gun. So long as you keep our ranks united, they can't beat us—so hold that line!'"[72]

The mourners of Memorial Day instead expressed their indignation in a mass meeting inside the Chicago Opera House on June 8, 1937, which symbolized the changed nature of the movement and the strength of the growing Popular Front of groups backing the CIO. Previous to the meeting, the mainstream press, led by William Randolph Hearst's antilabor *Chicago Tribune*, had continued to report that the strikers had been at fault. In one such article, James Petrillo, head of the Chicago Federation of Musicians of the AFL, condemned these "imported rabble rousers" who "organize marchers and arm them to attack police" and "blacken the labor movement." Meanwhile, the Paramount Company had edited film of the massacre into a news-reel, which showed what had really happened, but shelved it from the fear that "crowd hysteria" might result, which might lead to "riotous demonstrations in local theatres."[73] The meeting in the high culture locale of the Opera House featured speeches by Paul Douglas and Robert Lovett, distinguished University of Chicago professors, which preceded poet laureate Carl Sandburg's rise to the podium. Almost in a trance from seeing A. Philip Randolph and other black unionists in the audience, Sandburg chanted "The Brotherhood of Sleeping Car Porters" over and over again. Medical doctor Lewis Andreas, who had been at the scene on Memorial Day, later described the wounds of those shot during the incident to the audience while an organ played accompaniment. "Almost everyone in the place was crying," he later recalled to Studs Terkel, who was also at the event. This mass mourning led to the creation of a Citizens Joint Commission of Inquiry composed of well-respected Chicago liberals, which brought the nation's attention to the truth of the incident and changed the dynamic of support for the CIO nationally. The La Follette Committee in Washington confiscated the camera footage from the event to investigate it and screened its contents. The subsequent Senate investigation by the La Follette Committee upheld the story of Tisdale's wife, as the footage and other witnesses proved that police had fired on unarmed strikers who were running away from them. Locally, the national embarrassment caused Democratic mayor Ed Kelly to intervene on the side of the CIO in the events to come.[74]

This meeting helped create a culture of unity in Chicago among workers, but it alone would not win the steelworkers' battle. During the course of the six-week strike, the Ku Klux Klan tried to drive Joe Cook out of town, and a white supervisor told him that he resented that "God damned Hank Johnson you brought out," who "had no business trying to represent white men." Workers, white and black, escorted Cook to and from the picket line to ensure his safety. The union movement began to affect racial conditions outside of the plant as well. When a local bartender refused to serve Cook a beer, white SWOC members made him change his mind and forcibly integrated the saloon. John P. Davis, who visited the Indiana Harbor to bolster the morale of the striking workers, was "particularly impressed with the respect, admiration and loyalty of the workers in Valley Mould for Joe Cook, their elected president," a previously unimaginable position for a black man in an integrated labor union. Cook and his fellow strikers made sure not a single scab entered the plant until the strike was settled on July 8, 1937. The first day back on the job, however, Cook almost led them right back out again when the men saw posters on the factory wall that read "We have signed no agreement." The workers sat down until management removed the posters—in their place, the foreman posted a signed statement that the plant would honor overtime as stipulated in the new contract.

The subsequent National Labor Relations Board balloting resulted in swoc besting the union organized by employees loyal to the company by a mere six votes, making it one of the first Little Steel companies to win sole bargaining representation for the cio and "raising the standard of living of our fellow workers."[75] Speaking soon thereafter as the director of the Calumet Labor League, Cook claimed that the nnc fight for "jobs at decent living wages" in "democratically controlled trade unions" had become a reality in Valley Mould and elsewhere. "The Fight for a bona fide union," Cook wrote "is a fight for democracy."[76]

The first year and a half of swoc and nnc activism in Northwest Indiana and South Chicago was remarkable. Thousands of black steelworkers entered swoc lodges alongside whites, with relatively little discrimination. Black ministers and other leaders came to admit that the nnc and swoc brought job security and better standards of living at home. "On the matter of race," one Urban League report concluded, "the situation [because of swoc] has radically changed." Just as important, a newly empowered group of black workers had taken it upon themselves to become labor and community leaders. George Kimbley, an organizer in Gary, wrote John Davis of the "pride" he had in the nnc. He believed that its "efforts will not be in vain for the very spirit filtrates into the minds of the Negro workers throughout these United States." Due to the "tireless [work] of our Congress," he and others had built "bonds of . . . unity between black and white workers."[77]

The energy from the steel drive made the Second National Negro Congress, in Philadelphia in October 1937, a spirited and unified convention. Once again sharing the platform with the nnc's Davis and A. Philip Randolph was Phil Murray. Just as important, black steelworkers like Olabel Francis, who had helped bring about the victory at the Wilson & Bennett Company the previous spring, watched as delegates from the audience. In his speech, Murray did not mince words. He explained how swoc represented economic freedom that would "set in motion . . . the instrument that might make possible . . . political freedom." He urged all of the nnc delegates to "return to your homes and communities and render every assistance you can to this crusade" because it would bring out "economic and political salvation." Randolph shook the hand of Murray after his rousing speech, and Davis surmised that the unity established within the NNC's Popular Front between liberal and radical African Americans, as well as the interracial labor movement fostered as a result, would allow them to author a new set of antiracist democratic values, bringing the black Magna Carta to fruition.[78]

▨ ▨ ▨ With success in the steel industry at hand, the NNC hoped this momentum would spur a drive for first-class citizenship. Its leaders saw organizing workers as step one of a two-step process. The first step, they concluded, was to "get in on the ground floor." Having accomplished this unprecedented goal of interracial union membership, blacks would parlay their newfound power into community activism and municipal politics. "Once Negro workers are in the union," the NNC's Davis wrote, "it must be our task and theirs to see to it that there is complete trade union democracy."[79] Then, he hoped, labor's tactics would benefit black communities outside of the union. "Suppose *every* Negro family in Indiana Harbor were organized?" Davis asked Reverend Mitchell. "Couldn't we force high schools not only to welcome our children . . . but as well to give our sons and daughters jobs in these classrooms?" Boasting of the daily pay raise from $4.20 to $5.00 for many area steelworkers, Davis and others believed that the infusion of more than a million dollars in yearly income for black communities would feed new working-class institutions.

While SWOC's success created a model for industrial union organization, its white leaders began to resist the NNC's efforts to create a broader social movement unionism. Despite the rhetoric of Phil Murray, as early as 1937, the goals of SWOC and the NNC clashed. Davis hoped for SWOC members to lead civil rights campaigns beyond the shop floor, but SWOC's Van Bittner thought that this type of activity would endanger the goal of organizing workers. In a Chicago meeting of SWOC organizers, Bittner laid down a series of fifteen commands that illuminated both his narrow vision for SWOC and the forthcoming focus of the union. He told SWOC leaders that they should not attend meetings of other organizations except when engaged with a specific steel issue. "Forget Spain situation, auto situation, and other world problems" and spend "24 hours a day" organizing steelworkers, he said. African American organizers conversely saw these so-called distractions as part of a larger progressive movement that would fight for racial equality. Bittner, however, evinced a narrow view of how to best organize the union and cared little for developing a democratic union or antiracist movement. "We are dictating policies of all lodges until steel is organized," he concluded. Bittner told local organizers not to hire any lawyers for grievances without his approval, gave credit to the UMW, not SWOC, for the success of the campaign, and replaced organizers who disobeyed his leadership. In short, Bittner saw SWOC as a dictatorship until further notice.[80]

Soon after this meeting, SWOC's national leaders showed their disregard for the union's rank and file. The "nonelected outsiders" who led SWOC were made up of former UMW organizers like Bittner and Philip Murray, whose loyalty was to John L. Lewis rather than to steelworkers. In March, Lewis negotiated a backdoor agreement with Myron Taylor of U.S. Steel for recognition of SWOC and a basic contract. While hailed as a significant achievement for the newly founded CIO, the insistence by SWOC leaders that only the UMW names appear on the contract showed their lack of consideration for the workers themselves. The resulting agreement featured an eight-hour day and forty-hour week, a ten-cent raise, a weak seniority clause, and no change to the vacation policy, but many local union members believed that had the union leadership allowed them to engage in a strike, they would have achieved more substantial gains. This agreement portended troubles for other SWOC locals when Tom Girdler of Republic and other "Little Steel" companies decided to fight against the union. Having little trust in its own membership, SWOC only tacitly endorsed strikes when Girdler began lockouts of steelworkers to drive the union out. By the Memorial Day Massacre, the rank and file was out on strike with little help from the national leadership. Despite the killing of ten men (including Lee Tisdale) in fields outside of Republic in South Chicago and others in Ohio and Pennsylvania, SWOC abandoned this strike in defeat by November 1937.[81]

The lack of democracy in the union and low morale created by the failed strike negatively impacted the union over the next two years. Federal spending cutbacks and the tightening of the money supply triggered what became known as the Roosevelt recession of late 1937 and 1938. This renewed national economic crisis, from the perspective of SWOC, made concentration on building and maintaining the union paramount. Inside steel plants like Valley Mould and Wilson & Bennett, workers had to fight to preserve the previous gains they had made as employers sought to cut wages back to pre-CIO levels.[82] Yet many black union members in Chicago did not see the situation as a choice between union solidarity and community activism. The NNC vision of civil rights unionism required grassroots democracy to filter into the community, but the lack of local autonomy in steel deterred many workers from taking part in a wider movement. Membership in the Chicago district fell dramatically from a peak of 31,819 in the spring of 1937 to 19,684 by 1939. It was the Second World War, not union activism, that locked unions and companies into agreements (like a union dues checkoff) and thus allowed SWOC to survive and become the United Steel Workers of America.[83]

What did this larger unionization scheme mean to NNC activists? The correspondence of John P. Davis reveals his optimism that a better relationship would develop between himself and union executives. In the midst of the impressive organizing campaign in the summer of 1936, Davis wrote that SWOC "shows a disposition to do everything I have so far suggested." Yet by November Phil Murray answered Davis's request for more staff and pamphlets with a curt letter claiming that SWOC was unable to hire any more organizers. After the successful conference of black steelworkers in early 1937, Davis argued that SWOC desperately needed to appoint an organizer in the South (at the same pay rate). He surmised that 60 percent of steel's labor force was black, and that it was imperative for SWOC to act on its promises of racial solidarity below the Mason-Dixon Line to bolster the union's national power. The regional director in the South felt differently. He wrote Davis expressing "regret [at the] improper treatment of Negro workers in the South" but put any such racial work on hold until "the union is establish[ed]."[84]

Despite the recalcitrance of SWOC's leaders, the local NNC council forged ahead with broad community-based actions. On the South Side of Chicago, housing became the most salient issue. Hemmed in by restrictive covenants, many migrants to Chicago lived in kitchenettes and other apartments neglected by absentee landlords. Rent was higher than in other parts of the city because blacks had to live within a circumscribed area. In the spring of 1937, the South Side Tenants League, led by George McCray, organized over 1,000 households to protest their living conditions and present petitions to Mayor Ed Kelly. Playing ignorant, Kelly told the *Chicago Defender* that he "regretted that he knew nothing of said conditions." The Tenants League included John Gray of the NNC youth division, Joseph Jefferson of the Negro Labor Relations League (an organization that sought neighborhood jobs for blacks), and NNC attorney Orion Page. In April, the league won court cases against landlords who had raised rents without making any improvements to the property. After saving "tenants $720 yearly in [the] first [building] and $1200 in [the] second," John Gray reported that they had organized twenty other buildings and that "petitions are coming into the office faster than we can take care of interviews with landlords." Meanwhile, local SWOC lodges (contradicting national union policy) wired in support of the Wagner-Steagall Amendments to the U.S. Housing Act to create more public housing and drafted "proposals for the building up of large blocks of workers' homes through the entire country." Local NNC members like Joe Cook pushed this broad SWOC endorsement by organizing mass meetings and protesting the workforce composition and delay of the first African American public housing project in Chicago. Ishmael Flory, an NNC leader who had just moved from Oakland to Chicago, worked with the American Consolidated Trades Council of plumbers, lathers, and steamfitters, to press for more construction jobs for black unionists. Formed in 1928 by NNC member Ed Doty, the council lobbied the Chicago Housing Authority to get more blacks hired in these building trades and demanded "more active policing" to enforce contracts that required the hiring of a certain number of black workers on public construction projects in their neighborhoods. Elected as the South Side's delegate at a mass meeting, Joe Cook served as a representative at a public forum on housing sponsored by Chicago's city council to demand the completion of a public housing project in a black Chicago neighborhood. Thanks to Cook and many other black Chicagoans, the Ida B. Wells Homes in Bronzeville opened in 1940.[85]

The NNC drive in steel also influenced other South Side jobs campaigns. Top black labor organizers from steel and other industries met regularly at a building called the Forum on Forty-third Street to discuss strategies for "jobs and prosperity for Chicago's workers." In 1939, they formed the South Side Labor Council, with Mary Redmond of the International Ladies Garment Workers Union, Ed Doty of the American Consolidated Trades Council, H. C. Roberts of the Federated Hotel Workers Union, Willard Townsend of the Transport Service Workers Union, and NNC insiders like attorney Orion Page, Joe Cook, Henry Johnson, and the head of the new council, Ishmael Flory, who had become an organizer for the AFL Joint Council of Dining Car Employees. The council sought to cultivate pro-union sentiment and militant forms of activism as the means for economic emancipation. It held speakers' series, issued press releases, organized a massive antilynching rally, and fought for public utilities jobs. The South Side Labor Council came to exemplify the sprit of the Forty-third Street Forum—personifying the connection between labor and black community activism.[86]

This connection to working-class politics also influenced the decision of Chicago's black artists to join the CIO. The AFL had previously represented these artists, and the union did not protest when the Illinois Arts Project hired only artists who promised "no nudes, no dives, no social propaganda" and often purposely fell short in filling artists' quotas based on federal mandates.[87] Chicago's union local severed ties with the AFL in 1937 and affiliated instead with the United Office and Professional Workers of America, a decision that would greatly impact black artists.[88] Now part of the CIO, artists engaged in sit-down strikes and pickets at the Merchandise Mart and Works Progress Administration offices on Erie Street, succeeding in getting Increase Robinson removed as head of the Illinois Arts Project in 1938. "My first lesson on the [Illinois Arts] project," painter Charles White remembered, "dealt not so much with paint as with the role of unions in fighting for the rights of working people."[89]

But more than in any other field, the NNC's work in steel transferred energy into a parallel drive in Chicago's meatpacking houses. Located in the Back of the Yards neighborhood west of Bronzeville's South Side black neighborhood, these packinghouses were also divided by skill, ethnicity, and race. Fifteen years before, the Stockyard Labor Council had tried to sustain a biracial union movement but had failed due to intimidation from the packinghouse companies and because the 1919 Chicago race riot had deepened animosities among workers.[90] Indeed, although African Americans worked in the packinghouses in the Back of the Yards, they were not welcome to live or socialize there after dark. Before the CIO campaign in steel, a few former Stockyard Labor Council activists and a small number of Communists in various packinghouses tried to put a new union together. One such organizer, Herbert March, a Communist organizer working at Armour, reported in the summer of 1935 that the union campaign had reached its "lowest point." The Amalgamated Meat Cutters (an AFL craft union), "working hand in glove with the big packing interests," had enough of a presence in some of the smaller plants to "sabotage" efforts for an industrial union. Company and union interference had combined with a lack of coordination between Communist organizers to stymie the development of a union. "Most of the comrades carry on work in an individual manner," March admitted, "with the result that many things we should have accomplished long ago . . . have been delayed." Organizers focused on dangerous "speed-ups" of the pace of packinghouse work along the disassembly line where workers slaughtered and packaged "everything but the squeal." Though disgruntled, the workers feared dismissal from their jobs for even discussing a union.[91]

This fear began to dissipate in 1936. Inspired by the steel drive, a group of packinghouse workers approached SWOC to ask for a charter for a Packinghouse Workers Organizing Committee (PWOC).[92] SWOC eventually allowed these organizers to use the name but did not have $600,000 to put into a drive like that of steel. Thus, workers inside the plants had to do it on their own. They began with a group of black workers on the "killing floor" of smaller packing plants. Managers had supposedly placed African Americans in these critical positions because they considered them unintelligent and docile. Any attempt to shut down a plant, they reasoned, would fail without the support of this all-black department. The racist reasoning behind this placement backfired, however. Led by African Americans on the "killing floor," a work stoppage at an Armour "sheep kill" plant in 1933 had shown organizers the potential for militant unionism.[93] As one packinghouse organizer remembered, organizers who became PWOC leaders had realized that a "great well of leadership amongst black packinghouse workers . . . was suppressed" and saw these workers as the core of a potential union.[94]

The most direct link between SWOC and PWOC was one key black leader: Hank Johnson. In the spring of 1937, SWOC agreed to transfer Johnson to PWOC and continue to pay his salary as previously negotiated by the NNC. By July, Johnson had organized enough packinghouse workers to bring eighty of them to a picket line in South Chicago during the "Little Steel" strike.[95] Interacting with Johnson on this picket line and elsewhere, packinghouse workers got to hear of his organizing techniques in steel as well as experience his oratory at mass meetings on "CIO corner" outside of the main Armour hiring office by the stockyard's gates. This "marketplace of unionism," as one organizer called it, often featured the "great preacher," Hank Johnson, as a main attraction. In his speeches, Johnson employed a "poorboy southern accent" to put an "amusing twist" on day-to-day interactions between foremen and black workers who pretended to play the subservient racial role expected by their supervisors.[96] Seeing this enacted on the CIO corner, black and white workers alike would laugh about racism while at the same time becoming educated about the divisive role of race on the shop floor. Johnson's effectiveness would eventually earn him a promotion to the full-time assistant national director of PWOC.[97] He stood as a symbol to all black packinghouse workers that the new union took African American members and grievances seriously.

During the spring of 1938, a peak time of organization for PWOC, the NNC organized a mass meeting of several thousand blacks in South Chicago to bring this labor energy into civil rights activism. At the Du Sable High School, Hank Johnson chaired the meeting, which represented a "broad strata of the

From left to right: Labor leader John L. Lewis, PWOC director Don Harris, and Chicago NNC leader and PWOC assistant director Hank Johnson at PWOC rally, Chicago, July 16, 1939. Johnson personified the leadership connection between the NNC labor and civil rights campaigns and the CIO's successful organizing of unions among steel and packinghouse workers between 1936 and 1940. Courtesy of the Illinois Labor History Society.

Negro population in Chicago, artists, teachers, businessmen, physicians, trade unions and many other fraternal groups."[98] The program at the meeting featured dances, skits, and a theater troop that performed Theodore Ward's play *Even the Dead Arise*.[99] As participants entered the auditorium, they walked by large murals "depicting the struggle of the Negro for freedom," painted by "a group of young South Side artists." The main speakers, A. Philip Randolph and Charles Burton, both expressed genuine enthusiasm about the prospects for the NNC in 1938. Soon after, Randolph wrote Davis: "The opportunity for the service of the Congress in the liberation movement of the Negro people is greater now than ever before."[100] After this rally, in an unusual gesture for SWOC, Phil Murray wrote to Davis to "urge" the NNC "to continue its fight for anti-lynching legislation."[101]

Though Johnson's leadership was pivotal in transferring energy through the NNC from the community to the shop floor and back, the decisive force in organizing Chicago's African American and white packinghouse workers was the rank-and-file workers themselves. Aside from Johnson, PWOC did not have the luxury of paid NNC organizers, but it also did not have the burden of SWOC's authoritarian leadership. This autonomy complemented Johnson's organizing approach. "Speeches at an occasional mass meeting don't organize a union," he wrote; "what they do is to clear up any questions [and] do educational work. But the real job of organizing has to be done every single day by the men and women who work right in the plant."[102] Inside the packinghouses in Chicago, black workers became presidents in nine of fourteen Chicago PWOC locals.[103]

Meanwhile, with the CIO moving forward with interracial unions, the NNC wanted to push the AFL to do likewise. During the late 1930s, the NNC pushed the AFL to stop discriminating against black workers, while it also fostered the CIO's militant tactics and industrial organization. For example, NNC members supported the SWOC drive at the same time as they sponsored the "Randolph Resolution," an ultimatum named after their president, which they hoped would force the AFL to admit black workers and organize them alongside whites. The resolution demanded that AFL unions comply with antidiscrimination measures, to which they had long paid lip service. Chicago NNC members organized meetings about the resolution, distributed 10,000 leaflets, and provided thousands more leaflets for their dining car employee allies to distribute across the country. The strategy, John P. Davis believed, complemented the organization of steelworkers into the CIO.[104]

Yet many BSCP and CIO members saw these two aims as competitive, not symbiotic. In 1937, Davis would write to John Gray of the Chicago youth division of the NNC that the "tendency . . . to work away from [Chicago NNC head] Dr. Burton instead of toward him" caused a rift within the organization. Rye, Johnson, and others in the local council complained of Burton's foot-dragging, seeing it as symptomatic of the BSCP at large. Davis acknowledged that Burton had "many weaknesses," but for the sake of unity he demanded that other NNC members give him time to improve.[105] Meanwhile, Randolph pocketed his resolution at the AFL convention. His union was on the verge of recognition in late 1936 by the Pullman Company, and the BSCP leader saw it as his first priority. He told Davis he would take up discrimination with the executive board of the AFL but "merely from the point of view of a delegate." Some NNC members were disappointed, no doubt, to push a resolution that its president refused to put to the AFL leadership. "To my mind, Randolph took a rather weak-kneed position," Ishmael Flory wrote. "When he is in Chicago," he continued, "I am going to discuss with him the matter very frankly and freely."[106]

As BSCP leaders concentrated on their own union, top black Communists made matters worse. James Ford, a leader of the "Negro Section" of the party, gave credit to the NNC for its work among steelworkers. "The National Negro Congress as a body and its officers," Ford wrote in 1937, "won their citizenship in the steel drive." Yet his overall assessment of this NNC movement revealed his distance from the actual work that had taken place. For example, Ford claimed that the 1937 conference of African American steelworkers in Pittsburgh was "initiated and organized by us." The definition of "us" here remains key to understanding the CP's involvement in the NNC. If "us" referred to all members of the CP and its sympathizers, then Ford's statement taking credit for the Pittsburgh conference seems accurate. However, an important distinction needs to be made between the low- and mid-level black Communists and the "Negro Commission" of the party, in order to understand how the CP functioned inside and outside of the NNC. As one internal CP document recommended, "Communist work for the National Negro Congress" should be "based on independent activity of the C.P. among Negroes."[107] Thus, low- and mid-level Communists like Henry Johnson, Joe Cook, Ishmael Flory, and John Gray in the Chicago region became pivotal NNC members without much restriction from the CP leadership. These NNC members did not advertise their CP status (though some did little to hide it either), and the bulk of their work remained separate from that of top black CP leaders. When, for example, the Chicago-region CP (District 7) met in 1938, its top black representatives, like Ray Hansborough, Claude Lightfoot, and Beatrice Shields, had only a superficial connection to the NNC.[108] These Communists probably stayed away from the NNC council in order to assuage concerns that it would become known as a Communist-dominated outfit. Yet the practical effect of this policy divided top Communists from the NNC members who were associated with or members of the CP. Aside from CP leaders like Ford taking credit for NNC work, this relationship seemed to work without significant problems until 1939.[109]

The line between these black Communists eroded, however, when the CP abruptly changed tactics during the summer of 1939. The Hitler-Stalin Non-Aggression Pact, signed in August, led Communists in America to alter their strategy by opposing intervention in the developing European war and subsequently becoming more adversarial toward President Roosevelt and his New Deal administration, which seemed to increasingly support the militarization of the economy and possible involvement in the war overseas. This meant altering antifascism to preclude intervention in an "imperialist" war abroad and severing ties with liberal allies who supported the administration. This CP shift had a ripple effect and caused problems inside the NNC because its Communist members were now asked to follow a different policy from the antifascist Popular Front tactics they had embraced since 1935. This did not mean people like Johnson, Cook, and Flory resigned from the NNC council, but new demands from high-ranking CP members made their work much more difficult. First, they now felt pressure as party members to abide by anti-imperialist and antiwar rhetoric when they had previously been in the vanguard against Nazism. Second, the about-face licensed liberals to criticize Communists as self-serving. Even before the pact, SWOC's leaders had shown a penchant for anti-Communist rhetoric. In August 1939, two white Chicago district SWOC organizers complained that the union newspaper often wrote about Communism, Nazism, and fascism as indistinguishable terms. They believed these articles led workers to conclude "that *Steel Labor* is red-baiting, just as [much as] the Conservative Democrats and Tory Republicans." Rather than engaging the issue of red-baiting, Van Bittner, as head of the district for SWOC, condemned the men for writing the statement at all. Having been advised of "our indiscretion and lack of understanding in national policy," the browbeaten organizers asked to "retract it."[110] SWOC's antidemocratic structure would not bode well for Communists in its ranks, especially now that liberal anti-Communism was gaining more traction among some of the NNC's members and allies.

After the signing of the Hitler-Stalin Pact, Texas representative Martin Dies put an anti-Communist committee into action, which traveled the country to subpoena Communists and pressure others to blacklist them. In November 1939, Dies came to Chicago, only days before Armour workers would choose between PWOC and a company union. It was not a coincidence, then, that Dies chose Henry Johnson and Herbert March, two of the most important PWOC organizers and NNC stalwarts, to testify in his show trial. After testifying, Johnson turned this interrogation on its head in a speech in front of hundreds of packinghouse workers. "I understand that Mr. Dies came here from his home in Texas," he said, and "as one Texan to another, I can recommend to the Congressman that he stay in Texas and investigate the un-American activities of the Ku Klux Klan, and the lynch mobs [there]." The Dies committee persuaded few Chicago workers to turn against PWOC.[111] Yet the hearing targeted influential union leaders who had Communist affiliations rather than top black party leaders. This choice exposed the priority of the Dies committee to defeat the industrial union movement above its purported goal of defeating the CP. In the coming months, Ishmael Flory would have to resign his post with the Dining Car Cooks and Waiters because anti-Communist pressure caused the AFL to purge Communists from its ranks.[112] It would now be more difficult for these Popular Front Communists to hold larger NNC coalitions together. These internal tensions came at the very time that PWOC had congealed into a potential source for a mass NNC/PWOC union movement. Amid political confusion, the opportunity disappeared for the NNC, while PWOC would emerge in the 1940s and beyond as a strong civil rights union.

When PWOC and NNC activists did combine their strength in the late 1930s, their collaboration produced tangible results. In 1939, leaders of SWOC and PWOC formed a committee, Labor's Non-Partisan League of Illinois, to back Mayor Ed Kelly for reelection.[113] Although Kelly embraced the machine politics that had for so long stifled African Americans, he also considered himself a New Deal Democrat, and labor activists hoped to force him leftward once in office. The Memorial Day Massacre had stained Chicago as a violent antilabor city, and now Kelly gestured toward cooperation with the CIO. In fact, when, in December 1938, 600 livestock handlers went out on strike after the Union Stockyard and Transit Company refused to honor a previous National Labor Relations Board decision to recognize the union, Kelly clandestinely interceded. What had appeared to one PWOC organizer as "headed for a bloodbath" became a victory for the union when the police remained neutral throughout the dispute and Kelly threatened that the city would begin to charge the company for access to the Chicago River. The company recognized the union and signed a contract soon thereafter.[114]

During that same election year, another opportunity to apply progressive union aims in politics came from the election of Earl Dickerson as Second Ward alderman. NNC leaders Hank Johnson and Ishmael Flory allied with packinghouse organizer Herbert March to canvass the Second Ward, which convinced Democratic machine precinct captains to rebel and support Dickerson's candidacy. As a result, Dickerson won the city council seat and became the first black Democratic alderman from the majority-black ward. Attorney Dickerson had allied with NNC and labor networks since 1936 by attending their conferences, speaking at mass meetings, and supporting events like those at the Forum that espoused pro-union and antiracist politics. Once on the city council, Dickerson did not flinch from these politics. His participation in an NNC coalition to obtain skilled motorman and conductor jobs for African Americans on trains and streetcars, for example, led to the integration of the Chicago Transit Authority's workforce in 1943. The defiance of Dickerson to the political machine, however, led to his short stay of only one term on the city council. Nonetheless, for a few years, Dickerson championed CIO and NNC causes in city government and showed the potential for a political alliance between union and other black progressive forces.[115]

One year later, however, the black radicals and liberals that the NNC had brought together in 1936 drifted apart. The shift in CP policy, coupled with SWOC's antidemocratic structure and the reluctance of its liberal members to push for a more militant form of trade unionism activism, stalled the NNC's momentum. PWOC won its fight over the Armour Company, but its members had little reason to join a local NNC at a moment when its Chicago Council seemed fraught with political tensions. The NNC would regroup to fight for its antiracist agenda in Chicago again in the 1940s, but without the same industrial union base or strong institutional support from liberal African American organizations. Rather than attempting to implement a comprehensive Black Magna Carta, the Chicago Council thereafter concentrated on specific campaigns for economic justice and civil rights justice within unions and Chicago's South Side neighborhoods.

▦ ▦ ▦ A number of NNC members provided energy, resources, experience, and legitimacy for black workers to join the CIO and become local union leaders. As packinghouse organizer Leslie Orear explained, "Once you know that the black guys on the killing floor are in the union, and in the leadership like [Henry Johnson], then you can stick your neck out and put your [CIO] button on."[116] As many as 25,000 black workers in the Chicago region put on their CIO buttons during the late 1930s, positioning themselves as the "strategic grip" of union locals. That black workers constituted this "grip" matters because it explains their motives for unionism. The NNC role in reorienting black workers and communities changes our understanding of the CIO's "culture of unity" because it shows the central importance of black intellectuals, activists, and artists in making the New Deal work across the "color line." Blacks were not just another ethnic group but racialized "others" who had a long history in the United States of fighting discrimination, and their unique contribution to building industrial unionism has too often been taken for granted.[117]

By 1940, the NNC coalition had helped usher thousands of black workers into powerful unions. This process not only provided black unionists with newfound power but also changed the attitudes, however slowly, of white workers as well. Interracial social occasions at first described as "anxious" and "sometimes embarrassing" became easier, and taverns and diners began to welcome all workers near steel and packing plants. One group of white steelworkers, for example, discussed in late 1937 whether they would accept a black foreman. After getting challenged by his friends for saying, "I would work under him," one worker then admitted, "I tell you the truth, at first I wouldn't like a Negro boss" but "later on, I would get used to him" because "I think the CIO will get us away from thinking so much about color."[118] This transformation of attitudes about race, born of practical necessity, dramatically changed the labor movement in America. From 1936 to 1940, SWOC grew into a union of more than 500,000 total members; PWOC began one year later and reached 90,000 members; and the BSCP, with an overwhelmingly black membership within the white-dominated AFL, grew from 1,200 members in the mid-1930s to over 6,600 during the same four-year period.[119]

While black organizers delivered on their end of the bargain by organizing thousands of workers, the national unions did not reciprocate with a strong endorsement of civil rights. Black steelworkers, and to a lesser degree packinghouse workers, had to contend with national leaders who did little to enact the democracy they preached. Phil Murray headed SWOC and then the United Steelworkers of America from 1936 to 1952, which he ran as an authoritarian (and increasingly anti-Communist) dictatorship. Due in part to this leadership, black workers remained in mostly unskilled positions because departmental seniority, while preventing their outright dismissal, did not enable their promotion. In packing, Van Bittner ran the national organization until 1941, and during the war years, packing locals remained handcuffed by the "Little Steel" formula—incremental raises accompanied by a no-strike pledge—that the CIO signed with the federal government.[120]

The NNC's work had also contributed to a significant cultural shift in Chicago that has become known as the Black Chicago Renaissance. In contrast to its Harlem predecessor, this arts movement focused explicitly on the dignity of the black working class, and works from black Chicago artists depicting African American labor and resistance were featured in major national exhibits in Chicago and Washington and, most significant, within their own space at the South Side Community Arts Center. During the Second New Deal, the government sponsored approximately one hundred such centers nationwide, but few of them were located in African American neighbor-hoods. A dilapidated mansion at 3831 South Michigan Avenue became the projected site in Chicago, and artists like twenty-one-year-old Margaret Tay-lor Goss Burroughs became especially active in getting the center funded and opened. In 1941, one year after the center's opening, Eleanor Roosevelt came to Chicago to inaugurate it. In its first year alone, the South Side Community Arts Center staff organized two dozen exhibitions seen by 28,000 people and enrolled 12,000 members of the community in classes. And the center's artists also did not shy away from hosting political events. Despite harassment from the Dies committee for being "red," the NNC held a "folk party" at the center in 1941 to raise money and link its civil rights to the cultural work there.[121] For Charles White, the energy produced by the center made him more politi-cally ambitious in his art. Gordon Parks, whose photography studio occupied the basement of the arts center, remembered touring Chicago's poorest areas of the South Side with White to get a better sense of the plight of the people there. Amazed by White's "powerful, black figures," Parks claimed that they "pointed to the kind of photography that I knew I should be doing." Upon coming back to Chicago in the late 1930s to work on his book *Twelve Million Black Voices*, Wright was astonished by this group of artists. Gordon Parks remembered that Wright inscribed his copy of the book, which "became my bible" as "to one who moves with the tide."[122]

To NNC members, the tide that diverted its members did not seem in-evitable. As Davis optimistically predicted in 1938, "Current developments in the labor movement and in politics . . . make it possible for us as a group to use new and more aggressive methods to solve our problems." Davis and other NNC members believed in the untapped power of the thousands of black workers they had helped organize.[123] In addition to union gains, the Earl Dickerson election to the Chicago City Council reflected the influence of the NNC in seeking to change the political landscape of the South Side politics. The NNC hoped that Dickerson would replace Arthur Mitchell as the next South Side congressman. The NNC had previously battled with Mitchell over his lack of support or even acknowledgment of his constituents' demands. "I do not represent Negro people in any way," Mitchell had said after his victorious 1932 election; "I represent the First Congressional District of Illi-nois."[124] Dickerson, by contrast, took such militant and uncompromising civil rights positions on the city council that he only served one term. The Chicago Democratic machine pulled its support for his reelection bid and then under-mined his congressional campaign by backing William Dawson, former Republican and political pragmatist, who became the next black congressman from Illinois.[125]

While the NNC did not achieve formal political representation of its views in Washington, the work of black cultural figures on the South Side had made it the focal point for the arts nationally. Yet on the eve of the Second World War, many of the generals on this Chicago battlefront, hampered by political backstabbing and the Roosevelt recession, chose disunity. In fact, the bitter rivalries created around this split cost Hank Johnson his life in 1944 when a disenchanted Artel Shelton, another former packinghouse worker turned coal miner organizer, shot him dead over a union dispute. While the NNC changed Chicago and ushered in what Drake and Cayton called the "passing of the 'safe leader,'" its fissures highlight the difficulty of holding together such a diverse coalition of forces. For the NNC, these coalitions, both inside the black community and within labor unions, proved productive but never stable or easy.[126] Surveying Chicago as the vanguard of the CIO's organization of black workers, the *Chicago Defender* endorsed the possibility of an NNC movement. In one editorial, it called for "unity" and counseled that "we must stand together on the economic battlefront, or starve separately."[127]

The Chicago Council did not die. George McCray, Lillian Summers, Ishmael Flory, St. Clair Drake, William Patterson, and others reorganized it into an effective catalyst and supporter of community and labor struggles during the 1940s. In South Chicago and Indiana, NNC activists like Joe Cook became lifelong community and union leaders. Ed Sadlowski, who would become a key white challenger to the steel union's national leadership during the next generation, admired Cook. He was a man of "sharp intelligence," Sadlowski remembered, who voluntarily became "my first teacher in the art of organizing the unorganized."[128] Under the restructured Council in Chicago, the NNC would organize tenants, rally against lynching, protest police brutality, and fight to desegregate workplaces in the Chicago region.[129] In these fights, they often joined packinghouse trade unionists leaders such as Herbert March and Peter Davis, but still they often lacked the forces and finances to produce lasting victories. However, they did succeed in opening up wartime factory jobs to blacks, and, perhaps most significant, with strong political support from Earl Dickerson, they desegregated skilled employment jobs on Chicago's local transit system.[130]

These gains notwithstanding, with only a few dozen "energetic members" rather than a sustained movement of thousands across the city, the NNC's Magna Carta of transforming race and class relations would go unrealized in

Depression-era Chicago. Nevertheless the expanding base of trade unionists within the South Side of Chicago stood out to African American and white workers across the nation as a prime example of pushing the industrial labor movement, despite its leaders' reluctance, as a base for a labor-based civil rights movement. Below the Mason-Dixon Line, the Southern Negro Youth Congress hoped to organize black workers based on this model, and in places like Richmond, Virginia, this goal became a reality well in advance of CIO endorsement.

CHAPTER TWO

Negro Youth Strike Back against the "Virginia Way" in Richmond, 1937–1940

As a child in 1920s Richmond, James E. Jackson Jr.'s earliest memories were the sound and smell of tobacco workers. "When the quitting whistle blew," Jackson exited his father's pharmacy and anticipated the arrival of the black factory workers by the noticeable smell of tobacco in the wind. These workers had no washing facilities or locker rooms at the factories, so they walked home in soiled clothing, and in the colder months they fashioned overcoats out of burlap tobacco sacks. The smell of tobacco was unmistakably sweet but came to represent something far more bitter. The majority of these black employees—including the young, the old, and the disabled—worked at rehandling plants, where they removed the stems from the tobacco leaves, a grueling task that stripped the skin off their fingers. They labored from sunup to sundown and made only a few dollars a week. When Jackson greeted these workers until "the last straggler had passed," they seemed "joyful to taste the fresh air," but he realized their happiness was only a brief respite from work that no human should have to endure, especially for such a meager paycheck.[1]

Jackson initially responded to this daily scene by working hard in school to ensure his escape from it, but his attitude began to change during the early 1930s. Jackson grew up at the Frederick Douglass Court project, a tract of land bought by his father and other black professionals to extend the overcrowded black neighborhood in Richmond just outside the city limits. This neighborhood was shielded from some of the day-to-day assaults of Jim Crow, and as a young man Jackson excelled at the Moore Street public school, became an Eagle Scout, and as a sixteen-year-old entered Virginia Union University, located on the outskirts of town near Richmond's tobacco and textile plants. As president of his freshman class, Jackson gave a speech in the chapel, "The World beyond the Campus," in which he tried to get his fellow students to notice the factories and workers on the horizon. He challenged his classmates with the insistence that the privilege of higher education mandated a responsibility to those African Americans who struggled for basic survival, and this responsibility soon led him to check out the rumors that hunger marches into Richmond's downtown had begun to take place on Saturdays.[2]

In 1931, he attended a march from the sidelines, and what he saw changed his life. When a group of policemen blocked the path of the demonstrators, a large black woman, whom everyone called Sister Davis, took a billy club from an officer and proceeded to lead the march to the steps of City Hall. There, in a dramatic spectacle, hungry and unemployed people chanted together to demand jobs and relief from the government. Inspired, the next week Jackson marched with them, and back on campus he joined the Communist-led National Student League, which put him into a network of young black and white students who attended conferences to discuss their dissatisfaction with Depression conditions and American racism. At Virginia Union University, Jackson formed a Marxist club as well as a Cooperative Independents Club, debated against Lincoln University on whether blacks should join the Communist Party, picketed the A&P store for its hiring policies, and demonstrated on behalf of the Scottsboro defendants. In the summer of 1935, Jackson and a white student leader from the University of Virginia named Palmer Weber organized a student conference at Virginia Union University, which culminated in an interracial march of students to the capitol building, where they proceeded up the steps and into the chambers of the legislature. Interrupting the state house while in session, Weber announced: "We have business." Thereafter, Jackson read a prepared statement, which demanded an end to segregated education, including the denied application of his sister, Alice Jackson, to the University of Virginia graduate school. When the National Negro Congress (NNC) formed in 1936, Jackson eagerly joined its youth division. One year later, Jackson graduated from Howard University with a degree in pharmacology, returning to Richmond to work alongside his father—but also to help lead a new organization called the Southern Negro Youth Congress (SNYC).[3]

James Jackson symbolized the kind of leaders that emerged within the SNYC, who, during the New Deal, organized a "new kind of union" in Richmond, Virginia. Jackson and other young black activists formed an alliance with tobacco workers and waged several successful strikes to obtain better pay, working conditions, and hours. These gains fostered a new sense of pride among Richmond's black working class. In struggling to ameliorate the horrid conditions and meager remuneration at tobacco processing plants, these workers rejected the "natural" order of the Jim Crow South. The union meant much more to them than simply a means to address workplace grievances, and its actions reverberated across the city. The secretary of the local Urban League, for example, considered the alliance between SNYC members and tobacco workers as "the most significant thing that has happened to Richmond Negroes since Emancipation."[4] The managers of white supremacy in Richmond seemed to concur; they worked hard to limit the challenge. While the battle that ensued changed the terrain of the city's racial politics, Richmond tobacco companies and craft unions—despite labor shortages and the creation of the federal Fair Employment Practices Committee—conspired to keep African Americans from making significant employment and civil rights gains. But the SNYC also established a model for the CIO and its left-led United Cannery, Agricultural, Packing, and Allied Workers of America (UCAPAWA) to make region-wide gains for black workers during the Second World War.[5]

This chapter analyzes how the SNYC, tobacco workers, unions, and policy makers converged during the New Deal in the former capital of the confederacy. In February 1937, over 500 delegates attended the first SNYC conference in Richmond to "Dream, Organize, Build—For Freedom, Equality, Opportunity."[6] Three months later, black tobacco stemmers stopped work at the Carrington & Michaux factory. The SNYC and workers of Richmond openly challenged labor exploitation as the core of Jim Crow and in the process also attacked Richmond's racial and gender boundaries. As a result of this challenge by a new generation of black southerners, established institutions in the black community, the political machine, the tobacco magnates, and the unions shifted gears, chose different tactics, and learned lessons that altered approaches to both African American protest and the management of white supremacy. These boundaries, as the SNYC would discover, were formidable. They stretched back a half century and at least two generations. The perpetrators thought of themselves as welfare capitalists who operated on the basis of local southern customs. But what ultimately kept the SNYC from sustaining its movement in the tobacco factories were aspects of modern capitalism that proved anything but local or pastoral. SNYC activism in Richmond from 1937 to 1939 tested both the possibilities for industrial unionism as a means of economic justice below the Mason-Dixon Line and the limits of the Second New Deal's liberal proponents in the struggle to secure first-class citizenship.[7]

◈ ◈ ◈ Since the antebellum period, African American workers had processed nearly all of the tobacco grown in the South. Originally the workforce consisted mainly of slaves, hired out by their masters in the hinterland to urban factories during the peak season (from spring to fall), but this pattern changed after the Civil War. With the abolition of slavery, a new wage labor system continued the exploitation of black workers by keeping them desperate for jobs in urban environments. In addition to exploitation, tobacco companies began to develop cigarette-making machines, which displaced unskilled jobs for black workers with skilled positions for whites. The fine-tuning of these machines, which could produce up to 120,000 cigarettes a day by the 1880s, coincided with the rise of Jim Crow. As machines became more prominent, so did white operators, and segregated workplaces followed. Although a few white women had worked in the industry in the 1850s, by the turn of the century many more of them sought out this work as it became acceptable (although not necessarily respectable) employment.[8]

By the onset of the Great Depression, Richmond's tobacco workforce was half white and half black, half women and half men. Companies had segmented the labor force to such an extreme degree that anyone with a basic knowledge of the industry could describe jobs in racial and gender terms. Black men handled the leaf and dropped it off at centralized markets. From there, black women unpacked it at redrying plants, where they cooled it and packed it into hogsheads for production at another facility where other black women removed the leaves from the hogsheads. At this point, the leaf may or may not have been stemmed, the process by which workers remove the central stem of each leaf to ready the tobacco for processing. Most companies hired independent stemmeries to prepare the tobacco for processing. These "independents" hired an all-black labor force, with women mainly doing the stemming and the men supervising and cleaning the waste. If the tobacco arrived with its stems, the company hired black women to stem it at its own plant. After stemming, black men and boys blended and flavored the tobacco and then fed it into cutting machines for shredding. To finish the process, white women hand-packaged the cigarettes for delivery. Meanwhile, at every stage of the process, white men oversaw the work, ensuring it met quality and quantity standards and occasionally operating the machines themselves.[9]

This segregated employment pattern was profitable for employers but a miserable experience for their employees—especially black workers, in terms of health and pay. Companies assigned blacks to redrying, stemming, blending, and shredding work because these jobs were dangerous and often separate from the main processing factory. In these rehandling plants, humid conditions resulted in a better product at the expense of the health of the black workforce. Stemming and shredding produced huge clouds of dust particles, which workers, inside damp rooms, unavoidably inhaled. Flavoring tobacco exposed the lungs to chemicals, and cutting machines often resulted in the loss of fingers and limbs. Moreover, gender- and race-segregated job classifications also allowed companies to pay huge wage differentials. Black women in stemmeries, paid by the pound of discarded stems, made as little as five dollars a week. Black men made little more. White women made about double what black women did, and only white men earned a living wage. Moreover, unlike other industries, tobacco corporations did not suffer from a decline of sales during the Depression years; sales totals for the major companies ranged from $55 to $250 million a year during the 1930s. The discrepancy between company profits and workers' pay cried out for effective union organization.[10]

Four decades earlier, tobacco workers had founded the Tobacco Workers International Union (TWIU) to put forth their grievances. Although blacks sat on the first executive board and the union constitution forbade discrimination, by 1900 organizers had expelled black members from leadership posts and accepted employers' race-based job classification system. In fact, the TWIU allowed employers to organize many of its first locals as they saw fit. When in 1911 the U.S. Supreme Court broke apart the American Tobacco Company Trust into what became known as the Big Four—R. J. Reynolds (Camel), Liggett & Myers (Chesterfield), American (Lucky Strike), and Lorillard (Old Gold)—the union gained more control over its locals but not more power in the major factories. The TWIU continued to operate on the fringes of the industry because the Big Four tobacco companies refused to bargain with its leaders. Rather than provoke these companies through strikes, slowdowns, or other agitation, the union chose to start a boycott against them during the two decades preceding the 1930s. This boycott of the Big Four was largely ineffective because few consumers adhered to it. Only smaller firms that wished to capture a niche in the market sought the union label. They signed contracts to get the TWIU's stamp of approval in exchange for minimal concessions and union recognition. By the 1930s, the union seemed more like an obstacle to organizing workers than a vehicle. The TWIU in Richmond, James Jackson concluded, acted like "mosquito repellant, a union to repel the unions."[11]

In 1935, black sociologist Charles S. Johnson completed a national study for the federal government called *The Tobacco Worker* that analyzed wages, unions, segregation, job classifications, and the attitudes of workers on the job. "The question of race . . . has a long history heavily freighted with the social traditions," he concluded, which put tobacco workers into "self-destructive competition." Johnson's study unsurprisingly uncovered that the industry's white workers had acquired deep-seated forms of race-based attitudes, encouraged by employers and union alike. But what also interested him was how these notions sometimes contradicted each other and how white workers felt threatened due to the capital-intensive expansion of the industry during the Great Depression. Overall, white workers in the study expressed a desire for separate job classifications that promoted them to do the skilled work while leaving blacks with the dirty tasks, because, as one white worker claimed, "they can stand it better." But black laborers recently noticed how unemployed whites began to ask for any job in the plant, which meant that racialized employment categories began to break down, albeit to the detriment of black workers. Meanwhile, mechanization threatened jobs, and while new machines had traditionally led to the promotion of whites to run them, this was not always the case. One white worker in Richmond, for example, claimed a "race war" would result if blacks got promoted to operate machines in the tobacco factories. Yet Johnson noted that there already were a few African Americans employed in these jobs in Richmond. Another white employee, presumably one who worked alongside black workers, expressed empathy amid racial epithets. "My father told me once," he said, "you'll find lots of people in the factory as good . . . as you are, and a nigger ought to make as much as a white man."[12]

Outside of the factory in middle-class Richmond, segregation by tobacco companies reinforced a polite form of white supremacy. Contrasting themselves with the racially violent Deep South, Richmond's white elite took pride in the tranquility between local blacks and whites and believed that the best way to deal with problems was to avoid conflict, maintain good manners, and express paternalistic concern for the less fortunate. This southern civility led black leaders to exchange racial deference for a basic level of services and peace. The paternalism and accommodation put a smiling face on a highly exploitative political economy based on race, but also on class and gender, making it feel so peaceful and natural that it was seldom discussed. Arthur Dean, a columnist for the white daily *Richmond News Leader*, epitomized this attitude in a response to a reader's inquiry. He addressed a question from a

"Working Girl" who asked, "Should Persons of Different Races Marry?" His answer, of course, was no. But the way he answered the question reveals how race relations operated in Richmond. First, Dean wrote, "Some things are difficult to write about . . . because one must not show prejudice." He then admonished the girl's mother for suggesting she would shoot her if she married outside her race. "A working girl," Dean wrote, "who has the ability to support herself . . . is not influenced by threats of a shooting party." Instead, Dean suggested, that while "every race has behind it a fine background and splendid traditions," some races "have more real depth and interest in cultural things" than others. Dean's answer effectively mirrored Virginia's stance on white supremacy: silent "separation by consent," otherwise known as the "Virginia Way."[13]

⊞ ⊞ ⊞ For the new generation of educated black youth, however, the lives and position of blacks within southern society seemed increasingly unsatisfactory. Their college educations in the context of the Depression led to a growing willingness to not only challenge the existing social order but also draw explicit connections between economic and racial oppression.

Like James Jackson, Edward Strong had grown increasingly convinced of the responsibility of young African Americans to develop a youth movement that extended beyond the campus. Born in Texarkana, Texas, in 1914, Strong grew up in a devout Baptist family. At the age of twelve, his family migrated north to Flint, Michigan, where he became involved in the youth division of the NAACP. During the early Depression years, Strong lived in Chicago where he attended the YMCA College, and through his youth work in the church he helped John Gray, Ella Baker, James Jackson, and others organize a Negro Youth Conference in Chicago in June 1933. The conference and other National Student League activity generated a "pledge" for youth to fight "racial supremacy," to "popularize the culture of the Negro people," and to "serve untiringly in the promotion of unity of Negro and white students."[14] Locally, the National Student League tacked on a resolution condemning the practice of Strong's YMCA College for barring black students from using the swimming pool.[15] When the NNC met in Chicago three years later, Strong saw it as a new opportunity to further develop and sustain the youth movement agenda. During the preparations for the first NNC convention, executive secretary John P. Davis took Edward Strong under his wing. In Davis's mind, Strong stood out from the rest of the youth delegates because of his experience. Strong assisted Davis with organizing the NNC in Chicago, and after-

Edward E. Strong, ca. 1940s. A protégé of John P. Davis in the NNC, Strong helped lay the groundwork for the formation of the SNYC in Richmond in 1937. From box 2, National Negro Congress Photograph Collection. Courtesy of Photographs and Prints Division, Schomburg Center for Research in Black Culture, The New York Public Library, Astor, Lenox, and Tilden Foundations.

ward Strong moved to Washington to complete a graduate degree in political science at Howard University, where Davis helped him develop the initial program of a southern youth division of the NNC.[16]

After the NNC formed in Chicago, the youth delegates met again that summer in Cleveland, where they decided to concentrate their efforts on the South. The formation of SNYC, the delegates concluded, was urgent because "life for Negro kids after ten is little else but hard labor, low pay and no chance for education and advancement."[17] Louis Burnham, born in Barbados and raised in Harlem, was a student at City College in New York and American Student Union leader, a Popular Front national student activist federation, when he first heard of the SNYC. Writing in the *Norfolk Journal and Guide*, he applauded the idea of the SNYC (and would later become one of its most significant leaders). Taking seriously Langston Hughes's criticism of black students as "spineless Uncle Toms, full of moral and mental evasions," Burnham wrote that the bravery of the Scottsboro defendants and Angelo Herndon— young black men on death row who had fought back—had caused educated black youth like himself to reconsider professional careers. "Negro youth," he concluded, "have steadily been gaining the strength and the will to fight back."[18]

As a result of their higher educations and the circumstances of the Depression, many organizers of the SNYC had come to understand the racial politics of the South from a different angle of vision. Disfranchised, threatened with lynching, and segregated into the worst occupations, these black youth had neither a receptive environment nor significant material resources to draw upon. Far from intimidated, however, Ed Strong took comfort in the "great tradition [that] flows with the blood in our veins." If Frederick Douglass, a self-educated black man who escaped from slavery, would not rest until he and his race achieved freedom, who was Strong to cower and hide? Besides, Strong wrote, "Southern culture largely has been built upon our labor."[19] Burnham also came to reject the mythology of the South. White southerners romanticized the southern way of life as noble and chivalrous, and northerners expressed nostalgia for its simplicity. But Burnham could not reconcile these myths with the reality he saw during the Depression. "For [black] young men and women the South is not 'exotic,'" he wrote; "it is real and tangible— for them the South is life. A successful All-Southern Negro Youth Conference will be an investment . . . in building a really democratic South."[20]

The SNYC call for the founding conference declared that by "bus, trains, automobiles, on foot—they're going to Richmond!" Since organizers expected over 500 delegates, they began in January to prepare for their visitors and persuade the local black community to embrace them. An initial breakthrough came when Ed Strong made arrangements to speak at the Leigh Street AME church at a forum sponsored by the Reverend C. E. Queen. Other ministers had hesitated to endorse the conference because they feared upsetting the racial status quo; Queen gave the SNYC organizers moral legitimacy and a place to hold meetings. A reporter for the *Richmond Planet*, the black newspaper in Richmond, attended this church meeting and became persuaded of the SNYC's intentions. He described Strong as "not a 'blood and thunder' speaker" but someone "who deals in facts and figures with the dexterity of a master." By the end of the month, the Reverend C. C. Scott agreed to host the SNYC at his larger Fifth Street Baptist Church, and the *Planet* officially endorsed the conference as "pregnant with possibilities." It instructed "every patriotic man and woman to give comfort and support to these youthful warriors enlisted in a righteous cause."[21] The white press did not endorse the conference, but neither did it object, and one report even mentioned that the local government appropriated $500 to "entertain" the delegates.[22] Without fear of condemnation or violence, SNYC organizers saw Richmond as the best place to begin their new organization.

Over 500 delegates and 2,000 spectators filled the church on the second weekend of February 1937. Dr. C. C. Scott, the church's pastor, gave an opening invocation on Saturday morning. But it was the NNC's John P. Davis who set the tone for youth delegates to decide their own destiny. Davis suggested that adult delegates should waive their right to vote on all matters at the conference. The youth delegates (mostly in their twenties) approved this suggestion by giving him a "big hand" before breaking into roundtable discussions that afternoon. The roundtables all focused on the responsibilities of this younger generation. Christopher Columbus Alston led a discussion, "Youth on the Job." Angelo Herndon (whose 1932 arrest for causing an interracial "insurrection" in Atlanta and subsequent death row case made him a cause célèbre) spoke on "Youth as a Citizen." James Jackson talked about "Youth as a Student."[23]

At the mass meeting on Saturday night, the delegates listened to some of their most respected elders deliver speeches. Max Yergan, having spent more than a decade of his early life in South Africa, spoke about the parallels between imperialism in Africa and the American South, a system that "uses labor without compensation and destroys the culture of a people." Seeing both situations in terms of class and race, he stated that "I do not believe that

the poor white element . . . is responsible for lynching [in America]. I believe that the responsible people . . . are the ones [in power] who could have
stopped it long ago and have not done so." Yergan advised the youth delegates
to prepare themselves for a long and hard struggle against white supremacy
to reunite the working class.[24]

Following Yergan, two of Howard's most distinguished scholars spoke with
invectiveness rarely heard at a public meeting in the South. Prior to their
speeches, the youth delegates had "heated discussion on the social restraints
placed on students by many schools of higher education in the South."
Whether influenced by this discussion, which one reporter deemed a "rebellion," or chosen by the SNYC because of their opposition to this restraint,
E. Franklin Frazier and Mordecai Johnson of Howard University encouraged
black youth to fight. Frazier, the famous sociologist who left Fisk University
in 1934 for the academic freedom of Howard, commanded the audience to
reject established methods for interracial betterment in favor of militant and
even revolutionary actions. Both African American and interracial groups,
Frazier said, "have been making surveys for the last 25 years and none of
them have meant anything." Frazier told the young men and women not to be
"bamboozled" into "getting sophisticated" or "being good," because "it won't
do you a damn bit of good here." Frazier advised the SNYC audience to mis-
behave, organize, and act. "The Negro is not over-organized," he thundered,
"but organized too much for futility."[25]

Dr. Mordecai Johnson, the acting president of Howard, who had changed
the university into a black intellectual powerhouse over the previous decade,
followed Frazier by urging black youth to wake up from the "hypnotic influ-
ences of the world." Many African Americans "of the intelligentsia," he told
the packed Sunday morning audience, "feel [Jim Crow] has been in existence
since I was a boy and will probably be in existence long after I am dead." Johnson then quoted from Romans 12:2: "And be not conformed to this world: but
be transformed by the renewing of your mind, that ye may prove what is that
good, and acceptable, and perfect will of God."[26] To Johnson, this biblical passage legitimated the radical thinking that would undermine the psychology
of Jim Crow, something that both he and Frazier had tried to do from inside
the academy.

The SNYC forum gave both of these intellectuals a chance to explain how
to fight racial inequality in the South as they had done, but also how to go
much further. These Howard intellectuals, who increasingly saw inequalities
in class and racial terms, had "performed a daredevil act," according to one

historian, to maintain their places at the helm of black institutions while trying to implement social change in the 1930s, which included fending off an investigation by the government after Howard hosted the initial NNC conference in 1935.[27] Unrestrained by such institutional ties, young southern blacks had more of an opportunity to perform their own brave daredevil acts. Frazier and Johnson urged the audience to become intellectuals as a means to act, not as a means to show sophistication, respectability, or social conformity.[28]

The conference's impact on the young delegates echoed throughout the larger Richmond citizenry. The white *Richmond Times-Dispatch* and the African American *Richmond Planet* provided extensive coverage of the sessions. The black-owned *Norfolk Journal and Guide* also reported on the event and later sent an "Inquiring Reporter" to ask local blacks, "What is your opinion as to the outcome of the Southern Negro Youth Conference held here a week ago?" A student from the local Virginia Union University commented that "lots of good will be accomplished as the result of this movement." James Jackson's mother, Clara Jackson, claimed she was "astonished" by the resolve of the youth in attendance, her son included. Dr. W. T. Johnson, a civic leader and First World War veteran, concluded that he now "believed in the movement," and the head of a local benevolent club claimed the sessions "got at the very heart of conditions" in Richmond.[29] With the endorsement of both black intellectual leaders and many local blacks, the SNYC leadership in Richmond came away from the conference in search of an issue to activate the rebellion.

Organizing industrial laborers stood out as the preeminent issue before and after the conference. Since early 1937, SNYC leaders took careful note as the Richmond press reported on union drives in the coal, steel, and auto industries by the newfound Committee for Industrial Organization (CIO). Protected by the Supreme Court's recent affirmation of the Wagner Act, thousands of workers went on strike. After the success of the sit-down strike at General Motors in Flint, Michigan, and the launching of the NNC-backed drive in steel, John L. Lewis of the CIO announced that the new movement hoped to venture south and organize textile workers.[30] SNYC leaders saw this as a great opportunity. The SNYC proclamation drafted at the Richmond conference stated: "We shall join our hands together to build trade unions in the South free from prejudice."[31]

After the conference, the SNYC organized a delegation from Richmond that took the youth movement into the White House. During the previous year, Ed Strong, as youth chairman of the NNC, and other future SNYC leaders testified during Senate hearings in favor of the American Youth Act, which would provide more adequate government employment for young people on a nondiscriminatory basis than had the New Deal's National Youth Administration program. Now organized as the SNYC, they joined youth from around the nation who traveled to Washington, D.C., in late February 1937 to renew their lobbying campaign. The Richmond SNYC delegation joined "hundreds of white and colored youth from other cities," and Strong was among the seven delegates chosen to meet with President Roosevelt. In the White House, the delegates gave the floor to Angelo Herndon, who told the president of his imprisonment. His lawyers were in the process of appealing his eighteen- to twenty-year sentence on the chain gang to the Supreme Court, Herndon explained to the president, and his false arrest for asserting his citizenship represented the story of many other black youth in the South. The delegation demanded more funding for the National Youth Administration by passing the American Youth Act and supported Roosevelt's plan to appoint new liberal members to an expanded Supreme Court to overturn cases of southern injustice like that of Herndon. Although the bill for the Youth Act would fail to pass in the coming months, the demonstrations that weekend helped stop Republican plans to cut National Youth Administration funds for the next fiscal year and solidified ties between progressive blacks and whites in support of a jobs campaign.[32] This delegation inspired the newly formed SNYC because its leaders now saw how an interracial youth movement had the potential to overturn Jim Crow. Symbolizing this optimism, SNYC members took pride in the news that the Supreme Court set aside the conviction of Herndon in a five-to-four decision in April.[33] They hoped this foreshadowed more decisions by the Court to protect civil rights, and SNYC leaders in Richmond eagerly sought to begin a local program of action for economic and racial justice.

Outside of SNYC, black and white leaders in Richmond reacted to news from Washington about the progress of New Deal legislation, especially in the unionization of industrial workers, with uneasy anticipation. The modern urban world, and particularly unrest around labor, presented a challenge to Richmond's peaceful management of white supremacy. The *Richmond Times-Dispatch*, a white and relatively liberal paper, for the South, applauded the right to organize but also hoped that the Wagner Act would be "amended to the end that it be fashioned into an instrument for the promotion of industrial peace, instead of an implement for stirring up strife." A political cartoon on its editorial page illustrated this unease: a white male worker, armed with a sledgehammer labeled "power," stood poised to hit a brick labeled "responsibility," which was in turn held up by a base labeled "Wagner Act Decisions." The newfound power of this laborer, granted to him by the Supreme Court's recent validation of the Wagner Act, came with important "responsibility" to preserve law and order and the status quo. In a similar fashion, the white *Richmond News Leader* also approved labor organization but made it clear that "a strike, ninety-nine times in 100, is an inexcusably wasteful method of settling any labor dispute." Even the African American *Richmond Planet*, whose editors commended the militant SNYC conference, fretted over the potential strife that the CIO would bring to Richmond. In response to what it termed an "epidemic of sit-down strikes" elsewhere, an editorial condemned the tactic as "an unhealthy sign [of] anarchy." The governor responded to these fears by declaring sit-down strikes illegal in Virginia, although he added that state authorities would obey national laws and not intervene unless local leaders requested assistance.[34]

To everyone's surprise, a black woman at South Richmond's Carrington & Michaux Tobacco factory was the first to yell: "STRIKE!" On the morning of Friday, April 17, 1937, fifteen machine operators at the plant stopped working, but, threatened with dismissal by the white foremen, they went back to work fifteen minutes later. During lunch break, however, word circulated among the 300 employees about the incident. When the break ended a half hour later, the entire workforce, in response to the strike call by a female stemmer, refused to return to their stations. The plant sat idle for the next three hours until management decided to pay employees for the previous week, call in the police, and send employees home until Monday. The employees abided by this, and the police escorted them off the property without incident. W. W. Michaux Jr., vice president and general manager of the plant, told a reporter that his employees had not gone out on strike but were fired. The plant had shut down early on Friday to "get rid of some agitators," and "when we reopen we'll take back the ones we want." Meanwhile, T. M. Carrington, the head of the company, told the *Richmond News Leader* that "we could shut down until next season" but would rather not for the sake of those who "need the work."[35]

Over the weekend, the workers contacted both the AFL and the CIO about organizing a union. The newfound CIO claimed it did not yet have a tobacco union to organize these workers. The AFL's TWIU, which had active locals at several Richmond cigarette factories and had just signed an agreement with the American Tobacco Company the previous week, refused to let them affiliate. The president of TWIU, E. Lewis Evans, came to Richmond over the weekend to announce plans to organize the white employees of Philip Morris.

When asked about the black strikers at Carrington & Michaux, Evans dismissed the right of these black workers to strike, calling it "unauthorized." "We have not had a strike since 1900," Evans boasted, "and we don't want to start off with one here now." A reporter among the workers gathered at Loving Union Hall, not far from the plant, described their situation as "hopeless." Without the support of any established labor union, it seemed that workers would return on Monday and that W. W. Michaux, after firing some of the workers, would allow the rest to come back to work under the same conditions they had protested on Friday.[36]

While both the company and the white press discounted the resolve of the workers, Christopher Columbus Alston of the SNYC stepped in to help them organize their own union. Five years earlier, in Detroit, Alston, a self-described "nosey little kid," had skipped school to march alongside 5,000 unemployed workers in front of Ford's River Rouge plant. At this infamous demonstration, police had fired on the demonstrators, killing five and wounding over a hundred others. Among those murdered was George Busell, a Jewish friend of Alston. "Instead of jobs we got bullets," Alston later recalled, and the events of that day led him "to [become] a confirmed radical." Later, having dropped out of school for a job at the Ford plant, Alston began to meet with other workers to discuss their grievances. Overheard by Ford's legion of security spies, he was escorted out of the plant a week later and told to not come back.[37] To Alston and other SNYC members, the walkout at Carrington & Michaux offered an opportunity to implement the resolutions of their founding conference and bring the militancy of Detroit to Richmond. Over the weekend, Alston began to organize the striking workers into a union and to rally the African American Richmond community behind them.

By Monday morning, Alston and the strikers had accomplished both goals. They had recruited Josephus Simpson, managing editor of the *Richmond Planet*, to take part in a negotiating committee, which also included himself and three elected employees from the new union, John Shaw, Levi Hansley, and Mildred Hansley, to represent the 300 workers. All five people that the "Richmond Inquiring Reporter" interviewed expressed strong support for the strike, seeing it as a hopeful sign of changes to come. One observer hoped they would "have courage enough to stick out until they get what they want." Another saw the strike as the beginning of a larger movement, calling it "the best thing that has ever happened in Richmond." He continued, "Everywhere Negroes are underpaid and overworked. Somebody must make a start and these tobacco workers who have had the courage to venture out should receive the support from every Negro." A third respondent agreed and also indicated that the larger black community had rallied to their cause. "It is encouraging," he said, "to see those few Negroes who were making a decent salary support those who were getting little or nothing. That shows cooperation."[38]

Word of the strike spread statewide over the weekend, and Frank Kruck of the Virginia Department of Labor was deployed to Richmond to ensure its peaceful settlement. On Monday, the strike committee showed Kruck several pay envelopes from the last week as proof of the "scandalous" wages. Many workers earned as little as $1.20 a day for 65,000 stems. The most privileged stemmers handled the heavier three-year-old Burley-dried tobacco. If a worker produced the maximum of thirty-five pounds in a day, he netted about $1.75 in pay. However, those handling the Georgia Leaf, a green tobacco, could not make more than fifty cents a day at a nickel a pound. With the highest wages around $9 a week, no one at the plant earned a living wage. Cora Born, a seventeen-year-old stemmer, explained to Kruck what these low wages meant. She told Kruck that she had earned $4.42 in the previous week at the plant but had had to pay $2 a week in insurance and $2.50 a week to rent a room. These two payments alone left her in debt; all other items had to be bought on credit. Another unidentified stemmer sobbed as she explained to Kruck that buying food from stores on credit led these establishments to garnish her wages. Following this testimony, the committee described the abominable conditions of the plant. Only one fan worked on the shop floor, and management would not allow workers to open the windows to ventilate the humid air and clear dust particles from inside the factory. In addition, both male and female workers lacked adequate restrooms or changing areas. According to a reporter from the *Richmond Planet*, the women's lavatory "has the appearance of a horse stall, with five antiquated fixtures lined up on a concrete floor and one on which an attempt has been made to make it private to some extent." At first Kruck listened as an impartial arbitrator, but he later conveyed sympathy for the strikers in a private meeting with the committee, expressing his amazement at how these workers survived.[39]

The committee demanded that the company provide a wage increase, shorter hours, and improved sanitary conditions and promise that all workers would be allowed to return to work once an agreement was reached. After negotiating with W. W. Michaux and the rest of the plant's management, Kruck obtained all of the workers' demands except a per-hour wage increase. The strike committee rejected these terms but offered to split the wage difference to a five-cent-per-hour raise. The company returned with a proposal for two and half cents. The workers vehemently rejected this offer, and finally the company agreed to the five-cent wage hike and improved sanitary conditions and limits on hours. Having met them "about half-way," Michaux publicly announced that all the employees (including fifty who had been laid off the previous week) should come to work on Monday. Upon hearing of the settlement, the workers "took on new life" and "rejoiced."[40]

An editorial published in the *Richmond Planet* best encapsulated the changed mood brought about by this spontaneous strike and subsequent SNYC alliance. Recounting these "peonage jobs," the editor echoed statements from the SNYC conference. "Why lose time discussing health and crime statistics and inter relations? Why worry about being decent, when such indecency prevails?" The New Deal and the Wagner Act, the paper suggested, meant nothing if a plant like Carrington & Michaux could expose workers to horrible health conditions and leave them with "starvation wages" to take home. While the *Planet* stuck to its previous condemnation of sit-down strikes, the editorial ended on a more ambiguous note. "In the instant case," the editors concluded, "we are bewildered in making a decision as to whether the ends justify the means."[41]

This strike spirit proved contagious. Workers at I. N. Vaughan and Company did not waste much time debating the merits of the action at Carrington & Michaux. On the last day in April, they met at C. E. Queen's Leigh Street Methodist Church, the key SNYC meeting place and the "only church that would come to the rescue of the striking workers." This space had become a headquarters and refuge for union members to pray, sing, and congregate off the street in Richmond, and at this particular meeting workers from the recent strike congregated with 250 Vaughan employees. Asking them to join together, Christopher Columbus Alston spoke of the recent victory and the need to spread the unionization drive. By the end of the night, the majority of Vaughan employees in attendance had joined the second local of the Tobacco Stemmers and Laborers Union (TSLU).[42]

Vaughan employees went out on strike five days later, with demands similar to their predecessors: higher wages, better health conditions, shorter hours, and recognition of the union. Yet not all Vaughan workers immediately understood why they had stopped work. "I am just following the gang," one female employee told a reporter. "I worked so hard this morning and until I am aching all over," she complained, "and I would not like to lose my money." Leslie Smith, a local student at Virginia Union University and SNYC

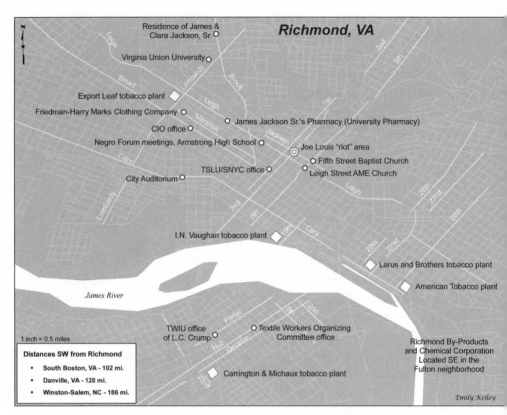

The snyc and the tslu in Richmond, 1937–1940. Map by Emily Kelley.

organizer, stepped in to allay any confusion about the local union's intentions. He appealed to the workers by showing them respect as "ladies and gentlemen" and by making the union "fun," with picnics, banquets, and especially singing. Organizing pickets in groups of fifteen, Smith gathered materials to make placards for the workers.[43] One such sign read, "Officials get $150,000 One Year Extra Bonus: What Do We Get?" Another striker pasted wage slips on a placard, writing on it, "The Proof Is in the Pudding—Could You Live on This?" Even more effective in fostering unity were the booming voices of the strikers, which could be heard from blocks away. According to reports, the workers chanted such phrases as "We cannot live on bread alone" and "Free us from wage slavery," in between singing Negro spirituals. snyc organizers also taught the workers the famous union song "We Shall Not Be Moved." The workers quickly embraced the song, adding verses such as "Mr. Alston Is Our Leader" and "We Want Better Wages." A *Richmond Planet* reporter described the scene as "a soul-stirring sight." This group of "black workers 460 strong, in defiance of custom and tradition," he wrote, encircled "the plant of their employer singing with a gusto born of courage and determination."[44] Only one-half of the plant had been unionized before the strike, but the combined effect of the walkout and the subsequent unity fostered through church meetings at Leigh Street, performances outside the Vaughan plant, and the backing of SNYC organizers brought 467 of 469 Vaughan employees into the TSLU.[45]

The solidarity of the strikers became essential when the company's managers tried to process the tobacco that was inside the plant. They got a few black men and women into the plant by having them claim that they needed to use the bathroom inside. When the scabs did not emerge and a few others tried the same tactic, strikers outside the plant "menaced them with sticks" until they left the neighborhood. Rumors circulated that the company would next try to move the tobacco from inside its plant to other local stemmeries. To ensure that such a move would not occur, male TSLU members organized an all-night vigil to guard against anyone entering the Vaughan factory or tobacco leaving it. Carrington & Michaux employees, in a show of solidarity, announced that they would not stem any tobacco coming from the Vaughan plant. These actions effectively closed off other means to process the tobacco inside, which would soon spoil, making the company more anxious to settle. Vaughan soon agreed to all of the terms the union demanded except wages, offering a 20 percent rather than 40 percent increase. TSLU representatives, encouraged by the growth of the local and seeing this agreement as the first of many, signed the contract.[46]

With this second strike victory, many of Richmond's African Americans began to see the emergence of a movement. For Robert Davis, a black worker, New Dealers had finally recognized the plight of America's southern laborers. "Our President," he told an audience at the Leigh Street Church, "has fixed it so the laboring man can't be beat over the head any more." Such protection, he believed, would allow organized labor "to fix it so that in the State of Virginia when one wheel stops all will have to stop." Alice Burke, writing for the *Richmond Planet* in late May, also envisioned this movement spreading across Virginia so that tobacco magnates would have to pay their black workers a "decent living wage" of twenty dollars a week. "When every worker is organized," she wrote, "the boss will have to deal with the Union and will have to pay what the workers demand—or no work!"[47] Edward Strong, whom Burke praised as one of the "young people of the Southern Negro Youth Congress who have led the Stemmers to victory," expressed a similar optimism. He believed that the collaboration between the SNYC and the tobacco workers showed that "it will be possible . . . to secure liberation from economic slavery." Currently at 900 members, the TSLU would continue to grow so long as young people remained committed to helping these workers. "If the young people working with the unions will continue to display the same courage . . . and the community will continue to back them heretofore," Strong boasted, "we may say that the success of the drive is a foregone conclusion."[48]

⊞ ⊞ ⊞ Other evidence from these first strikes, however, suggests a more complicated picture of the prospects of this union movement. Because of the success of the new union, larger institutions took notice and responded. African American attorney J. Thomas Hewin, who had allied with the union, warned that the TSLU should "not get intoxicated by the fruits of their victory." Hewin's statement portended that these strikes would cause a negative reaction inside the black community and greater Richmond that would keep anything from being a "foregone conclusion."[49] Notions of respectability and civility, both black and white middle-class Richmonders realized, might come undone by a black-led movement of workers that exposed the city's racial status quo by linking it to labor exploitation. Both the AFL and the CIO had originally turned down aid requests from these tobacco workers, but the TSLU's victories prompted them to take a second look. For its part, the CIO reacted with enthusiasm and caution. On May 11, John Suttle, a former coal miners' union organizer who now worked for the CIO, arrived in Richmond to establish a regional office. Although he declared as his first priority the establishment of a CIO haven for the independent TSLU, the national office had actually sent him south to organize textiles, and union representatives from the white clothing workers' union began to attend meetings of the independent tobacco workers' union. At one such meeting, Albert W. Cox of the Textile Workers Organizing Committee spoke to the tobacco workers and claimed that there was not a color bar in the CIO.[50] Perhaps not—but the workers also knew that textile workers remained a practically all-white employment field by "custom." Suttle eventually agreed to help the TSLU, allowing Jackson, Alston, and others to become CIO organizers, albeit on a voluntary basis. Without the financing that their counterparts in the clothing industry received from the national CIO, SNYC organizers had to find other work to survive.[51]

John P. Davis, executive secretary of the NNC, saw an opportunity to put the "prestige" of the newfound CIO behind the TSLU. He contacted John Brophy of the CIO's leadership in Washington, D.C., to suggest a wide-scale

organizing campaign. Davis had spent several months in 1934 with black tobacco workers in North Carolina, making contacts and conducting an extensive survey of five local plants. The results of the survey showed that the
President's Reemployment Agreement raised hourly wages, but speedups in
production had caused the weekly wage to decrease. Most important, the
TWIU of the AFL had done little to address these concerns. Davis found that
the TWIU organized separate locals and only negotiated for the white employees. When Davis testified on behalf of blacks in the industry during the
1934 National Recovery Act hearings, he met with the leadership of the TWIU,
whom he described as all being over seventy-five years of age and "in bed with
the company." Davis discovered, for example, that the secretary of the Anton-
Fisher Local of the TWIU also served as the secretary to the general manager
of the company. The TWIU had negotiated "secret contracts" with companies
to receive dues payments from their employees in exchange for a no-strike
policy and only minimal improvements for the workers themselves. Davis
encountered the undemocratic tactics of the union firsthand when he helped
organize a North Carolina Tobacco Workers Council. The council voted, as
required by the TWIU constitution, to override the president's decision to
never hold a convention of the locals. When the resolution passed by the two-
thirds vote required, the president, E. Lewis Evans, traveled to North Carolina, suspended the leaders in the workers' council, and "bought off other
union officials."[52]

This time, Davis promised the CIO's John Brophy minimal costs and excellent organizers. He told Brophy that the dues of the workers would pay for the
organizers after eight weeks. As for the organizers, Davis suggested that the
union hire SNYC leaders, whom he described as "capable and alert young men
who have grown up in tobacco cities[, which] naturally led to a new attempt
to aid tobacco workers."[53] As the union grew, SNYC organizers like Alston
and Strong conferred with Davis in order to harness the national momentum
of the CIO to their work. Davis knew of their dedication and militancy and
therefore recommended them with complete confidence.[54]

The TSLU strikes also led the TWIU of the AFL to recognize these black
workers. After the first strike, the TWIU offered membership to the independent union. "You should have seen how the A.F. of L. rushed to us with open
arms to take us over after all the fighting was done," John P. Davis wrote,
"but we said no." Meanwhile, a "Congressional source" leaked information
to E. Lewis Evans, president of the TWIU, that AFL unions in Richmond and
Durham were "going 'COMMUNISTIC' 'C.I.O.' and with the John P. . . . DAVIS

crowd." The TWIU began to panic and defined this new movement as a return to the days of Reconstruction. "It would be a shame," Evans wrote, "if this movement were to develope [*sic*] into something similar to the old CARPET-BAGGER campaign." To the AFL, these new organizers sought nothing other than "SOCIAL EQUALITY."[55]

Although the *Richmond News Leader* concluded that friction between the AFL and the CIO was "not a local but a national dispute," the reaction to the strikes showed otherwise. Over the next weeks, Evans planned a rejuvenation of the TWIU by solidifying the secret agreements it had previously made with the companies. Behind closed doors, Evans suggested to Richmond TWIU organizer J. E. Lentie that the union should coerce these companies into signing agreements with the AFL as the lesser of two evils and should conspire to keep the CIO out. "I have an idea," he wrote in July, "that the FIRMS will object to the NIGS getting into the C.I.O. or in that Communist bunch that they have been training with . . . but they may not want their appearance in the idea." Race-baiting, sabotage, and more secret deliberations, which had been the leadership's method before the rise of the TSLU, now became even more central to the AFL union's organization strategy.[56]

The workers who defied the TWIU's no-strike policy and formed the TSLU certainly acted in "defiance of custom and tradition," but their actions also showed just how entrenched the Jim Crow "Virginia Way" of civility had become. All press accounts remarked on how "orderly" the demonstrators were, which suggests that both the strikers and the press tried hard not to alarm the larger public. SNYC organizers stressed that the strikes would "remain orderly," and the press noted their "unusually orderly conduct." Richmond had braced itself for the arrival of labor disturbances, and the highlighting of order by the white and black press tried to allay these fears. In a column in the *Richmond Planet*, the reporter described the Vaughan strike as "not marked by bitterness either on the part of the employees or employer."[57] The employer, Mr. Vaughan, "appears to be a kindly old gentleman at heart," the reporter concluded, and "had never been overbearing in his attitude and had always been kindly disposed to his employees."[58]

The organizers in the SNYC felt otherwise about this paternalistic rhetoric. The SNYC did not share the sympathy of southern white progressives for people like Vaughan. They instead believed that this emphasis on Vaughan's good manners meant that liberal whites privileged civility above the confrontation that would bring about changes in the racial and class caste system of Richmond. Strong wrote that a "rotten liberalism . . . has too long . . . characterized race relations in the South." Sick of the "patronizing, back-slapping kind of attitude," Strong outlined new goals for black youth that no longer included accommodation to Jim Crow. These black youth, he believed, "show fair promise of removing the unwholesome taint from the phrase, 'Some of my best friends are Negroes.'"[59] Both the supposed orderliness of the employees and the kindliness of the employers would be tested in the coming months, as Richmond blacks and whites responded to the growing black labor movement.

▨ ▨ ▨ On the last day of June 1937, over 2,000 TSLU members and their supporters marched through Richmond. In support of the striking local, the marchers began at the Tobacco By-Product and Chemical Plant in the Fulton neighborhood and ended in a mass meeting at the City Auditorium. If anyone living in Richmond had not yet witnessed the new black union movement, this performance made its presence impossible to ignore. One week after the meeting, the *Richmond News Leader* editorialized about African Americans and the new industrial unionization attempt in the city. Calling "the enlistment of Negro workers in the same organizations with whites" the "most interesting aspect of the invasion of the South by the CIO," the editors gave their tacit approval. "Some of us deplore the methods that are being employed in the CIO strikes," the editorial concluded, "but we should welcome a change that cancels the old, unjust industrial doctrine that the wages of a Negro are to be low because he is a Negro." The support for this movement from the white *News Leader* and the white *Richmond Times-Dispatch* indicated to the TSLU how the racial environment in Richmond contained room to maneuver, at least in theory.[60]

The strike at the Tobacco By-Product plant carried on into July. Unlike in the previous strikes, these 160 workers complained more about their job classifications than their wages. They did not stem tobacco but handled and extracted chemicals from tobacco that was unfit for other uses. Most of these workers performed skilled tasks at the chemical plant, but the company classified them as "helpers" and "laborers." Black workers—despite what they actually did at the workplace—more often than not fell into semiskilled or unskilled classifications, which had been created either by AFL craft unions to exclude them or by companies in order to downgrade the pay of blacks and women. The company's representative, H. K. McConnell, showed his reluctance during negotiations to change this system, and the strike dragged on as a result.[61]

On the Fourth of July, strikers remained on the picket lines, smoking cigarettes, watching fireworks, and carrying "badly worn placards." During the previous two weeks of round-the-clock picketing, the summer heat had taken a toll. Yet Carrington & Michaux and Vaughan TSLU members provided "substantial support," and the SNYC organizers and strikers erected makeshift shacks around the plant to provide a refuge from the heat. Now resolute in staying outside the plant, the TSLU negotiated from a position of strength. Four days later, representatives from the TSLU local, along with John Suttle from the CIO and Henry Shepard and Christopher Columbus Alston from the SNYC, met with state labor negotiator Frank Kruck, and the company conceded to almost all of their demands.[62] On the issue of job classification, the company reclassified several positions "to recognize the worker's pride in his position." Increases in pay, however, were not based on these new job titles but on the previous wages of the workers.[63]

Meanwhile, during the slack winter season, the SNYC expanded its efforts to reorient black Richmond into a more militant and cohesive community. SNYC members, led by Augusta Jackson, revitalized the Richmond Negro Forum by making the series of lectures into discussions on black labor, culture, and history. The SNYC leadership hoped to make up for the "silence of many of our textbooks" on the "role the Negro people have played in building our American democracy." The speakers included Ralph Bunche, the nationally renowned Howard University scholar, who lectured on the "African background"; Thomas Morton, the state commissioner of labor, who spoke on the "Negro in the American labor movement"; and Arthur Davis Roscoe Lewis, state director of the Federal Writers' Project, who spoke on the role of blacks during Reconstruction in Virginia.[64]

No transcripts exist of these talks, but Lewis published *The Negro in Virginia* in 1940, which included a large section on nineteenth-century Richmond. The study recounted how blacks called political conventions, elected legislators, established schools, and even sat on the jury that tried Confederacy president Jefferson Davis for treason in Richmond. Yet in 1890, black candidate Joseph Holmes from Charlotte County was gunned down in cold blood. This intimidation was widespread, according to the study, which resulted in Democratic candidates sweeping the elections and subsequently implementing Jim Crow laws. This Writers' Project study introduced Reconstruction with the quotation, "De bottom rail's on top An' we's gwine to keep it dere." To the audience of Lewis's November 8, 1937, lecture, the new union movement must have seemed like a revival of a lost tradition. Quoting Harlem intellectual Arturo Schomburg's statement that every "ounce of fact is worth a pound of controversy," the SNYC staff believed that a person "equipped" with this historical knowledge "is better prepared to face the problems of his community."[65]

The SNYC encouraged working-class blacks to attend these and other cultural activities. Thomas Richardson, an aspiring actor, playwright, and SNYC founder, created a community theater in Richmond to bring socially significant plays to the black community there. Beginning in late 1937, this new group of young African American actors performed plays at the local Booker T. Washington Theatre to packed audiences.[66] The SNYC avidly recruited working-class blacks for these events. For example, in late September 1937, the SNYC hosted a meeting at the Leigh Street Church to elect delegates to the second conference of the NNC, to be held in Philadelphia the following month. In addition to delegates like Alston and Jackson from the SNYC, C. E. Queen and Milton Randolph from the Negro Forum, and Urban League and NAACP representatives, the group elected eleven tobacco workers from TSLU locals. Ed Strong wrote that these "young women from tobacco factories in Richmond" would have a unique opportunity to travel outside of Richmond and "exchange experiences" with other union delegates. In Philadelphia, they heard speeches from John P. Davis, Max Yergan, and other NNC leaders, who, in early 1938, also came to speak at the Negro Forum in Richmond.[67]

Perhaps the most prescient Negro Forum event, however, was a speech by Louise Thompson in February titled, "The Place of Women in a Changing World." Born in Chicago, Thompson lived in Harlem during the 1920s and 1930s. In New York, she served as a leader of the International Workers Order, a Communist Party offshoot, and took part in the arts movement there. In 1932, she organized a trip of black artists and young intellectuals to Russia. Two years later, she was arrested in Birmingham for trying to organize interracial International Workers Order chapters. Thompson's discussion of the changing role of black women and words of encouragement fell on receptive ears in Richmond's black community. During the previous year, reports of the union rarely mentioned the fact that women made up the majority of workers in tobacco stemmeries. This silence suggests a discomfort with the prominent role women had in the union. For James Jackson, the bravery of Sister Davis from the 1931 hunger march showed the deep tradition of black women in the movement for economic justice. "The ones who talk to the press and take the bows very often are men," Jackson recalled years later about the Richmond strikes, but "women and black women have borne the great part of the heroism."[68] The few exceptions to this silence evince an image of a movement made up not only of militant working-class blacks but one with black women in the trenches. Writing in the *Richmond Planet*, Alice Burke noted that a woman at Carrington & Michaux had first yelled "STRIKE" to start the work stoppage. Bolstering Burke's claim of female leadership, when a reporter asked a local black man named H. Harris about the strike, he highlighted the importance of female leaders. "If the women hold out," he stated, "the men can't work, as the women are the ones who control the machines."[69]

The dual role of black women as workers and mothers had long been a necessity for African American families, but their additional roles as strikers was new. Burke noted that female laborers "are the ones who first hear the cries of their children for food," and a living wage would mean "more education for the young ones." Whether women would also have a role as union and even civil rights leaders, however, was still uncertain. During the Reconstruction era, black women in Virginia participated in a broad range of political activities until men began to circumscribe their role in the church, at conventions, and at polling places.[70] If speakers in the Negro Forum and SNYC members sought to resurrect militant forms of activism from Reconstruction, did that also indicate a revival of the egalitarian gender roles in terms of race leadership? Despite the press emphasis on male SNYC organizers, a black female leadership had emerged to make the TSLU successful, and it remained to be seen whether it would alter gender norms both inside and outside the black community in Richmond.

▦ ▦ ▦ The success of the TSLU worried Richmond TWIU organizer L. C. Crump only if it encroached on his domain: cigarette plants and white employees. Crump had noted the progress of the TSLU the previous year but told the union's president that if he paid attention to blacks "other work will suffer." Besides, Crump reasoned, the TSLU had only organized stemmery and chemical plants, both of which had been traditionally ignored by the TWIU. "The only thing that bothers me," Crump wrote, "is that they may attempt to [organize] the American [Company's] Negroes."[71] By August, TWIU president Evans recommended that Crump conspire with American Tobacco Company management to dismiss the CIO as an illegitimate union. "The main problem is to prevent the C.I.O. from turning the 'Black Sheep' away from your fold in the American factories," he wrote, and "I do not doubt that you will have the moral support of the company in this respect. If you can enlist [its] aid," he concluded, "the C.I.O. goose is cooked."[72] Crump must have followed directions. By December, American Tobacco promptly broke off negotiations with the TSLU and signed a one-year contract with the TWIU.[73] The TSLU (now CIO Local 472) filed a complaint with the National Labor Relations Board (NLRB), which prompted an investigation. This pivotal battle would continue, but not until the NLRB had finished its investigation.

The postponement did not bode well for the TSLU. The union movement as a whole, according to Jackson, had "taken a turn for the worse by the spring." The pressure from the TSLU locally and the promise of a new Wage and Hour Act nationally convinced employers to rethink how to best manage their labor forces. Owners of tobacco stemmeries went on the offensive in early 1938 to "wreck the unions and demobilize the workers' unity" rather than capitulate to new contracts. The union movement had taken them by surprise the previous year, but now companies sought to delegitimize, subvert, and destroy the TSLU and its leaders. During the winter, Carrington & Michaux closed down, "throwing all of its workers into the streets." I. N. Vaughan introduced "rationalization" to its stemmery to reduce actual wages to precontract rates. And when other means failed, foremen attacked union members on the job, "thereby provoking fights" that gave the company cause for "laying them off."[74]

The SNYC and the TSLU expected support from the CIO to fend off these attacks from employers and the TWIU. John Suttle, the CIO's regional representative in Richmond, attended TSLU meetings and empathized with the workers' plight. His participation, in fact, had led the TSLU to affiliate with the CIO during the summer of 1937. In March, Suttle reported to John P. Davis that "Mr. Strong and Mr. Jackson sure went to the bat 100% for the C.I.O. organization" during three recent meetings. Worried about both independent and AFL union competition, Suttle told Davis, "God knows they have been divided long enough by the employers and it shall continue to be my duty to do everything under the Sun for them." Although James Jackson appreciated the work and commitment of Suttle, he complained that one man should not represent the whole state of Virginia. The lag in union dues over the slack season put the SNYC organizers back on a volunteer basis. "Unless we are freed from the necessity of earning a living in order to devote our full time to reforming the ranks," Jackson confided to Davis, "we will have a house of cards on our hands when the time to negotiate contracts comes up."[75]

Acting as a broker between the Richmond SNYC and the national CIO leadership, the NNC's Davis told the young organizers not to expect the aid of John L. Lewis and other CIO officials. The CIO had overextended itself with the campaign to organize steelworkers in the North. Under this "heavy financial load," Davis was "sure they would not consider the appointment of an organizer at the present time." However, the lack of support "did not mean that [SNYC organizers] should take a hopeless attitude to the problem." Davis was especially encouraged by the addition of Francis Grandison as a volunteer organizer, whom the SNYC appointed when someone the CIO sent was not up to the task. Similar to Jackson, Grandison hailed from Richmond, came from a respectable family (his father was a barber), and had even joined the same Boy Scout troop. But rather than study and go to college, Grandison became disaffected during his high school years and left home. He eventually joined a Civilian Conservation Corps camp to do hard manual labor and returned to Richmond to work with the SNYC in 1937.[76] Davis encouraged Grandison, Jackson, and the SNYC to persevere without CIO support by demanding relief for the laid-off TSLU workers, petitioning relief administrator Harry Hopkins for federal money, filing petitions with the NLRB because "this tends to bolster up the spirit of union members," and starting a community drive to "save the tobacco unions." If they could hold out for the next few weeks, Davis hoped that a new CIO convention could bring new policies, while relief efforts would bear fruit and the NLRB would step in to punish the tobacco companies.[77]

This plan was easier made than done. In May, Ed Strong and Francis Grandison recruited the NAACP state president, J. M. Tinsley, and the head of the Liggett & Myers tobacco local of the TWIU, Henry McDougall, to issue a joint press release. It protested the inadequacy of the recovery program and urged the passage of the more expansive bill that had come before the U.S. Senate. It addressed Harry F. Byrd, senator from Virginia, who opposed the bill. "We cannot help but point out," the release read, "that you have opposed every measure in this session of the Congress that has been in the interest of the people." Byrd's position showed the recalcitrance of southern Democrats regarding Roosevelt's New Deal measures. During the early years of the Depression, many southern Democrats accepted federal relief measures so long as they could control the distribution. Agricultural workers, processing workers, and domestics—all mainly African Americans—were excluded from New Deal measures such as those in the National Industrial Recovery Act and the Wagner Act. With Roosevelt's second term, these Democrats became more suspicious of what the work of New Deal agencies would mean in the long run. The mobilization of the CIO and the Supreme Court's validation of the Wagner Act indicated that the old ways of the South were becoming threatened by federal protection of labor unions and the aid New Deal agencies like the NLRB provided for black tobacco workers. Yet Roosevelt himself had contributed to the crisis by cutting money from relief agencies in 1937 in an attempt to reduce some of the federal deficit. This economic policy contributed to what became known as the Roosevelt recession, which gave southern Democrats further excuse to limit relief budgets. To the SNYC, the New Deal seemed to have two faces. One face was that of Frank Kruck, state labor mediator, who had aided the TSLU in getting unprecedented improvements in wages and working conditions. The other was Democratic senator Harry Byrd, whose "wanton disregard of the citizens of this state" left "thousands of workers in tobacco, textile, and other industries [who] have been thrown out of work during the last two weeks" without recourse.[78]

As the stakes became higher, all parties in Richmond became more antagonistic. In June, Joseph Arrington, the African American pastor of Sixteenth Street Baptist Church, held an event to "develop friendship" between workers and management of the tobacco plants. Attending the meeting, James Jackson quickly saw that it was a ruse. Jacob Harris, a Larus company employee, and Newton Miller, the white personnel manager of the company, gave speeches to sell a company union in the guise of an independent union. Jackson added his name to the list of speakers and condemned the chicanery of Harris and Miller as a trick to defeat the CIO in the upcoming September election at the plant. Arrington asked Jackson to curtail his speech, but the workers in the audience overrode the minister, insisting that Jackson finish. Arrington responded by telling the press he would no longer hold meetings that promoted "labor wars," and a choir member demanded that Jackson apologize for taking advantage of the church's forum to cause unrest. Jackson expressed regret but also said: "The workers present knew no apology was necessary for they understand conditions." This meeting, according to press accounts, was the third in Richmond held during that summer to dissuade members from joining the CIO.[79]

Later that month, boxer Joe Louis's knockout of the German Max Schmeling further exposed both the potentialities and the pitfalls of interracial collaboration in Richmond. Louis, known as the Brown Bomber, had become the preeminent sports celebrity among African Americans since his professional debut in 1934. Schmeling had defeated Louis in the twelfth round in a June 1936 fight, and African Americans anxiously awaited the rematch, which would take place two years later. With the rise of the Nazis in Germany, the fight took on a resonance well beyond the sports pages.[80] The local black press followed Louis's every move, and the national press portrayed the Louis and Schmeling rematch as a battle between democracy and fascism.

When Louis defeated Schmeling by knockout, it was understood as a symbolic victory for all those in America who opposed fascism. To African Americans, it also offered irrefutable proof that "scientific" racial ideologies had no merit. Black Richmonders thronged onto Second Street "about twenty minutes after the German was wiped out of fistic existence" to celebrate Louis's defeat of the Nazi fighter and his blow to white supremacy. Scores of whites had also come into the neighborhood to celebrate in a demonstration that CIO members in Richmond and elsewhere saw as a show of interracial solidarity against fascism.

The joyous mood in Richmond, however, soon turned sour. When the white driver of an automobile, unable to pass through a busy intersection due to the crowds, proceeded to drive through the crowd instead of around it, the spontaneous celebration degenerated into fisticuffs. Authorities quickly dubbed the disturbance the "Joe Louis fight riots," and police with "guns drawn" invaded the black section of town. The police injured many pedestrians as they tried to "contain" the situation. After the streets had been cleared, white reporters focused on the damage done to automobiles while the black press focused on the driver of the car that injured five people. The *Richmond News Leader* detailed the "disastrous aftermath" of "cut faces and hands and bruises from bricks and stones hurled through automobile windows." Before the driver plowed into the celebration, the black press reported, the crowd had been jubilant but peaceful. Further, the *Baltimore Afro-American*, Richmond edition, discovered that forty of the forty-five people arrested for disorderly conduct were white pedestrians. If anyone had caused a disturbance, it was the white people "slumming" in the neighborhood after the fight, not the black community.[81]

The reaction to the so-called riot showed the great division between Richmond's liberals and the new union movement. "More has been done [by blacks] to damage interracial goodwill," Richmond mayor Fulmer Bright said in a statement, "than anything in my memory." According to the mayor, the "outrageous conduct on the part of our Negro population" was to blame. The members of the Virginia Interracial Commission, composed of both white and black civic leaders, largely concurred with the mayor's assessment when they met behind closed doors to discuss the incident. "White leaders," one account reported, "were quick to ask what had gone wrong with the well-behaved colored people of Richmond who have known their places all this time." Some black moderates also fell back on previous habits of blaming the behavior of certain members of the black community, despite evidence to the contrary.[82]

Only the SNYC and the TSLU challenged this chorus of condemnation. The SNYC issued a statement protesting Mayor Bright's interpretation that thousands were guilty of "outrageous conduct." "Whatever undesirable incidents may have occurred from that celebration," SNYC leaders in Richmond wrote, "cannot be interpreted by any stretch of the imagination as a riot." Redirecting attention to the boxing match, SNYC leaders argued that the Louis victory, rather than damaging interracial goodwill, "represents a distinct international gain for interracial understanding because it struck a body-blow at the mythical Nazi theories of racial superiority." This symbolism frightened the mayor and other white authorities because it threatened their own homegrown fascism. The TSLU, claiming to represent 4,000 members, called the mayor's statement a "slander of the colored people." The TSLU believed that the crowd represented a "spontaneous demonstration" against those who "jim-crowed [and] exploited" workers. Although the crowds that night may not have had such an overt political agenda, these black workers saw the response to Louis's victory as related to their own resistance of Jim Crow. When the mayor fumed that he did not give a "continental damn" about the TSLU's objection, his response reinforced the idea that the battle over Joe Louis's victory had as much to do with the insurgent labor movement as the incidents surrounding the heavyweight title. With the renewal of tobacco contracts on the horizon, the mood in Richmond became anything but conciliatory.[83]

▨ ▨ ▨ Despite this new antagonism, the TSLU managed to forestall layoffs by tobacco companies, and during the next tobacco season it struck at the heart of the industry. In need of a victory to regain momentum, over 200 workers from the Export Leaf tobacco company went on strike on the first of August. Francis Grandison said the workers' demands would reflect the minimum set by the federal Wage and Hour Act, which would become effective in the fall. The workers demanded a closed shop, an increase in men's wages from thirty-two to thirty-eight cents per hour and women's from twenty-two to twenty-eight cents per hour, one week of vacation with pay for employees on the payroll for more than two years, and the checkoff system for union dues. Yet this strike represented more than just demands made on this rehandling plant—Export Leaf was a subsidiary of the Brown & Williamson Company, and the giant British American Tobacco Company owned both companies. The TSLU was now competing on an entirely new level of the industry. The Carrington & Michaux and Vaughan factories had a history stretching back into the previous century in Richmond that imbued them with a local and pastoral image of kindly paternalism, but British American Tobacco by the 1930s was an international conglomerate with little concern beyond production and profit. Its Richmond factories alone had twenty different gates stretching over acres of property. By getting in the door at the Export Leaf plant, the TSLU hoped it would lead to its goal of organizing the entire industry. And this vision was not only that of the SNYC organizers—the strikers at Export Leaf also expressed a broader vision for social change than the previous year. When ten employees decided not to join the strikers, George L. Corbin, the general manager of the plant, said employees not taking part in the strike would not be allowed to work because "it might lead to trouble for them." With one striker's placard reading, "Brother, beyond these walls is slavery. We fight for freedom on this line. Join Us," Corbin's assessment seemed accurate. The rhetoric changed from specific demands to the idea of "freedom," and this placard evinced a sense that a movement was afoot to change the balance of power in the former Confederate capital.[84]

And join they did. The Reverends C. C. Scott, president of the Baptist Ministers Conference, and W. L. Ransome of the First Baptist Church collected money to support them. For the first time, black clergy, other than the stalwart Reverend Queen, had openly joined the ranks of this labor movement. Within the larger labor circles, the TSLU informed the national CIO of its walkout. In response, a new and fast-growing CIO union, the UCAPAWA, donated fifty dollars to the strike fund. At a mass meeting at the Leigh Street church in August, the CIO's Suttle told the strikers to "stick together" and persevere until the peak production season began at the end of the month.

Meanwhile, James Jackson showed his contempt for the "Virginia Way" in negotiations with the company. Although the immediate negotiator and supervisor at the plant was George Corbin, who had lived in Richmond and worked for British American Tobacco since 1909, Jackson knew that the company's executives in New York and London cared little about racial traditions in Richmond if they might further damage their profit margin. Thus, Jackson got revenge on behalf of the workers when he explained that if he had to address Corbin as "Mr.," then Corbin ought to do the same. Corbin had often been disrespectful of the black workers inside of the plant, and on lunch break he made money selling them overpriced food on payday. Jackson knew this

Richmond tobacco workers on strike against the Export Leaf company, Richmond, 1938. Young black organizers in the SNYC joined forces with the largely female and African American tobacco workers of Richmond to enact a New Deal for tobacco workers in advance of the CIO. From Augusta V. Jackson, "A New Deal for Tobacco Workers," *Crisis*, October 1938; lot 13089, nos. 91 and 92, NAACP Photographs Collection, Library of Congress. Courtesy of the Crisis Publishing Company, Inc.

comment would infuriate Corbin, and he later recalled how the look on the supervisor's face "would turn old Jefferson Davis over in his grave." Corbin refused to negotiate on this basis of equality, but the company overruled him by bringing in lawyers from its New York office to act as a conduit between local plant managers and the TSLU union negotiators. This activity stirred the tobacco plant owners in Richmond. One concluded that "times had changed," saying, "I remember when I used to fire a nigger for just walking into my office."[85]

While this confrontation occurred behind closed doors, a public demonstration of white women in support of their black female counterparts amplified the message of racial equality over the supposed tradition of separation by consent. In August, John Suttle put action behind his words when he arranged a show of support from the CIO's white female textile workers, who had organized since 1935 into the Amalgamated Clothing Workers. In a sympathy march, over 200 white CIO workers from clothing plants marched from the Friedman, Harry, Marks Clothing Company's textile plants nearby to Leigh and Lombardy Streets, where the strikers picketed at one of the company's gates. As these women approached in white uniforms four abreast, Jackson recalled, from several blocks away they looked like marchers of the Ku Klux Klan. But then he saw them in the sunlight and heard them shouting labor union slogans. When they met, several of the white women embraced their black counterparts and both groups began "weeping and singing."[86]

Although the locals of the clothing workers and tobacco workers had not yet been integrated, this symbolic march showed the potential for an interracial and working-class movement in Richmond. And just as important, the demonstration showed that this movement was fueled by white and black women, who made up the majority of workers in the tobacco and clothing industries. Although press accounts of the strike still focused on the male leadership, articles noted that Mrs. Pearl Winston and Mrs. M. Harris of the Export Leaf plant served on the negotiating committee. Moreover, the sight of black and white women mingling around the plant must have been astonishing in a city whose Jim Crow restrictions had become entrenched during the past four decades.[87]

On the last day of August, the strikers' perseverance was rewarded with a new contract. Export Leaf Local No. 582 won checkoff of union dues, $22,000 in increased wages, a union bulletin board inside the plant, employee seniority, and a clause on vacations with pay. At the CIO Hall on West Broad

Street, the strikers and their supporters sang and danced in jubilation. They presented James Jackson with an award for his leadership and also honored Francis Grandison and Thomas Richardson of the SNYC, as well as John Suttle of the CIO. Better wages and better conditions had been achieved at the plant, and the larger goal of economic freedom seemed within their reach. Or, as the headline in the *Amsterdam News* of New York read, "Tobacco Workers Win; Dixie Jolted."[88]

The success at Export Leaf made organizers Jackson and Grandison confident that their grievances with I. N. Vaughan would reach a successful settlement as well. Over the summer, Vaughan had instituted a task system to speed up production and threatened to fire those workers who did not meet their daily quotas. The company introduced this new system in anticipation of the Wage and Hour Act. If he had to pay his workers higher wages, Vaughan reasoned, he needed to increase production to retain the level of profit his plant had experienced in previous years. The TSLU objected to this policy, and when negotiations broke down over a new contract in September, more than 400 workers went out on strike.[89]

Showing little sympathy for the union this time, Vaughan hired strikebreakers to stem and prepare the tobacco and requested that the police protect their entry into the plant. When the first twenty scabs arrived at the Tenth Street plant, a fight broke out. The police arrested nineteen of the strikers but not a single replacement worker involved in the scuffle. Six other strikers received medical treatment following the brawl. Again, black women led the way. Police arrested twice as many black women as men on misdemeanor offenses and charged Lessie Dixon and Ruth Armstrong with assault and battery.[90] The arrested strikers also included James Jackson. A policeman had told Jackson to move from the sidewalk, and he complied, but he also let the officer know that the pickets out in front of the plant were in compliance with the law. When the policeman heard Jackson's reply, he arrested him and had him held on $500 bond. "You can talk bold to these 'niggers' down here all you want," the officer told Jackson, "but don't talk back to me." After this incident, police protected more than 100 strikebreakers as they entered and left the plant each day of the strike.[91]

This skirmish was no accident. All sides in the conflict had become bolder since the previous year. A Richmond reporter for the *Baltimore Afro-American* reported that Vaughan had boasted of his admiration for Hitler and Mussolini, and the black press increasingly drew parallels between Hitler's rise in Europe and similar methods in the South.[92] But rather than look overseas for

Vaughan's racial logic, the SNYC looked back to slavery. To James Jackson, the civility of Richmond smacked of the paternalistic ideology from the previous century. During the course of the negotiations, Vaughan and his wife refused to accept that their black employees would want a union to come between them. As owner of a tobacco stemmery that went back generations in his family, Vaughan thought of his workers as childlike dependents. Over the course of the negotiations, which Vaughan insisted on handling himself, he suffered a heart attack and his wife ended up in a mental institution. Not unlike the wives of plantation owners who could not believe their loyal slaves wanted to leave after Emancipation, Mrs. Vaughan's worldview seemed to fall apart when black workers openly challenged her and her husband.[93] As the SNYC challenged the racial status quo, violence and intimidation began to belie the peaceful facade of Jim Crow in Virginia.

The trial of the arrested strikers, however, demonstrated a surprising degree of tolerance for the defendants. Charles Tinsley, the company attorney, argued that the black female defendants, Lessie Dixon and Ruth Armstrong, should be convicted for assault and battery for their connection with the brawl, a sentence that would have landed them in jail for a year. Black attorney J. Thomas Hewin defended the strikers. He argued that inconsistent testimony presented by the prosecution and the high level of labor exploitation should lead to not guilty verdicts. To the surprise of the prosecution, Justice Elben C. Folkes dismissed the charges against thirteen of the nineteen arrested and reduced the charges to small fines for the rest. He also issued a warning to the police officers that they had no authority to interfere with peaceful pickets. Hewin, Jackson, and members of the TSLU considered the judge's decision another victory. Soon thereafter, Vaughan made concessions to settle the strike (although he did not sign a new contract), and Carrington & Michaux reached a similar agreement with the TSLU.[94]

The success of these local battles emboldened the SNYC activists and TSLU members to extend their work across the Piedmont area. In late August, they formed a Tobacco Organizing Committee, with Grandison as director, Alston as an organizer, and James Jackson as educational director from the SNYC, along with the five current presidents of locals in the area. They also established an advisory board consisting of John P. Davis of the NNC, the Reverend C. E. Queen, local attorney J. Thomas Hewin, and two white CIO officials—John Suttle of the Virginia CIO and Mike Smith of the Amalgamated Clothing Workers. The preliminary goals of this committee were very ambitious. It discussed organizing 5,000 workers in South Boston (near Richmond) and over 8,000 in Danville, Virginia, as well as initiating drives in Winston-Salem, where the formidable R. J. Reynolds Company was located.[95]

To the TWIU, R. J. Reynolds seemed impenetrable because, unlike other tobacco companies, Reynolds had hired many blacks throughout the plant and provided company welfare programs to quash any chance for a union to take hold. Without organizing black workers, any possibility of organizing Reynolds would be ineffective. Yet the black press also seemed allied with the company. Since Reynolds hired many black workers at the same wages as whites, reporters like A. T. White asked why blacks at Reynolds would want a union. Any such attempt, he and others believed, would jeopardize the employment of thousands of black workers, many of whom held positions well above stemmers. The Tobacco Organizing Committee considered Reynolds the next logical step because of the number of black workers there. When the committee met that summer, its plans were nothing short of a region-wide labor and civil rights movement. The committee would organize these workers into unions as a means to obtain better wages and conditions, but it also wanted to encourage union organizers to fight for the rights of blacks across the Piedmont area.[96]

❖ ❖ ❖ When the Wage and Hour Act finally took effect in late October 1938, however, the movement derailed. I. N. Vaughan, still furious over losing the strike and the subsequent court battle, dismissed 127 members of the workforce, all union members. The very next day, Vaughan contacted the local branch of the federal employment office, asking for more workers. Following Vaughan's lead, the Larus Company fired 153 workers and threatened 250 more if the union protested this decision. Rumors spread that Carrington & Michaux would also soon reduce its workforce by half. Francis Grandison fired off a letter to Elmer F. Andrews, the wage and hour administrator in Washington, protesting this abuse of the new law. The companies, Grandison fumed, increased the task load of the remaining employees by 50 percent as a way to comply with the law without losing any revenue through the increased wage requirements. Production quotas for a single day now hit outrageous levels, which put the TSLU immediately on the defensive.[97]

How did the momentum shift so suddenly? With labor agitation and the prospect of government-mandated minimum wages facing them, tobacco re-handling plants made an end run around their black labor force. As early as the 1920s, mechanization was becoming an important option for employers in their efforts to retool the industry's labor arrangement. Between 1920 and

1930, the labor force of black tobacco workers in Virginia dropped from 10,457 to 7,142; and from 1930 to 1937, productivity increased by 50 percent while employment continued to drop. This decline indicates that some mechanization had already taken place, although mostly in larger plants.[98] When the National Recovery Administration minimum wage codes excluded stemmery workers, these companies had little incentive to further invest in machinery because they were able to continue exploiting workers at low wages. Thus productivity rose by demanding more out of fewer workers.[99]

By 1938 the Wage and Hour Act and the challenge from a new union movement provided incentive to employers to rethink the structure of the industry. At the annual meeting of the Tobacco Association of the United States two months earlier, the largest tobacco companies had planned concerted action against the new law. A dominant theme of the meeting, one reporter noted, was "how to defeat the minimum wage requirement of $10." For the time being, companies agreed to pay higher wages by firing the least efficient workers and increasing production quotas. With a surplus labor force of unemployed workers, those left with jobs had little leverage to complain about the increased quotas. Although this system would not work forever, the companies reasoned it would take awhile for the CIO to regroup. In the meantime, companies retooled their factories with machines. By 1940, over half of these plants had become mechanized.[100]

Increasingly threatened by the CIO's plans to organize not just rehandling plants but also manufacturing and packaging plants, the TWIU started to pay attention to black workers for the first time. The previous battle between the TWIU and the TSLU over the American Tobacco Company's Smoking Branch made its way onto the NLRB's docket by October 1938. The decision made by the regional director thwarted the TWIU's plans to form a bargaining unit consisting only of white production employees in the company's plants in four different cities. In a precedent-setting decision, the NLRB found that whiteness was not an appropriate category to form a bargaining unit. The board rejected a unit consisting of the white workers in several plants, choosing instead to hold an election for union representation at the Richmond plant.[101]

This long-awaited decision appeared to favor the TSLU at a time when it desperately needed to make inroads. While the alliance with the white Amalgamated Clothing Workers union bolstered symbolic interracialism, it had little practical effect on the TSLU. As the *Norfolk Journal and Guide* had illustrated a few months earlier in a political cartoon, southern white workers

"If the Fellow on the Ladder Would Just Get Up and Face Forward," *Norfolk Journal and Guide*, April 8, 1938. Courtesy of the *New Journal and Guide*.

blocked the ladder for black workers to climb onto the road of "progress" that unions had forged in "Other Sections of [the] U.S.A." The new union movement needed to become interracial in Richmond, because in order to gain leverage against the layoffs at the subsidiary rehandling plants, the TSLU needed the support of white production workers.[102]

The TSLU won the battle, but the TWIU had the resources to win the protracted war. The TWIU appealed this NLRB decision on five different technicalities; the NLRB agreed to hear the appeal, which did not overturn the result of the finding but bought the TWIU much-needed time to coerce the black workers at this American Tobacco plant to join their union.[103] The TWIU had a distinct advantage because the union had more funds to employ organizers due to the checkoff agreements they had signed. In addition, despite the grumbling by the TWIU's Evans, the union decided to waive the reinstatement fee of three dollars for those workers who had left the union. In contrast to the TWIU, the CIO's coffers had been drained by the strike of "Little Steel" in the North and the strike's subsequent defeat in 1938. The ambitious plans outlined by SNYC members and local CIO officials, although encouraged by the national CIO officers, received little financial backing from them.[104]

The prediction of a TWIU triumph over the CIO by President Evans seemed to come true by the end of the 1938. On November 22 of that year, NLRB officials ran the election at the American Tobacco Richmond Smoking Branch plant. The TWIU won a narrow victory, receiving 342 votes, as opposed to 334 for the CIO's TSLU.[105] Thereafter, the TWIU called its first strike in thirty-nine years in Richmond. Over 2,000 workers at six Liggett & Myers plants in Richmond won wage gains and the right to represent the workers in all of the plants. Local 194 of the TSLU, worried about further losses of its jobs to machines or white employees, honored the strike, even though Evans reaffirmed his commitment to segregated locals. "Freedom of action," he stated, "will be hampered with the two races acting together." This statement showed that the TWIU cared little about expanding its labor movement to cover all workers. Evans admitted to Richmond organizer Martha Cosby that "the Negro is a check [by the companies] against too great a growth of the Whites," but he nevertheless continued to treat blacks as second-class members.[106]

Black workers had to circumscribe their demands for freedom and equality within this AFL union movement or face retribution. If blacks did not join the TWIU on his terms, Evans reasoned, the TWIU and major tobacco companies would conspire to eliminate their jobs. This did not seem like an idle threat by the TWIU and was in fact a real possibility by 1939. Reports in the black press uncovered plots in small towns in North Carolina in the summer and fall to hire white women in stemmeries to replace blacks, thus reversing the hope of the TSLU to bring women together in solidarity to bolster the labor movement. Now that the Wage and Hour Act had gone into effect, these jobs paid somewhat better, and new machinery made certain jobs at these plants less arduous, so companies reconsidered the racial hierarchy of their job classifications. In both St. Louis and Kentucky, the TWIU conferred with local management and convinced them to hire white women and lay off "unorganized" black employees. Meanwhile in Richmond, tobacco companies celebrated a new record for the largest amount of tobacco stored and awaiting processing in the city's history.[107]

Since the CIO had made few inroads with white workers in the tobacco industry, Richmond's progressive leaders had no way to counteract the layoffs and speedups, because their members had become expendable employees, while the unionized plant workers belonged to the competing union or had no organization at all. As a result, correspondence between organizers dwindled as they watched the momentum of their movement slow to a stop in a matter of months. With the New Deal Wage and Hour Act, company intransigence, and competition from the TWIU all working against SNYC organizers, the mood of the TSLU members became despondent.

In 1940, the SNYC moved its headquarters to Birmingham, Alabama. The pull of a stronger union movement and a small cadre of dedicated black Communists in the mining and steel trades there drew the SNYC to this Deep South setting as a permanent headquarters.[108] In addition, the prospects of a war abroad precipitated a widening chasm between the SNYC and Richmond's liberals—black and white—that may have convinced the SNYC to relocate.[109] Most of all though, the reversal of the union movement in Richmond led its disheartened leaders to make a fresh start elsewhere.[110]

The experience these SNYC leaders had in Richmond made them lifelong activists for the black working class. James Jackson decided to give up his somewhat comfortable lifestyle as a pharmacist in Richmond. He moved south and became one of the most dedicated black radicals in America for the next three decades. Christopher Columbus Alston moved back to Detroit, where he became a key civil rights figure and United Auto Workers organizer. Ed Strong would lead the SNYC in Birmingham, fight in World War II, become a leader of the NNC after the war, and then work directly for the Communist Party. These SNYC members had gone from inexperienced youth leaders to savvy organizers within a few years. Though bitter at its end, the Richmond campaign furthered the SNYC organizers' educations and cemented a lifelong devotion to struggles for economic justice.[111]

But most important, the SNYC and TSLU had effectively laid out a road map for CIO leaders to follow. In 1942, the remaining faction of the TSLU became UCAPAWA Local 24, while the Tobacco By-Product plant fell under the jurisdiction of the Gas, Coke, and Chemical Workers of America of District 50 of the United Mine Workers.[112] As historian Robert Korstad concluded in his study of tobacco workers in North Carolina during the postwar period, "the main impetus" for UCAPAWA's decision to target tobacco workers "came from tobacco workers in Richmond, Virginia." Before the SNYC and TSLU, even well-intentioned organizers did not feel confident that this segment of the working class, largely African American and female, could be organized. The movement in Richmond showed not only that organization was possible but also that, if given the right amount of resources, it could become the vanguard of southern organization for the CIO. "From this base," Korstad concluded, "the union [the UCAPAWA and then the Food, Tobacco, Agricultural, and Allied Workers (FTA)] started organizing workers across the South."

SNYC organizers kept in touch with tobacco organizers across the region. The CIO granted UCAPAWA the authority to organize tobacco workers in Virginia and elsewhere during the Second World War. UCAPAWA efforts expanded by leaps and bounds, including organizing a few plants in Suffolk, retaining the gains made by the TSLU in Richmond, and launching major organizing campaigns in Memphis, Charleston, and other southern locales. Leading the charge were local organizers who worked with the NNC and SNYC, like Theodosia Simpson in Winston-Salem, Owen Whitfield, who became a UCAPAWA organizer across the South during the war, and Mrs. C. E. Jackson, a secretary of one of the TSLU-turned-CIO locals in Richmond.[113] Although they abided by the CIO's no-strike pledge, their campaigns forced the War Labor Board, the successor to the NLRB, to intervene, hold elections, certify contracts, and raise wages for tobacco processing workers.[114]

After the war, the CIO launched Operation Dixie to organize tobacco and other industrial workers across the South. The national CIO leadership had become convinced that organizing northern industrial workers would become compromised by the flight of more companies south across the Mason-Dixon Line without a concomitant effort to unionize southern laborers. With a 1-million-dollar budget and a staff of 250 paid organizers, the CIO provided the resources that the SNYC organizers and TSLU members had desperately needed a decade before. Although Operation Dixie as a whole fell far short of expectations, an exception to this trend was the tobacco industry. Theodosia Simpson, who helped engineer the watershed FTA victory at R. J. Reynolds in North Carolina, became a SNYC organizer in her spare time.[115] And in 1946, the CIO named two black female stemmers, Evetta Hampton and Emma Howard, as the lead organizers in Richmond. Far from dying on the vine, the Richmond movement spawned efforts across the South to unionize tobacco workers and created a civil rights movement from this CIO organizational base.[116] The successor to UCAPAWA, the FTA compiled twenty-three union contract victories and increased its membership to more than 8,000 workers in Virginia and 20,000 members in North Carolina during Operation Dixie.[117]

The TSLU organizing campaign had also helped change the environment within the TWIU. Indeed, the challenge from the TSLU and the CIO had emboldened the TWIU's black members to fight for equality within the organization. On previous occasions, locals of the union had called for a convention, only to have President Evans arrive and disqualify the local or the request on technical grounds. In early 1939, a new challenge came from Kentucky. Local 185 from Louisville furtively polled other Kentucky locals to force a national meeting. Although the locals voted for the meeting, President Evans asked for a revote and then claimed both failed on technicalities. The Kentucky Federation of Labor contested Evans's claim. By August, the case went to court, and a Louisville judge ruled against the TWIU leadership. In October 1939, the union held its first convention in thirty-nine years. The convention resulted in the ouster of Evans, a promise to hold conventions every four years, and, perhaps most important, a reconsideration of organizing black tobacco workers. The new president, Warren Smith, hired black organizers to compete with the CIO in places like Winston-Salem.[118]

Yet the democratization of the union was far from complete. After the Second World War, Richmond's TWIU Local 219 reneged on its promise to integrate black workers, and these workers then took the union to court. Rather than capitulate, the union argued for separation of the races using *Plessy v. Ferguson*, the Supreme Court case that had affirmed segregation in 1896. By the 1940s, even William Green, the cautious head of the AFL, worried about the foot-dragging of the TWIU. With over half of the membership African American by the Second World War, Green told President Smith that the negative press concerning the racism of white members had compromised its organizing drives and weakened the standing of the entire AFL.[119]

The tobacco workers' struggle also indicates that even at the peak of the New Deal, Richmond's moderate leaders showed an unwillingness to allow a labor and civil rights movement to develop. Scholarship by historians has implied that such a movement would have been possible at the time if more places in the South had featured less violent forms of Jim Crow, as in Richmond.[120] Yet the movement to unionize black workers indicates that this form of southern civility, defined by historian William Chafe as "the progressive mystique," became a "masterful weapon of social control" because "the enemy was elusive and flexible, not immediate and brutal."[121] Moreover, these entrenched lines of racial separation blocked an alliance between white women organizing in the textile factories and their black counterparts in the tobacco plants, who in some cases worked right down the street from each other. Both became part of the CIO in late 1930s Virginia, but one group did not become intertwined with the other, except for that brief shining moment in August 1938 when they converged at Lee and Lombardy Streets. The SNYC would need to continue to put forward the strategy of the TSLU in the war years: lead the movement in the South by intertwining race and class identities and by imploring like-minded white colleagues to come along for the ride.[122] Unfortunately, for every Palmer Weber who had come to embrace civil rights activism in the student and labor movement as a Christian necessity, there were two or more like E. Lewis Evans of the TWIU who sought to derail all forms of resistance to the Jim Crow status quo.

Moreover, the racial hierarchy of employment put black tobacco workers at such a disadvantage that "progress" in the form of further mechanization and modernization actually jeopardized the very basis of their employment. The Wage and Hour Act, the NNC's John P. Davis protested in Washington, would force many black tobacco workers out of jobs rather than raise their wages within them.[123] Just as organizers gained a foothold in organizing tobacco workers, their jobs, the dirtiest and most labor-intensive, disappeared. The SNYC tried to leverage international capitalist logic against the local customs of "Virginia Way" paternalism, but sixty years of unfettered profit in the industry worked to promote the continuance of a local system of race and gender apartheid in Richmond's factories.

Organizers in Richmond and elsewhere in the South discovered that employment discrimination had become incredibly difficult to remedy without a more comprehensive agenda. The stony silence of Monument Way honoring the leaders of the Confederacy in Richmond mirrored the powerful and silent grip of many paternalistic whites there. Racial tranquility, for Richmond's liberals, was based on inequalities and a free market capitalism that trumped human rights. By contrast, the SNYC and the NNC would formulate controversial plans to adjust union seniority for black workers in the 1940s. Adjusting seniority, they contended, would deal with the problem of organizing workers whose jobs, due to four decades of Jim Crow discrimination, had increasingly disappeared because of mechanization or had often made them the last hired and first fired.

As the SNYC activists discovered in Richmond, the organization of southern labor and racial equality went hand in glove. Without a living wage, civil rights seemed insubstantial to working-class blacks. Lucy Randolph Mason, a white organizer for the CIO and a granddaughter of elite Confederates, concluded in 1937, "The South Is Fascist—its domination of the Negro has made it easy to repeat the pattern for organized labor." Mason understood how race oppression intertwined with class and gender oppression in the South. Despite her southern manners, she knew that conflict had became necessary

to change this system, which meant forgoing traditional notions of southern civility. The TSLU forged such a pathway through the labor movement,
reintroducing human rights below the Mason-Dixon Line by defining civil
rights as protection against both labor and racial abuses, and its derailment
has left a long shadow over the rights of all workers in the South.

CHAPTER THREE

Civilization Has Taken a Holiday

Violence and Security in the Nation's Capital

In February 1940, John P. Davis walked south from the Florida Avenue office of the National Negro Congress (NNC) to Capitol Hill for an appearance before the Senate Judiciary Committee. The committee had reopened hearings on the Wagner-Capper–Van Nuys antilynching bill and had offered Davis the opportunity to testify in its favor on behalf of the NNC. Davis, the NNC's national secretary, declared that his goal in appearing was to "expose the fallaciousness of the reasoning of the opponents of the bill who declare that lynching as a crime is on the decline." Davis believed that the southern senators who had filibustered antilynching legislation during the previous year had not only succeeded in taking the bill off the Senate's agenda but had gained control over the terms of the debate itself. He reminded the Senate committee that "it is not lynching alone but the *lynch spirit* which threatens the peace and security of minority groups in America." Rather than considering lynching as an aberrant southern crime, Davis explained that its real purpose was to instill a debilitating terror in African Americans. "To put it another way," Davis continued, "every time a Negro is lynched in America the whole Negro people shudder with justifiable fear and apprehension—the whole Negro people are lynched in spirit." The lack of federal protection, Davis concluded, stripped every African American of a "feeling of security and peace of mind to which he as an American citizen is justly entitled in our democracy."[1]

Beginning in 1936, the NNC fought parallel national and local battles against the "lynch spirit" in the nation's capital. As federal representatives debated the antilynching bill on Capitol Hill, NNC leaders extended this fight to include racial violence in urban neighborhoods. NNC members believed that a long-standing and widespread pattern of police brutality by metropolitan police forces against African Americans constituted "urban lynching."[2] They made the connection between police terror in Washington and southern lynch mobs because both violently perpetuated a culture of white supremacy. Over the previous dozen years, the NNC discovered, the metropolitan police had shot to death an average of one African American every three months.[3] Indignant over this use of lethal force, the NNC applied mass-action tactics to eliminate all forms of racialized violence in Washington, D.C., and the nation—whether from large mobs or from officers of the law. Its members and allies sought to build a coalition of organizations whose activists would directly challenge this racial subordination, a challenge that began with trying to transform abuse into protection of civil rights and then extended to issues like labor exploitation and access to wartime jobs. They saw police violence as central to this fight because it limited mobility, infringed on privacy and property, and caused grave physical harm. Moreover, the cumulative effect of this daily harassment by the protectors of the law insulted the humanity of the District's black populace right in the shadow of the nation's Capitol.

By looking at the development of the Washington Council—seen as a vanguard NNC council because its leaders believed the District of Columbia's racial politics set the model for the nation—this chapter provides a different understanding of civil rights during the late 1930s. How did NNC leaders develop ideas about citizenship and foster aggressive tactics to combat this "lynch spirit" in Washington? And what influence did they have on the District and the nation? Historians who have studied African Americans during the New Deal have not yet fully made this broader critique of racial violence. They have concentrated on "legal lynchings" like the Scottsboro case in Alabama, heinous acts of violence by groups like the Ku Klux Klan in the Deep South, and the political debate over the federal antilynching bill.[4] Focusing on the grassroots NNC coalition in Washington reveals how issues like the shelving of federal antilynching legislation became intertwined with the quest for fair employment. Moreover, this chapter delves into the local context of Washington, D.C., where police brutality, restricted urban mobility, and lack of employment security had become defining characteristics of Jim Crow. Those who objected to these local policies had little recourse since Congress controlled the District's local government, which effectively prevented residents from choosing their own leaders. Thus, local and national struggles connected because success on both fronts became essential for transforming either one. In the 1930s, the NNC publicly resurrected an expansionist view of freedom that included equal access to public spaces, institutions, and employment by focusing on police power, which should protect rather than curtail these rights. When D.C. activists confronted the local white supremacist power structure and put this vision of freedom on the urban activist agenda nationally, they foreshadowed President Roosevelt's "Four Freedoms" speech of January 1941, in which the president argued that "unity of purpose" of "millions of free men and women" would establish "freedom from fear" coupled with "freedom from want" to establish "the supremacy of human rights everywhere."[5]

Roosevelt's robust 1941 definition of freedom did not exist in late nineteenth-century Washington. During the Reconstruction era, Washington's black citizens clashed with the all-white police force over restrictions of their civil rights. As soon as they gained the franchise, black citizens exercised their newfound political power to pressure the local government to hire several black officers. As historian Kate Masur explained, the local Republican Party "briefly dominated Washington politics and developed policies that favored laborers, municipal development, and an expansive vision of racial equality before the law." Yet after citizenship rights expanded in the late 1860s, local blacks noticed that segregationist ideas began to creep into the city government's debates. Parallel to the demise of Reconstruction across the South, narrow definitions of citizenship came to dominate in the decade that followed, and in 1874 Congress placed the District under control of a presidentially appointment commission.[6] Thereafter, although a bill to segregate streetcars failed, the federal government backed many other institutions that began to separate their clientele by race. "For fifteen years I have resided in Washington," one black resident wrote in 1906, "and while it was far from being a 'paradise for colored people' when I first touched these shores, it has been doing its level best ever since to make conditions for us intolerable."[7]

As Jim Crow restrictions mounted at a gradual but effective pace, the deterioration of black citizenship in the District became especially apparent in the policing of crime. Calvin Chase, the editor of the black-owned *Washington Bee* newspapers, recalled with indignation how after the murder of his father by a white man the police made little effort to find the killer. Chase editorialized about racism within the police department but felt helpless to do any more about it. "The fever is spreading," the *Bee* noted in 1905, and "the Negro is afraid to complain." During the 1910s, the informal segregation effort by white elite Washingtonians became formalized by the Taft and Wilson presidencies. The white supremacist policy included a concomitant criminalization of African Americans in Washington. The number of arrests of blacks exceeded that of whites each year, and black newspapers reported story after story of policemen, particularly Irish ones, beating black citizens and prejudicially suspecting them of crimes before finding any evidence of their involvement.[8]

By the First World War, black citizens began to fight back. Washington's black elite raised money to build self-sustaining institutions, like the YMCA on Twelfth Street in 1914, making strong black institutions out of segregated spaces in Washington. Meanwhile, less organized working-class blacks began to challenge more openly the enforcement of racial containment in Washington. Their acts of defiance led white newspapers like the *Washington Post* to report stories about them as criminals rather than as resisters of their own racial subordination. As happened in other cities after the First World War, the confluence of working-class militancy and enforcement of white supremacy resulted in a "riot" in Washington. Stirred up by the Red Scare atmosphere of the Palmer raids and sensational news reports of black men preying upon white women, on July 19, 1919, white soldiers stationed in Washington began to indiscriminately attack black citizens. This riot and others that summer differed from previous "riots" in that blacks fought back on a large and widely publicized scale.[9] African Americans in the District had brought in guns from Baltimore and distributed them at Seventh and T Streets to blacks who had just returned from the armed services. This militant self-defense, many blacks would later conclude, brought the violence to an end in five days and minimized the number of black victims. Moreover, black residents predicted that the police would intervene in the riot to protect whites and contain blacks. In the five days of fighting that followed, the police proved them correct; of the more than one hundred arrests made, over 90 percent were African Americans. During the decade that followed, white politicians and officials in the District tried to ignore the outbreak. The white press muted some coverage of black crime during the riot's aftermath, and Congress never investigated the cause of the racial disturbance. The House Committee on the District of Columbia instead quietly reinforced Jim Crow barriers in the hope of quashing further disturbances.[10] By the early 1930s, District police began to enforce segregation in public parks for the first time since the Civil War. Meanwhile, government bureaucrats ignored civil service requirements about job performance and tenure to fire black employees solely based on their race.[11]

Thus, Washington became a Jim Crow city by the 1930s, but during this decade, a new phase of black resistance began to emerge on the campus of Howard University. Founded during Reconstruction and largely funded by federal appropriations, Howard exemplified W. E. B. Du Bois's idea of a talented tenth. In the 1920s, a campaign against white paternalism inside Howard University led to the 1926 appointment of its first black president, Mordecai Johnson.[12] Over the next few years, Johnson changed the dynamic at Howard. As he would later acknowledge, any teacher who did not have a strong concern for the rights of African Americans was not worthy of teaching at Howard.[13] Thus, Johnson hired young African American intellectuals, including Ralph Bunche, Abram Harris, E. Franklin Frazier, and Emmett Dorsey, whose work in the social sciences in the 1930s focused on economic-based solutions for racial discrimination. "Patience with older, more traditional social remedies was fading with each passing year," one scholar concluded about these professors, and "socio-economic policies of the New Deal became intertwined with daily life in black Washington."[14] At the depth of the Depression, in 1932, students created the Liberal Club to protest social ills that went beyond the campus. Advised by Ralph Bunche, the organization's members immersed themselves in New Deal politics and experimented with more confrontational forms of activism. After Liberal Club member Lyonel Flourant attended an International Student Congress against War and Fascism in 1934, he and other students became particularly interested in stopping the spread of fascism to places like Ethiopia and began to seek remedies for homegrown forms of fascism. The following year, the Liberal Club at Howard joined over 100,000 other college students in a nationwide strike against war and fascism. Singing "Ain't Going to Study War No More" as they marched across campus, antiwar protesters became an annual spectacle at Howard in the late 1930s. Moreover, these students increasingly sought to join political movements outside campus by joining in protests against fascism and racism in Washington.[15]

Coordination between these intellectuals and activists came as a result of a 1935 conference by John P. Davis, head of the Joint Committee on National Recovery, and Ralph Bunche, faculty member in the Social Science Division of Howard. This historic conference laid the groundwork for the establishment of the NNC. Titled "The Position of the Negro in Our National

Economic Crisis," the campus conference at Frederick Douglass Hall featured a broad political spectrum of participants, including intellectual and scholar W. E. B. Du Bois, socialists like A. Philip Randolph, Howard professors like Bunche and Emmett Dorsey of the Economics Department, Communist leader James W. Ford, and Howard Myers, a government adviser to the New Deal's National Recovery Act. After the conference, some of the leaders in attendance retired to the home of Ralph Bunche for further discussions. Through their conversations, they decided on the need to unify black organizations into a "United Front," which led to the formation of the NNC.[16]

Howard students attended the conference and took inspiration from its intellectual and activist energy. After the conference, Liberal Club meetings debated the New Deal with a new sense of urgency and focused on galvanizing student support for the February 1936 inauguration of the NNC in Chicago. In the span of just a few months, the club's members endorsed the NNC, formed a youth sponsoring committee, held a mass meeting on campus, and distributed pamphlets explaining the NNC's purpose. By February, these students had raised enough money to sponsor the trips of four Howard delegates to Chicago. "A permanent militant organization was formed to enable the Negro to use mass pressure," one delegate reported, "in gaining those rights which have long been denied." The "entire student body," one reporter claimed in the spring of 1936, seemed to be "wholeheartedly interested" in the NNC, an interest that was "most refreshing in view of youths' past indifference to social problems." By the following fall semester, the Liberal Club announced its intention to get involved in Washington NNC campaigns, concluding that "we may be assured that students at Howard will not again be labeled 'lazy,' 'disinterested,' or 'frivolous.'"[17]

In December 1936, youth movement leader Edward Strong reported that Professor William P. Robinson of the Political Science Department and "several [other] people are anxious to get started" on "organizing a local council of the NNC."[18] The creation of the NNC Washington Council was significant in part because it spread the Howard activism into black churches, community organizations, and neighborhoods. This diffusion of activism also helped take some pressure off President Mordecai Johnson, who after the May 1935 Howard NNC conference was accused by conservative professor Kelly Miller of hosting a gathering that was "communistic in tone and red in hue." Miller convinced Harold Ickes of the federal government's Department of the Interior to investigate the matter, which threatened to result in revocation of federal appropriations, upon which Howard's administration depended. Thelma Dale, then a student at Howard, remembered that when graduate student youth leader James Jackson created the Marxist Club, Abram Harris of the faculty tried to dissuade members from continuing the club during such a sensitive time. Thus the 1936 creation of the Washington Council of the NNC shifted activism into Washington's neighborhoods and away from the campus.[19]

Once the NNC moved off-campus, many Howard faculty stopped participating, leaving the more radical intellectuals at the helm. Ralph Bunche, Abram Harris, E. Franklin Frazier, and Emmett Dorsey, whose ideas had shaped the early direction of the NNC, mostly stayed on campus, while a younger group of faculty became the NNC's backbone. Doxey Wilkerson and William Alphaeus Hunton, both young professors at Howard in the mid-1930s, helped organize a Howard Local 440 of the American Federation of Teachers and advocated that it become more connected with Washington's larger labor movement. "Never before had black university teachers formally aligned themselves with the organized labor movement," Wilkerson later explained, and this showed that the faculty was "concerned with labor as a force for social progress."[20]

The organization of the faculty put the Howard union in contact with other labor organizations in Washington such as the United Federal Workers and the Hotel Workers. In addition, a second group of faculty joined the New Negro Alliance (NNA), a "Don't Buy Where You Can't Work" organization created in 1933 after the firing of three black employees at the Hamburger Grill on Twelfth and U Streets. This group, like similar ones in other cities, used boycotts and pickets to pressure white businesses in black neighborhoods to hire African American employees. Howard faculty like Howard Naylor Fitzhugh and Eugene Davidson, a Howard law graduate, became central actors in the NNA. Meanwhile, campus-anchored intellectuals like Emmett Dorsey criticized the NNA for "[intensifying] the consciousness of the job competition relationship between white and black workers," while Ralph Bunche called the NNA's strategy "utterly stupid."[21] The NNC activists agreed that the NNA attempt to gain a few jobs in black neighborhoods was shortsighted. However, many NNC members also understood the community-building possibilities created by the group's activism. Thus, Wilkerson and Hunton participated in the NNA, even though they remained more committed to the Washington Council of the NNC, whose vision included an interracial labor movement for jobs that would stretch beyond the Black Belt of Washington.[22]

As Bunche, Frazier, Harris, and Dorsey watched and criticized from the confines of campus, younger lions on the faculty immersed themselves in local activism.

◈ ◈ ◈ The Washington Council of the NNC sought to galvanize local working-class blacks by focusing on issues of discrimination that mattered to them. Unlike Chicago or Richmond, Washington lacked a large industrial base in steel, packing, or tobacco that could serve as a foundation for union-based civil rights activism. Since 1933, the NNA had concentrated on obtaining jobs for African Americans in retail stores in black neighborhoods, but the NNC wanted to broaden this activism into a wider movement. Apart from high unemployment, the most acute local grievance was policing. Among the resolutions passed at the NNC founding meeting in Chicago regarding "Lynching and Civil Liberties," NNC leaders called for the "abolition of police brutality." Back in Washington, in April 1936 the Scottsboro Defense Committee met to discuss the issue. John P. Davis and William Hastie, a Howard professor appointed to a position in the Interior Department, shared the podium at the Metropolitan Baptist Church that spring evening to appeal for the freedom of the Scottsboro defendants but also to widen the fight against racial violence in America. "Unless we have the substance of law," Hastie declared, "it doesn't matter whether a person is hanged by an unauthorized mob or by an organized mob known as the law."[23] African Americans in Washington, especially of the younger generation, responded to this message because they personally witnessed or experienced police abuse in their own neighborhoods. One month after this meeting, for example, a seventeen-year-old student at Dunbar High School suffered severe injuries after police clubbed her near her home at 1432 D Street, Northeast. Called in to quell a disturbance on a city bus, the police ordered everyone off. Martha Lloyd then remembered hearing the sergeant "say something about having trouble with those colored people in that section and stating that they should arrest any they get their hands on." The next thing she remembered, two white police began indiscriminately beating all of the black passengers and onlookers on the sidewalk. Events like this one convinced the NNC to form a coalition around the issue of police brutality.[24]

In order to build that coalition, however, the NNC needed to convince existing Washington organizations to join it. After the Chicago conference, some black church leaders had criticized the NNC for its radicalism and lack of clergy participation. In Washington, Davis sought to preempt such criticism by making church leaders central to the NNC council. Davis was fortunate to get the endorsement of the Reverend W. H. Jernagin, a progressive black preacher in the District who had attended the Chicago meeting. Jernagin returned home to Washington and made a report on the NNC to the Interdenominational Ministers Alliance, and this distinguished body of African American clergy voted to endorse it and become an affiliate. By the following year, NNC members elected the Reverend Arthur D. Gray as the head of the Washington Council, drawing his congregation and other churches into the fight against police brutality. The involvement of clergy allowed the NNC access to dozens of churches in Washington, but, more important, gave the local council a level of immediate respectability that it had to fight to attain in other cities. From a very early stage, these church leaders convinced the Elks of Washington, the NAACP, the NNA, and other civic groups to become involved with the NNC.

Of the list of civic groups that joined the NNC coalition, the Improved Benevolent Protective Order of Elks of the World stood out because it had a large membership base of African Americans that had never been specifically oriented toward protest politics. Known for their fraternal lodges and lavish annual parades, the Elks had a significant reach into cities and small towns across the country—from Mississippi to New York, from Ohio to California—and by the mid-1930s, the organization claimed over 100,000 total members. The "powerful Elks," one black newspaperman claimed, "occasionally press for Negro rights," but "for less than what it costs to stage an Elk convention" they could have employed a full-time Washington lobbyist for civil rights. Their leader, James Finley Wilson, nicknamed the "little Napoleon" for his short stature but commanding presence (and sometimes dictatorial leadership), had become the Exalted Ruler of the Elks in 1922 and operated its national headquarters in the District. Although Wilson had urged the membership to vote Republican in 1932, he, like many other African Americans during the New Deal, began to reconsider this political allegiance. This hesitation was not lost on President Roosevelt and the Democratic Party in the North, who saw how the black vote made the difference in a number of midterm elections in 1934. During the summer of 1935, the president invited Wilson and other Elk leaders to the White House before their annual conference; thereafter Roosevelt watched the Washington parade of thousands of Elks through the streets of the District. Meanwhile, the NNC courted the Elks as well. John P. Davis invited Wilson to attend the 1936 Chicago convention of the NNC and thereafter met regularly with Wilson and other Elk leaders to bring them into the NNC Washington Council's protest plans.[25]

Black Washingtonians like the Elks rallied around the NNC because police brutality struck a nerve. The long-standing pattern of police abuse, based on personal experience or the stories of others, had given virtually every black citizen of Washington reason to distrust the metropolitan police. In late 1936, the NNC Washington Council outlined the most egregious recent cases of brutality to Major Ernest Brown, the longtime chief of police in Washington, listing at least fifty known killings of blacks by police over the past decade. "For the sake of fairness," the memorandum stated, "many of these killings occurred while the officers were strictly within the line of duty." However, the NNC believed that "a study of the gruesome records must convince any fair-minded person that altogether too much of the hair-trigger method has been employed—shoot first and investigate afterwards." Many cases fell under the category of "slaughters" rather than police work, and while cases have "smelled to high heaven" of guilt by the officer, only one policeman had ever been reprimanded in these killings.[26]

The NNC provided specific evidence in five recent cases, including the police shooting of Lawrence Basey, which provided evidence that police and the members of the coroner's jury, the investigating body for police shootings, believed blacks were inherently violent criminals. In August 1936, a group of black Civilian Conservation Corps workers were headed home from a project in the Northeast quadrant of Washington. As they approached Officer V. H. Landrum, he shot at them at close range, killing Lawrence Basey, and arrested the others for inciting a "riot." Despite evidence presented at the coroner's trial that Landrum shot before any altercation occurred, that he had a past record of shooting at Civilian Conservation Corps workers, and that he had beaten a black man without cause a few years before, the jury exonerated him. The jury concluded that if the officer believed he was under threat of bodily harm, even if evidence showed otherwise, he had cause to shoot. Upon hearing this logic, even District Attorney Leslie C. Garnett called it a "damn-fool verdict." In addition to demanding the immediate suspension of this policeman, the NNC charged that he "requires the attention of a psychiatrist" because he, like many others on patrol, operated under the illusion that blacks were pathologically violent.[27]

In 1937, the Washington NNC expanded its activities against incidents of police abuse. Since the NNC was the relative newcomer among black organizations in the nation's capital, John P. Davis proceeded with caution. First, because the federal government controlled Washington's police department through a House Committee on the District of Columbia, an NNC delegation pinpointed a first-term congressman from Los Angeles, Byron N. Scott, to press for reform. Reminding Scott of the number of black voters in his home district in California, they urged him to adopt this cause of police brutality. In late January, Scott proposed a House resolution to establish a subcommittee for an "investigation to determine whether and to what extent the use of unnecessary and unlawful use of force by police officers . . . have become a menace to life, liberty, and the general security within the District of Columbia." Second, the NNC lobbied for an African American candidate to fill the recently vacated position of police judge for the District. Representatives from the Elks, the local NAACP, the *Baltimore Afro-American* newspaper staff, the Interdenominational Ministers Alliance, the YMCA, the Washington Bar Association, Howard University, and a half dozen other organizations met with the attorney general in March, hoping to persuade the police commissioner and federal officials to influence President Roosevelt's choice.[28]

During these negotiations, NNC members organized a mock trial of the police under the auspices of the Joint Committee on Civil Rights at the AME Zion Church. A parade of victims, eyewitnesses, and journalists "provided a complete picture of the lawless police terror which [had] reigned in Washington over the past ten years." Attorneys from the prestigious black law firms Houston and Houston and Cobb, Howard, and Hayes presented other evidence, and black leaders from the YMCA, Howard, the Elks, and churches acted as judges. This event demonstrated the new-style tactics of the NNC: with theatrics in front of a large public audience, the mock trial showed how the District ought to protect citizenship rights through democratic governance. Events like this one also allowed activists to cross class lines in Washington, as police brutality based on racial profiling affected the poor and the wealthy alike. It broadened the practical day-to-day exercise of freedom for District residents, rejecting both Jim Crow in Washington and its brutal enforcement. The court of public opinion, the NNC knew from the Scottsboro case, mattered as much as backroom negotiations in rallying the community around shared indignation to break down barriers to freedom of mobility and equal access to institutions in the capital.

This kind of mass pressure, however, had not yet produced enough political leverage to influence federal policy in 1937. William King, a Democrat from Utah who had chaired the House Committee on the District of Columbia over the past four years, cared little about African Americans in Washington—his electoral district back home had no black constituency. For the District judge position, the White House floated the names of Hobart Newman, a young white attorney, and William L. Houston, the African American lawyer who had founded the firm Houston and Houston and served as a professor at Howard and whose son Charles was the force behind the NAACP's legal defense division. Lacking sufficient pressure to promote Houston, D.C. officials quashed his nomination, complaining that it would be seen as far too radical to replace a longtime Republican judge with a black Democratic one in Washington. The White House concurred and in August put forth only Newman for the vacant position. This "failure of the President" to nominate Houston, the *Chicago Defender* concluded, "was quite a disappointment."[29]

The lack of progress in curbing police abuses in 1937 led the NNC to become more aggressive in implementing militant tactics. Incidents of police brutality continued to pile up. A Howard student accused of picking pockets was beaten; a twenty-year-old black man who had fled a traffic accident was shot to death, and then the coroner's jury exonerated the officer; and a black man and his pregnant wife were beaten after the man did not move his car fast enough from where it was parked.[30] Even Washington's Works Progress Administration guide, published in 1937, mentioned the conflict between the police of D.C. and poor black residents. "Efforts of the police to ferret out crime," the federally sponsored guide concluded, "are not helped by the furtiveness of alley dwellers, who consider 'John Law' to be their natural enemy—with good reason, at times, in light of police brutality."[31] Meanwhile, these police brutality stories ran side-by-side in the Washington edition of the *Baltimore Afro-American* with stories like "Anti-lynch Bill Set-Back Is Bitter Blow to Father Whose Son, 15, Was Killed in '32."[32]

▨ ▨ ▨ John P. Davis sought to connect these campaigns to more than just the headlines. During the summer of 1937, he met in Detroit with Walter White, national secretary of the NAACP, to coordinate plans between the two groups. Once back in Washington, Davis contacted White on several occasions, always expressing deference to the NAACP for its "splendid fight" on the antilynching bill but also suggesting that "tremendous public sentiment must be built up during the next few months." Busy with the lobbying effort in Washington, White largely ignored Davis, until the bill was passed over once again by a Senate filibuster in February 1938.[33]

Davis, seeking to counteract the dismay felt by many African Americans over this setback, decided to organize a Washington conference in March 1938 to expose the senators who had fought against the antilynching bill. After conferring with a sympathetic Charles Hamilton Houston of the NAACP, Davis informed White about this conference of "100 outstanding people" for the purpose of planning a nationwide lobbying campaign. White responded with a request that Davis postpone the conference because "certain steps are now being taken to which publicity cannot be given," and when Davis did not cancel his plans, White became furious. In a flurry of correspondence to other NAACP leaders, White referred to the conference as a "typical Johnnie Davis trick," charging that the "unscrupulous" NNC leader only wanted to "cut in on our program" for "ballyhoo purposes."[34]

White and Davis both had cause to criticize the other. As historian Patricia Sullivan's NAACP study explained, much to the chagrin of other leaders in the NAACP like Charles Houston, White took on the lynching fight as his personal mission and zealously guarded against collaboration with the NNC, which engaged in more militant protest politics than political lobbying in Washington. As Houston advised White earlier about the NNC, "To keep [Davis] from running off with the show—unless he breaks his neck in the meantime—is for the Association to put on a bigger and better performance," which meant broadening the NAACP campaign, which only focused on "the manifestation of the evil" of lynching "while ignoring the causes." But as Houston's comment also suggests, the NAACP had never fully trusted Davis's loyalties. In fact, in the mid-1930s, Walter White asked a staff member of Davis's NNC precursor, the Joint Committee on National Recovery, to report on his activities and find out "what really motivates him." Meanwhile, White also promoted dissension between Davis and Du Bois out of fear that the two of them allied might force him out of the NAACP leadership. Beyond concerns over personal power, however, White saw the NNC competing with the NAACP. When the NNC was formed, its leaders promised not to duplicate the work of the NAACP; although Davis saw this antilynching work as complementary, White clearly did not agree. In addition, the Communist participation in the NNC had concerned White since its inception, and he no doubt had heard about Davis's well-publicized trip to the Soviet Union for the December 1937 twentieth-anniversary commemoration of the Russian Revolution, which had occurred two months before the argument over the NNC's proposed antilynching conference. While nobody (including Davis, it turns out) knew if he was an actual member of the CP, NAACP leaders clearly had reason to suspect him of fostering a closer relationship to the party over the past year.[35]

Despite this growing antagonism between Davis and White, the conference drew 123 delegates from around the country. These delegates included the Bishop L. W. Kyles from Winston-Salem, who gave a fiery speech, and grassroots NNC organizers like Stanley Cotton from Gary, Indiana. The delegates at the conference agreed on a resolution that "the shelving of the antilynching bill shows a grave crisis in the political life of our country" and hoped to form a coalition with the Labor's Non-Partisan League, the CIO, and other groups to "drive from political life" the "small minority" who continued to oppose the bill by a "shameless filibuster." Despite the lack of NAACP participation, the delegates nonetheless complimented the NAACP and looked for its "continued leadership in this vital struggle." The NNC sought to cooperate with these groups "in bringing the bill back before Congress" and made a point to equate racial violence in America with "the murderous onslaught of fascist forces against the people throughout the world." At the conference's conclusion, the delegates listened to local leaders report on their campaign against police brutality, sent thousands of telegrams to senators, and planned a follow-up march for two weeks later.[36]

By holding the conference without White's approval, the NNC sent a clear message that it would no longer allow the NAACP to dictate the pace of racial activism in Washington. Although organizational jealousy probably caused much of the friction between White and Davis, it also unearthed key differences in vision and strategy between the two groups. The NAACP had prioritized legislative lobbying behind closed doors and public appeals in its literature to push the antilynching bill, whereas the NNC opted for mass-action tactics to apply pressure. Furthermore, the NAACP saw lynching primarily as a southern phenomenon, whereas the NNC saw it as a much wider pattern of "domestic fascism."[37]

Proceeding with its strategic brand of political lobbying combined with street theater protests, the Washington Council of the NNC frontally challenged police brutality in a widely publicized case in 1938. Aside from the defeat of the antilynching bill, the case that mobilized community outrage was that of Leroy Keys. Keys, a shell-shocked veteran of the First World War, ran from police when ordered to halt and barricaded himself inside a nearby apartment building. Soon thereafter, Keys appeared in the window of the apartment, muttering to himself, and set a small fire. The police, after calling in backup, opened fire on the window and shot Keys dead. Although there had been other recent police killings, this one happened at a moment when many black citizens had reached their limit of patience. Also, Keys's status as a sick veteran of the First World War triggered indignation among older black Washingtonians who still harbored resentment over the postwar 1919 riot. Still others connected this killing to the current spread of fascism in Nazi Germany. "We think Hitler is a tyrant and a brute, a ruffian and a cur. We detest him for the way he is crushing the Jew," the editors of the *Baltimore Afro-American* newspaper wrote, but "don't forget that there is a man right here at home who has his heel on our neck." In the aftermath of the killing of Keys, a black American Legionnaires Post passed a resolution to "express its unqualified condemnation," the United Federal Workers called it an "urbanized form of lynching," the AME Ministerial Union endorsed the campaign, and the Inter-Racial Committee of the NAACP asked the NNC, "Can you send someone or a delegation to help us?"[38] In all, thirty-six organizations joined the Keys coalition, which continued to build momentum into the summer. The coroner's jury, unable to come to a decision on the case after two investigations, sent the case to the Grand Jury, which "ignored" the charge of homicide. With the "community still seething" over the case, the coalition further escalated its protest campaign to reopen the investigation.[39]

The NNC also increasingly reached across the physical and social barriers of Washington's segregated neighborhoods in search of white allies, finding them in local labor, youth, civic, and Socialist Party and Communist Party (CP) leaders. For example, Thelma Dale and other black youth in the Washington Youth Federation, an affiliate of the Southern Negro Youth Congress (SNYC), reached out to white youth leaders in the District such as Howard Ennes of the Washington Youth Council, while the NNC elders allied with Charles Russell, who headed the civil liberties group called the Inter-Racial Committee.[40] NNC activists also knew well that the CP had committed its resources to fighting racial injustice in the South, most famously defending the Scottsboro Boys, and they now sought white CP members and other fellow travelers in the Popular Front coalition to fight brutality. Invited into action, the CP's Washington, D.C., division began holding open-air meetings in June that connected local violence to lynching. At one of these meetings, Martin Chancey, the CP's city secretary, told a crowd gathered at Tenth and U Streets, "We don't hear of lynchings in Washington in the same manner as in Georgia or Alabama but lynchings are perpetrated by those who are supposed to protect human life and property, the members of the District police force."[41]

The following month, all of these allied groups made up a crowd of 2,000 people that marched through the streets of the District to demand an end to police violence. The marchers brought black coffins for each of the police victims over the past decade, including one for William McKnight. The previous month, McKnight had run from a policeman on his way home because he carried a small package of "foodstuffs" that he had taken from the restaurant where he worked. The officer's immediate response to a running black man was to discharge his weapon; the bullet hit McKnight in the abdomen and killed him. "Because of the record of the police department for the last eleven years," the Reverend R. W. Brooks surmised, "McKnight not knowing what officer John Sobolewski might do, took [his] chances on running away." During the demonstration, a car occupied by the widowed Mollie McKnight led the marchers on foot. Estimated to be about one-fifth white, the crowd demonstrated a newfound interracial solidarity in the streets of Washington during that summer day. Although the police forced the marchers to put away the coffins as well as any signs calling for Superintendent Brown's dismissal, the crowd got the point across by chanting, "Major Brown must go!" and "Stop Legal Lynching."[42]

The police brutality campaign of the NNC challenged the very notion of American civil society. In their speeches and editorials, these activists recast the so-called Negro problem into a white problem. They showed how whites, not blacks, perpetrated violence in the nation's capital. In July, for example, an editor of the Baltimore Afro-American penned an editorial titled, "Civilization Takes a Holiday." As "another victim bit the dust in Western two-gun fashion," the writer claimed, it had "aroused the indignation of a civilized community to unprecedented heights." Rather than merely placing blame on individual officers, the editorial argued that the "perpetrators reflect the policy of their superiors" and that "the blood of every victim of police lynching is on their hands."[43] Civilization, these activists demonstrated in their nonviolent protests, had indeed taken a holiday in Washington, and the NNC coalition, not the police, sought to return it to the nation's capital.

If police violence was a systemic problem, the NNC activists argued, then all citizens were affected by it. At the turn of the century, Washington had more black professionals than either New York or Chicago. During the 1920s, the NNC believed that the black elite had largely turned its back on the problems of working-class blacks in Washington, and by the early 1930s even the Washington Tribune complained about the lack of a "representative militant organization."[44] To repair this class division within Washington's black communities, NNC activists brought together a coalition that crossed ideological and socioeconomic lines. During the mass march in July, many of the placards read, "You May Be Next," to imply that police violence did not spare the respectable.[45]

This applied to both sexes. Citing a case where police broke into an elderly black woman's home and beat its female occupants in a search for a suspect named Manassas, one NNC member published a pamphlet titled, "Make Washington Safe for Negro Womanhood." In vivid detail, the statement described the scene at Julia MacKay's home: "If you are a colored woman awakened in your home at 5 o'clock in the morning and a police sergeant . . . pushes his night stick into your stomach and calls you a God d—n dumb N——r, there is NOTHING you can do about it. I know, because the acting District Attorney told me so."[46] Although the Washington police shot mostly black men, other forms of police intimidation of black women led to the "demand that Washington be made a safe place for Negro womanhood." Activists argued that racial violence also affected white Washingtonians. Stretching back to Howard student demonstrations, these activists concluded that violence perpetrated by "uniformed constabulary paid to protect human life and property" was evidence of the erosion of the civil liberties of all Americans. The same police violence that hemmed in African Americans, they argued, also broke apart labor unions and protected strikebreakers. Thus, acts of police violence affected all citizens, not just black ones. "No, there was no war," a *Baltimore Afro-American* journalist wrote, but "citizens were shot down in the streets of the nation's capital."[47]

The NNC sought to harness this frustration to apply to both local and national campaigns. At a mass meeting of 1,200 people cosponsored by the NNC and the Interdenominational Ministers Alliance, the leaders announced plans to obtain thousands of petition signatures against police brutality and submit them to President Roosevelt. They saw Roosevelt as potentially sympathetic because a few months before, at a mass meeting in Philadelphia, the NNC had invited the First Lady to speak, and she had expressed her support for its civil rights goals. "We are getting to a point when we are going to insist that all human beings have certain basic rights in modern civilization," she said, "that all should be equal before the law, that there should be no discrimination in citizenship rights." After this event, the NNC distributed literature containing this quote and used it in its mission statement during its antilynching conference and the campaign against police brutality.[48]

The petition to Roosevelt was very specific. It demanded that the federal government suspend and bring charges against five particular officers, remove Commissioner Brown, issue pensions for the families of victims, and appoint a citizens' committee to hold public hearings and then make recommendations to the commissioners of the District.[49] The coalition, which included new allies like the Dining Car Employees Union, American League for Peace and Democracy, American Civil Liberties Union, and Washington Insurance Underwriters Association, organized "flying squadrons [that] went from house to house in Washington collecting several thousand signatures."[50] Even NAACP legal strategist Charles H. Houston, in contrast to Walter White, joined the campaign by offering free legal services to the victims. "We have been forced to conclude," John P. Davis wrote to the president in August, "that the responsible officials of the District of Columbia will not or cannot act to protect the lives and liberties of American citizens living under their jurisdiction. The time has come when we can no longer keep silent."[51]

Just outside of Capitol Hill, the NNC took to the streets to back its petition, generating a mass movement against brutality in Washington. With several demonstrations of more than 1,000 people and 24,000 petition signatures collected during 1938, these activists achieved a new kind of visibility in the capital and became widely recognized for their work. In June 1939, the *Baltimore Afro-American* announced a remarkable achievement: not one African American had been killed by police in the past year. "Modestly the officials of the [National Negro] Congress have stated that it is not their victory alone," the editorial continued, but the "job could not have been done had it not been for the tireless energy and leadership the National Negro Congress gave to other organizations in this fight against police crimes on the Negro people of Washington."[52]

In addition to the cessation of police killings, the NNC coalition brought about the creation of a new civilian trial board. "In place of a trial board composed of police officers," the civilian board made a significant difference in curbing police brutality. According to the NNC's Arthur Gray, "The number of . . . incidents has markedly decreased," because the board made recommendations for indictments and obtained suspensions against some of the policemen accused of abuse.[53] Having shown the NNC's muscle, Davis suggested that it now "carry the issue of police brutality to Congress." He outlined a plan to pressure specific members of the House Committee on the District of Columbia in their home voting districts, many of which had a substantial number of black voters, CIO unions, and functioning NNC councils. Then, having made an appointment for representatives to see the House Committee in early January, he hoped to convince Congressman Scott from California to reintroduce his resolution calling for an investigation into police brutality in the District.[54]

The NNC also linked its work against police brutality to its struggle for jobs. NNC leaders knew that not all black crime stemmed from racially biased police methods but that other forms of insecurity led some blacks to take desperate measures. As Davis explained in 1938, "We declared as part of our policy the extension of the fight of police brutality to a struggle for jobs."[55] The Labor Committee of the NNC, headed by Clarence Johnson of the Dining Car Workers, organized thirteen locals of hotel workers in Washington by educating the half-white, half-black workforce about the racially divisive tactics of employers. The NNC and these new unions called for National Labor Relations Board (NLRB) elections in 1939; all but one of these elections resulted in union recognition and job security. The Labor Committee of the NNC proved "more successful than any of my efforts," Miguel Carriga of the Hotel Workers union wrote, and "whether our people [in the American Federation of Labor] realize [it] or not," the "credit for these victories belongs to the National Negro Congress."[56]

John P. Davis emphasized the successful hotel workers' campaign to ensure that the New Deal administration of President Roosevelt understood its importance in relation to the NNC's quest for all Americans to have the freedom from fear. As part of his congressional testimony in opposition to potentially diluting amendments to the Wagner Act, Davis retold the story of recent District hotel workers' victories to emphasize the crucial role of impartial NLRB elections. He explained that the NNC and the AFL had made inroads for black and white hotel workers alike in D.C. because the NLRB and "the act, have done more to aid the underprivileged" who "lived in mortal fear" of forming unions due to "coercion of the employer" than "any other act Congress has enacted."[57]

As Davis outlined before the federal government, the NNC strove to make the hotel victory into a widespread struggle for black placement and security in existing and new employment fields. To aid black women, Wilhelmina Jackson and other members opened an employment bureau for domestics out of the NNC offices. Jackson aimed to place candidates immediately in openings and ensure minimum wages and working conditions and, in the long term, hoped to form a citywide union for domestic workers.[58] In addition to organizing unionized and unemployed workers, the NNC organized picket lines in front of "sweat shop" employers in the District. In one such protest at the National Pants Company, Edward Strong, the newly elected head of the SNYC, joined John P. Davis and a group of over seventy men, white women, and students to protest the piecework pay system that netted full-time workers less than five dollars a week. When Davis led the picket line in singing the "Star Spangled Banner," white policeman A. L. Fridette arrested him. (Two months later, Fridette was spotted in plain clothes taking notes at an NNC police brutality meeting and became the "target of boos, hisses and cat-calls from the audience.")[59] Aside from picketing and other public airing of grievances, the NNC filed and won charges with the NLRB against employers like the Arcade Sunshine Laundry, whose manager fired employees for trying to organize their co-workers. The NNC aimed to organize service workers into a domestic workers union through the CIO, but at the very least, it sought to shame employers into providing better conditions.[60]

Complementing the jobs campaign, the NNC also targeted poor health conditions in black neighborhoods as another aspect of economic and physical security. Beginning in January 1939, its members sponsored a yearlong health campaign of eighty affiliated organizations. This coalition organized a conference with experts on health education, who explained that blacks were six times more likely to contract tuberculosis and twice as likely to have still-born children, which contributed to a life span of at least ten years less than white Washingtonians. To combat these discrepancies, black activists distributed literature and protested against unsanitary conditions in black neighborhoods.[61] The NNC also defined the problem of poor health as not only stemming from terrible housing conditions but also from a lack of recreation spaces for African Americans in the District. Without other options, young blacks in the District congregated in the streets and sidewalks, which in turn exacerbated the police problem when white officers tried to move them from street corners. To tackle this problem, the NNC commissioned a survey of recreation in the District. Directed by Thelma Dale, a Howard graduate and Washington Youth Federation leader, the report demanded that the government uphold the mission of the Department of Recreation's former director, who claimed that "preserving and perpetuating democracy" was its purpose, "and therefore [the Department] must accept responsibility in looking toward the building of a democratic environment." The report found a lack of recreational spaces in black neighborhoods, widespread segregation in federal and city parks, and prohibitive fees at certain public facilities.

Blatant forms of recreational segregation in Washington grew into a national controversy during the spring of 1939 when the Daughters of the American Revolution (DAR) refused to allow internationally renowned black opera singer Marian Anderson use of the federal government's Constitution Hall. In February 1939, Doxey Wilkerson, according to one historian, "took the lead" in preparing and presenting a detailed proposal to the school board to hold the concert instead at Central High School, the only other hall in D.C. large enough to accommodate several thousand people. The school board, taking a page from the DAR, voted five to one to reject the proposed concert. Following this setback, several Washington civil rights groups, like the NAACP, the Brotherhood of Sleeping Car Porters, and the United Mine Workers, as well as several clubs from Howard University, formed the Marian Anderson Citizens Committee, which held a mass meeting in late February 1939 to publicize its case. Unbeknownst to the committee, the meeting and other publicity convinced Eleanor Roosevelt to take a stand. The First Lady wrote a telegram of regret that no venue would host the Anderson concert and thereafter resigned from the DAR. This action transformed the Marian Anderson Citizens Committee campaign from a District issue to a national one. Harold Ickes, a former Chicago NAACP head and now a Roosevelt cabinet member, worked closely with the NAACP's Walter White and a host of other groups to pull off a magical reversal of fortune: Anderson, on Easter Sunday at the Lincoln Memorial, memorably sang "My country tis of thee, sweet land of liberty, to thee we sing" in front of 75,000 people. Careful listeners noted that Anderson had changed the lyrics of the patriotic song "America" from the original "of thee I sing" to "*to* thee *we* sing." The revision reflected the civil rights movement of 1939; "to" noted the unfinished promise of American liberty, and "we" referenced the collective struggle to achieve that goal. This event, one historian concluded, signified "the first black mass action to evoke laudatory national publicity and earn a positive place in American public memory." The NNC played a less prominent role in comparison to the NAACP, whose leaders had the ear of Eleanor Roosevelt and other White House staffers, in making the final concert arrangements. Nonetheless, NNC members took pride in their past three years of civil rights activism, which had helped produce this moment when African Americans and their allies symbolically took back their country as the "Sweet Land of Liberty."[62]

Over the next year, NNC members sought "the perpetuation of the Marian Anderson Committee for a continued fight against discrimination." "The concert showed," according to the NNC Washington Council, "the artistic excellence" and "the richness of possibilities of Negroes," as Anderson's voice "had [even] greater echoes than those heard over Constitution avenue."[63] But now these groups needed to do the "anti-climactic" work necessary to break down segregation across the District. With their comprehensive report in hand, which specified all of the spaces in the city that barred blacks, the NNC and its affiliated allies pressured Department of Interior officials to desegregate facilities in Washington. Harold Ickes pledged to ban all forms of federal discrimination, and early desegregation campaigns won black access to parks, baseball diamonds, tennis courts, and a tourist camp, the latter opening just in time to house sharecroppers, industrial workers, and other delegates arriving for the April 1940 national convention of the NNC in Washington.[64]

▨ ▨ ▨ The flurry of NNC activity in the District to break down segregation, end police brutality, and foster economic security provoked the ire of conservative legislators, who sought to thwart this new militancy. In 1938, Congress created a new committee, chaired by Martin Dies, to investigate "un-American activities." Using an earlier federal report on Howard University that had been commissioned by Harold Ickes, the Dies Committee attacked the NNC in an attempt to break its coalition. Papers like the *Chicago Defender* blasted the committee, noting that its "unbridled assaults threatened their limited liberties" and, more important, because Dies "directs his main fire [at] the staunchest champions for equal rights for Negroes." In 1939 and 1940, Dies Committee reports singled out the NNC and the SNYC (without having ever informed either group that they were under investigation), summoned John P. Davis to appear before the committee in September 1939, and in 1941 investigated Alphaeus Hunton, an NNC board member and Howard University professor of English, who had played an essential behind-the-scenes role in the police brutality campaign.[65] The *Defender* made this connection in late 1939 by pointing out that "Black men have been indiscriminately and in cold blood murdered on the streets of the nation's capital," but thanks to NNC members, who worked "so effectively," this un-American violence had been checked. "We do not know where Mr. Dies was during these struggles for the rights of the most forgotten sections of America," the editorial continued, "and it seemed that the NNC, not Dies, had come time and again to the 'Defense of American Democracy.'"[66]

John P. Davis also went on the counterattack against Dies, submitting a fiery eleven-page open letter to the Speaker of the House of Representatives in early 1939. Communists participated in public NNC meetings and at least five members of its fifty-member board were Communists, the statement explained, because the organization "welcomes free and democratic discussion by speakers of every point of view." Davis believed that Dies's real motive was to "discredit the attempt of Negro citizens to win their constitutional rights as free citizens in Democratic America." He pointed out that "Dies has been a bitter opponent of federal anti-lynching legislation" and explained that racial violence helped keep blacks from voting in Dies's home state of Texas. His committee, Davis advised, would be better suited to "investigate the Ku Klux Klan, lynchings, [and] mob violence in Texas," rather than to attack the NNC, which continued to fight for "every letter of the American Constitution (including the 13th, 14th, and 15th amendments)."[67]

The Washington Council of the NNC alluded to the application of the Thirteenth Amendment when it extended its policing campaign against the "lynch spirit" in another direction: debt peonage. Beginning in 1939, Bob Wirtz and William Henry Huff, attorneys for the CP's International Labor Defense (ILD), worked with the NNC Chicago Council members within an Abolish Peonage Committee to locate over one hundred refugees from Georgia who now lived in Chicago, Cincinnati, and Baltimore. ILD lawyers took affidavits from these peonage victims and submitted them to the nascent Civil Rights Division of the Department of Justice. In one affidavit, an escaped worker recounted how farm owner W. T. Cunningham hit Ben Hale over the head with a "wagon stander" and shot his son "with his pistol in the groins" when he rushed to his father's aid. Then, since Cunningham had seriously injured both men, he summoned the sheriff, also a peonage farm owner, to send them to the chain gang. Cumulatively, these firsthand accounts of servitude at W. T. Cunningham's farm in Oglethorpe County included graphic details of the conditions these farmworkers faced: without pay, except for a couple of dollars at Christmas; beatings and whipping of black men and pregnant women to coerce them to hoe cotton; and enforcement by the local sheriff of vagrancy laws (and even cooperation of the Chicago police to extradite escaped workers) to confine them to this farm.[68]

The graphic evidence of police-backed violence to enforce involuntary labor, the NNC believed, provided legal justification for federal action. In a detailed and pointed letter to Attorney General Robert H. Jackson, John P. Davis wrote that the Department of Justice "has the duty to proceed speedily and with utmost vigor," based on the evidence the NNC provided of Klan violence against blacks in late 1939 in Greenville, South Carolina, and the peonage evidence from Oglethorpe, Georgia. For the Klan cases, Davis argued that the federal government had made previous exceptions to its "Lindbergh law," which held that federal courts had no jurisdiction unless the actors crossed

The NNC Washington Council fostered a diverse coalition of forces within the black community and political left against all forms of racial violence. This photograph shows an NNC delegation prior to meeting with U.S. Assistant Attorney General O. John Rogge to demand that the Justice Department pursue cases against southern farmers who held blacks in virtual slavery through debt peonage, April 1940. *Left to right*: Louis Colman, New York ILD; William L. Patterson, Chicago ILD; Charles Hamilton Houston, counsel for the NAACP; J. Finley Wilson, Grand Exalted Ruler of the Negro Elks; and John P. Davis, NNC executive secretary. Photograph by Scurlock Studio. Courtesy of the National Museum of American History, Behring Center, Archives Center, Smithsonian Institution, Washington, D.C.

state lines but also that the Department of Justice believed that "collusion between local offices of the Ku Klux Klan" may have occurred across state boundaries "in the acts described above." For the Oglethorpe victims, Davis had an even more persuasive argument. Based on the existing federal peonage statutes, which even Assistant Attorney General O. John Rogge admitted were "clear violations of federal law," the Department of Justice had cause to prosecute under the 1866 Peonage Act because "involuntary servitude" violated the Thirteenth Amendment.[69]

The NNC took the campaign a step further by bringing the actual victims of this violence to testify in Washington. Not unlike the previous ILD campaign around the infamous Scottsboro case, the Washington NNC and its allies in the ILD and the National Council to Aid Agricultural Workers pressured the Department of Justice by exposing these acts in the court of public opinion in the nation's capital. At the Lincoln Temple Congregational Church on March 19, the NNC hosted an "Abolish Modern Slavery" mass meeting, which featured two Chicago refugees from W. T. Cunningham's plantation in Georgia and two victims of the recent spate of Ku Klux Klan terror in Greenville, South Carolina. An advertisement for the meeting explained that "here in Washington" these issues "are not isolated" and "concern us." In March 1940, the same month that Senator Tom Connally of Texas denounced Davis's call to abolish the "lynch spirit" in America, the dramatization of all forms of police-backed violence in Washington made it clear to many citizens that lynching, police brutality, and peonage were all connected in a nationwide pattern. As stated in the advertisement for the mass meeting: "All of us, white and colored, owe it not only to those who have been injured but to ourselves and the future of our children to protest—more than protest—to defend ourselves."[70] The NNC coalition in Washington held together and even pressured Dies to start denouncing groups like the Ku Klux Klan. And significantly, this defense by the NNC aggressively defined "civil rights" for the nation. This was a relatively new term in the 1930s in relation to African Americans, and the NNC used it to mean federal protection against the intertwined evils of racial discrimination and labor exploitation of American citizens.

Despite the NNC's counterattack, the Dies Committee's targeting of the NNC as "Red" also portended pejorative consequences. According to Thelma Dale, a youth leader and NNC member in Washington, the black community was less susceptible to red-baiting in Washington because it valued the work the NNC had accomplished over the past years. "In Washington, in the fight against police brutality," Dale explained, "were we going to put a circle around a Communist?" The NNC "wanted to accept whomever" would help them fight against police violence. "Martin Chancey . . . the head of the Communist Party in Washington D.C.," Dale concluded, "functioned fully, openly. So who were we to turn them away? We didn't."[71] Yet federal officials, yielding to the pressure of the Dies Committee, forced the resignation of Dale from her government day job because of her connection to this NNC activism. In addition, the NNC campaign to compel the House Committee on the District of Columbia to create and enforce local civil rights laws stalled, and this political atmosphere exacerbated internal political fissures, which came to a head during the NNC's third national convention in Washington in the spring of 1940.[72]

The Reverend Arthur Gray, president of the NNC Washington Council, officially opened the NNC's third national conference in the Department of Labor's Auditorium on Friday, April 26, 1940. Approximately 175 local delegates discussed tactics for ending Jim Crow with others who traveled from across the nation to Washington. Northern delegates, no strangers to discrimination, still hesitated once in D.C. because they knew of its southern reputation. "When we entered the suburbs of Washington I noticed the car moved more slowly than before," Ralph Ellison wrote about his trip to the conference, because "there was always that fear of Negroes going from the North into the South of running afoul of Southern custom [and] the driver knew we were driving into the capital of the United States—and of legal Jim Crow." In addition, the Washington NNC had organized two campsites, one within yards of the Washington Monument, as well as several rooms in private houses so that the delegates would not have to stay in unsanitary or segregated hotels. Both black and white delegates wore "Stop Lynching" pins that referenced the NNC's campaign against all forms of racialized violence. One delegate epitomized the mood of the conference when he yelled from the floor, "Peonage, Anti-Lynch Bill, poll tax, these are our issues," and "Some of us will have to die for them!" Echoing this outburst of indignation, the speakers at the conference represented the most militant leaders of labor and civil rights, including John L. Lewis, the head of the CIO, A. Philip Randolph, the NNC's dignified president and head of the Brotherhood of Sleeping Car Porters union, Hank Johnson of the steel and packinghouse workers, and John P. Davis, the executive secretary of the NNC. The speakers and delegates alike embodied both the expansion of the NNC's network over the past four years and its future potential to lead a mass movement into the 1940s.[73]

This exhilarating conference atmosphere seemed to promise further growth of a united movement for civil rights, so it came as a surprise to the delegates when A. Philip Randolph refused to continue as the NNC's president. Although confusion resulted over this announcement, the spirit of militancy did not subside after the conference. Instead, it splintered into different paths as many liberal NNC members followed Randolph's lead into a new all-black group that would become the March on Washington Movement (MOWM). Thereafter, Washington NNC members watched as Randolph threatened a mass march on the capital during the next summer to demand that the federal government provide access to wartime jobs. Fearing that Randolph and his allies in the NAACP and other African American groups would make good on their threat, President Roosevelt signed Executive Order 8802 on June 25, 1941, establishing a new federal agency called the Fair Employment Practices Committee to ensure nondiscrimination in employment.

But NNC members did more than watch. During the same period that the MOWM threatened its march on the capital, the NNC redoubled its regional efforts for job security by targeting the largest airplane factory in the eastern United States. As the war between the Nazis and Britain and France expanded overseas, the NNC saw a growing number of well-paid industrial jobs as a new target for economic security. War jobs not only promised steady wages but were based on government contracts; thus, the NNC planned to apply pressure to both employers and the federal government simultaneously for antidiscrimination measures in hiring. The NNC was already active in places like Detroit in assisting the United Auto Workers' battle to organize the Ford Motor Company in the spring of 1941. There, activists like Christopher Columbus Alston, having moved back north after his stint organizing tobacco workers, took a job in an auto plant and worked with a strong council of the NNC in the Motor City to sever the paternalistic ties between Ford and black churches, as well as to educate workers on the benefits of the interracial United Auto Workers. John Davis traveled to Detroit during this period and was inspired by what he saw. "Jobs afford economic security," Davis said in a March 1941 speech to a crowd in Detroit, "and out of this develops the social and economic standard of a people."[74]

Back in Washington, Davis and the NNC found Ford's regional equivalent in Glenn L. Martin. Like Ford, Martin's status as a titan of industry was accompanied by a defiance of unions, but Martin diverged from Ford's paternalistic stance in hiring black workers. Instead, Martin openly vowed to never have anyone but white, male workers employed at his aircraft manufacturing plant. A dozen years before, Martin had built the most modern aircraft manufacturing plant in the country in a town ten miles east of Baltimore named Middle River. Although the company almost folded during the early Depression years, Martin stayed the course long enough for the war to begin in Europe. Contracts with the French government followed in 1939, and after a period of uncertainty in the year that followed, the plant rebounded with an unprecedented $375 million in U.S. military contracts. The plant went to three-shift production and began a massive expansion of the factory into several new buildings, which opened during the summer of 1941. With a new

B-26 prototype ready for production, the only issue slowing down Martin's $375 million dollars in government contracts was enough metal from Alcoa. Martin publicly protested to the Office of Production Management (OPM), and in turn new methods of ordering and a national scrap metal drive were initiated that summer.[75]

The NNC also protested to the OPM, arguing that barring blacks from munitions jobs compromised all-out war production. In March, NNC representatives met with Martin officials. Company representatives told them they had no intention of "pioneering in the field of defense jobs for Negroes." The need for qualified labor was so great that Martin established training courses in Virginia, North Carolina, and Appalachia to bus white male workers into the plant rather than hire African Americans or women. Undaunted, the NNC vowed it would return, meanwhile stepping up protests in Washington. It blamed Sidney Hillman, the former union leader and now head of the OPM, for effectively conducting a sit-down strike against black workers, as he aided and abetted corporations that openly discriminated. NNC leaders also befriended employment experts like Bertha Blair, "formerly employed by the Women's Bureau of the Department of Labor," who now "was one of the principal white individuals actively engaged" with the NNC. In early April, Blair and others organized a mass meeting in Washington's Mt. Carmel Baptist Church and planned a second "jobs conference" in Baltimore for the end of the month. The NNC demanded 7,000 jobs for blacks at the Martin factory and vowed to keep sending qualified applicants to the Middle River plant until they were hired.[76]

In the midst of its militant campaign for jobs at the Martin plant in Baltimore, the NNC organized a benefit concert featuring the internationally famous artist Paul Robeson. This April 1941 concert, the NNC believed, might create national civil rights attention for its jobs campaign, much like the Marian Anderson concert had done two years previous. Unfortunately, the DAR's attitude toward an integrated audience had not changed since Anderson had stoically sung in front of the Lincoln Memorial. So when similarly blocked from using Constitutional Hall, the NNC found another indoor option: the recently constructed Uline Arena in Washington. Under pressure from sponsors, the Uline's management agreed to desegregate its seating for the Robeson event. The concert would be a joint benefit held with the Committee for Aid to China and featured Eleanor Roosevelt as a sponsor.[77]

But just ten days before the concert, controversy erupted. Cornelia Pinchot, the wife of the governor of Pennsylvania and friend of Eleanor Roosevelt, announced that both she and the First Lady would withdraw their support because they had not been made aware of the NNC's joint sponsorship. Mortimer Graves of the Committee for Aid to China responded in the press that the shared proceeds "cannot be accepted as a valid reason" to withdraw, especially since he had approached the NNC about co-sponsorship—the China committee had feared it would not sell enough tickets alone. For his part, Davis responded to Pinchot that the NNC would withdraw as long as it got reimbursed for its promotion and advertising expenses and on the condition that the Uline Arena would vow to extend its integrated policy to all future events. Meanwhile, in a private letter to Robeson, Pinchot explained that she had to withdraw because of the segregation issue, even though Robeson knew that the NNC had been the only group to previously object on that basis. In the end, the hubbub obscured a reason much less technical and much more political. In recent months, the NNC had become a critic of the Roosevelt administration's laggard response to job discrimination in the war industries. Just weeks before the scheduled concert, John P. Davis had shared the podium with Eleanor Roosevelt at a New York University civil rights forum with more than 300 students in attendance. When during the question-and-answer session students asked Mrs. Roosevelt if the president should issue an executive order banning all forms of discrimination in the military and war industries, the First Lady stated she believed such a step might cause trouble during this time of international crisis. Then she turned to Davis and asked if he agreed. "In a quiet but positive voice," a reporter explained, "Davis traced the ramifications of job discrimination against the Negro through steel, aircraft, coal, the federal agencies [and] the Army and Navy to the door of the White House." A roar of applause followed Davis's answer that apparently "drowned out his last words" and undoubtedly put the First Lady in an uncomfortable position. This confrontation and the NNC threat to picket the OPM had caused quite a stir among the FBI agents, who had noted the Communists who attended recent meetings; these agents in turn reported back to the White House and no doubt advised Eleanor to withdraw.[78]

The First Lady missed quite a show. On Friday evening, April 25, 1941, more than "six thousand people of every race sat elbow to elbow" and, according to one reporter, "made the place rock with their applause and shouts of adoration." Emceed by John P. Davis, the event had an "air of informality" as members of all races mingled in stands and the concession area. Robeson sang several international numbers but did not sing "Chee Lai," the Chinese "March of the Volunteers Song," which he had previously learned to per-

The NNC picketing the Office of Production Management in Washington, D.C., as well as the Glenn A. Martin aircraft factories in nearby Maryland to integrate war production jobs, 1941. Photograph by Scurlock Studio, copy in Schomburg Center for Research in Black Culture, The New York Public Library, Astor, Lenox, and Tilden Foundations. Courtesy of the National Museum of American History, Behring Center, Archives Center, Smithsonian Institution, Washington, D.C.

form in perfect Mandarin, instead calling to the stage Liu Liang-mo, a leading vocalist among the Chinese soldiers, to sing it. Thereafter, the climax of the evening came when Robeson sang the famous "Ballad for Americans," backed by four local choirs, which totaled "a chorus of 150 voices." Since the ballad had debuted on radio in November 1939, the song had topped the American charts and had become something of a national anthem, embraced not only by groups like the NNC and CIO but also by the Republican Party and even, in one instance, by a Boy Scout troop. The song traces the history of the United States since the Revolution and ends with the question, "Say, will you please tell us who you are?" Robeson's sonorous voice responded with a list of different jobs, ethnicities, and religions of people who make up "America." And since "our country's young" and "the greatest songs are still unsung," these people would fulfill "America's" unfinished democratic promise.[79]

The NNC received a morale boost and much-needed check for almost $900 from the concert, and better yet, Robeson stayed in town to attend a mass meeting in Baltimore on Sunday for the jobs campaign.[80] This meeting featured Elks national leader J. Finley Wilson and Baltimore Elks head Ida Cummings and took place at their organizational lodge, which became the NNC's hub for activity over the next six months. Wilson and Cummings spoke for the NNC, detailing its plan to distribute 75,000 leaflets, picket government offices back in Washington, and send rotating delegations of applicants to the Martin plant. In the evening, the conference attendees, 1,500 strong, marched to the Baltimore Coliseum, where Robeson sang, Doxey Wilkerson and Jack McMichael of the NNC and American Youth Congress spoke, and Frank Bender, the head of the CIO in Maryland, pledged his support for their jobs drive. The next day, NNC members began to put the plan into action. They distributed fliers and picketed federal offices, following the lead of Davis, who told the press that the OPM "had the power to force holders of defense contracts to drop their discriminatory practices" and that "deeds, not talk, are needed to secure jobs."[81]

Neither Martin nor the government flinched at first. Even with the late June creation of the Fair Employment Practices Committee, thanks to Randolph and the MOWM, Martin remained defiant. In July, he testified to Congress that he would not jeopardize production by hiring blacks, because white workers "would walk out when Negroes walk in." Moreover, he would not "do anything to disturb a social problem until someone else has straightened it out." Furthermore, he claimed exemption from Executive Order 8802 because his government contracts had been received before President Roosevelt signed the order. Meanwhile, the FBI grew increasingly attentive to the NNC in D.C. and Baltimore. Agents noticed one picket line that included black men in army uniforms with signs about "Jim Crowism in national defense" and rashly concluded that only Communists could inspire such protests. The government should hold the line, the FBI warned, because the jobs campaign really only sought "infiltration of communist workers in the plant to sabotage production rather than secure jobs for negroes."[82]

Despite these warnings and excuses, Martin's hand was forced by the NNC's mounting pressure over the summer to hire African Americans. In June, Howard Jackson, Baltimore's mayor, signed a statement of endorsement of

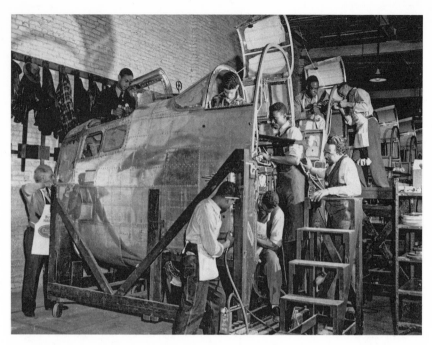

Above and opposite: Workers at the Glenn A. Martin aircraft factory in Canton, Maryland. The NNC's wartime jobs campaign in Washington led to the integration of the workforce in war production industries. Courtesy of Glenn L. Martin Maryland Aviation Museum, Baltimore, Maryland.

the NNC jobs campaign, citing the 17 percent black population statistic in his city and insisting that blacks should get equal access because the "cornerstone of democracy is the right to its citizenry to jobs." Threatened with a lawsuit by the Baltimore Urban League, the company opened select training classes to black candidates; the following month a vice president stated in a letter to John Davis that the Martin Company would make "an honest endeavor to give members of your race the opportunity"; and thousands of blacks got hired to work in the Canton plant in the months thereafter. Over the next two years, the United Auto Workers, with NNC help, organized the Martin plant and won representation of its workers, and the NNC in turn pushed the union to fight for black workers' demands for better health conditions, more skilled jobs, and employment at the Middle River plant rather than just at the subsidiary Canton plant. In all, the NNC Martin campaign created about 5,000 jobs for blacks, 66 percent of whom were women. One-seventh of them were skilled positions, representing 5 percent of the company's total workforce.[83]

Meanwhile, the NNC Washington Council in 1941 focused its energy back into its campaign for jobs in the capital as well as physical security. The Washington Council succeeded in getting the D.C. Employment Center to change its policy of accepting word-of-mouth referrals that in effect led to white-only hiring practices.[84] Moreover, NNC members became active in a strike of laundry workers that showed the overlap between the police brutality campaigns and labor struggles. As the tension between strikers and strikebreakers mounted outside of the Arcade-Sunshine plant, police intervened on the side of the company, beating male and female strikers and arresting them for intimidation and disorderly conduct. The NNC coalition, renamed the Citizens Committee against Police Brutality, carried on the fight against police brutality in this case and many others, forcing the department to indict many officers.[85]

In September 1941, the NNC even pressured the new District commissioner, Major Edward Kelly, to attend one of its mass meetings. This meeting, held at the Metropolitan Baptist Church, demonstrated the continued strength of the NNC coalition of forces. The FBI counted eleven hundred blacks and forty whites ("the majority being Jewish") in the audience and recounted that Howard University professor and NNC leader Doxey Wilkerson introduced the event by stating that over the summer District police had without cause killed four more blacks. Washington, Wilkerson said, was a "southern city," where police made certain that blacks "were segregated in living conditions and public affairs and [there was] also discrimination in employment." Hugh Miller, the white leader of the Washington Committee for Democratic Action, followed Wilkerson by explaining how the "problems of the negro were also the problems of the white" and urging attendees to fight "Hitler's theory" of "racial superiority," which was manifest in the District's abusive police tactics. John P. Davis, the next speaker, "received quite an applause by the audience present." Davis reminded the packed church audience that, due to the NNC's previous efforts in 1939, the police department had not killed a single black citizen. Despite this accomplishment, however, few structural reforms had resulted and the police department had returned to its old form. "Don't take no for an answer," he shouted. "Restore law and order. Bring back Democracy." Wilkerson then introduced Police Chief Kelly, "an honest cop," as the next speaker. Kelly outlined a new policy for the force. He claimed no more discrimination would occur, he supported the NNC demand for a police trial board, and he planned to hire at least fifty black officers. He finished his speech by exclaiming that he would not stand for police brutality in the department any longer.[86]

After an intermission during which the United Cafeteria Workers quartet sang "various negro spirituals," Wilkerson introduced J. Finley Wilson, Exalted Leader of the Negro Elks organization, representing 100,000 African Americans. The FBI agents described Wilson as "a violent type of speaker, shouting at the top of his voice [which] made quite a show." The elder Wilson warned of another round of riots like those of 1919 if the police did not protect the civil rights of black men and women. He stated jokingly that "we can lend a lease" to Stalin in Russia if he "will defend us." Only if the government protected the rights of all people in both army camps and civilian life in Washington, Wilson said, would the Elks "battle and defend America and make it safe for the black and white under the 'Stars and Stripes.'" Finally, Jack Zuckel of the Industrial Union Council confirmed that 15,000 local workers would back the campaign, and that the "CIO is carrying on the fight for you" at the Glenn Martin plant in Baltimore to allow all citizens to "defend America." The meeting ended with agreement from the audience to march in the streets of Washington in a parade against police brutality; one week later, people lined the sidewalks and others drove cars with placards at four locations in the District. The NNC and its allies in the Committee against Police Brutality, the FBI concluded, appeared stronger than ever in the fall of 1941.[87]

This flurry of activity, however, would come to represent the apex of the campaign against the "lynch spirit" until after the end of the Second World War. After the United States entered the war in December 1941 with the Soviet Union as an ally, liberals, Communists, CIO members, and others in the NNC coalition shifted tactics by supporting the war effort as a first priority. Thus, by the summer of 1943, the FBI was relieved to report that the local NNC Council had been "entirely inactive for the past two months." Doxey Wilkerson had resigned his post at Howard and had joined the CP to work full-time in the Baltimore-D.C. area instead of for the NNC. Alphaeus Hunton, another dynamic NNC leader, left Washington for New York to become the head of a new international organization called the Committee on African Affairs. Meanwhile, other members of the NNC entered the armed forces to fight fascism abroad.[88]

Most important, John P. Davis, the NNC's architect and executive secretary since 1935, left the organization. While Davis said he resigned to focus on voting issues as an assistant to Congressman Vito Marcantonio, his decision was more emotionally and politically complicated than that. When interviewed in 1953 and 1954 by the FBI, Davis explained he left the CP because he had never accepted its discipline and increasingly got into personality conflicts with its leaders. Davis admitted he considered himself part of the CP from the mid-1930s until he left the party in late 1941, though he never had a membership card and did not become a representative of either the CP's Negro or National Commission. He met on several occasions with black Communist leader James Ford but received only suggestions. Davis claimed that he had free rein to run the NNC how he saw fit and that it never was a "Communist

Front." But after Hitler's invasion of the Soviet Union in June 1941 resulted in the second abrupt CP foreign policy shift in two years, Davis felt politically compromised by his CP ties and believed that continuing on might sabotage the NNC's need to reinvent itself. In short, he felt the ideological whiplash and did not want to compromise the organization he had worked so hard to create. He left the organization in younger hands, as many former NNC and SNYC youth leaders now rose into the NNC leadership. The NNC continued in Washington and nationally, but, signaling its shift of priorities and personnel, it relocated headquarters to New York City in 1943.[89]

During John P. Davis's 1920s student and literary days in Cambridge, he penned a poem that imagined the crucifixion of Christ from the perspective of a black victim of lynching in the United States. He called it, "To My Lord, Jesus Christ":

> They say you suffered and I doubt it not;
> But your body was not left to rot
> Hanging from the limb of a charred spruce tree
> In a land where the sons of God are free.
> A Roman soldier took your body down
> And Joseph freed your head of its crown.
> The Marys took your body from your foes,
> My body, rags and all, was left for crows.
> No Pilate washed his bloody hands of me
> Nor tried to make a blind mob think and see.
> I did not rise up from the sleeping dead
> With a halo around my curly head.
> I called my Father but I called in vain:
> My prayers too heavy laden with my pain.
> And yet I do not grudge you of your fame.
> For there is little left you but your name.
> You are the great failure of the skies,
> Who sowed in men's hearts truth and reaped but lies.[90]

To the young Davis, the victim of American racial violence "did not rise up from the sleeping dead with a halo around my curly head" nor inspire a "blind mob [to] think and see," but instead represented a ritual of unapologetic and debilitating white supremacy. Rather than looking to the sky "in vain," Davis came to see his job as the head of the NNC as a means to channel his anguish and that of other African Americans. This meant avenging the dead and the brutalized victims of southern lynching, police violence, slavelike work conditions, and the denial of work. Beyond simply exposing these acts of racial sadism and discrimination, the NNC sought to destroy them by taking to the streets in order to force a vote on the federal antilynching bill, pressure the Department of Justice to investigate brutality under the Thirteenth Amendment to the Constitution, access living-wage jobs for blacks who would otherwise remain unemployed and desperate, and transform the police force from a preserver of second-class citizenship into an integrated force that protected civil rights for all. These acts and their remedies cumulatively amounted to a battle to overturn the "lynch spirit" in America's capital during the late 1930s, with that battle quickly expanding from the local issue of police and jobs, to the national issue of neo-slavery and lynching, and increasingly to the international stage of fascism and Nazi brutality by the Second World War.

The NNC's Washington campaign against the "lynch spirit" made remarkable strides in exposing everyday violence against black people in the nation's capital. Its members did so by taking back the streets and by holding mass meetings, canvassing for petition signatures, picketing, and marching with thousands of African Americans and their white allies. The Washington NNC coalition made officers accountable for their actions, won a civilian review board, and, at its peak in 1938–39, stopped District police killings altogether. As Charles Houston of the NAACP concluded, "The persistent and forceful campaign which the Washington Council and allied organizations have waged against police brutality in Washington has been one of the most significant battles for civil rights and personal freedom and security ever conducted in the District of Columbia."[91] Furthermore, the specific police campaign widened to include successful strikes of hotel workers, access for blacks to wartime factory jobs, and investigations into peonage by the Department of Justice.

The block of southern senators in Washington, however, dismissed virtually all legislation to protect the civil rights of blacks. The NAACP push for an antilynching bill (with or without the NNC) failed due to the efforts of Senate Democrats, who had both the power to silence President Roosevelt from taking a public stand and the seniority to quash and filibuster legislation introduced by progressive New Deal representatives. As one NNC election report detailed, thirteen legislators from the South won with only 1 to 3 percent of the total population voting in 1942. Putting this into perspective, the report concluded that more votes were cast in "little" Rhode Island than in the five southern states that encompass "that vast sweep of country from the Atlantic Coast to the Mississippi River and Gulf of Mexico."[92]

This southern group of legislators also wielded the balance of power over the District's fate. Local activism won victories in the policing of space and the protection of civil rights as well as access to jobs, but Washington as a whole continued as a symbolically powerful, racially desultory, southern city. Davis admitted to Alphaeus Hunton that the police brutality campaign had succeeded in achieving certain reforms, but that it "seem[ed] to be going around in circles" because permanent changes would require the NNC to target specific legislators and jeopardize their reelection in districts back home, if the congressional oversight of Washington was going to be changed.[93] This paralleled the poll tax and antilynching fight and represented one reason Davis stepped away from the NNC in 1942. He conducted a nationwide study of voting patterns for Congressman Marcantonio of New York while also continuing to serve on the board of the Southern Conference on Human Welfare, an interracial progressive group that had begun in 1938 and that had more southern inroads than the NNC did by the Second World War. As the next chapters explain, the SNYC would attempt to register black voters in the South, while the NNC, with its headquarters in New York City, would concentrate mostly on northern civil rights campaigns. In short, a new strategy would have to go outside of D.C. to change its governance inside the District. As one prominent example, the NNC helped get Adam Clayton Powell elected to Congress in 1944 so that he could not only take responsibility for his own district but also serve as "Congressman-at-Large for half of the District Columbia," which was "rule[d] by men who came from areas that were against the Negroes' dreams and hopes."[94] Echoing Powell's fight, Thelma Dale reminded the NNC in D.C. that Theodore Bilbo from Mississippi, perhaps the most openly white-supremacist senator, had become in 1945 the "Chairman of the Senate Committee on the District of Columbia Affairs which makes him virtually the Mayor of Washington. . . . We cannot expect any change in the situation" unless the NNC and others removed him from power.[95]

The NNC wanted to "Blast Jim Crow out of Washington," but its attack tragically came apart at the seams right at the moment when its constituents reloaded their weapons. The NNC broadened the conception of civil rights by challenging all forms of extralegal violence as a systemic flaw in American democracy. Its members deemed freedom from fear of "Nazi tactics" and "brutal persecution" by law officers as the essence of democratic citizenship.[96] And this conception of citizenship, put into action by the Washington NNC, helps explain how the NNC's antiracist activism made physical and economic security the basis of American citizenship during and after the Second World War. The battle its activists waged represented an important first phase of a long and protracted struggle against the "lynch spirit" in America. But this campaign also speaks to the divisions that emerged in the black-led left's movement during the late 1930s New Deal. What follows, therefore, explores in detail the NNC's April 1940 Washington conference, at which A. Philip Randolph announced his refusal to continue on as NNC president, and what this meant for the dawning 1940s decade of civil rights protest.

Black and White, Red, and Over?

The Congress Splits in Washington

More than 1,200 delegates came to Washington, D.C., in April 1940 "to close ranks, lock hands, and courageously deal with the crisis which today threatens the security of every Negro in America." The National Negro Conference (NNC) purposefully held the conference in the nation's capital when Congress was in session in order to declare to the federal government that civil rights activists would not be intimidated by the Dies Committee or filibustering southern senators. In a letter to the NNC greeting its upcoming conference, President Roosevelt wrote: "It is now more than ever important that the place of a minority group in a democracy not be obscured by ignorance and prejudice" and that all people should "consider . . . these problems of the minority in order that the processes of democracy may work to bring about their solution." Although Roosevelt's statement seemed intentionally vague, at the very least it evinced his knowledge of the significance of the NNC conference. The *Chicago Defender* surmised that over the past four years some of the NNC's "cardinal objectives" had "become national issues of sufficient urgency to influence far-reaching government measures." The president greeted the NNC not because of its polite request to consider racial discrimination but because the organization had forced civil rights onto the New Deal agenda.[1]

Delegates filed into the grand new Department of Labor Auditorium on Friday afternoon to witness their president, A. Philip Randolph, share the speakers' platform with the head of the CIO, John L. Lewis. Presented by the Reverends W. H. Jernagin and Arthur D. Gray of the Washington Council,

NNC leaders meet with labor leader John L. Lewis (far right) just before the start of the Third National Negro Congress, April 26–28, 1940, Washington, D.C. A. Philip Randolph and John P. Davis are to Lewis's immediate right. Photograph by David E. Sherman, Time & Life Pictures Collection. Courtesy of Getty Images.

Randolph and Lewis needed little introduction—they were the most important black and white labor leaders in America. Randolph had helped organize the Brotherhood of Sleeping Car Porters (BSCP) and won its recognition by the American Federation of Labor (AFL) and the Pullman Company, while Lewis, the head of the United Mine Workers, helped create the CIO, which had organized millions of workers over the past four years.[2]

John L. Lewis began his speech by quoting Frederick Douglass. "There may be a wages of slavery only a little less galling and crushing in its effect than chattel slavery," Lewis read, and "it is a great mistake for any class of laborers to isolate itself and thus weaken the bond of brotherhood between those on whom the burden and hardships of labor fall." Giving high priority to domestic labor solidarity, Lewis saw no reason why the movement for "the highest degree of security" for all Americans needed to be sidetracked by "foreign entanglements and political circuses." Lewis staked out an isolationist foreign policy position for the NNC and the CIO; instead of fighting abroad or between each other, they would fight together to expand the New Deal to encompass antilynching legislation, abolition of the poll tax, and guaranteed suffrage for all Americans. "If it is our mission to save Western civilization," he continued, "then let us begin by saving it right here in our own country." After his speech, two black miners presented Lewis with a plaque for his dedication to interracial labor unions, and he in turn invited the NNC to affiliate officially with Labor's Non-Partisan League. By all accounts, Lewis's speech "drew thunderous applause."[3]

Perhaps A. Philip Randolph felt like a second act to Lewis on Friday night, but by the closing of the NNC convention on Sunday he had gained everyone's attention. In his Friday speech, Randolph lambasted the Dies Committee and endorsed trade unions as the path to freedom for African Americans. The NNC president claimed that the "NNC is not communistic nor a communist front," and he went on to denounce the Communist Party (CP) as "not working for the interest in the American people as a whole or the Negro people

Registration desk in the lobby of the U.S. Department of Labor Auditorium, where the Third National Negro Congress convened. Photograph by David E. Sherman, Time & Life Pictures Collection. Courtesy of Getty Images.

A. Philip Randolph (left) and John P. Davis (right) hold the plaque to be awarded to John L. Lewis for his distinguished service to black labor as head of the United Mine Workers and the CIO at the Third National Negro Congress. Photograph by David E. Sherman, Time & Life Pictures Collection. Courtesy of Getty Images.

John L. Lewis speaks on the opening night of the Third National Negro Congress. Photograph by David E. Sherman, Time & Life Pictures Collection. Courtesy of Getty Images.

in particular." Only a smattering of applause followed, and according to one delegate, the disapproval of his "Red-baiting made [many delegates] forget some of the finer points of Randolph's speech." Ralph Ellison, sitting in the audience and identifying with the leftists in the NNC, heard Randolph's "deep, resonant voice" but found his arguments "strange in the mouth of one who was supposed to be their leader." Randolph suggested that the presence of white delegates and "Red" foreign policy resolutions made the black-led NNC no longer viable. With a "feeling of betrayal," Ellison concluded, "I did not realize it, but I had witnessed a leader in the act of killing his leadership."[4]

On the following day, Davis urged that the NNC accept the invitation to join the Labor's Non-Partisan League and deepen its collaboration with the CIO. "What distinguished this Congress," he said, "is that today the Negro people are not fighting alone." Davis recounted the past years of NNC activity, which included intervention into the "great steel, auto and packing house industries [where] we have seen Negroes flock by the thousands into the ranks of organized labor." The "greater job security" afforded by the successful interracial

A. Philip Randolph speaks after John L. Lewis on the opening night of the Third National Negro Congress. By the end of the conference, Randolph had announced his refusal to continue as the NNC's president. Photograph by David E. Sherman, Time & Life Pictures Collection. Courtesy of Getty Images.

labor movement led to "increased earning power" and possibility of "buying homes," which "has strengthened the position of the Negro professional and businessman." This meant that the NNC and the CIO had brought about a significant blue-collar black middle class, and now Davis urged the Congress to continue the fight that had proven so successful, as well as join the Labor's Non-Partisan League because the NNC needed to harness the power of "four million votes in the North" to force the major political parties to "guarantee the ballot to the voteless people in the South."[5]

Davis's speech echoed both John L. Lewis's speech and the CP line. He used phrases like "the Yanks are not coming" and "we shall not die" to argue that the "enemy of American democracy is at home," so "let us fight the enemy here." But he also explicitly linked this antiwar stance to the Communists. "I have visited the Soviet Union," he said, referring to his 1937 trip abroad, "and I have witnessed their accomplishments" and "know of their ideals" of "genuine equal rights and freedom." Davis outlined a direction for the NNC that to some audience members confirmed their suspicion that he had become much closer to the CP. While this was certainly the case, Davis saw the most productive path for the NNC as deepening its collaboration with the CIO in an interracial movement to overturn Jim Crow at home and by not getting involved in the "imperialist war" abroad, which would divert attention from expanding the New Deal to cover the civil and human rights of all Americans.[6]

Upon hearing the applause, which "lasted for five minutes" after Davis's speech, one delegate claimed that this speech "seemed to signal what was to happen later—the decision of A. Philip Randolph not to run for President of the N.N.C." Although this delegate and some others began "whispering" about divisiveness on Saturday, most of the Sunday audience was shocked when Randolph parted ways with the NNC. Due to "donations from CIO unions and the Communist Party" to the NNC and the organization's "sympathy for the Soviet Union," Randolph said he would not seek reelection, declaring that "when an organization is tied up it loses . . . its mass character." Silence, mixed with "ohs and ahs and a few scattering bits of applause," followed Randolph's declaration. To replace him, the NNC nominated Max Yergan, a former YMCA administrator in South Africa, professor at City College in New York, and NNC executive board member, to become its next president.[7]

At the conference and thereafter, Randolph explained that the NNC convention had too many white delegates, took donations from the CIO and the CP, and was too sympathetic to the Soviet Union. All of the above allegations had truth in them: 370 of the 1,264 delegates to the Washington conference were white; the NNC had requested funding from the CIO in 1936 and 1937 and again in 1940, which amounted to a few thousand dollars; the CP had provided some funding and short-term loans to the NNC since 1936; and many of the resolutions passed in 1940 followed the new line of the CP, which advocated staying out of the "imperialist" war.[8]

Of these criticisms, the last point became the essential one for Randolph. When in August 1939 Stalin and Hitler signed a nonaggression pact, the international CP line went from a staunch antifascist take on the Nazi regime to one that urged its followers to stay out of the war. A Socialist since the 1910s, Randolph had long-standing ideological problems with Communists for embracing the "totalitarian state" of Stalin but had largely put his reservations aside in the mid-1930s for the sake of working in a larger Popular Front coalition. The nonaggression pact and Russian "imperialist" invasion of Finland in November 1939, however, became too appalling for Randolph to stomach. When the NNC adopted an isolationist approach at the Washington convention, Randolph concluded that Communist ideology and not the ideas of African Americans now controlled the fate of the organization. This ideological path, according to the NNC's former leader, would not lead to a genuine mass movement but was instead "suicidal folly." In previous years, Randolph had condemned the red-baiting of the NNC, calling blacks "yellow" for allowing the "red label" to get in the way of unity. By May 1940, he had changed his mind. "It seems to be beyond the realm of debate," he concluded, "that the Negro people cannot afford the handicap of being black, the handicap of being red."[9]

Why, then, did the vast majority of 1940 delegates stay in the NNC? When looking at Randolph's decision from the perspective of the NNC members who remained, other reasons for this split also become apparent. Randolph corresponded with John P. Davis on all major NNC decisions but was not involved in the day-to-day organizing work of the organization because of his commitments as head of the BSCP.[10] The NNC welcomed Randolph as its president because he gave it respectability. His reputation of fighting for the rights of black laborers in the BSCP predated the NNC and earned the grudging respect of less militant leaders like Walter White of the NAACP, who had done his best to work with Randolph on issues like the antilynching campaign but had kept the NNC at arm's length. With this modicum of legitimacy provided by Randolph and the BSCP, the NNC avoided much of the criticism from elite black leaders when its members crossed class lines inside urban black communities in order to raise funds and initiate new forms of direct-action protest.

However, by 1940, many NNC activists had diverged from their president's understanding of how best to effect social change. Those in the trenches in the battle against "Jim Crowism" in Washington, Chicago, and elsewhere knew that many Communists—black and white, inside and outside the NNC—expressed sincere dedication to antiracist activism and made effective organizers. They tried to build alliances with any and all groups that would aid their cause and saw this process as a democratic exchange of ideas to achieve practical activist goals. From 1936 to 1940, the two groups that became their staunchest allies were the CP and the CIO. As Ralph Ellison reported about the Washington conference, the mood "among the delegates was one of militant indignation." Citing the speeches of Owen Whitfield, sharecropper and "Negro folk preacher" who had led other Missouri farmers to the roadsides in protest the preceding year, and Hank Johnson, the "urban hero" of steel and packinghouse workers who showed how "indignation had found a direction," Ellison concluded about Randolph's resignation that "we cannot stop for controversy!"[11]

It made sense that NNC delegates pushed for an isolationist position since John L. Lewis on the one hand and the CP on the other endorsed an idea that was not too dissimilar from the slogan "We Ain't Going to Study War No More" of Howard University's Liberal Club, which linked war with the spread of fascism.[12] Moreover, many Africans Americans also linked war to imperialism, especially after the Italian attack on Ethiopia. In 1935–36, the NNC demanded that the United States and the League of Nations intervene and impose strong sanctions to repel the invasion. Western democracies balked, and Ethiopia fell under the control of Benito Mussolini's fascist military dictatorship. The anemic response by the League of Nations confirmed to many African American activists that the Western powers prioritized imperialism over democratic self-determination.[13] Thus, at the 1940 convention, the majority of NNC delegates in Washington did not feel duped, controlled, or bribed by the CIO and the CP in 1940; instead, they saw these groups as important allies in the fight against fascism in America and held similar objections to American intervention in another world war.

Randolph largely concurred with the "indignation" Ellison felt at the NNC convention but worried over its "direction." In a rebuttal to a *Chicago Defender* reporter who blasted his decision to leave the NNC over Communism, he revealed his core political faith: "There is one chief, main and invaluable quality for which the Negro people are distinguished, honored, trusted and respected, and that is loyalty to the United States of America. If we should ever be suspected of abandoning this priceless jewel, our loyalty to our father-land, God help us!"[14] The NNC, due to CP and CIO involvement, had become increasingly adversarial toward the Roosevelt administration. Moreover, the sudden shift in politics after the Hitler-Stalin pact of 1939 convinced Randolph that these allies could not be trusted. Randolph strategically chose to leave the NNC to instead pressure the government and the AFL from the inside; he still advocated rebellion against Jim Crow but within the parameters of liberal anti-Communism. Despite the entrenched racism within the AFL that BSCP leaders knew all too well, Randolph sought to apply leverage based on loyalty to the U.S. government to remove racial barriers within American institutions.[15]

The NNC had in its first four years defined police brutality, lynching, disfranchisement, and government-backed employment discrimination not as aberrations of an otherwise healthy American society but as part of a systemic racism that had infected American culture and politics. What changed in 1940 was its idea of the best pathway to attack this racism and enact a second emancipation for African Americans. The NNC after the convention sustained ties to the CP and the CIO and became an increasingly vocal critic of the Roosevelt administration's rush to war, which diverted energy away from civil rights at home. By contrast, the BSCP's 1940 convention featured a patriotic parade, a resolution condemning Communists, and keynote speeches by New York mayor Fiorello La Guardia and Eleanor Roosevelt. Even though the BSCP was politically nonpartisan, journalists noted that the organization more than ever before supported Roosevelt's Democratic administration and defense program.[16]

Most black press accounts of the NNC split in Washington reported on all of the salacious details but in the end drew sober conclusions that both parties had roles to play in the black-led civil rights movement. Lester Granger of the Urban League explained in an article that the "very nature of the organization" made the NNC split "predictable." The attempt to represent hundreds of organizations had an "intoxicating appeal" but never held the potential to sustain itself, since the NNC also advocated dramatic social and political changes in black communities and American society. "It was specifically promised that the Congress would not wander all over the map, duplicate efforts by existing organizations, would not desert its coordinating role," he wrote, "but this promise, of course, would have been difficult to keep, with the best of intentions." The "empty treasury" of the NNC, the animus between the CIO and the AFL, the charge of duplication by the NAACP, and political party loyalties (Socialist and Communist, but also Democrat and Republican) all made holding the NNC together in this way practically impossible. Yet, Granger explained, the "courageous" speech of Randolph had done the NNC a favor because now it could sharpen its weapons against Jim Crow. Black leaders should not "openly repudiate the Congress [the NNC]," Granger concluded, because it "has a job to do in the field of political and labor action." Other pundits concurred with this last statement. The popular "National Grapevine" column in the national edition of the *Chicago Defender* echoed the NNC claim that its work might become more effective. "Keen observers noted that the 'chaff' and 'packing excelsior' having fallen away," the column stated, "the remaining membership of the congress is a 'hard core' of real fighters for down-to-earth race champions." Although black press editorials differed in tone, all seemed to agree with an editorial that simply concluded that the NNC "has a great place in our life" and that its vision "cannot be ignored."[17]

Yet, in the year that followed, it was Randolph who devised a plan that got the attention of the nation. As BSCP leaders witnessed the mobilization of the economy for wartime production, they saw it as an especially opportune moment for blacks to pressure the federal government for antidiscrimination in employment. This idea, based on black indignation and mixed with the leverage of patriotism, became the foundation for the March on Washington Movement (MOWM). Its leaders threatened a national march on July 1, 1941, of 100,000 African Americans to the Capitol unless President Roosevelt established a mechanism to provide access to war industries employment on a nondiscriminatory basis.

By June 1941, the MOWM, much to the envy of the NNC, had reached the Oval Office. The president met with Randolph and Walter White of the NAACP on June 18 to play a game of political poker. The president asked White how many people would march, and he replied that no fewer than 100,000 people would descend upon Washington. In response, "the President looked me full in the eye for a long time," White recalled, "in an obvious effort to find out if I were bluffing or exaggerating." With his eyes focused intently upon White, Roosevelt undoubtedly recalled the mass protests of the NNC in the nation's capital. In fact, in discussing the proposed march during a previous meeting, Eleanor Roosevelt specifically referenced the police problems in the District. "You know where I stand, but the attitude of the Washington police, most of them southerners, and the general feeling of Washington itself," Eleanor Roosevelt said, "are such that I fear there may be trouble if the march occurs."[18]

After the meeting, FBI reports hastily prepared at Roosevelt's request concluded that the MOWM had the troops to descend on Washington, both because of its own organizers and due to the threat that Communist-influenced groups would join them. Quoting black Communist leader James Ford, one FBI memorandum explained that the CP embraced the "trends of militancy" in the MOWM and "all efforts of the Negro people to fight against jim-crowism" and would "use the occasion" to make the demonstration one against "imperialist war." During this 1941 period, when public opinion polls showed the nation decidedly opposed to entering the war, President Roosevelt and other members of the Democratic Party, including many southern segregationists, increasingly sought to garner support for the war effort to assist the urgent British and French efforts to stop Nazi expansion. Thus, a demonstration in Washington about racial discrimination in employment was threatening enough, but one that also protested the upcoming war as an imperialist battle between the British and German empires made its potential all the more politically damaging. Although Randolph had severed connections with Communists when splitting from the NNC in April 1940, the FBI nonetheless defined Randolph as the "former head of the National Negro Congress," and a confidential informant claimed that a number of leftist groups—all of them allies of the NNC—had plans to convene "twenty-five thousand delegates" to picket the White House to publicize the potential entry of the United States into the war against fascism at a time when racial discrimination continued on American soil.[19]

Meanwhile, during the three months leading up to the proposed July march, the NNC and the Southern Negro Youth Congress (SNYC) pursued a strategy that criticized Randolph but did not seek to thwart the MOWM. "A great many people have come to me recently," John P. Davis wrote in May, "to ask the question 'How can we head off, how can we counteract, how can we nullify and destroy Randolph's march?'" But Davis saw "danger" in these remarks. Like many on the Communist left, he believed that "Randolph has adopted a bankrupt position" because he allied the MOWM with "such fascists as Senator Carter Glass in calling for all out aid to the British Empire" and threatening to "barter away our lives for empty promises of work" and "support for the Roosevelt war plans." Davis also criticized the MOWM for its all-black membership rule because it cut off assistance from progressive white labor unionists, further splitting civil rights forces. But Davis also explained to the SNYC's Ed Strong that "the mood of the Negro people is one of militancy," and any attempt to discredit the march would thwart the objectives of people "sincerely seeking jobs for the Negro people." Therefore, the NNC encouraged its members to participate as individuals but would not try to join the MOWM as an organization. While Davis discouraged direct NNC affiliation, he saw no reason that the SNYC "should not participate" and encouraged Ed Strong to contact Randolph and endorse the SNYC members' continued participation in significant and growing local MOWM chapters in Richmond, Atlanta, and elsewhere in the South.[20]

During the MOWM campaign in 1941, the NNC determined to show a "constructive effort" of its own rather than "engage in a civil war."[21] The NNC pursued this policy, which both followed the wishes of black CP leaders like James Ford and revised them by not meddling directly with the MOWM. The sustained jobs campaign against Glenn Martin in Washington and Baltimore showcased this approach. During the summer of 1941, the NNC engaged in a widespread jobs campaign by doing what it did best: picketing, petitioning, and pressuring the government and employers from its working-class base.

Would the MOWM have been able to bring 100,000 African Americans to Washington? A wide variety of black leaders, including John P. Davis and Ed Strong, believed the MOWM had the forces to pull it off. Even conservative critics like Claude Barnett of the Associated Negro Press believed that although "Mr. Randolph has lost caste with radical elements," Roosevelt's attempt to thwart the march in June made it more popular among blacks. Others, however, were skeptical of its numeric potential because of the previous split with the NNC and the explicit bar on white participation, but unlike Barnett, many did not think the NNC was "definitely out to sabotage the march."[22] Whether the march would have resulted in a few thousand demonstrators or ten times that amount cannot be determined. What mattered during the negotiations was that J. Edgar Hoover deemed the threat real, and Roosevelt calculated its potential occurrence as politically disastrous. The FBI concluded that groups like the NNC and other leftist allies had proven they could organize mass protests. As Charles Collins of the AFL's hotel workers explained, the "idea grew out of the nation-wide movement to end discrimination, especially in defense industries, and this movement has been mainly led by the National Negro Congress." The MOWM leadership emerged from those who left the NNC, but the preceding years of concerted mass action played a role in the political calculus and made the threatened march all the more potentially militant.[23]

Thus, the president did not dare to call the proposed march a bluff. In exchange for canceling the march, Roosevelt signed Executive Order 8802 on June 25, 1941, to "reaffirm" antidiscrimination policies in all defense programs and to establish the Fair Employment Practices Committee to monitor the legislation's enforcement. Having invoked only the possibility of wartime dissent, Randolph took the significant concessions offered by Roosevelt and called off the march.[24] After the creation of the Fair Employment Practices Committee, the NNC used it as a tool for its own campaigns. In addition to the victorious Glenn Martin campaign, the NNC launched wartime jobs campaigns, often on the heels of Fair Employment Practices Committee hearings—at West Coast aircraft plants, at Detroit and Chicago auto factories, and at plants owned by Bethlehem Steel in the Midwest and Baltimore.[25] Therefore, while the NNC/MOWM rupture seemed tragic to many black activists, the two groups in 1941 waged complementary fights to gain access to war industries jobs.

Much more debilitating to the NNC's coalitions in Washington and other cities were the international circumstances that once again changed the direction of the organization by 1942. Hitler's invasion of Russia during the summer of 1941 and the entry of the United States into the war after Pearl Harbor in December produced a sea change in American politics that led to the CIO's no-strike pledge, the CP's cooperation with U.S. war aims above other concerns, and the transformation of the NNC and the SNYC into "win-the-war" agencies. The shift to prioritizing the war effort gave many NNC members ideological whiplash, and their activism now became less conspicuous. As a result of the organizational turn to a win-the-war strategy, Davis became one of the movement's casualties because he had thrown his hat in with John L. Lewis in 1940 and had argued against the "imperialist war." Davis believed that "for the first time a leader of labor—not a philanthropist or politician— has captured the imagination of the great Negro minority in this country." But the NNC alliance with Labor's Non-Partisan League and Lewis failed to produce a powerful labor–civil rights coalition. With the benefit of hindsight, Davis's decision to ally with Lewis harmed the NNC since Lewis went on to endorse the Republican presidential candidate in 1940 (whom the NNC did not support), stepped down from the CIO leadership, and became a symbol more of labor disunity than of unity.[26] Davis's faith in Lewis came from the

CIO backing of NNC campaigns and led him to the overly optimistic conclusion that "no person in America can be more certain of future support of the Negro people than Mr. Lewis."[27] Thus, when in late 1941 virtually every labor and civil rights leader but Lewis got behind the war effort against Germany and Japan and other NNC members seemingly transformed their rhetoric overnight to support the war, Davis resigned as the executive secretary in an attempt to save some of the organization's credibility from charges of hypocrisy.

Randolph's forces, however, also did not succeed in sustaining a wartime civil rights movement. At the AFL's national convention in 1942 and at several others thereafter, Randolph's passionate plea for an antidiscrimination resolution "was strongly condemned by some of the AFL leaders for even raising the issue." Several black leaders wondered why Randolph continued to keep the BSCP in the AFL when the federation so openly derided him and the role of African Americans in the labor movement. "Why is it that ten thousand, able-bodied intelligent Pullman employees," Adam Clayton Powell wrote, "will continue to stand the downright insulting and stultifying treatment meted out to them when they have another choice?" Despite some dissension among Pullman porters who favored joining the CIO, the BSCP remained in the AFL in order to "fight harder from the inside," as the *Amsterdam News* (New York) approvingly put it, despite the "martyrdom that loomed for [Randolph] in his apparent inability to make a dent in the rock-ribbed anti-Negro policies of [the AFL]."[28] After calling off the Washington march in 1941, the MOWM staged mass meetings in New York, St. Louis, and Chicago during the summer of 1942 and held a national convention of sixty-six delegates in Detroit in September. But the MOWM also drew increasing criticism from the black press for lacking organization and not having a definite program. In 1942, Roosevelt, now with public opinion fully behind the war effort, refused to grant the MOWM an audience, and its leaders cancelled its proposed Washington mass meeting. Meanwhile, Randolph became increasingly defensive in trying to explain why the organization demanded integration and disavowed black nationalism while restricting its own membership to only African Americans. In addition, others within the MOWM became disaffected because its leaders did not seem willing to bring an actual Washington march to fruition.[29]

In 1940 and 1941, both the MOWM and the NNC aggressively fought for and won major employment gains for blacks, but both groups also became somewhat ineffectual after the United States had entered the war. Neither group, however, was ready for an epitaph. Randolph, backed by unions and liberal allies, continued as a nationally known and respected leader of civil rights for the next two decades.[30] And the NNC also continued to fight, though first it had to regroup. At the end of 1942 the NNC moved its headquarters from Washington to New York, and during the rest of the war it would take the leadership of a dedicated group of black women to rescue it from sectarianism and loss of morale.

CHAPTER FOUR

Finding the North Star in New York
Home Front Battles during the Second World War

In the fall of 1942, Captain Hugh Mulzac launched the newly built *Booker T. Washington* Liberty Ship into the Pacific Ocean. As the ship made its way from California to Panama, the captain surveyed his crew of "forty-two fine sailors" of "eighteen different nationalities . . . from thirteen different states" and asked himself, "What sweeter triumph could a man wish for himself, his race, and his country?" The departure of the 10,000-ton war supply ship marked the climax of a twenty-year struggle for Mulzac. Though he had obtained a captain's license in the early 1920s, with the exception of a "two-year trick as skipper" on Marcus Garvey's Black-Star Line, Mulzac had been shut out of skilled employment, forced to work jobs on the deck and the dock rather than command a vessel. After completing his first mission, he docked the *Booker T* in the Harbor at Thirty-ninth Street in Brooklyn for a two-week respite before making his maiden voyage across the Atlantic. "As we tied up," Mulzac wrote, his crew encountered "hundreds of enthusiastic well-wishers . . . shouting and waving little American flags."

Mulzac's shore leave and subsequent Atlantic journey were anything but restful. In New York, he spent his time in meetings, celebrations, and other rallies, including the "biggest affair of our stay," a banquet sponsored by the Greater New York Industrial Council. Held at the Hotel Commodore, this event on January 2 attracted 1,200 guests, including prominent black trade unionist Ferdinand Smith of the National Maritime Union (NMU), white unionist Michael Quill of the Transport Workers Union, Harlem politician and minister Adam Clayton Powell Jr., and black artists Paul Robeson and

Langston Hughes. With "only a few hours rest" during his stay in the city, Mulzac led the *Booker T* out to sea, established its position in the convoy of ships, and went straight to sleep. He awoke the next morning to find that his steward and watchman had lost the convoy the previous night. Stranded in an ocean filled with German submarines, Mulzac chose to continue, weathering a powerful storm along the way, until he reached the harbor at Belfast, Ireland. As crew members unloaded a cargo of seventy-five airplanes, they learned that their ship had arrived ahead of the convoy, which had lost several ships en route. This perilous yet successful journey represented the first of many maritime adventures for Mulzac and proved to him "that colored and white can achieve together what they cannot even aspire to singly."[1]

The left-wing coalition that toasted Mulzac at the Hotel Commodore—unionists, politicians, and cultural figures—had largely become the nexus of the National Negro Congress (NNC) network after it relocated its national office to New York in mid-1942. During the previous year, Mulzac had approached two dozen organizations to "press my case in Washington" for fair employment. Yet the NAACP told Mulzac that it needed to concentrate on "civil liberties in the South"; the Reverend Adam Clayton Powell said "he would see what he could do" but nothing resulted; and Ferdinand Smith of the NMU "was not," according to Mulzac, "optimistic about my chances and did not play a decisive role in the final victory." Instead, Mulzac found allies in the Brooklyn Council of the NNC, which petitioned government officials, issued press releases, and held a citywide mass meeting to demand his employment as the first black captain of a wartime vessel. Once Mulzac was appointed, these other organizations feted him, but among the celebrities in attendance that night at the Commodore, NNC activists Steve Kingston, Dorothy Funn, and Thelma Dale applauded Mulzac with special enthusiasm because they had made his journey possible.[2]

Mulzac's remarkable journey as captain of the *Booker T* paralleled the turbulent yet productive path of the NNC on the home front during the Second World War. After the tide of political alliances shifted dramatically during 1940 and 1941, the NNC needed to make a fresh start to regain its legitimacy and efficacy as a civil rights organization. With only about thirty councils operating in any capacity during this NNC nadir, a younger group of black women took over much of the NNC's operation in New York City.[3] Like Mulzac, they sought a "star to steer by" and often felt adrift in unknown seas. War brought dramatic new circumstances, and the NNC worked to make factory floors the equivalent of the deck of Mulzac's ship: a veritable United Nations of racial and ethnic groups working together for victory. To do so, however, they had to find new leverage to fight for African American job security and civil rights. With their allies and members in the Communist Party (CP) and CIO defending the no-strike pledge, and many others enlisted in the armed forces, their previous mass action tactics required modification. They put energy into three primary areas: education, alliances inside trade unions, and political campaigns. While these directions had mixed results, NNC leaders did manage to once again steer the organization by the end of the war to the forefront of the fight for African American equality.

By looking at the NNC's journey during the war, this chapter will examine the claim by historians that the Second World War represented a watershed for African American activism. Between Richard Dalfiume's late-1960s, oft-cited pioneering essay, "The 'Forgotten Years' of the Negro Revolution," and Howard Sitkoff's more recent questioning of the assumed wartime civil rights boom, a consensus viewpoint had accepted that the war spawned the modern-day civil rights movement. This consensus also relates to a secondary debate over whether Communists quit fighting for civil rights to support the Soviet Union's war effort abroad above all other concerns. As one historian put it, while the CP's antiracist agenda did not stop during the war, it was forced into "narrow channels."[4] This chapter will analyze the influence of CP ideology on its African American leaders during the war to determine how they steered a course using the "Red Star" of Marxism, the North Star of African American culture, and even the stars that "fell on Alabama" in the South. Moreover, looking at the NNC's campaigns during the Second World War will show how the war quelled all forms of permissible dissent by activists while the government's rhetoric promoted equality. As the historian Leon Litwack concluded, the "persistence, even the heightening of racial tensions and violence" during the war, "suggests" that the wartime rhetoric of equality "failed to alter white attitudes and practices."[5] Judging by the number of 1930s-style demonstrations, the war quelled racial protest. Yet racial activism also ventured into new fields of work, which were far from "narrow." As NNC leaders sought a new direction to revive the organization, they poured energy into education, labor, and politics, making the Second World War also about their liberation.

▨ ▨ ▨ During the wartime state of emergency, NNC leaders created cultural outlets in New York to express their ideas. First, they influenced the content of the *People's Voice*, a progressive newspaper in Harlem that began as the

"Soap Box" for the Reverend Adam Clayton Powell. Born in New Haven in 1908, the college-educated minister of the huge Abyssinian Baptist Church in Harlem had become a central political figure by 1942, when he won a seat on New York's City Council. Powell used the *People's Voice* as a vehicle for his political career and wrote most of its editorials. Yet while presenting a progressive alternative to Harlem's *Amsterdam News*, the pages of the *People's Voice* also contained the intellectual stirrings of NNC leaders, who had become Powell's allies. Max Yergan, the NNC's president, wrote guest columns and provided behind-the-scenes financial and editorial support; Ferdinand Smith, who became the NNC's national treasurer in 1941, wrote a weekly column on labor; and Doxey Wilkerson, a Washington NNC leader who resigned from Howard University to join the CP, became a *People's Voice* editor. With Smith's labor column and Yergan's articles on Africa and other issues, the newspaper offered an unprecedented arena for the NNC to publicize its meetings and hash out its plans to desegregate the armed forces, abolish the poll tax and lynching, and remove employment barriers. Half kidding, Powell once referred to the *People's Voice* as the "Lenox Avenue edition of the *Daily Worker*," New York's Communist paper, because its pages reflected a mixture of Communist and African American thought. Yet when the FBI went so far as to call the *People's Voice* "Communist controlled," it exaggerated, since the paper expressed multiple perspectives. Harlemites found the *People's Voice* attractive because its columns, editorials, and letters to the editor expressed a wide range of opinion.[6]

During the war, the NNC also published a journal of its own. Beginning in 1943, the *Congress Vue* (later renamed the *Congress View*) offered an NNC-specific vision of the war; unlike the *People's Voice*, the *Vue*'s direction came from a group of black women. With many NNC men enlisted in the military and others working for the NNC's wartime offshoot, the Negro Labor Victory Committee (NLVC), these women largely ran the NNC day-to-day. They came from diverse backgrounds, though all possessed a college education, teaching experience, and youth movement participation. Their leader, Thelma Dale, had studied social sciences at Howard and served as superintendent of the Campbell AME Church Sunday school. She became a Washington Youth Council leader and helped found the Southern Negro Youth Congress (SNYC) in 1937. Thereafter, Dale affiliated the Youth Council in D.C. with the SNYC's activist campaigns across the South. Also from Washington, Mayme Brown had earned a music degree and then a master's from Howard and had taught high school in 1940 and 1941. Feeling, however, that she "could make a greater contribution toward fuller integration of Negroes in all phases of American life" through the NNC, she resigned her teaching post to become more active in the NNC's Washington campaign for public utilities jobs. Jessie Scott Campbell, from New Jersey, had graduated from Montclair Teachers College and then got involved with the NNC through its Newark jobs campaign. In 1938 she moved to Brooklyn to become the YWCA Girls Work secretary and joined the NNC as director of organizations. "Petite, vivacious, dauntless," and older than many in her cohort, Dorothy Funn taught in the New York public schools from 1923 to 1941, worked on the Brooklyn NNC's jobs campaign in the early 1940s, and during the war alternated time between the NLVC and the NNC. Jeanne Pastor, while attending night school at the City College of New York, began a job at the Urban League's Jobs for Negroes Campaign in Westchester before becoming the NNC's office manager. And then there was the Jett family. Soon after the Jetts moved from Birmingham to New York in the 1930s, all three daughters became active in NNC work. Maude Jett, who had graduated from Miles College in Alabama, developed programs "on Negro History and Culture" at Harlem's Washington Business Institute. Her sister Ruth "first realized she could do something about the many problems confronting the Negro people" when she served as president of the student council at the Harlem Evening School, making contacts with students all over the city, though especially in Spanish Harlem. Meanwhile, their other sister, Jenny, worked for the NMU, one of the NNC's most important union allies. "We tell Ruth," one NNC member joked, "that letters from the Jett family alone could almost serve to get the permanent F.E.P.C. passed."[7]

As part of their mission to reenergize the NNC, these female leaders created the *Congress Vue* to support the campaign to "win the war and to win full citizenship," deliver news from "other parts of the world," and be a "link among progressive Negroes throughout the country." Although its circulation never reached more than a few thousand copies, the NNC distributed it to union locals and army bases so that dozens of people read each copy. Soldiers met to discuss the contents of the *View* on military bases, the Teachers Union bought thousands of copies of a special education issue, NMU agents distributed it at ports around the country, and copies even reached a Japanese relocation camp in Arizona. As one press release claimed, "There is a lot of dynamite packed in the eight printed pages" of the *View*. Although less prominent in New York than the *People's Voice*, the publication charted the

Thelma Dale speaks at an NNC event, 1943. As the acting executive secretary of the NNC during the war years, Dale led a remarkable group of women who reoriented the NNC's work in New York City. From box 2, National Negro Congress Photograph Collection. Courtesy of Photographs and Prints Division, Schomburg Center for Research in Black Culture, The New York Public Library, Astor, Lenox, and Tilden Foundations.

NNC's vision during the war. Moreover, both of these publications helped fuel the "Double V" campaign of the mainstream black press for victory against fascism at home as well as overseas.[8]

After finishing their day's work at the NNC office, many of these leaders made their way to 57 125th Street in Harlem to teach classes at night. Created in 1943 by a group of progressive educators and activists, the George Washington Carver School had no entrance requirements and minimal class fees and opened its doors to "all men, women, and children of Harlem and elsewhere, regardless of creed or color." The school received funding from part of a larger Robert Marshall Foundation grant to the NNC and from staging "benefits, concerts, [and] forums." Between 200 and 500 students enrolled each term, with one-quarter coming from trade unions. Members of its steering committee included NNC president Max Yergan, who had previously taught a pioneering course, "Negro History and Culture," from 1937 to 1941 at the City College of New York, and Gwendolyn Bennett, chosen as director of the school because of her previous experience as head of the Harlem Art Center.[9] Both of these educators had lost their positions in 1940 due to the repercussions of the Rapp-Courdert Committee of the New York State legislature, which had sought to "ferret out" Communists from publicly funded educational institutions.[10]

The Carver School's founders sought to create an autonomous educational institution whose curriculum and funding was not beholden to politicians and red-baiters. Three white board members resigned because they claimed it was "Communist Dominated," but Adam Clayton Powell believed their annoyance stemmed from paternalism rather than from Communist influence. "When we have projects in Harlem we want [whites] to come and work WITH us, not dominate us," he wrote of the 1943 controversy, "and the intellectual droolings of New York University . . . are not applicable for the day in and day out needs of the common man of Harlem."[11] While many Communists worked at the Carver School and influenced the school's direction, its courses were less doctrinaire than other CP-sponsored schools, like New York's Jefferson School.[12] Carver's Board of Directors had prominent black intellectuals like E. Franklin Frazier of Howard University and Dr. Alain Locke, the preeminent cultural critic who edited the 1926 *New Negro* during the Harlem Renaissance, as well as Dr. Lawrence Reddick, who had recently taken over the prestigious post of head curator of the Schomburg Library, the central archive of black intellectual life in Harlem.[13]

Called a "People's Institute" by its creators, the Carver School hired teachers "who have not only distinguished themselves in their fields of study, but have proven themselves to be interested in the problems of the Negro people by active participation in their struggles." This combination of intellectual and activist requirements drew many NNC members to the school as teachers. Max Yergan and Alphaeus Hunton, of the NNC and the Council on African Affairs, respectively, jointly taught a course on international politics, reasoning that "it is essential for Americans to understand the Colonial Peoples." Thelma Dale offered a course on domestic racial conditions, "Racial Equality for All," and Gwen Bennett taught African American history courses, believing that "in these classes will be found the only weapons to combat prejudice and discrimination . . . the true facts about the history of the Negro people." The Carver School also fashioned a strong arts department to accompany its political and historical courses. Mayme Brown offered a class on choral music, blues singer Josh White and stride pianist James P. Johnson guest lectured in a jazz class, and two of the most nationally distinguished young black artists, Charles White and Elizabeth Catlett White, became regular faculty members. Living in New York until he enlisted in the army, Charles White taught drawing courses at the Carver School. Elizabeth Catlett taught sculpture and pottery, as well as one of the school's most popular courses, "How to Make a Dress." When not teaching at the school, both served as the staff artists for the *Congress View*.[14] "Art is one of the strongest social weapons," Catlett declared, "but at the Carver School people get to develop politically as well as culturally."[15] The Carver School was distinctive, according to its staff and students, because of this combination of ideology and practice, politics and culture. Moreover, the school's faculty and students alike "reserve[d] the right to examine the national and international political scene and to act upon their findings in a forthright, courageous manner." The school hoped to prepare Harlem's working-class black community to "take their rightful place in society after the war is won."[16]

Taken together, these journalistic and educational activities supply a rich portrait of the NNC's cultural politics, which extended the "Double V" from fiery journalism to education backed by activism. In looking at this activism from an intellectual perspective, three themes in particular stand out: a revisionist interpretation of the Civil War in relation to the current war; the focus upon creating a national African American cultural front; and the promulgation of new theories on race as a social construction rather than a biological certainty. These themes revealed both wartime synchronicities and tensions between African American and Communist ideas, the two intellectual foundations NNC members drew upon most in thinking about their alliances, goals, strategies, and tactics.

The NNC looked to African American history to better understand the current war. In the first issue of the *Congress View*, the NNC published a poem by Carl G. Hill, a merchant seaman who had gone missing during the current hostilities. In his poem, "Of Frederick Douglass," Hill reflected upon the life of this seminal black intellectual and activist to better understand the coming of the Second World War. The poem concluded:

> We see him yet:
> Douglass the strong, the bold,
> Still teaching,
> Still leading us upward
> Out of our special hell,
> Still holding high the blazing taper—
> The beacon of all oppressed!
> Here lies the pathway, stretching
> Endlessly upgrade;
> Here lies the bold unshaken footprints
> That lead to freedom . . .
> Let us take heart again.[17]

In the 1940s, the NNC sought to tread the path of Frederick Douglass from decades before. Since its 1936 founding, its activists embraced historians and intellectuals whose Marxist reinterpretations of black history confirmed their economic agenda. W. E. B. Du Bois's 1935 *Black Reconstruction in America* rebuked the "Lost Cause" thesis by highlighting black achievements as vital to the Union victory and the expansion of democracy, while Herbert Aptheker detailed black resistance during slavery in numerous Communist publications.[18] Based on this mix of scholarship and activism, Charlotta Bass, the editor of the black-owned *California Eagle* newspaper and an NNC activist, concluded that these academic works "had completely exploded the previous 'standard history.'"[19]

Well-versed in this revisionist history, NNC members compared the cause of the Second World War to that of the Civil War. Dorothy Funn, for example, noted that by late 1862 the Union army needed black troops to win the war. "President Lincoln signed the Emancipation Proclamation as a wartime necessity," she stated, because "the united hands of black and white were needed to abolish the fascist forces operating against our country's interests."[20] Ferdinand Smith compared Lincoln's Emancipation Proclamation to Roosevelt's Executive Order 8802, arguing that both were wartime necessities to generate "maximum unity of the American people . . . to effectively defeat the enemy." NNC leaders thus applied black history to fit the Communist left's win-the-war strategy, which prioritized the war abroad and the opening of a second front in Western Europe to beat back the Nazi army over domestic struggles for economic and racial justice. These two ideologies fused together because African Americans, the NNC believed, would gain new employment opportunities resulting from U.S. needs to maximize productivity. A second front would spur an even greater demand for wartime unity as well as assist the "courageous Russian army."[21]

The war analogy also provided a cogent case for the NNC to call for unity across racial lines. Alliances based only on skin color would prove dangerous, Thelma Dale thought, and "Frederick Douglass, Sojourner Truth and the other great emancipators worked with white abolitionists to secure the freedom of the Negro people."[22] Thus, the NNC criticized A. Philip Randolph's all-black March on Washington Movement as having "little faith in white friends of the Negro people."[23] Rather than a war of the darker versus the lighter races, the NNC believed that the conflict against fascism paralleled the conflict to abolish slavery. "In the Civil War," Ferdinand Smith wrote, "Douglass said 'Slavery must expand or die.'" And today, he explained, "fascism is not different."[24] In short, the NNC believed that the Second World War aligned the "dominant interests of the nation" with "the freedom goals of the Negro people," and NNC members hoped that their support of the conflict against fascism would force U.S. democracy into action as an "urgent war measure."[25]

The NNC's interpretation of the Civil War came in conflict with the dominant narrative of states' rights and the "lost cause" that had accompanied the rise of Jim Crow in America. During the Second World War, these contrasting interpretations of history became most apparent in the debates surrounding the 1942 Hollywood film *Tennessee Johnson*. The biography of Lincoln's presidential successor Andrew Johnson, the film portrayed him as a "misunderstood man," in contrast to Thaddeus Stevens, the radical Republican legislator and abolitionist, who "is made out to be the disrupter of the nation's unity." The NNC organized a coalition of nineteen organizations to protest the film after viewing a special screening of it in New York. They petitioned the Office of War Information to ban its release, calling it "one of the most dangerous films in the history of the motion picture industry."[26] To the NNC, Johnson, who once wrote that "Negroes have shown less capacity for government than any other race of people," was comparable to Hitler.[27] The NNC did not succeed in getting the film banned, but its rebuke of *Tennessee Johnson* spurred a national debate among mainstream press outlets. The tenor of this debate exposed how the NNC's view of culture differed from their liberal win-the-war allies. The NNC fought such films because it did not want the current war to embolden contemporary Johnsons to again follow a war for freedom with the violent imposition of white supremacy. Mainstream journalists discussing the film's contents ranged from the *New York Times*, which declared, "It tells a fine story . . . [and] we don't see how it could harm anyone," to a review in the *Chicago Daily News* that concluded, "We can't call Tennessee Johnson a lesson in United States history but it will serve a purpose and arouse curiosity enough to make you read up on your history." The innocuous white reviews of the film contrasted sharply with accounts in the black press. "Education is not merely a department of civilization like art and religion," one *Chicago Defender* columnist wrote, "it is an indispensable condition for civilization."[28] The NNC agreed, calling the genre of film "the most powerful instrument in mass education." During the summer of 1943, the NNC formed an emergency committee of forty prominent New York cultural figures to discuss "Negro Culture in War Time." The committee's "first requirement was that artists and audiences alike get rid of their complacency and realize the significance of what is at stake in this matter of democratizing America's entertainment."[29]

The NNC aroused audiences by promoting its own vision of history through the arts. Its leaders spoke frequently on radio programs, organized Negro History Week celebrations, sponsored art exhibits, and held massive rallies in New York to promote plays like "New World A-Coming."[30] Staged at Madison Square Garden in front of an audience of 25,000, the play by Owen Dodson was the highlight of the 1944 NLVC's annual Negro Freedom Rally. The interracial cast featured some of the most famous African American artists of the 1940s, including dancer Pearl Primus, singer Josh White, and actor Canada Lee. The script included American historical figures like Tom Paine, abolitionist Sojourner Truth, and recent war martyr Dorie Miller as characters who had come back to life to present the way forward for African Americans to win their freedom.[31] In the final scene, contemporary black and white progressives bury "Jim Crow, White Supremacy, and Jew-Murderers" on stage and then ask their historical equivalents for advice:

Negro Soldier (to Tom Paine): Is it true? Tell me Tom Paine, are they really buried for good and all?

Tom Paine: The people bury them. It's up to them to keep them buried.

Negro Soldier: How?

Paine: Use the ballot like a gun to shoot the bad ones out and the good ones in.

Negro Solider: Sojourner, how we going to keep them buried?

Sojourner: We gotta keep the friends we're winning the war with. . . . And those unions — you keep them growing, you hear me!

Dorie Miller: Unless everybody is free, nobody is free.[32]

Followed by the "New World A-Coming" theme, the cast marched off to victory through their progressive interracial alliance.

The wartime drive to maximize productivity also provided opportunities for the NNC's message to reach a wide audience — ironically, through collaboration with the propaganda arm of the federal government. *The Negro Soldier*, a film sponsored by the War Department to improve black morale, exemplified this cooperation of the NNC and the government. Carlton Moss, the film's director, showed "how Negroes fought side by side with Union troops in the Civil War," according to Augusta Jackson's review in the *Congress View*. Due to its sympathetic depiction of black troops, conservatives within the War Department made sure the film was not widely distributed. However, NNC activists in cities like Detroit, New York, and Los Angeles hosted free screenings of the film for large audiences. These rallies boosted morale of African Americans, connecting victory in the current war with that in the Civil War in the hope of bringing about a new Reconstruction era. This time, however, black and white activists would fight to keep the white supremacists from eroding the democratic goals of the war.[33]

As part of its unity strategy, the NNC also sought to make black culture an integral part of mainstream American culture. As war employment spurred new migrations to the West and North and more than 1 million African Americans entered the armed forces, NNC activists sought to make sense of these spatial transformations in relation to African American identity. Every issue of *Congress View*, for example, included a drawing of Douglass accompanied by his words that became the NNC slogan: "From East to West, from North to South, the sky is written all over, 'NOW OR NEVER.'" The movement of people and ideas due to the war, the NNC postulated, would remake African

American culture if activists and artists connected contemporary struggles across geographic boundaries.[34]

NNC leaders in New York emphasized cultural events that crossed boundaries of rural and urban, folk and modern, and "highbrow" and "lowbrow" culture. Under the leadership of Max Yergan, the NNC sponsored a conference on "Negro Culture in War Time" and other meetings with black artists, who assailed stereotypical roles, comments about the "primitive" qualities of black art, and unequal access for black performers to the mass media and radio.[35] Charles White, for example, had as a teenager participated in the 1930s Chicago arts movement, producing paintings that depicted the humanity of black laborers and scenes of struggle from African American history. During the war, White painted a massive mural, "The Contribution of the Negro to Democracy in America," unveiled at Virginia's Hampton Institute in 1943. This mural connected White's art and the NNC's vision of black history by featuring slave rebels like Denmark Vesey and Harriet Tubman, cultural figures like the blues singer Leadbelly, contemporary political rebels like Max Yergan of the NNC, and the internationally famous singer, actor, and activist Paul Robeson.[36] Meanwhile, Teddy Wilson, a jazz bandleader and member of the NNC's cultural committee, had recently finished a tour with Lionel Hampton, Gene Krupa, and Benny Goodman, "showing America that Negro and white musicians could appear with a really 'big name' outfit on an absolutely equal basis."[37]

These artists departed from the Harlem Renaissance of the 1920s by infusing their art with social protest. They embraced the "New World A-Coming" in Owen Dodson's pageant rather than the book by the same title by journalist Roy Ottley, who had glorified the 1920s arts movement and largely ignored the cultural achievement of the 1930s. According to Louis Burnham's review of Ottley's book in the *Congress View*, African Americans had had enough of "the vapid carryings-on of the 'smart set' which gathered around Amelia Walker during the gay twenties—activities that have been (Heaven knows!) sufficiently documented by Carl Van Vechten and others who made no pretense of being interested in anything more than the surface phenomena of Negro life." The NNC's Committee for Democratic Culture dismissed what members saw as the "flash exterior" of the 1920s art scene in favor of immersing themselves in working-class struggles.[38]

NNC leaders sought something more, however, than pushing African American culture across class and racial lines; they also wanted to fuse black

Above and opposite: NMU and NNC leader Ferdinand Smith and blues singer Josh White (with Josh White Jr.) at the Negro Freedom Rally in Madison Square Garden on June 26, 1944. Smith and White represented the political power and cultural movement that the NNC helped catalyze during the Second World War. From box 1, National Negro Congress Photograph Collection. Courtesy of Photographs and Prints Division, Schomburg Center for Research in Black Culture, The New York Public Library, Astor, Lenox, and Tilden Foundations.

rural folk traditions with the recent urban experiences of African Americans. The 1930s followed two decades of migration to cities, and black intellectuals within NNC circles debated how black rural traditions fit new cosmopolitan ways of life. After having led the 1936 cultural panel at the NNC in Chicago, Richard Wright continued to grapple with the juxtaposition of Marxism and black culture. "In the absence of fixed and nourishing forms of culture," Richard Wright wrote in 1937, the "Negro has a folklore which embodies the memories and hopes of this struggle for freedom." This folk tradition, Wright

believed, had potency when combined with Marxism, to "unify [the artist's] personality, organize his emotions, buttress him with a tense and obdurate will to change the world." If Marxism was "the bones," according to Wright, then folklore encompassed the flesh of black identity.[39]

Like Wright, the NNC blended forms of African American culture and connected them to its protest politics. At a panel at the 1940 NNC convention on "Cultural Freedom," Gwendolyn Bennett, poet Sterling Brown, and others discussed how culture informed protest politics. For his part in the session, Brown challenged mainstream forms of art that distorted black history, such as the enormously popular film *Gone with the Wind*. Mainstream producers of culture did not know black folk culture, Brown explained, and instead "imagine a play about sharecropping and suddenly in comes a chorus of girls from the cotton field where they whoop it up as they go, and that's why we were born." This remark prompted the audience to respond in knowing laughter. Following Brown, Bennett described the "problem of culture with quotation marks around it." Instead of separating art from life, she explained how culture had to contain "action" to portray "the sum total of the experience of a group of people," a pedagogical vision that she applied as the director of the Carver School. This vision, expanded from the time of the New Deal into the Second World War, defined a generation of black artists in the audience that day, from painters Bernard Goss and Norman Lewis to writer Ralph Ellison, who concluded, "My experience with the Congress [the NNC] was almost mystical in its intensity."[40]

In addition to these mainstream depictions, NNC members also learned about black cultural achievements in less formal settings. During her student days at Howard, Thelma Dale remembered after-school sessions at the home of professor and poet Sterling Brown, where he would read his poetry and play on his phonograph the field recordings of folk music that musicologist Alan Lomax had made of African American workers in the South. This music, Dale remembered, "was very influential" because she had not known about "that part of . . . Negro life." Years later, when teaching at the Carver School during the 1940s, Dale wanted to bring this kind of experience into her classroom, and she invited Brown to guest lecture for her "Race on Minority Problems" course, believing this cultural fusion to be a significant part of the "path to equality."[41]

In New York, the NNC sought to host public events that combined these rural folk traditions with contemporary urban black culture. Performances like that of Aubrey Pankey, an African American pianist who had trained and lived in Europe during the 1930s and then returned to the United States to escape the Nazis, exemplified this trend. During his NNC-sponsored Carnegie Hall concert in January 1944, Pankey blended Beethoven, Schubert, folk songs from South America, and African American spirituals in a single performance.[42]

Similar in his genre crossing, Josh White, the blues and folk singer from the Piedmont region of South Carolina, also collaborated with the NNC. White had often been dismissed as inauthentic because of his "mannered" and "sophisticated" style, but according to historian Michael Denning, the "Piedmont blues were more explicitly political" than other regional styles. Once in New York, White's cabaret performances made his music all the more significant to the NNC because many of his songs had aspects of both rural and urban traditions. In fact, in 1941, White recorded a three-disc song cycle, "Southern Exposure," which featured lyrics from poet and SNYC member Waring Cuney. This recording featured notes by Richard Wright, who deemed the songs "fighting blues" for their overtly political nature concerning the war. In "Defense Factory Blues," Josh White echoed the NNC campaign for wartime jobs when he sang, "I'll tell you brother/Well it sure don't make no sense/When a Negro can't work/In the National Defense." White connected through music what activists had attempted to do through social protest. In the song "Uncle Sam Says," he summed up the NNC's wartime vision with these lyrics: "Uncle Sam says, 'We'll live the American way.' Let's get together and kill Jim Crow today!" Given the content of these songs, it is not surprising that the NNC chose White to perform at the Negro Freedom Rally and other benefits and put him on the cover of its pamphlet, "Forward through Unity to Full Citizenship for Negro Americans!" He represented the kind of black cultural front they had embraced: a militant amalgam of black folk culture, urban cabaret, and leftist politics.[43]

The NNC's "cultural front" also included a campaign to reinterpret the concept of race. The NNC collaborated with Edmonia Grant of the American Missionary Association and Columbia University anthropologist Dr. Gene Weltfish, who had helped put together an exhibit at the Cranbrook Institute of Science in Michigan called "The Races of Mankind." The original exhibit featured twenty-two six-foot panels, which explained that "nationalities are not races," that the "bloods of all men . . . are alike except for factors which control blood clotting," that "no race is [the] most primitive—each race is specialized," and that "culture is not inborn."[44] The exhibit presented the latest scientific proof that outcomes of race were a product of environment and not biologically determined. Since the 1930s, Adam Clayton Powell noted in the *People's Voice*, Franz Boas had "looked at nazism with his objective mind [but] was a voice crying in the wilderness." Now that the war pitted Nazi race theories against American democracy, the time had come to promote Boas's "test tube and graph" and refute the biological racism that had accompanied the rise of Jim Crow in America.[45] To show that cultural factors shape ability, one poster in the exhibit asserted that northern blacks outperformed southern whites in entrance examinations administered for the armed forces. Education, not race, determined intelligence, the exhibit's sponsors argued. The display depicted African Americans as a relatively recent combination of "African Negro, American Indian and American white," but alongside this claim the achievements of W. E. B. Du Bois, Paul Robeson, and Marian Anderson were cited so as to also show the significance of black culture. In particular, the displays entitled "Negroes Are a Part of Our Culture" and "America Was Built by Its Minorities" showed that African Americans did possess a significant heritage, but not one biologically determined by their race. The exhibit, although somewhat overdone (part of the "lively humor" of the exhibit asked, "Who are the Aryans?" and answered "as blonde as Hitler—as long headed as Rosenberg—as slender as Goering—and as tall as Goebbels"), provided a powerful platform for the NNC to dismiss notions of racial inferiority.[46]

NNC members applied the lessons of the "Races of Mankind" exhibit for use in their own programs. Their allies at the Carver School taught it; the *People's Voice* serialized it in the spring of 1944; and NNC members sold posters made from the original exhibit to unions as a means to help "your trade union members understand basic facts about race and cultures necessary to improved working relations." When the head of the United Service Organizations (USO) banned copies of a "Races of Mankind" pamphlet after protests from Kentucky representative Andrew May and other southern House members, the NNC helped organize "thirty-nine scientific and semi-scientific organizations" to endorse it and convinced the National CIO War Relief Committee to distribute 400,000 copies to union members across the nation.[47] In 1943, with hate strikes and riots over integrated employment and housing erupting in Detroit, Los Angeles, and Beaumont, Texas, the NNC saw this education campaign as one means to tie racial prejudice to fascism. "In order to take away the liberty of individuals," one NNC member wrote, "fascism has to suppress scientific truth." The NNC knew that "the information is not new in any sense of the word, but it has never reached those large sections of the American nation who accept without a thought the idea of Protestant Anglo-Saxon superiority."[48]

NNC members connected the exhibit to their activism against the Red Cross's practice of segregating blood. During the war, blood became important to saving lives on the battlefront and also represented a tangible symbol of the battle between biological and cultural explanations of race. In 1942, for example, Mississippi senator John Rankin declared that "to pump Negro blood into the veins of our wounded white boys" would "mongrelize America and drag it down to the level of Siam." His demand for blood segregation went hand in glove with white supremacy; he called groups like the NNC the "enemies from within" for attempting to change the policy of the Red Cross.[49] Undeterred by Rankin and others, the D.C. Council of the NNC and the United Federal Workers in 1944 distributed handbills about blood segregation and staged a demonstration in front of the Blood Donor Center in Washington. The following year, Thelma Dale, with help from Adam Clayton Powell, led a delegation to meet with the Department of War and the surgeon general's office in Washington to discuss how segregating blood "denies fighting men blood that in most instances would prevent the loss of lives." The Red Cross admitted it continued the practice as "a matter of tradition and sentiment rather than science." Though the NNC exposed this policy as life threatening, the Red Cross continued to segregate blood until 1950, bowing to political pressure from powerful Dixiecrats over scientific evidence.[50]

The NNC also expressed concern that African Americans would define the current conflict as a "race war" against Japan. There is a "necessity for refuting the Japanese theory of protection of the darker races," Thelma Dale wrote. "Unfortunately," she continued, "there is still in high circles, both Negro and white, too much talk of a race war in the Pacific," and she believed that "cartoons in the daily press . . . are much tinged with white chauvinist propaganda and Negroes tend to react to such provocations with a defense of the Japanese, or a . . . hope that the 'white chauvinists' will get a real beating before *they* finally win." The race-based interpretation of the war was not without some truth. Indeed, before the NNC advocated entering the war in late 1941, Max Yergan and other leaders had cautioned against entering into an imperialist conflict. However, to the NNC, imperialism stemmed from class exploitation. Alphaeus Hunton of the NNC and Council on African Affairs, for example, contested W. E. B. Du Bois's interpretation of the war. Hunton criticized the new book of his friend Du Bois, *Color and Democracy*, because

Du Bois depicted "aggression in terms of racial rather than economic motives." Although Hunton admitted "that nearly all people in colonial bondage today are black, brown or yellow," he believed that "the decisive common denominator of these and other 'unfree' peoples is not skin color but a backward stage of economic development which makes them susceptible to exploitation by imperialism in more advanced countries." The "Races of Mankind" supported the NNC's Marxist interpretation of race prejudice as a "by-product" of exploitation rather than its root cause.[51]

The cultural currents of Red and Black, however, did not always mix so easily. The NAACP rebuked the hopes of a cooperative postwar world as naive. Why, the NAACP asked, would whites suddenly give up their white supremacist ethics? It seemed that the NNC, because of the CP's focus on winning the war, had forgotten Douglass's famous statement that nothing would be achieved without struggle. This feeling even led to a roundtable in *Negro Digest* that asked, "Have the Communists Quit Fighting for Negro Rights?" In the article, Horace Cayton, an academic and journalist who was far from conservative about social protest, concluded, "Most damaging to Communist prestige is their failure to formulate any program in the armed forces and their tacit acceptance of the Jim Crow practices in the Red Cross."[52] While the NNC did have a program to protest these forms of discrimination, its leaders still quoted Douglass's call to arms from 1863 as one that emphasized "action!" in winning the war over "criticism" as the "plain duty of this hour."[53] Mayme Brown, for example, criticized the NAACP's Walter White for his book *Rising Wind* because of its dogged focus on lynching. She believed that "White had little confidence in the new and more democratic world that is emerging" and "fails to note that the pattern of reaction was definitely in the process of decay." If Brown had made such a statement during the NNC's previous campaign against the "lynching spirit" in Washington, it would have been derided. The war had clearly brought a more patriotic and optimistic approach from the NNC.[54]

Despite this optimism, conflicts over representation and activism between the CP and the NNC occasionally surfaced in public. Back in 1939, NNC members had picketed movie theaters showing *Gone with the Wind* because the film depicted happy slaves and white planters as the real victims, yet the *Daily Worker*'s movie critic praised the film. Complaints from NNC members and Ben Davis resulted in this critic's dismissal and a new series of articles on the "Negro in Hollywood Films."[55] During the war, tensions between the white CP members and the black left also emerged over tokenism. Although events like the Negro Freedom Rally succeeded in drawing large interracial crowds, Communists sometimes embraced African American celebrities without realizing the movement they represented. Why, Thelma Dale asked the director of the Council of American-Soviet Friendship, do the council's programs "restrict the participation of Negroes to either Paul Robeson or Mary McLeod Bethune?" Dale complained that the council "fails to recognize the wealth of leadership amongst the Negro people in America." Because such tokenism neglected the "varied contributions [of blacks] to American life," she urged the council to "help to break that stereotype." The extent to which the cultural front mixed at the top but not below would become an increasingly important topic of conversation by 1944.[56]

Nonetheless, the NNC's cultural work depicted African Americans as essential to the war effort and the history of the nation. Its activists and educators believed that they could make this war one of economic emancipation by equating discrimination against African Americans at home—with special emphasis on employment—with fascism abroad. NNC ideas left a powerful imprint on African Americans and their allies. By combining folk and cosmopolitan, rural and urban, and historical and contemporary ideas, the NNC attempted to make black identity part of a new world that would embrace African Americans as distinct yet quintessential Americans.

▨ ▨ ▨ The blending of regional forms of black culture in New York led the NNC to explore the idea of stretching its protest networks into the South. In the fall of 1943, its leaders proposed that Thelma Dale take a trip south and report back on the potential for beginning NNC chapters in places like Virginia and Alabama. The SNYC's Lou Burnham endorsed the trip, explaining that while the NNC should not compete with the NAACP's successful wartime membership drives, the NNC still had a "job to do in the South" that "must be taken up . . . where the NAACP leaves off" and must begin with the "wide dissemination of the *Congress Vue* as an indispensable key factor" in providing information on civil and citizenship rights in otherwise isolated southern communities. Rather than envision southern NNC councils as the hub of activity, Burnham urged the NNC to initiate "clubs" in cities and rural communities where members would advocate for labor unions and galvanize support for crucial issues like voter registration. If the NNC had found the "North Star" in New York, they did not want that to come at the expense of southern work. Because, after all, Burnham wrote, the SNYC strove during the war for "Stars, not bombs, to fall on Alabama."[57]

With the blessing of NNC leaders, Dale headed south. Her trip took her through Virginia, to Tuskegee in Alabama, and then into the hub of SNYC activity in Birmingham. As a former vice president at large of the SNYC and Washington Youth Federation leader, Dale's trip represented something of a homecoming, in which she could pursue collaboration with longtime friends and recruit new allies. In Alabama, Dale spent several days in Birmingham meeting with trade union leaders and black middle-class civic leaders, delivered speeches at mass meetings in Smithfield, Bessemer, and Fairfield, and then traveled into the hinterland Black Belt sections of the state with two dedicated activists, Dorothy Burnham and Oscar Bryant.

Dorothy Challenor Burnham was born and raised in Brooklyn. While studying biology at Brooklyn College from 1932 to 1937, she became a youth activist leader around issues like the Scottsboro case. In 1941, she married fellow New York youth leader Louis Burnham, and the following year the couple moved to Birmingham to take up leadership positions in the SNYC.

Oscar Bryant was a black unionist and Communist from Alabama who represented the radical base that went back to the early years of the Great Depression. His real name was Andy Brown, but after he agreed to do the dangerous work of organizing rural NNC clubs, he began to use the pseudonym as a means of protection as well as to obscure his CP status. Meeting Bryant and these local union, youth, and Communist leaders in Alabama, Dale saw firsthand the richness of the network that the SNYC had built upon since moving its headquarters there in 1939.[58]

During the war, the SNYC was embodied by its dynamic executive secretary, Esther Cooper. Like Dale, Cooper grew up in a middle-class household and attended Dunbar High School in Washington. In Arlington, Virginia, Cooper remembered her mother's activism as branch leader of the NAACP, including her protest over school textbooks (both in content and supply) and her work organizing a picket line in front of a local theater showing the film *Gone with the Wind*. Through the experience of picketing the theater, Cooper's mother joined the NNC and the NAACP in the 1930s, both of which contested the film's distortion of American history and its glorification of the white South during slavery. Because Cooper's mother was from Ohio, Esther enrolled in Oberlin College from 1934 to 1938. In college, echoing her pacifist father, Cooper maintained a strong opposition to the upcoming war, even joining the Fellowship of Reconciliation, which opposed all wars on principle. Yet the deaths of classmates who volunteered to fight for loyalist Spain challenged her pacifism. After graduating from Oberlin in 1938, Cooper moved to Nashville to pursue a graduate degree at Fisk University. There she studied under a number of left and liberal faculty members, including Addison D. Cutler, an economics professor, who invited Cooper to join a small discussion group of faculty who met privately in a room full of Marxist literature. At one of those meetings, she joined the CP. This decision did not seem to her like a life-changing one, but, unsure of her new affiliation, she kept her CP membership a secret. Marxism then seemed more of a useful tool of social scientific explanation than a way of life for her. During her studies at Fisk, she delved into a thesis project on the potential unionization of black domestic workers.[59] In her analysis, she included comparisons to England, Russia, Switzerland, and Denmark, concluding that the "assumption that domestic workers are unorganizable has been proven false in certain European countries."[60] This thesis research led her to thoughts of becoming an organizer of black female workers, but when an offer came to continue her academic work at the University of Chicago, she made plans to enroll there in the fall of 1940.

Before Cooper moved north, James Jackson convinced her to spend the summer in Birmingham to help SNYC with campaigns to fight police brutality and register voters. Arriving in Birmingham, Ed Strong (then of the SNYC) and James Jackson took Cooper out for lunch in the black business district at Nancy's Café. As they sat down to discuss the summer plans, Strong and Jackson first asked Cooper how much money she had brought with her and whether she might loan it to them to pay overdue bills and get the typewriter out of "hock" at the pawnshop. "They were supposed to be paying me!" Cooper recalled, but she nonetheless gave them all of her money, a donation that she repeated when, during the war, she won a Rosenwald Grant to study black soldiers' attitudes but ended up spending the money on SNYC campaigns. Though in the 1930s, Cooper never would have believed she would join the SNYC, let alone become its executive secretary during the war, working with the group changed her life—first professionally as she developed into a youth leader in Birmingham and then personally when she fell in love with James Jackson and married him in Birmingham in May 1941.[61]

During her visit to Birmingham, Dale discussed the past and present activities of the SNYC with Cooper as a means to consider future collaboration. Dale had attended the Third All-Southern Negro Youth Conference in Birmingham in April 1939 and had great admiration for her SNYC friends in the Deep South. Dale had helped coordinate the campaign against police brutality in Washington, but she also knew that establishing a parallel, if smaller, police brutality campaign in Alabama was an entirely new level of commitment. Although the NNC galvanized support for marches and mass meetings in the District of Columbia, its actions did not risk provoking southern sheriffs and lynch mobs. In 1940, for example, the Caravan Puppeteers, a traveling group of SNYC members who put on skits about voter registration, peace, and farmers' problems, learned about the case of Nora Wilson after a performance in Elmore County, Alabama. Wilson, a teenager and domestic worker, had stood up for her younger sister when her employer accused her of stealing ears of corn. After the argument, police arrested Wilson, and a jury later found her guilty of assault and attempted murder. The SNYC launched a publicity campaign that spread as far as Washington and prompted allies to send telegrams to Wilson's tiny hometown of Millbrook and to the prison in Wetumpka, Alabama. Less than a year later, local police dropped the charges. On June 22, 1941, the SNYC hosted a celebratory breakfast for Wilson to demonstrate that black youth could reverse injustice in the South.[62] Over the next year, the SNYC launched similar campaigns against the Birmingham-area police by combining lawsuits filed by black Birmingham attorney Arthur Shores with publicity and mass meetings to expose the unjustified and ubiquitous abuses by police, which the SNYC equated to "Hitlerism" in the South.[63]

Similar to the Washington campaign against "the lynch spirit," SNYC activism in Alabama saw police brutality and the issue of mobility as beachheads for parallel struggles for jobs and suffrage. That vision was bolstered by the experiences of people like O'Dee Henderson, a steelworker, who was arrested for inadvertently "bumping into a white mill employee" on the job. Henderson was then taken to the police station in Fairfield and beaten to death in May 1941. During the SNYC's "Abolish the Poll Tax Week" later that month, white ally Joe Gelders of the Southern Conference for Human Welfare had been out collecting petition signatures when he witnessed a "young Negro worker" named Foster Powers getting beaten by a local policeman for disturbing the peace. (The only disturbance, the SNYC discovered, was that Powers had epilepsy.) Gelders immediately asked the crowd gathered around to provide witness statements, and then the police arrested him as well. Similarly, the SNYC's "Right to Vote" campaign drew support from members of the International Union of Mine, Mill, and Smelter Workers and the United Steel Workers of America, as well as from local black youth who had already become involved in fighting police brutality.[64] From 1939 to 1941, the struggle for the vote made headway for the first time since Reconstruction in the Birmingham area—voter registration rose from fewer than 500 to 3,000 voters registered there. Yet, with a total black voting population of approximately

150,000, this increase indicated that the campaign had only just begun, and the SNYC and its allies needed assistance on voter registration from groups like the NNC to continue their work.[65]

During her November 1943 visit, Dale was particularly impressed that the SNYC had recently established three youth centers. These new education and recreational spaces paralleled the programs of the Carver School in New York City by offering young blacks opportunities that segregation had previously restricted. Cooper organized a session for Dale at the Smithfield Center so that Dale could meet with trade union leaders and explained to her how that center and others in and around Birmingham offered classes in black history, Spanish, unions, and voter registration, as well as hosted political meetings, art exhibits, music concerts, and basketball games.[66] Dale also empathized with the fact that SNYC staffers like Cooper, Dorothy Burnham, Mildred McAdory, and Sallye Belle (Davis) did double duty by serving as youth center directors and teachers, even as they worked on SNYC campaigns and, in the case of Cooper and Bell, took care of newborn baby girls. "I'm finding it almost impossible," Cooper wrote to her husband in the army, "to do a good job in the Youth Congress or here at home with no one living with me." Sallye Bell, who joined the SNYC after having Augusta Jackson as a teacher at Miles College, was more fortunate. She worked "evenings at the Smithfield Center" while a cousin living with her took care of her newborn daughter, Angela Yvonne Davis (who would become a famous black activist two decades later). Cooper realized, however, that Bell's free child care might not last, explaining that the SNYC had to find a "small sum for her work" because the "kids love her in the community."[67] Despite the long hours spent running them, these youth centers increased local SNYC membership; the Fairfield center alone increased SNYC membership in the neighborhood sixfold, to over 300 members, with an additional 1,500 people participating in the center's activities. The other two centers had similar results, all of which showcased the potential for NNC growth in Alabama. With enough funding and personnel, the centers represented a great base from which to renew campaigns for civil rights and could very well be replicated in other SNYC locations across the South.[68]

The discussions Dale had in Alabama illuminated the potential for coordination between North and South, as well as the obstacles to those efforts. "The trip," Dale wrote to Strong in New York, "has been one of the greatest experiences of my life." She came away enthused about combining the forces of the SNYC with the NNC in places like Alabama, as well as through contacts in Virginia and Louisiana. "The South has the need and potentialities for real

SNYC youth center, Birmingham, Alabama. Such youth centers symbolized the important range of cultural and political work undertaken by activists like Esther Cooper Jackson, Dorothy Burnham, and Sallye Belle (Davis) during the war. From box 1, National Negro Congress Photograph Collection. Courtesy of Photographs and Prints Division, Schomburg Center for Research in Black Culture, The New York Public Library, Astor, Lenox, and Tilden Foundations.

growth of a Negro people's movement," she concluded on the trip, "and the NNC can fill the bill." Esther Cooper agreed that it was "quite a successful trip," and she hoped that the NNC would carry out plans to move into the South since "the Youth Congress, with its new orientation on Youth Centers, cannot do all the things it formerly tried to do." The visit revealed to Cooper what "we take for granted," noting that Dale "was amazed at the friends we have here, and our complete acceptance among all kinds of people." Dale noticed how Cooper, the Burnhams, and other SNYC members lived out the kind of world they wanted to create, both in their personal lives and in their activist work. They may have abided by segregation laws in Birmingham, but they did not accept either their racial or their gender proscriptions. Despite the hostile climate, they engaged with allies and their communities with a stubborn conviction and dignity.[69]

Underneath her defiant exterior, however, Cooper found that the South during the war might be romantic to visit but was much tougher to endure as a resident. In her letters to her husband in the military, Cooper mentioned how "every day for four long years since I've been here, there has been some incident"—being called by her first name by a young girl at the tailor, sitting in the dank Jim Crow waiting room at the optometrist, or leaving a doctor's appointment when she had trouble with her pregnancy because the doctor used old, rusted instruments to examine black patients. "These humiliating things," she explained, "warp a person's personality," and unless she occasionally took "a vacation" out of the South she feared "becoming a Negro nationalist or of physically hitting back at some insulting white person . . . or the alternative, of becoming apathetic and selfish." To be sure, Cooper appreciated her northern NNC friends, but she grew frustrated by northern assumptions about the South. For example, the NNC had taken away Ruth Jett from the SNYC staff in "meetings in New York without our consent," and Cooper wondered why they get to "decide what she is to do." "I just get so damn mad," she concluded, because "there are few people who want to 'take' the difficulties of living in the South" and the "glamour of mass meetings and demonstrations in New York appeal to them too greatly."[70]

After her return to New York, Dale proposed to open a southern regional center of the NNC in Birmingham. Unlike her colleagues, whom Cooper privately blasted, Dale now saw the NNC's work in the North as "inseparable with the spread of democracy in the South" and volunteered to "take the job" of running the NNC office there. But once again the war intervened. Writing a couple of months later to H. D. Coke, a Birmingham newspaper editor and the newly elected NNC leader there, Dale explained with regret that "Ed Strong's induction in the Army on Feb. 16 caused us to drastically change our plans for my extended stay in the South." Replacing Strong, Dale became the executive secretary of the NNC and stayed put in New York.[71] With few resources and a one-person staff—Oscar Bryant—the various rural "Work Together Clubs" and city chapters of the NNC only had a few dozen members. The exception was Montgomery. There an NNC group led by Deacon William Anderson coordinated with the SNYC and local unionists like Pullman porter E. D. Nixon in a 1944 voter registration campaign. But cash strapped and lacking personnel themselves, NNC leaders in New York City could do little to assist from the North. Mayme Brown, for example, responded to Anderson's complaints of the "terrible conditions that exist on buses and trains," not with assistance from New York but by telling him "how important it is to organize more and more people from day to day who, though they may not be able to do much now, will be ready when the blow is struck." As the NNC knew, one year earlier Mildred McAdory, a SNYC staffer and Fairfield Youth Center director, was on a bus on her way home from work when she and others got arrested for moving the "board" on the seat that divided the black back section from the front white section. Police arrested her, hit her, and put her in jail. Released the next day, McAdory vowed that "if the people will use this incident" to launch a "mass effort to end the intolerable treatment . . . on street cars and buses," then "the hardship and misery I have suffered will be avenged." But such a movement did not emerge. Fueling Cooper's complaint about New York siphoning away southern leaders, McAdory, a native of Homewood, Alabama, moved to New York for civil rights and journalism work. With or without her, neither Montgomery nor Birmingham managed a sustained bus boycott during the war, which Montgomery achieved during a different historical context more than a decade later.[72]

▨ ▨ ▨ While organizing in the South represented more ambition than logistical reality for the NNC, its leaders determined that expanding its labor and political alliances in New York was within immediate reach. During the 1940–41 period before Pearl Harbor, as the NNC fought successfully for thousands of jobs in aircraft manufacturing outside of Baltimore and on the West Coast, the New York Council agitated for jobs more than ever before. In analyzing the CP in Harlem during this period, the historian Mark Naison argued that its efforts "were at once pathetic and impressive," placing the denunciation of the war in the former category and the NNC's fight for jobs in the latter category. Thus, despite occasional pronouncements from Max Yergan condemning the "imperialist war" abroad, the practical work of the NNC New York Council centered upon jobs. The NNC had always made organizing blacks into progressive unions and breaking job ceilings in places like Chicago and Richmond a high priority, and this strategy continued despite the apparent dissolution of the Popular Front. The New York NNC, however, had not been as active in the late 1930s on the job front but instead had protested lynching and Works Progress Administration cuts while promoting the black arts scene in Harlem. It was not until *after* the split from A. Philip Randolph in

1940 that the NNC took on new life in New York by working through the progressive wing of the labor movement.

In November 1940, the NNC sponsored an emergency statewide conference for African American rights to implement its new "job hunt" strategy and expose discrimination in industry. For the next six months, NNC activists from both the Brooklyn and the Manhattan Councils sent representatives to meet with defense contractors about hiring African Americans. Nowhere was their success more apparent than with the Sperry Gyroscope Company. In Brooklyn, they formed the Joint Committee on Employment with other local organizations like the NAACP and the Urban League and proceeded to picket the plant. With cooperation from the United Electrical, Radio, and Machine Workers of American (UE) in making hiring recommendations, the coalition broke apart the company's race-based hiring and job classifications and won over the president of the company to interracial employment policies. Once blacks had these jobs at Sperry and elsewhere, the NNC and Local 1224 of the UE fought to keep them there, promote them, and address their grievances. The Brooklyn NNC, for example, held meetings at which these new industrial workers spoke about their experiences and strategies for breaking employment barriers, as well as on how to "get along well" with fellow workers once hired. This antidiscrimination agitation led the NNC to coordinate efforts with the UE — in certain defense plants the union leaders signed agreements to actively fight discrimination in their locals.[73]

In the transit industry, the NNC worked with a left-wing union to fight job discrimination, but this campaign featured more complicated loyalties and tactics. The Transport Workers Union (TWU), since its formation in 1934, had a strong Communist presence among the leadership, which preached antidiscrimination. When, in the late 1930s, the TWU received complaints from black workers that the Interborough Rapid Transit (IRT) and Brooklyn-Manhattan Transit (BMT) lines discriminated in hiring and promotion, TWU leader Mike Quill and the Executive Board took them seriously and held special membership meetings and promised upgrades of a token number of black transit workers. What they did not fully anticipate was the membership's response. Rumors spread among white workers that the TWU leaders sought to replace them with black workers. Despite emotional meetings that resulted in resolutions about the importance of nondiscrimination within its ranks, the TWU retreated from upgrading these aggrieved black workers. As a result, anger grew within the black community in Harlem, fueled especially by the Harlem

Labor Committee (HLC), a black nationalist organization that openly condemned interracial unions. The NAACP, no supporter of the HLC for sure, nonetheless also acted against the TWU when it backed Mayor Fiorello La Guardia's proposal that the newly acquired IRT and BMT would become part of New York's public transit system as nonunion lines. Therefore, when in March 1941 the TWU called a strike against the 5th Avenue and Omnibus Company, which affected routes in Harlem, the New York Age, a black newspaper, spoke for a variety of black New Yorkers when it advised that the company hire black strikebreakers.[74]

This strike left the NNC in a dilemma; its members wanted to continue to fight for the hiring and promotion of black workers but also did not want to break the union apart. Since the NNC's founding, it had sought to build power to achieve economic justice for blacks through the labor movement. Thus, the NNC stood by the TWU as the sole African American organization to offer public support. Fortunately, the union won the strike. But that still left the question of job discrimination unresolved, as HLC members and other Harlem activists renewed their denunciation of the TWU. This put added pressure on the NNC to put its rhetoric into effective action, and in April 1941 the NNC formed a coalition to work with the TWU but also pressure it from Harlem to live up to its pledge of racial equality on the job. Hope Stevens, the leader of the Manhattan NNC council, joined forces with Adam Clayton Powell to form the United Negro Bus Association. The NNC pressured the TWU leadership to push its antidiscriminatory demands among its membership and in the process galvanized thousands of African Americans under the roof of Powell's powerful Abyssinian Baptist Church in Harlem in support of a bus boycott. The bus companies tried to divide the TWU membership from the Harlem activists by claiming that union leaders and the NNC wanted to eliminate the seniority of white workers by hiring blacks immediately. But the TWU and NNC leadership held together and minimized the fallout from both the TWU membership and the Harlem community to force a settlement of the BMT and IRT (and the TWU membership) — to hire 170 black employees by suspending seniority and then commit to a racial hiring goal to make 17 percent of the workforce African American. Inspired by this New York campaign, NNC activists in San Francisco and Chicago also successfully pushed to integrate skilled transit employment during the war. These transit campaigns symbolized important breakthroughs, the NNC believed, because the conspicuous nature of motorman and conductor positions proved to skeptics that skilled employment could be integrated.[75]

These New York stirrings impressed John P. Davis. In one of his last acts as the NNC's executive secretary, Davis pressed for the continuation of a militant alliance with labor, despite the CP's shift to a "win-the-war" strategy. Meeting with union representatives from the NMU, the TWU, the Furriers Union, and the State County and Municipal Workers of America in New York, Davis recounted the work the NNC had done for the labor movement since 1936. Ferdinand Smith of the NMU followed by arguing that the NNC "must look to labor for the necessary support to carry out its activities." Now that the war called for maximum production, Davis and these New York unionists agreed to attack the discrepancy between the claimed shortage of manpower and the reservoir of available black labor. These unionists formed a War Production Committee of the NNC, with demands for 50,000 black workers to be trained in the next three months and for representation on the War Manpower Commission, a federal board created by President Roosevelt in April 1942 to manage wartime labor efficiency.[76]

Ferdinand Smith led the NNC's wartime unionist charge. The NNC's relationship to maritime workers began during the 1936–37 waterfront strike, when its members appealed to black workers on both coasts to support the strike and not allow African Americans to become strikebreakers.[77] As chief steward of the SS *Luckenbach*, the Jamaican-born Smith led a walkout of his crew on the East Coast and then served on the strike committee that raised $85,000 to keep the strikers financially afloat. Moreover, Smith accepted his role on the strike committee on the condition that "if we win[,] the new union will not tolerate segregation or discrimination of any sort." On May 3, 1937, this group of seafarers formed the NMU and elected Smith as a vice president; the NMU began to operate on a rotary hiring system rather than a racially preferential one.[78]

Over the next few years, a remarkably open debate about racial issues unfolded among NMU members in the pages of its paper, the *Pilot*. Members discussed whether to have mixed crews and how to best change the racially discriminatory policies of shipping agencies. In Baltimore, for example, Port chairman Pat Whalen declared, "The Negro people either go out of [the hiring hall] in rotation or we do not ship any other men." During the previous strike, "Negro brothers walked the picket line for 87 days," "lived in lousy flop houses," often sleeping "under the same blanket" with white strikers, and "ate our very thin stew." Progressive members of the union argued that the NMU now had to practice the same kind of interracial brotherhood that had made the strike victorious. In southern ports, however, NMU members were slower to embrace interracial crews. The *Pilot* printed many letters from members who rejected mixed crews in southern ports as impractical and dangerous. While ports like Norfolk still shipped separate white and black crews, all-white crews began to refuse to replace all-black ones in the rotation, defying the orders from many shipping companies to not employ blacks on voyages.[79]

As only 10 percent of the membership, black NMU members needed the NNC to help push their antiracist agenda. In 1941, the NMU supported the NNC's drive to end the lily-white employment policies of the Glenn Martin aircraft plant. Additionally, the union's wartime "Keep 'Em Sailing" motto bolstered the NNC's focus on winning the war as a first priority. Anything less, the NNC argued, would dishonor the heroism of these interracial crews, such as that of Captain Hugh Mulzac. At the Negro Freedom Rally in 1942, the NNC and the NLVC honored the 1,600 NMU members (200 were black) who had lost their lives to enemy torpedoes since the beginning of the war.[80] In its alliance with the NMU, the NNC maintained it had not abandoned the fight for racial equality because the overall racial policy of the NMU continued to improve over the course of the war. In return, Smith secured thousands of dollars from the union's coffers to support the NNC's work.[81] During the war, hundreds of white members of the NMU competed for slots on Mulzac's crew, making a powerful antiracist gesture that white members preferred inter-racial assignment.[82] Like Mulzac's, Ferdinand Smith's star rose as a black labor leader during the war. He served as NNC treasurer and NLVC director, and the CIO elected him as a vice president of its national body. Perhaps most important, the antiracism of the NMU had grown so strong during the war that Smith, backed by President Roosevelt's 1942 mandate that race should not be considered when hiring on ships, helped inspire the desegregation of union hiring halls in Mississippi and Texas. In 1944, despite the continued recalcitrance of some white NMU members, Smith leveraged his power to insert an antidiscrimination clause into the NMU's contract with shippers. In the seven years since the union had formed, the NMU record on race gave Smith and the NNC reason to be optimistic about spreading its culture and practices to shoreside sectors of the CIO.[83]

With Smith and other NNC leaders at the helm, the NLVC became an important trade union organization during the war. Though the personnel of the NNC and the NLVC overlapped and the NLVC would merge back into the NNC after the war, the NLVC had a separate task in mobilizing war workers. Its leader, Charles A. Collins, had worked with the NNC in its previous New York jobs campaign, and he held the position of business agent for the Hotel and Restaurant Employees Union of Local 6 of the AFL, an 18,000-member union local with 3,000 black members.[84] Another key member was Moran Weston, a Union Theological Seminary graduate and former secretary of the Manhattan NNC, who returned from organizing domestics in Baltimore in 1943 to take up full-time work for the NLVC.[85] In all, the new organization claimed participation from over fifty unions, organized the annual Negro Freedom Rally, held employment conferences, and, most important, fought behind the scenes to get blacks jobs in New York and New Jersey. This jobs strategy represented a departure for the NNC from its 1930s use of pickets and strikes to gain union recognition and foster interracial solidarity. Many of these CIO unions had already largely won recognition by 1942, and the guaranteed contracts and wage increases (however meager) of the no-strike pledge during the war locked gains in place. For those employees who did not yet have recognition, spirited union organizers like Thomas Richardson, formerly of the SNYC and now an elected vice president of the United Federal Workers of America (UFWA), organized grassroots petition campaigns for collective bargaining. For the 5,000 Italian, Jewish, and African American employees at the Brooklyn Naval Clothing Supply Depot, the largest clothing factory in the United States, this meant winning significant wage increases and seniority through interracial organizing drives, which the NNC pitched as patriotic participation for wartime unity.[86]

This kind of union activity did not have the same theatric visibility as the 1930s sit-downs and pickets but was nonetheless significant. The NNC and its union allies applied pressure on employers and the War Labor Board (WLB) for recognition and wage increases. Moreover, the NNC indirectly benefited from the actions of former ally John L. Lewis. Although the NNC condemned Lewis's wartime strikes, the WLB became a more effective agency because of his agitation; and in an effort to abate wildcat actions, the WLB rewarded those who played by its rules.[87] By mid-1943, the NLVC claimed to have opened 6,000 jobs to black men and women as merchant marines, fur workers, and warehouse workers, and especially in workplaces organized by the UE. During the war, the left-wing UE expanded to 600,000 members, making it the third-largest union in the CIO, and through coordination with the NLVC and NNC at plants like Ford Instrument, Western Electric, and Sperry Gyroscope, it succeeded in getting black workers hired. By 1944, Sperry had hired more than 1,200 blacks in twenty-four different occupations, including mostly semiskilled jobs and two dozen shop stewards. This showed the NNC that progress on the job front was possible with different tactics due to wartime exigencies.[88]

With these noteworthy employment gains in place, the NNC began to concentrate on how to preserve African American wartime jobs. Economists predicted major layoffs after the war, and the NNC worried that African Americans would become the first fired since racism in these industries had made them the last hired. A direct application of seniority rules would mean that even progressive unions would contribute to a massive decline in black employment. With the support of left-wing unions and the CP, the NNC conducted a study at the Sperry Nassau factory at Great Neck, Long Island, the plant with the company's largest number of black workers. Predicting that a 50 percent layoff would occur at that plant at the war's end, the NNC survey forecasted disastrous results. Black workers at the plant would drop in percentages from 7 to 3, from 2 to .1, and from 2 to 0, in key departments.[89]

This study portended disaster, and the NNC began to discuss the idea of "adjusted seniority" as the only remedy. Putting this concept into action would require making agreements with unions and employers for the maintenance of a separate seniority list for black workers in order to preserve their wartime percentages in particular workplaces. The NNC floated the issue for debate in the press, at conferences, and in its educational institutions. At the leftist Jefferson School in New York, for example, an early discussion among progressive teachers and students "was about equally divided" on whether the measure was a wise course of action. Meanwhile, the NNC asked that other unions conduct similar surveys to predict the impact of layoffs on the racial composition of their labor forces. Some unions, like the NMU, did not require adjustment because the percentage of blacks had not increased substantially during wartime, and because industrial employers in defense had only recently begun to hire black workers.[90]

The NNC initiated talks with its closest union allies to convince them to adopt adjusted seniority, which could then serve as a model for the CIO. A key early battle occurred when Arthur Huff Fauset, a longtime NNC leader and educator from Philadelphia, pressed the case for seniority adjustment at the 1944 UFWA constitutional convention in New York. Fauset reminded the delegates that labor movement gains "have come from unity" and that if "these Negroes are turned loose . . . you will have a reservoir of labor which will be unpredictable." The resultant political manipulation of race by employers and politicians, Fauset portended, would create "no less than the specter of fascism itself" in postwar America. Following Fauset's rousing statements, rank-and-file delegates engaged in a heated exchange over seniority. Delegate John Harmon stated that "until the President issued the Executive Order 8802," black workers had not entered the federal service and that it had taken a concerted campaign in the union to make "those prejudiced people" change, a gain that should not be lost to a strict application of seniority. Other delegates demurred. Howard Ziegenfuss of the Philadelphia Navy Yard believed that the UFWA's call for full employment after the war would make the question moot and that calls for adjusted seniority "[say] in effect that our program is not realizable and full employment is but an idle dream." Still others argued that the rank and file would "not support the position of the majority resolution" of adjusted seniority because it would mean the loss of jobs for whites in favor of blacks. "We have never asked one group to do the sacrificing and another group to do the gaining," another delegate concluded; "it is not going to work." After the debate, the UFWA passed a resolution in favor of "maintaining employment gains by Negro and women industrial workers," instructing its national officers to "take whatever steps are possible" to bring about an "equitable layoff policy." Although Thomas Richardson refused to call it a "compromise" resolution, its failure to mention the adjustment of seniority left the resolution without any mechanism to retain black employees.[91]

During this battle for "adjusted seniority," the NNC's harshest and most powerful critic was a black trade unionist named George L. P. Weaver. Born in Pittsburgh, Weaver had become a member of Local 1001 of the Transport Service Employees Union, which had about 500 members among station attendants in Chicago. During the war, Weaver rose to the upper echelons of union leadership. He became secretary-treasurer and director of the CIO's Committee to Abolish Discrimination, significant leadership posts for an African American, which were rivaled only by Ferdinand Smith and Willard Townsend, who also became national board members. "The answer is full employment," Weaver claimed, and "any type of proposal that would tamper with established principles of seniority would serve to undo many years of constructive effort to secure equality in the trade union movement for the black worker."[92] This position, Charles Collins of the NLVC complained, treated seniority like the "Ten Commandments." By becoming the CIO's most outspoken opponent of the NNC seniority plan, he made it easier for white unionists like Philip Murray to endorse a similar position.[93] Although respectful of Weaver in public, the NNC worried that the adjusted seniority debate showed him to be "in strong opposition" to its role in the CIO. NNC members feared that Weaver and Willard Townsend had allied to undermine their leaders. A takeover of the black leadership agenda of the CIO by Weaver and Townsend, the NNC believed, would be disastrous because the two men lacked militancy and both had expressed aversion to working with Communists.[94]

These differences came to a head during a debate at the NNC's January 1945 Conference on Post-War Employment, at which the NNC proposed a plan that presaged affirmative action in employment. The NNC stacked the deck at the conference by surrounding Weaver with panelists who either overtly supported or at least sympathized with adjustment. Its leaders and allies believed that the CIO needed to account for previous discrimination that had kept black workers from accruing seniority before the war. Thelma Dale called for the CIO's Committee to Abolish Discrimination to launch a massive education campaign modeled on labor seminars at the Carver School to explain the necessity for this adjustment as a uniter rather than divider of labor. The NNC made a strong argument but failed to convert liberal African Americans and white unionists. Full employment, the *Chicago Defender* agreed, was "idle, loose dreaming," and layoffs without adjustment would be "dooming the Negro to unemployment again." Yet the idea of adjusted seniority as a solution seemed beyond the boundaries of 1945 American liberalism. "*The Defender* does not pretend to have the answer," its editorial concluded, advocating only "good faith" in making a "compromise which will benefit both sides."[95] NNC leaders did manage to secure an adjustment agreement with the UE's Sperry Local 450, but even in this model case, management did not accept the agreement. "The union's effort to impose even a limited affirmative-action-style plan," historian Martha Biondi concluded of the left-wing UE in New York, "had failed." Black workers continued to get laid off from this and other plants in disproportionate numbers (at least 400,000 of 2 million by mid-1945) as production decreased toward the end of the war.[96]

The NNC's failure in this particular effort had silver linings, however. Its labor and political alliances yielded fruit in 1945 with the passage of the Ives-Quinn Law, a state-level fair employment practices bill. That February, hundreds of workers testified during hearings at the New York State capital in Albany in favor of the legislation. When the governor signed it later that month, the NNC honored Hulan Jack, a longtime member of the NNC and New York assemblyman, who had first introduced a state Fair Employment Practices Committee (FEPC) bill in 1942 and thereafter fought off amendments to water down Ives-Quinn. "New York has started the triumphant march," an editorial in the *People's Voice* wrote of the New York law, and "now, let us all join in to fight it through [on a national level]."[97] The NNC followed the signing of this bill by redoubling its efforts to ensure enforcement. With the International Labor Defense, the CP-affiliated legal defense organization, the NNC coauthored a pamphlet, "It Is Against the Law," which outlined New York State's antidiscrimination laws and explained how victims could pursue civic and legal action on complaints. Moreover, the NNC's union allies in the UE signed an agreement in July with the New York regional FEPC to identify discrimination with surveys of employment by the NNC.[98]

But these agreements were not enough, and when the war ended in 1945 the NNC enthusiastically renewed its mass action tactics. NNC and NLVC members picketed the Empire State Building in a "Save the FEPC Demonstration"; 400 delegates marched on Washington in January 1946 to lobby for a permanent FEPC; and smaller groups picketed outside the homes of senators who opposed the FEPC bill. The NNC hoped that even though they lost the immediate battle over seniority, they would win the war for black economic emancipation by ensuring that postwar employers hired African American workers.[99]

As a result of the wartime demand for maximum productivity, female NNC members also helped inspire new modes of thinking about women's roles in America. An informal study conducted at the UE's Employment Service Office indicated that most of the women who had been hired during the war desired to keep their jobs. One woman, who was among the 7,450 laid off in New York City in August 1945, preferred her wartime factory work because of the better pay and hours in comparison to her previous job as a domestic. Representing a smaller percentage of those surveyed, another woman preferred to cut back to part time in order to be "both a housewife and a career woman."[100] Both of these women, NNC leaders concluded, felt a new sense of entitlement because they had performed well in industrial jobs during the war that had previously been reserved for men. Encouraging such work, the NNC opened jobs to women in defense industries, promoted their new roles by honoring a "Miss Negro Victory Worker" at the annual Negro Freedom Rally in Madison Square Garden, fought for the inclusion and expansion of black nurses during the war, and organized a "Women in Industry" panel as an integral part of its 1945 conference on postwar employment.[101] According to Naomi Kornacker, the executive secretary of the NNC's Manhattan Council, these new positions promoted "liberation" as they met "the nation's production needs." In 1940, four-fifths of all employed black women in New York worked as domestics. Seniority adjustment, Thelma Dale and others reasoned, would liberate these black women from white kitchens in favor of better-paying and less-demeaning industrial employment.[102]

Signifying the new importance of female leadership in the NNC, Thelma Dale was chosen as a delegate to the Paris conference of the Women's International Democratic Federation, an international antifascist organization of women dedicated to women's equality, security, and peace whose December 1945 conference hosted over 850 delegates from forty countries. For the American delegation, the Paris conference provided the opportunity for a group of progressive U.S. women to launch the Congress of American Women (CAW). The women of the CAW proposed far-reaching measures for women's equality, such as maternity benefits, government-supported child and health care, and equal educational opportunities. With the slogan "10 WOMEN anywhere CAN START anything," CAW exemplified the potential for a women's movement to develop out of the Popular Front coalition.[103] Gene Weltfish, creator of the "Races of Mankind" exhibit, which had worked to debunk notions of biological racial inferiority, joined the CAW and sought to extend the exhibit's thesis by denying that motherhood impeded women from having careers and public lives. Yet, for Thelma Dale, the NNC's civil rights work trumped her commitment to this nascent feminist movement. After the Paris conference, the Women's International Democratic Federation offered Dale the position of American secretariat to stay in Paris and represent the interests of progressive American women on an international level. She turned down the position in order to return to the NNC because she believed that the postwar civil rights movement at home took priority. Dale remained active in the CAW chapter in New York in order to ensure that wartime gains for black women did not slip, but, as she explained in 1947 after whites lynched two black women and their husbands in Monroe, Georgia, to keep them "from exercising their democratic right to vote," the fight for racial equality took precedence.[104] Although the CAW would later disintegrate under pressure from the House Un-American Activities Committee and the Department of Justice during the Cold War, a new commitment to equality for black women nonetheless developed out of its work in the NNC and the CAW. During the war, Dale confided to one of her female cohorts, "We skirts are trying to hold down the fort." The NNC agreed, touting Dale's leadership as a "symbol of emerging leadership of Negro women."[105]

◼ ◼ ◼ With union allies at their side, NNC leaders in New York also made an unprecedented leap into electoral politics during the war. This decision would make them mainstream Democratic insiders for the first time but would also cause friction within the organization as electioneering pushed aside other NNC protest campaigns. This shift from protest to electoral politics began in 1943 when NNC members campaigned for Ben Davis Jr., an African American and longtime CP member. After Davis announced his candidacy, many people in New York, including some of Davis's allies, were skeptical that an open CP member could win an election. Yet this challenge only made the CP, the unions, and groups like the NNC work with added diligence for six straight weeks up to the election. As Davis would later recall, "I would have liked to have more skeptics like them." The NNC and NLVC loaned staff and resources to produce flyers, hold street corner meetings, and, working alongside NMU members, cover 110 polling places in Harlem. After four days of counting, Davis won the city council seat by approximately 2,000 ballots, with a total vote of 43,000. Communists, civic groups, and a host of black musicians and artists supported Davis, but "it was black labor," his biographer concluded, "that was the locomotive."[106]

Emboldened by this victory, the NNC increased its grassroots activity the following year to fuel the campaign of Adam Clayton Powell Jr. for Congress from the Twenty-second District. The NNC's employment efforts in the early 1940s had convinced Powell of the organization's usefulness. Since 1942, the NNC and Powell had also worked together on the *People's Voice* in campaigns for poll tax legislation, army desegregation, and the dismantling of the Ku Klux Klan. During the peak of the 1944 primary campaign for Congress, the NNC held street corner meetings in Harlem, distributed ballots, and committed Dorothy Funn to full-time work as head of the women's division for Powell's campaign. Funn obtained endorsements from a diverse group, which included Amy Ashwood-Garvey, Pearl Primus, and Daisy George, an organizer for the Hotel and Club Employees. "The women of Harlem have a double responsibility in these elections," one NNC pamphlet for Powell read; "they owe it to their G.I. Joes to vote, and to vote right, to protect their homes, their families, their men." The NNC and its allies in the NLVC and CIO mobilized voters to bring victory. They organized "flying squads" that canvassed neighborhoods, held rallies, and convinced their union allies to release scores of members for full-time work at the end of July. Powell won the nomination of all three parties (Democratic, Republican, and American Labor) and went on to win the congressional seat unopposed.[107]

As Roosevelt's 1944 campaign rode Powell's coattails in Harlem, the NNC worked to ensure the reelection of the president nationally. Beginning with a September testimonial dinner for Ferdinand Smith in New York, the NNC organized a six-week political tour for Smith and Mulzac to convince blacks — especially those who had recently migrated to the North and the West for factory jobs — to register and vote for Roosevelt. The NNC argued that Roosevelt's reelection would ensure postwar jobs and extend federal programs, claiming that the president had "initiated and fought for a whole series of programs of direct and immediate benefit to the Negro people."[108] The NNC and the NLVC also condemned the Republican presidential candidate and New York governor Thomas Dewey for balking on FEPC legislation, for refusing to allow soldiers from New York to use a federal ballot, and for extraditing George Burrows back to Mississippi on a "trumped up rape charge" that meant certain conviction by an all-white jury.[109]

In supporting Roosevelt, the NNC had to downplay its past grievances with his administration's refusal to support a federal antilynching law, his lack of commitment against the poll tax, and the continued segregation in the armed forces. On the issue of military discrimination, the NNC claimed that its members were "much dissatisfied" over this "major grievance" but that "we applaud the series of steps taken by the Roosevelt Administration in the direction of progressive improvement." Moreover, NNC leaders made only minimal attempts to support their choice of Henry Wallace as the vice presidential nominee or the black delegation of Democrats from South Carolina who showed up in Chicago to contest the lily-white official delegation from their state. During the Chicago Democratic Convention, they quickly assented to Truman becoming the next vice president and to white South Carolina delegates taking their convention seats. The choice of Truman seemed positive when considering that South Carolina politician James Byrnes had almost won the party's nomination. Yet the NNC's electoral strategy offered support for Roosevelt and got little in return. NNC forces acted within Democratic Party circles in 1944 as political insiders and helped elect African American congressmen — Powell from New York and William Dawson from Chicago — by increasing black voter turnout for the Democrats, but in so doing, they also temporarily abandoned their role as militant critics of government-backed discrimination.[110]

The relationship between the NNC and the CP drove this decision to displace protest in favor of politics. Earl Browder, a longtime white Communist leader in the United States, became the CP's most compelling voice for wartime unity in 1944. If Communists maintained their wartime allegiance to Roosevelt and other liberal forces in America, Browder believed that the postwar period would be one of sweeping international reform in favor of working people. During a mass meeting at Madison Square Garden in July, Browder urged the audience to put aside "prejudices and ideological preconceptions" in favor of the unity that had been achieved when Roosevelt, Churchill, and Stalin sat down the previous December in Teheran, Iran. Browder and American Communists interpreted this first three-power conference of the allies as a sign that postwar unity would render the previous radical and sectarian positions of the CP unnecessary and therefore formulated a new policy called the Teheran line. With the support of top African American Communists, Browder dissolved the CP in May and created the Communist Political Association (CPA). For the first time in over a decade, the Communists did not put up their own presidential candidate, instead expressing unqualified support for Roosevelt and other win-the-war candidates.[111] The NNC followed the lead of Browder and his black Communist followers by putting its energies into the 1944 election. After his election to the city council, Davis believed he had become one of the great symbols of the acceptance of Communists in America and admitted being "deeply influenced" by Browder's vision for the Communists. And the influence went both ways. As historian Gerald Horne concluded, "Arguably Davis's election was a material factor in helping Browder form the Teheran line, for if Communists were being elected . . . then a new world *was* coming." This cross-fertilization spelled trouble for the NNC, however. At a conference on seniority adjustment at Powell's Abyssinian Baptist Church, Davis argued against it. Postwar unity, Davis believed, would accomplish integration of the workforce, and adjusting seniority would not be necessary. Moreover, in a report on its 1944 activities, the NNC explained how its plans had changed as an indirect result of Browderism and the influence of the CP on its vision. "The entire program projected last year for cultural development was of necessity dropped," the report concluded, "when all machinery of the National Office was geared to the re-election of Roosevelt and progressive local candidates."[112] So while the NNC had succeeded in its electoral work, its leaders knew it came at a cost.

After the election in November, the Teheran line became even more influential in shaping NNC policy. Communists both inside and outside the NNC began to whisper about whether to "liquidate" the organization, while others discussed how the NNC should transform into an "ideological and educational center" with "no emphasis on building local councils." Ben Davis, more than any other black CP member, pushed for full implementation of Browder's thesis for the NNC. "Years ago it was necessary for us to mobilize masses of people in the streets on every struggle," Davis said at a January 1945 NNC meeting, but "today that is not necessary except in rare instances . . . because we are working with all forces that are for winning the war." Davis argued that the NNC's tactics had been obviated by "legislative channels in the City Council" and concluded, "We shouldn't try to give attention to the building of still another mass organization." While Davis's perspective appeared to win over top New York CP officials, it did not win over the African Americans who led the NNC. Speaking for the NNC leaders in the trenches at this meeting, Lebron Simmons from Detroit offered a stirring rebuttal to Ben Davis.[113]

Simmons offered a different vision for the national NNC based on the significant history of civil rights unionism in the Motor City. Detroit NNC president Rev. Charles Hill of the Hartford Avenue Baptist Church had a reputation for opposing the paternalism of Henry Ford that predated the United Auto Workers campaign, and since 1936 he had brought a strong group of militant unionist autoworkers into the NNC, which included Simmons, Christopher Columbus Alston, Coleman Young, John Conyers Sr., and Shelton Tappes. During the spring of 1941, the NNC helped the United Auto Workers fight a campaign to organize Ford autoworkers, the success of which was anything but certain because of Henry Ford's long-standing paternalistic ties to the black community. Backed by a propaganda campaign that promoted racial division and the use of strikebreakers and company spies, the strike line broke out into violence, and although groups like the NAACP Youth Council came out in support of the union, other groups stayed silent. Christopher Columbus Alston, who on the orders of John L. Lewis returned to Detroit from working with both the SNYC and the tobacco unions in Richmond, wrote a pamphlet, which the NNC distributed, "Henry Ford and the Negro People." In it, he urged local blacks to resist Ford's "special appeal" to "be 'loyal' to the company" and quoted a telegram from state senator Charles Diggs, which declared that "Ford's program of rugged individualism and being a law unto himself had come to a climax." Thanks to an April 1941 conference of the NNC; speaking appearances by John P. Davis, Paul Robeson, and even the NAACP's Walter White; and, most important, United Auto Workers and NNC organizing inside auto factories over the previous years, the union won. During the rest of the war, the NNC there grew into a fighting organization of over 1,200 active members and developed important alliances within Wayne County's CIO and with progressive groups like the People's Institute of Applied Religion, a group led by a southern preacher, Claude Williams, that sought to orient workers for civil rights unionism through the Social Gospel. By 1944, Thelma Dale reported from Detroit that "folks are doing a tremendous job here, which puts practically every other council to shame. Vera [Vanderburg] and Lebron [Simmons] supported by a corps of new people," she concluded, "are making Detroit NNC conscious in a big way." Thus, when Simmons spoke at the January 1945 board meeting in New York, he represented the people who led the NNC rather than the CP members who thought they controlled it. Through pickets and other street protests, Simmons explained, the NNC had managed to get jobs for blacks in the war industries, and this energy translated back into the community campaigns, especially since the disastrous 1943 riot in Detroit. Simmons proposed a drive to get 5,000 members in Detroit and to "lay the seeds for growth" of the NNC on a national level.[114]

Many NNC members nonetheless initially went along with the proposal of Ben Davis and reserved their criticisms of it for private discussions only. FBI informants in places like Chicago began to report complaints that the new CPA was "attempting to put the National Negro Congress out of business" and wanted to "lay low on Negro issues."[115] Supported by French Communist Jacques Duclos, who published a critique of Browder for lacking a "judicious application of Marxism-Leninism," William Z. Foster publicly challenged the CPA and Browder. By the summer, American Communists had concluded that it had been a mistake to abandon the radical ideology and emphasis on the working class for the sake of unity.[116] Before and then in the midst of this challenge, many NNC leaders jumped at the chance to criticize openly the party's lack of support for their work. Doxey Wilkerson had disparaged Communists' "giving up socialism" well before the controversy and later claimed that the CPA had almost destroyed the NNC; Ruth Jett wrote that the NNC had to "struggle for mere existence" during 1944; and Dorothy Funn criticized James Ford, a high-level black member of the CP, for his "continuous association with top leadership and no contact with the larger sections of the population." She believed that "we have been so engrossed with attaining unity at the top that the masses have gone on their way and organized themselves for their many demands without our assistance."[117]

Most critical of Browder was one original NNC member, Ed Strong. Dale and Strong agreed in 1943 to either "build the NNC or bury it."[118] When the building of the NNC did not happen, they blamed the influence of the CP and began to reorient the NNC to a more working-class, mass membership, and militant perspective. Writing from an army post in Burma in early June 1945,

Strong felt a sense of relief to read the publication of the "Foster-Duclos" criticism of the CPA, which called Browderism a "disastrous policy" because it relied on an imaginary "enlightened bourgeoisie." He expressed pent-up frustration of being "sick in the stomach" over the direction of the NNC. "You know better than anyone of course," he wrote Dale, "how under the illusionary concepts of Ben Davis, the major emphasis of Negro progressive leadership has been on securing formal agreement among a handful of top Negro leaders at the expense of organizing the Negro masses[,] and this obviously false and dangerous line has been pursued in the name of 'Negro unity.'" He criticized the direction of the NNC's 1944 election strategy, noting that certain black CP members in the NNC rejected all proposals for "mass work." He called the previous electoral campaign a "fool's paradise" and believed that the defeat of the national FEPC and adjusted seniority both had "their origins in the Browder thesis."[119]

Although in New York there may have been reason for optimism for politics rather than protest, in the South many SNYC leaders quietly fumed. Without suffrage and with the poll tax still intact in several states, they wondered, how exactly would the SNYC work to elect candidates? While the Youth Centers had proven valuable in Birmingham as hubs of activity, they were never meant to replace struggles for jobs and protection under the Fourteenth and Fifteenth Amendments. While in the army in 1944, James Jackson noted the news of Wallace's dismissal as vice president, hinting to his wife that this should warn against "moods of over-optimism." A year later, his wife, Esther Cooper, reached her limit of patience for the CP's meddling in the SNYC. He might find her conclusion heretical, she wrote to her husband, but she had come to believe that "the new period with 'everything being rosy' just didn't work in the South." Writing back from Burma, James Jackson expressed great relief that his wife agreed with his own assessment. "I had to laugh when I read your line about 'divorcing you for such heresy,'" he wrote, because "for more than two years I have lived in fear of having my fight with the [southern CP] leadership exposed and los[ing] your respect and [you would] have to divorce me as a consequence!" Jackson "was so proud" that Cooper agreed that "progress will be won in the street and not in the drawing room."[120]

Back at the helm in late 1945, Thelma Dale, Ed Strong, and SNYC allies such as Esther Cooper had saved the ship. During that summer, Foster had wrested control of the CP from Earl Browder, and Ben Davis, Ford, and other black CP leaders had admitted their mistakes, shifting in favor of a new militant party line. Certain NNC members did not forget, however, how in 1944 high-ranking CP members in New York almost sank the NNC and the SNYC, and they worked diligently to reorganize both organizations as militant protest networks of working-class blacks.[121] This reorganization mission began with the demand that the NNC offer the executive secretary position to Revels Cayton, a black trade unionist who had become a Communist in the early 1930s in Seattle, had worked as a steward and labor organizer on the waterfront, and had become part of the state CIO's antidiscrimination committee in California. His labor background, West Coast origins, and family lineage as the grandson of Hiram Revels, who became America's first black senator when he took Jefferson Davis's Mississippi seat in 1870, made Cayton the perfect choice for taking the NNC into a mass-based union direction.[122] Upon accepting the position at a January 1946 mass meeting in Chicago, he promised to "take on the job with the fire and zeal of the unconquerable spirit of Negroes whose heritage goes back to the days of slavery." The significance of his first speech was not lost on the NNC leadership. They had fought hard for the Detroit model of mass membership over the previous New York model, which had not emphasized council building. Much to the CP's dismay, the following year NNC members even laid plans for moving the organization away from the Communist leadership in New York in favor of an industrial union base in Detroit. In early 1947, an FBI informant in New York reported, "Communist Party leaders were stunned by the knowledge of the change of headquarters of the NNC and they felt that all progressive forces should be centered around one central location."[123]

Putting the new vision of the NNC into practice, Revels Cayton and other trade union members took immediate action. In January, NNC delegates from New York, Chicago, and Baltimore, joined by SNYC members from points south, descended upon Washington to demand the removal of longtime Mississippi senator Theodore Bilbo for his white supremacist politics of disfranchisement and to lobby the Truman administration for the permanent FEPC. At a mass meeting in Washington, Cayton explained, "We are not a pink tea organization and this is no pink tea fight confronting us." With a quarter of a million black workers in the UE and with 60 percent of many more millions of packinghouse workers on their side, Cayton demanded that blacks fight to make the postwar world one without Jim Crow. Seconding Cayton, a converted Ben Davis said at this meeting, "We must keep a never-ending picket line around the House, Senate, the White House, and Bilbo's home." As the meeting closed with a performance by the Golden Gate Quartet and a dramatic reading by actor Rex Ingram of Langston Hughes's poem "Let America

Be America Again," the delegates seemed to have agreed to let the NNC be the NNC again.[124]

Those who knew the intricacies of the NNC's wartime work credited the "dynamic" women who had kept the organization together. In November 1945, for example, Max Yergan closed an upbeat executive meeting with the following praise: "I can't let this meeting go by without expressing appreciation for the devotion and work which we have had from the staff, for Thelma's untiring leadership against terrific odds. She has held things together and now has the ship ready for launching upon new and favorable seas. When we look back and see the difficult narrows that we have treaded the executive staff deserves a vote of thanks and confidence."[125] The network that had begun in Chicago during the winter of 1936 now started an impressive resurgence in late 1945. It would take an unprecedented wave of government-supported suppression of civil liberties, legitimized and enforced by white liberals and trade unions, to stop it from achieving the goal of its new motto, "Death Blow to Jim Crow."

▨ ▨ ▨ "The Negro's general morale" during the Second World War, wrote Richard Dalfiume, was "paradoxically . . . both low and high." The work of the NNC in the field of black cultural politics, civil rights unionism, and electoral politics shows that the war years harbored both a triumph of militant forms of activism and cracks in its allied movement.[126] The NNC helped revive black history in order to make the Second World War into one with emancipatory potential, opened up thousands of defense jobs for black workers, provided new opportunities for black women, and helped get progressive candidates elected to local and national offices. Yet at the end of the war, black war workers faced unemployment without adjusted seniority, the NNC had not made inroads into organizing in the South, and the organization's uncritical support of Roosevelt had yielded little political leverage. While blacks in industry nationally more than doubled between 1940 and 1944—to 1.35 million employed—after V-J Day in 1945, 20,000 blacks in New York, 25,000 in Chicago, 35,000 in Detroit, and 7,500 in Baltimore lost their jobs.[127] Among these workers was Captain Hugh Mulzac. "After twenty-two successful voyages during which we carried 18,000 troops and countless thousands of tons of material, the *Booker T. Washington* and I were consigned to the boneyard." The "racially united, politically alert" crew had during the war "carried the message of . . . hope for mankind to the ports of four continents." Now Mulzac and 200 other African Americans who had "served as deck or engine officers" had been removed from their commissions and not reassigned, and the Coast Guard now regarded the captain as a "security risk" due to his wartime participation in civil rights demonstrations.[128]

The NNC had mixed results during the war, but given the circumstances, few alternatives existed. Moving the organization to New York put the NNC in a comforting radical environment during the war, but it also left little space for the NNC to enjoy freedom from the influence of top-level Communist leaders who resided there. Moreover, Ben Davis's election as city councilman led to an overestimation of what the black left had accomplished, and the microcosm of New York never applied to other places to which the NNC and the SNYC wanted to expand their antiracist work. That said, the postwar mea culpa performances of black and white Communists about their embrace of Browderism did not necessarily diminish what the NNC accomplished from 1942 to 1945. With the war in Europe taking priority for nearly every liberal and progressive group in America and with a million blacks in the service, the NNC did not see strikes and mass protests as viable. While concentrating on building local councils would have helped in the postwar years, accruing longer membership lists mattered little in terms of action until the war ended.

The group of black women who ran the NNC, along with the NLVC, left-wing unions, and the SNYC, managed to steer through the shoals of new wartime circumstances and political currents to make the NNC a fighting organization again. Through its wartime cultural, economic, and political campaigns, this new group of leaders came to represent a new perspective from a new generation. In a revealing letter from the fall of 1944, Esther Cooper wrote to James Jackson: "Ed [Strong] proposes that . . . all of us . . . get together after the war and work out together what the future work of all of us shall be."[129] Among the people she included in "us" were Jesse (Campbell) Scott, Thelma Dale, Dorothy and Lou Burnham, and Augusta Jackson (Strong), as well as other SNYC and NNC members. All of these activists had entered the NNC and SNYC youth movements in the 1930s and had grown up through their activist experiences within it. They, not the top-level CP leaders from an older generation in New York, would direct its present and future course, as shown during the war. As a result, by the war's end, the NNC took off again in the Midwest and on the West Coast, and the SNYC grew in places like Alabama and Louisiana and especially South Carolina.

CHAPTER FIVE

The World's "Firing Line"

South Carolina's Postwar Internationalism

On October 20, 1946, in Columbia, South Carolina, W. E. B. Du Bois threw down the gauntlet. "The future of American Negroes," he told an audience of 861 delegates of the Southern Negro Youth Congress (SNYC), "is in the South." Breaking from the trend of black intellectuals who called for migration to the North and West of the United States, Du Bois instead cast the South as the "battle-ground of a great crusade." Southern youth, he declared, would need to make "the Great Sacrifice" to "rescue this land." He then referenced Moses on the edge of the Promised Land in the Old Testament Book of Deuteronomy: "Behold the beautiful land which the Lord thy God hath given thee." African Americans and working-class whites had built this "glorious land," and, Du Bois contended, "it would be shame and cowardice to surrender . . . its opportunities for civilization and humanity to the thugs and lynchers . . . who choke its soul and steal its resources." Du Bois spoke with tremendous optimism for a racial reconstruction of America after the Second World War. Looking out on the crowd of militant young southerners—black and white, male and female—Du Bois saw the potential for a mass movement to bring democracy to a "southland" burdened by three centuries of "the flat failures of white civilization."[1]

The SNYC and its allies envisioned a movement of black southern youth because they saw their local fight as a significant front in the battle for the fate of the democratic world. As the war against fascism came to an end overseas, they sought to develop a new analysis based on international events, past and present, to foster a postwar movement for racial and economic justice that linked activities in the U.S. South to those of other working-class people around the world. Historians have recently declared South Carolina in the 1940s the "vanguard of the movement," due to the level of black resistance there, and this chapter explores the extent to which these activists saw themselves as grassroots actors on a world stage.[2] International issues preoccupied not only diplomats and world leaders, but also activists, students, and workers in South Carolina. Black southerners did not directly participate in the Council of Foreign Ministries alongside their longtime nemesis, South Carolina politician James Byrnes, but their protests and voices mattered in national and international arenas. SNYC leaders wanted to transform notions of southern black identity from provincial to national and then international, because they believed this wider vision would change the concept of Jim Crow from natural and immovable to artificial and breakable. Thus, by applying internationalist, anticolonialist discourse to what Du Bois saw as the "firing line" in the American South, these activists tried to connect world events to local conditions to inspire new forms of resistance to Jim Crow. To the SNYC, a postwar world without racial hierarchies was not only possible but essential to save humanity from nuclear war, fascism, and colonialism.[3]

▨ ▨ ▨ The possibility that political and protest activities would develop among blacks in postwar South Carolina seemed remote in 1940. In what would become part of the research for Gunnar Myrdal's famous study on American race relations, *An American Dilemma*, a black woman named Wilhelmina Jackson surveyed race relations in Greenville, Charleston, and Columbia on the eve of the Second World War. What she found distressed her. Greenville, "known for its mills and [the] bad race feeling the mills have engendered," had the best prospects because a recent black voting drive had shown "how white supremacy . . . can be made almost impotent or ineffective." There, a local African American professor, a CIO attorney, and the president of the Greenville Workers Alliance had inspired local African Americans to register to vote. Over 700 blacks registered, but a concerted plan by the local Ku Klux Klan, the press, and the police intimidated most of them from casting ballots in the following election. John Bolt Culbertson, the white CIO attorney, complained to the NNC's John P. Davis that half of the county's court cases involved landlords who, with the blessing of the Justice of the Peace, "take all the household furnishings of negro tenants for a week's rent and pocket the difference." Despite NNC publicity in Washington that demanded federal intervention, local vigilantism reversed the emergent struggle for the ballot in Greenville in the late 1930s.[4]

Elsewhere in South Carolina, Jackson did not see many better prospects. She deemed the NAACP chapter president in Charleston "an intellectual snob" who claimed to have 400 members but, when pressed, could not cite a single achievement of the group. The only real critic of the status quo, Jackson reported, was a "fairly militant man" named John McCray, who had protested police brutality in 1935 when local police killed eleven blacks without cause in a matter of months. This campaign, however, had "tacked on" to McCray "the dreaded name 'radical' . . . and, as a result, he is not accepted by the community." In the state's capital city, African Americans represented more than one-third of the 50,000 residents, but, Jackson concluded, "there is little political organization among Negroes." The only active black protest group in the city, the Negro Civic Welfare League, had lobbied since 1938 for better health and recreation facilities without much success. Its secretary, Mrs. Andrew Simkins, a state tuberculosis agent, was one of the few residents who stood up against local acts of discrimination. Most black Columbians that Jackson interviewed saw "no point in trying to vote, in trying to get jobs, because [like one person told her,] 'The white folks is goin' to let you git so far and no farther.'"[5]

To make matters worse, politicians leveraged the threat of black equality as the primary means to win elected office. Despite the lack of activism in Columbia and elsewhere in South Carolina, blacks had become political pawns. Florence Derieux, editor of *The State*, a relatively liberal newspaper in Columbia, explained how, "as a backdrop, the Negro is the most powerful political factor in South Carolina" because "candidates' whole activities are based on the predicate that Negroes might get something[,] and one of the main appeals in their campaigns is keeping the Negro out of political affairs of state."[6] Accompanying the politicians, the Ku Klux Klan had "[carried] on sustained campaigns against progressive candidates and [raised] scares like *race* and communism in *C.I.O.*" The only cure for South Carolina, Jackson believed, would be to remove its white dictatorship and force the federal government to get involved. "The day when Negroes will participate freely in politics here will still be far away unless the bull is caught right by the horns . . . and steps are taken to get federal intervention."[7]

Beneath the pervasive levels of pessimism, these complaints also indicated that the seeds of change had been planted among blacks and whites in South Carolina. The New Deal brought unprecedented federal money into the state, even though South Carolina Democrats like Senator "Cotton Ed" Smith had made their political careers out of "states' rights." Though Smith at first claimed to be a New Dealer, he increasingly worked against almost every measure brought forth by President Roosevelt and had even walked out of the 1936 Democratic Convention because a black minister gave a prayer as part of the proceedings. Washington proponents of the New Deal in 1936, increasingly supported by black northern voters, had tried to pass social welfare legislation but continually hit a southern Democratic roadblock. To remove this barrier, Roosevelt actively campaigned against Smith and other southern reactionaries whose obstructionist views on social welfare—but especially on race—threatened to break apart the national Democratic Party. Roosevelt, however, lost his battle to unseat Smith and his allies—these southern politicians stirred up racial animosity to drive whites to the polls and kept the New Deal's southern working-class supporters disfranchised.[8]

Modjeska Simkins nonetheless saw this wedge in the New Deal coalition as an opportunity for blacks in South Carolina. Modjeska Montieth was born just days before the turn of the century to middle-class parents whom she remembered as "fearless people in a time when Negroes were supposed to cower." Her parents emphasized education and sent her to Benedict College from elementary school through college. Her mother had been part of Du Bois's Niagara Movement in the early 1900s, and Montieth attended local NAACP meetings as a teenager. In 1929, she married Andrew Simkins, a successful businessman, who enlisted the help of an elderly relative and a housekeeper so that Modjeska could continue her career outside the home. For the next decade, she traveled statewide as director of Negro Work for the South Carolina Tuberculosis Association, making contacts by fusing health and civil rights concerns. By 1942, however, she and her employer parted ways when Simkins's health advocacy became secondary to her civil rights commitments.[9] Civil rights activities became paramount for her, as South Carolina's black organizations seemed to gain new resolve as war broke out in Europe. In 1939, chapters of the NAACP united to form a statewide organization to revitalize an organization that had at the time 1,200 members in eight communities; during the war that number grew tenfold.[10]

In Charleston, John McCray readily joined this growing tide. McCray grew up in Charleston County and had the privilege of attending the Avery Institute, a private school for black elites, where he graduated as valedictorian in 1931. He then earned a bachelor's degree in chemistry from Talladega College in Alabama, but, finding no jobs for blacks in this field, he moved back to

Charleston in 1935 and worked as a debt manager while simultaneously beginning a career in journalism at a small paper called the *Charleston Messenger*. In the late 1930s, McCray made a bold move and started his own paper, which he named the *Lighthouse and Informer*. This paper, as much as the state NAACP apparatus, would bring together like-minded activists and disseminate information to black communities across the state "as the official 'mouth piece' of all militant movements." Soon after he started the paper, McCray became convinced that Charleston, where he was "not accepted by the community enough to actually offer much leadership," would not be the best setting for his new press venture. He moved to Columbia to be closer to like-minded activists like Simkins.[11]

Osceola D. McKaine joined McCray at the paper after returning from Europe. Born in Sumter, South Carolina, in 1892, he attended the Colored Common School there. Soon after graduating, he obtained work in Savannah on a merchant freighter that sailed the Caribbean, giving him a firsthand view of the colonialism of the Western powers. The ship then docked in Boston, where McKaine attended classes at Boston College before deciding in April 1914 to enlist in the army. His early assignments in the army included a stint with the all-black 24th Infantry in the Philippines, training in New Mexico, and participation in a cross-border raid into Mexico to capture Francisco "Pancho" Villa. By October 1917, McKaine had graduated from the Colored Officers School in Des Moines, Iowa. He left for France as part of the "Buffalo Regiment," the newly formed 367th Infantry. When the war ended, First Lieutenant McKaine sailed back to the United States and settled in Harlem. In New York, he fused his international experience with radical politics. He helped lead a black veterans' organization (initially formed in France), wrote for A. Philip Randolph's militant newspaper, the *Messenger*, and joined the League for Democracy, another veterans' group in Harlem. Probably due in part to the postwar "Red Summer" of violence that swept through America after the war, the League for Democracy collapsed in 1921. Soon thereafter, McKaine embarked upon a "new life" in Europe. By the late 1920s, he had settled in Ghent, Belgium, and, with a business partner, had opened a nightclub called Mac's Place. This jazz cabaret employed over thirty people during its 1930s heyday, offering African American culture far away from America's racial constraints. But for the spread of fascism, McKaine might never have come back to the United States. In May 1940, however, German troops reached Ghent and took over his club. Rather than remain open for the Nazi clientele, McKaine fled Belgium in early 1941 for the United States.[12]

Soon after his return, McKaine wrote about the racial fluidity he had witnessed in other nations. Europeans, he wrote, had respect for "jazz and spiritual music" and an admiration for the "American Negro."[13] The treatment by the French "was slightly tinged with paternalism," the Flemish Belgians had been "slower to accept Negroes" than had the Walloon population, and the "Balkan peoples as well as the Slavs were all without racial prejudice insofar as Negroes were concerned." McKaine deemed British people as the most prejudiced against blacks, but not "as brutally as many Americans." However, the rise of the Nazis in Germany made the status of people of color become much more precarious, and McKaine's fears of Nazi aggression became reality in the spring of 1940. He remembered experiencing two days and nights of air and naval bombardment in La Panne (near Dunkirk), where "the 5 stories of my hotel, trembled like leaves on a tree." While he was never "molested or offended" by the Nazi soldiers who occupied his Belgian club, he saw the devastation they caused. Traveling back to Ghent on back roads, he "passed the corpses of men, women, children . . . still unburied," and their gruesome sight convinced him to leave. McKaine's cumulative experience in the Caribbean, Europe, and elsewhere had exposed him to a multiplicity of racial constructions. Further, the occupation of the Nazis of Belgium showed him the horror that derived from notions of Aryan supremacy. Nicknamed the "Lieutenant," McKaine returned to his home state ready to fight for the freedoms he had experienced abroad.[14]

Back in the United States for the first time in two decades, it did not take long for McKaine to get involved in black protest networks in South Carolina, which led him to meet Simkins and McCray. He had left his hometown of Sumter because of racial segregation and limited economic opportunities and had returned with at least "a splinter" of resentment on his shoulder.[15] Like Simkins and McCray, McKaine was encouraged by the momentum he saw within the state's NAACP. In 1942, McKaine helped revive the Sumter branch of the NAACP, becoming its executive secretary and initiating a campaign for racial parity in teachers' salaries. When on a statewide speaking tour for the Palmetto State Teacher's Association and the NAACP's Legal Defense Fund, McKaine met Simkins and McCray in Columbia. The three hit it off and talked late into the night about McKaine's international experience and civil rights vision for South Carolina. By 1943, both of these activists had hired McKaine (he worked as an associate editor of the *Lighthouse and Informer* and managed one of Simkins's liquor stores) so that he too could settle in Columbia. With their backing, he filed and won lawsuits to obtain equal pay for teachers in Charleston and Columbia.[16] This collaboration emboldened all three and seemed to hold the potential for sustained collaboration in fighting for the citizenship of disfranchised and Jim Crowed South Carolinians.

Simkins, McCray, and McKaine all agreed that their efforts should begin with pursuing access to the ballot. On April 3, 1944, the national NAACP legal team won its most important victory when the Supreme Court ruled in the case of *Smith v. Allwright* that "the right to vote in a primary . . . is a right secured by the Constitution." South Carolina, like Texas, had used its primary election to exclude blacks from the Democratic Party's selection of candidates. As Wilhelmina Jackson explained, "Since [blacks] are excluded from participating in the primary which *is* the election, they feel that they are just parties to a farce when they participate in the general elections." The South Carolina General Assembly, panicked by the decision, responded in dramatic fashion. Only ten days after the Supreme Court decided the case, it met in a special session and proceeded to eliminate all references to primaries from the state's statutes. In so doing, the legislators hoped to circumvent the *Allwright* decision because the ruling was premised on primary elections as "conducted by the party under state authority." If no state-supported laws formally existed, then the primary could be made a private affair and the Court's decision did not apply.[17]

Sitting in the audience during this special session, Osceola McKaine grew more and more indignant. McKaine and McCray interpreted the closing remarks of Governor Olin D. Johnston as "a threat of violence upon Negroes — an open invitation for the Klan to get busy!"[18] The national press dubbed this new means of resistance of legislators the "South Carolina plan," and other southern states saw it as a model response to the Supreme Court. During the next month, McCray, McKaine, and others formed the Progressive Democratic Party (PDP). Using both the pre-established networks of the state NAACP and the black political organizations that had developed around the campaigning for a fourth term for Roosevelt, the PDP convened in Columbia only two days after the white Democratic Party met there. Over 150 delegates, representing 38 of the state's 46 counties, attended the convention to hear McKaine cry out for a "third revolution." The decision, he told the PDP, was either to remain "spineless serfs" or to act as "free men." The dichotomy of serfs and men suggested an international class struggle that went well beyond the Carolina coastline. The struggle for the ballot was about forming a power base necessary for blacks to overthrow their anachronistic status as serfs. The delegates responded with enthusiasm to the idea that "this day will be remembered . . . when Negroes allied with liberal whites [and] decided to make this state a decent place to live." With McCray and McKaine as cochairmen, the PDP elected eighteen delegates to contest the seating of the South Carolina lily-white Democratic Party at the National Democratic Convention in Chicago.[19]

The regular South Carolina Democratic Party worried about the potential power of this new party. The *Columbia Record* attacked McKaine's speech, claiming he "talked too much" and "unwisely." In response, McKaine wrote to the paper's editor admitting that he "knew in advance that many statements contained in my speech would displease certain white men." Yet, he said, "I wonder do [whites] know what is going on in the hearts of Negroes? I wonder do most of them care what's going on in their heads and in their hearts? I ask these questions because if the white people don't know what the Negroes are thinking about — that's alarming; if they don't know how they feel — that's dangerous; but if they are not concerned about either; that can be calamitous."[20] McKaine suggested that white southerners underestimated both the intellect and the potential for resistance by African Americans. The proposed "third revolution" by the PDP threatened the state's Democratic Party for the first time since Reconstruction. In response, white leaders expressed little concern publicly. In private, however, they were unnerved, concluding that any inclusion of blacks from South Carolina by the national party would require them to secede from the Democratic Party. If "any one of them should be seated in Chicago," a state supreme court justice told the governor, "then our entire delegation will withdraw . . . and I am inclined to think that . . . several other states will join our delegation."[21]

Fearing the fallout of a PDP challenge to the national Democratic Party, Robert E. Hannegan, chairman of the national committee, and William Dawson, African American Democratic congressman from Illinois, met with McCray in Washington to defuse the situation. McCray refused to capitulate or cancel the PDP's plans. In mid-July, the delegates, using money raised by the PDP over the previous months, boarded a train in Columbia for Chicago. Once there, they did not get a hearing before the regular credentials committee of the Democratic Party but instead pleaded their case before a special six-member subcommittee. The subcommittee persuaded the PDP delegates to declare their support for Roosevelt whatever the outcome and then dismissed the PDP's claim on technicalities while making vague private promises for future action against the lily-white southern delegations.[22]

The PDP delegation nationalized the struggle of South Carolina's African

Americans. By challenging the all-white delegation in front of the national party, the PDP forced Democratic Party leaders to confront the disfranchisement of potential southern Democrats. The PDP delegates also paid close attention to the fate of their former senator, James Byrnes, who had come to the convention expecting to become the next vice president. Meanwhile, the PDP, Congressman William Dawson, and organized labor threw their support behind the current vice president, Henry Wallace, who had become more progressive since his stint as Secretary of Agriculture during the New Deal.[23]

Byrnes was not a rabid race-baiter like "Cotton Ed" Smith, but the PDP still found him threatening. In the early 1930s Byrnes had befriended President Roosevelt and had helped him pass New Deal legislation, serving as a conduit between southern Democrats and northern and western liberals in the House and Senate. While Byrnes supported white supremacy, he had initially showed restraint when speaking about race relations and had rarely made it central to his platform. Yet after 1937, Byrnes's public demeanor changed. Though he won all but one precinct in South Carolina alongside Roosevelt in the 1936 elections, he now openly spoke out against black political participation. During the debate over the federal Wagner–Van Nuys antilynching bill, Byrnes led the opposition to the legislation, singling out NAACP head Walter White as one of the "Northern Negroes" who wanted to take over the Democratic Party. Confronted with 158 lynchings that had occurred in South Carolina since Reconstruction, Byrnes argued for the right of states to conduct their own affairs. Byrnes's support for the filibuster of the antilynching bill made him odious and dangerous to African Americans in South Carolina, who interpreted his politicking as advocating the "right" of whites to kill blacks with impunity. Thus, his actions had given cause for activists to form the PDP and to challenge the legitimacy of the state's Democratic Party.[24]

Labor and civil rights activists saw the vice presidential choice as essential to sustaining the New Deal coalition of liberals and progressives. With Roosevelt's health in question, most delegates concluded that the vice president would likely become the next American president. The PDP agreed "to [not] stage a scene" at the Chicago Convention, but its presence convinced many Democrats that nominating Byrnes would prove divisive. Sidney Hillman, representing labor as the head of the CIO Political Action Committee (CIO-PAC), refused to endorse Byrnes. William Dawson met privately with Byrnes and then told Chicago mayor Ed Kelly that he would not endorse him either. Before the convention, Byrnes and Roosevelt assumed that the nomination would not dissuade black voters, who adored the president and

First Lady. The arrival of the PDP from South Carolina suggested otherwise. Edgar Brown, a black Republican Party politician from Illinois, had met the PDP delegates at the train station in Chicago and offered them free accommodations at the Stevens Hotel, sponsored by the Republican owner of the *Chicago Tribune*, Colonel Robert McCormick. The PDP rebuffed the antilabor and conservative McCormick, but his offer raised the possibility of an exodus from the New Deal coalition. Meanwhile, Chicago mayor Kelly had warned Roosevelt that only the voting strength of the city's Black Belt would carry Illinois. Dawson's rebuke of Byrnes meant that the loyalty of blacks, many of whom were only recent converts to the party, might be in jeopardy. While Wallace lost the nomination for being too progressive, Byrnes lost for being too conservative, thanks in part to a political party that had been organized earlier that year.[25]

The delegates came home from Chicago optimistic about their new political party. "Both Washington and Chicago should have taught you," PDP leader and delegate A. J. Clement wrote to McCray, "that two years is not too long to wait to build the type of organization, that . . . would place us in a most impregnable position to bargain and collaborate." The party soon thereafter nominated Osceola McKaine to challenge Senator Olin D. Johnston in the November 1944 senatorial election. In October, "Mac" toured two dozen towns and cities in South Carolina and became a recognizable leader for African Americans across the state.[26] The surviving evidence of his stump speeches shows that he downplayed the international aspects of his politics to foster a larger coalition of voters. He mentioned his background as a soldier in France and Mexico, but otherwise McKaine spoke only of domestic politics. He called for a secret ballot and "economic security for all" in the postwar. Instead of declaring his radical intentions as he had the previous spring at the PDP convention, he reached out to moderates during the tour who might have shied away from internationalism. McKaine staunchly defended Roosevelt and the New Deal to persuade liberal whites to join the majority-black PDP.[27]

The election results disappointed. Fraud probably diminished the total vote of 3,124 for McKaine, but he nonetheless came in third. Olin Johnston received 94,556 votes, and Republican J. B. Gaston received 3,807.[28] In January 1945, McKaine went to Washington, D.C., to register a complaint with the Senate that voting fraud had occurred in several South Carolina precincts, involving "at least two instances of police assigned to precincts influencing Negroes to vote certain tickets."[29] A black man routinely got ten years on the chain gang for stealing, McCray said, while Johnston was rewarded a seat in the Senate. PDP leaders believed that a fight on the floor of the Senate would bring more national attention to the denial of voting rights in South Carolina. McKaine's protest, however, was largely symbolic. Even if a few of the ballots cast had been fraudulent, the PDP lost by a margin of 90,000 votes. With blacks outnumbering whites in twenty-two of the forty-six counties in the state, the PDP needed to expand its electorate.[30]

By 1945, McKaine believed that the Progressive Democrats needed a wider reach and saw one potential new source in the SNYC. He had come to regret that their delegation had not "staged a scene" at the 1944 Chicago Convention, admitting on the campaign trail that he wished the PDP negotiators had not capitulated. He also concluded that South Carolina activists needed to create alliances with groups outside their local contexts. In 1942, McKaine had attended the Fifth All-Southern Negro Youth Conference in Tuskegee, Alabama. At this SNYC conference, McKaine listened as Paul Robeson explained how he had "learned" in his international travels "that [the] suffering of human beings transcends race." However, internationalism did not mean forgetting local people. "We must remember the poorest worker out here on a plantation," Robeson said. "If they can throw him out they can throw me out too."[31] This understanding of the "Negro problem" in America appealed to McKaine. Soon thereafter, he wrote to the SNYC asking why they had no representation in South Carolina. "We shall be happy to push the movement," he wrote, "if you will send us one or two directives." The SNYC replied by reminding McKaine that his ally Modjeska Simkins had been a sponsor of the Tuskegee conference and had recently agreed to serve on the Adult Advisory Board to SNYC.[32]

Although the SNYC's Louis Burnham assured McKaine that "we have not . . . overlooked the important state of South Carolina," the organization had not made inroads there since its 1937 formation. The SNYC focused on Virginia and Alabama, and to some extent on Louisiana and Tennessee. As Louis Burnham put it in 1942, "Results are slow when the only resources we have are human."[33] Especially during the Second World War, the SNYC concentrated activities around its Birmingham headquarters. Yet this circling of the wagons was also partially attributable to the change in philosophy of the Communist Party (CP) to put the war abroad above all other concerns. The SNYC pitched itself as a "win-the-war agency," while also struggling against the poll tax, extralegal violence, and disfranchisement.[34] When these two aims came into conflict, the war took precedence. For example, a draft of Esther

Cooper's fiery 1942 SNYC speech, titled "Negro Youth Organizing for Victory," contained several excised passages concerning discrimination in the armed forces and the lack of black officers. "Mr. President," one such deleted passage read, "Negro youth want to be fully integrated into every phase of army life."[35] Thus, evidence suggests that the SNYC responded to pressure from the U.S. government, CP, and CIO to scale back protest during the Second World War, but a lack of resources to expand outside of Alabama would have kept the SNYC out of South Carolina in any case.[36] It was not until after the end of the war that the SNYC became more able to expand its membership, which coincided with McKaine's search for new allies to sustain South Carolina's movement.

McKaine's international experience spurred his connection to the SNYC. In early 1945, McKaine accepted a position on the SNYC's Adult Advisory Board. He was asked by F. D. Patterson, president of the Tuskegee Institute, and by Mary McLeod Bethune, founder of Bethune-Cookman College in Florida, president of the National Association of Colored Women, and former director of Negro Affairs in the National Youth Administration, and McKaine considered the appointment a "high honor."[37] Soon thereafter, he agreed to speak at the SNYC's "May First Voting Rally" in Birmingham. With the Nazis on the brink of surrender abroad, McKaine took the opportunity to show how the southern struggle for the vote was part of the worldwide movement for human rights. "Whatever we may do here in Alabama," he declared, "will affect the actions of the oppressed in South Carolina, in South Africa, in India and in Manchuria." Ordinary people had a responsibility to reorganize the world. "It is no simple coincidence that we have gathered here tonight to seek a solution to the problem of making democracy work in a limited region," McKaine said, "while, at the same time, most of the nations of the world are meeting in San Francisco with the same [intention] for the whole world." He believed that just as the newly formed United Nations must "not fail to bring to the earth universal peace and prosperity," the SNYC must "not fail to contribute our share to their efforts by [bringing] a full measure of democracy to our Southland." According to McKaine, minorities and working-class people had an opportunity to use the ballot in the United States and elsewhere to make the postwar world a democratic one.[38]

McKaine defined freedom in terms similar to his Reconstruction era ancestors from South Carolina. A generation older than most SNYC activists, McKaine saw a strong connection between this new movement and Reconstruction. The Second World War had inspired a "worldwide movement of the oppressed and underprivileged" and a new understanding that "certain undeniable rights all men should enjoy wherever they may be." One of these rights, the right to vote, was the "prerequisite to full citizenship." The ballot for McKaine represented the "badge of citizenship," because, quoting Frederick Douglass, he saw it as a means for African Americans to no longer "undervalue ourselves." A movement to secure the ballot would embolden blacks to destroy Jim Crowism. This movement would parallel the one by blacks in the 1870s, only now the "oppressed and underprivileged" would bring democracy to the world. "Emerging from our subconsciousness," McKaine told the crowd in Birmingham, "was the need again for history to repeat itself, as when during the first bright days of Reconstruction, the legislatures controlled by the newly freed slaves and the emancipated poor white gave our region its first democratic governments."[39]

McKaine's speech fell on receptive ears. More than any other southern liberal or left organization, the SNYC had sought international connections to other youth groups, concentrated on worldwide political developments in its publications, and used international circumstances to both inspire and inform its members' activism. The SNYC's *Cavalcade* featured a monthly column, "Youth around the World," which informed its readers of anticolonial struggles from Ireland to African nations to Cuba.[40] The SNYC's second conference in Tennessee had delegates from India, Ethiopia, and China; Max Yergan of the NNC and the Council on African Affairs spoke in Birmingham on "Africa and the War"; Louis Burnham fostered new contacts at the Latin American Youth for Victory Conference in Mexico City; and other SNYC members attended an international youth conference in Washington in the fall of 1942.[41] At the Washington conference, SNYC delegates heard President Roosevelt address the "youth of the world." They discussed the war and how to win the peace. "We . . . of many lands, races, cultures, religions," delegates from England, the Soviet Union, China, India, Africa, and elsewhere wrote, "affirm our determination to fight on to the complete rout of Fascism."[42]

Until the end of the Second World War, SNYC leaders mainly learned about international politics and cultures through leftist organizations and especially from the CP. SNYC members interacted with Communists during the 1930s, and many SNYC leaders either joined the party or were at least influenced by it. Exposure to the CP's international perspective benefited these SNYC activists by offering them a cogent analysis of race in a global context. It enabled them to understand their particular predicament in the U.S. South by comparing it to other contexts of class and color exploitation. Most of them had never traveled abroad, and the CP's foreign policy allowed them to imagine the Soviet Union as an alternative to American capitalism.

The reliance on the CP for international education also had its drawbacks. When Communists switched from their militant antifascism to nonaggression with Nazi Germany in the fall of 1939, the SNYC followed the same path. It declared Roosevelt a "war-monger" who only sought "new markets and colonies" for an "imperialist adventure," one which called upon the "common people . . . to do the dying," even though they were not "represented by either side." They argued that the British "[enslaved] Indian and African people," and its "ruling clique" had no democratic aims for the war. They insisted the SNYC should concentrate on "the most elementary democratic right" of voting at home.[43] In June 1941, however, the Nazis invaded the Soviet Union and the CP's foreign policy changed virtually overnight. Now the war effort abroad trumped all other causes, and again the SNYC fell in line, albeit with an emphasis on fascism at home as well. In May 1942, the SNYC made a "July 4th Declaration" in support of the war, calling Britain one of America's "mighty allies" and offering to show "our loyalty" to the war in exchange for a full right to jobs and job training in defense industries and the armed forces. When the SNYC articulated two opposite arguments for peace and war within the span of two years, it confused some of its members, but unlike the NNC, it did not suffer a major public split. In local southern contexts, the Brotherhood of Sleeping Car Porters, the NAACP, and other groups worked with its young black leaders as much as they had before. Nonetheless, even though the SNYC maintained an international vision through the war, it was not entirely of its own making.[44]

Yet the influence of international affairs also became more personal during the war years for the SNYC. Young black men enlisted and were drafted into the armed forces, traveling outside their local communities for training and then to the Pacific Theater at the end of the war. At home, news from the war dominated the press, and wartime propaganda filled the airwaves. The most important effect was that foreign affairs influenced the daily lives of southern Americans in an unprecedented way. Global circumstances now became central to the SNYC because of the war.

The growing internationalist perspective of Esther Cooper and James Jackson embodied this changed perspective. Cooper attended an International Youth Planning Conference in Mexico City in late 1941, meeting delegates from Central and South America. This conclave showed the potential for a pan-American antifascist youth movement. She concluded that the SNYC had a responsibility to change the southern United States to keep up with Latin American youth movements. Meanwhile, James Jackson became convinced that the war represented a battle between "Barbarism and World Slavery [and] freedom-loving people of the world." Like many other SNYC members, he enlisted in the army, and he spent the next three years in the service, training at Tuskegee and elsewhere before being deployed to Burma.[45]

Selections from James Jackson's letters to his wife, Esther Cooper, show an expansion of his perspective beyond the southern United States as a result of his service in the armed forces during the war. In 1944, he applauded news of Du Bois's speech about the war. He wrote that Du Bois had become the unofficial spokesman for "the silenced millions of the world's darker peoples." A year later, he concluded that the war would have a profound effect on international democracy. He had come to believe that the West "cannot honestly hope to attain a very high stage of democracy as long as the people of the Far East are held in colonial subjugation." The war produced a "ferment" among these people that "can never again be contained within the framework of ante-bellum colonial oppression." In late 1945, he declared the SNYC as part of this "ferment." After the war ended, he hoped they would "take the offensive against the Ku Klux Klan and for the fulfillment [of Roosevelt's] four freedoms." It was, Jackson concluded, a "great age to be alive in!"[46]

Chosen as a delegate to the World Youth Conference in London, Esther Cooper sailed across the Atlantic Ocean in October 1945. Sponsored by the International Youth Council, a Soviet-influenced British organization formed in 1941, the conference attracted 437 delegates from 62 countries. "There were soldiers and sailors, airmen and tankmen; former partisans and heroes from Yugoslavia and U.S.S.R.; men and women from colonial and semi-colonial countries including India, South Africa, Gambia and Nigeria; youth from Latin America and China," Cooper reported. She listened and participated in panels relating to "minority problems" in the postwar world. On one such panel, she was particularly impressed with Kitty Boomla, an Indian delegate, who described British racism against the Indian people and called for "youth in advanced countries to take practical steps to eliminate color and race discrimination in factories and workshops, trade unions, schools and colleges, and in literature." Cooper met Kwame Nkrumah, the future prime minister of Ghana, and other African leaders and reported with delight that Godfrey K. Amachree of Nigeria presented a resolution calling for "colonial countries . . . to be free and independent" as the "first need of youth" in the postwar world. When not attending official conference sessions, Cooper dined with the All-

India Trade Union representatives, visited the Africa House at the University of London, and even helped arrange a dinner for delegates of color to meet W. E. B. Du Bois, who had traveled to Manchester for the Fifth Pan-Africanist Conference. By late November, Cooper had visited with American soldiers in England, talked with the Anglo-American society in Gloucester, and spoken over the BBC about the "SNYC and conditions in the South." Finally, she secured a visa to the Soviet Union, the last destination on an itinerary that took her across war-torn Europe.[47]

Returning to the United States in February 1946, Cooper reunited with her husband, James Jackson, and together they set off on a tour of the South to speak about how their travels had informed their politics. They spoke at black colleges and in major cities, including Birmingham, Montgomery, New Orleans, and Columbia. Adult advisory board members of SNYC such as Tuskegee president Frederick Patterson and South Carolina's Modjeska Simkins helped them arrange and advertise their appearances. At churches, college chapels, and lodges, the Jacksons discussed international colonialism, the role of postwar youth, war reconversion in the United States and the Soviet Union, and their vision for world peace. They spoke about how they hoped the tour would show the "close bond of interest which exists between American Negro youth and democratic youth throughout the world." Meanwhile, in private conversations, Jackson had lambasted the CP leadership of Sam Hall during the war as "condescending paternalism to Negro members" and discussed how W. E. B. Du Bois had a better analysis of the postwar world than did black CP leaders. While neither Jackson nor Cooper abandoned the CP as an important international network and ally to the SNYC, they were determined not to be bullied by certain older CP leaders whom they thought had lost touch with grassroots people, especially in the South. Now with international experience behind them, they became more determined than ever to chart their own course, and the tour raised much-needed money for the SNYC to build its councils. Through education, organization, and militant action, they hoped to make the SNYC into a vanguard for a postwar movement.[48]

▨ ▨ ▨ McKaine and Simkins, for their part, argued that the SNYC's new path needed to go through South Carolina. They convinced SNYC members that they could reach South Carolina's younger black and progressive white populations and enter the already-established PDP network. In late 1945 and early 1946, they, along with Annie Belle Weston, a PDP leader, convinced the SNYC to focus on South Carolina for the first time. The SNYC agreed with enthusiasm and set an October date for the Seventh All-Southern Youth Congress in Columbia. They conceived the conference as a "mass mobilization of youth" with a twofold purpose. First, they would make the conference a launching point "to complete the struggle . . . begun by our forefathers in the Civil War and Reconstruction period, when they struck a mighty blow for freedom." Second, they would expand this historic struggle to encompass "the great contribution made by Negro servicemen and women in the recent war [because] we are fighting the same battle on the homefront." The planning committee hoped this past struggle would connect with the recent war for freedom and generate a new southern movement for equality.[49]

The connection between the war abroad and local civil rights struggles at home became tragically apparent in February 1946. Since the war's end, South Carolina's citizens had come into contact with returning black and white veterans on a daily basis. One such veteran, Sergeant Isaac Woodard, boarded a bus in Georgia to return home to his family in North Carolina. During his journey, Woodard asked the bus driver to make a rest stop. The driver did so reluctantly, in Batesburg, South Carolina. Once stopped, he chastised Woodard for taking too long and called the local police. Chief of Police Linwood Shull arrived and forcibly removed Woodard from the bus. A group of officers then proceeded to beat him in a nearby alley, gouging out Woodard's eyes and almost killing him. Rather then getting medical attention for him, they threw him in jail for disorderly conduct. McCray was the first person to publicize this case, which by the spring had sparked a national NAACP campaign and by the summer had become the focus of four national radio programs by Hollywood celebrity Orson Welles.[50]

The beating of Woodard reconfirmed the SNYC's decision to focus on South Carolina. The planning committee embarked on an organizing campaign across the state, training homegrown leaders with the potent mix of international politics and African American history and initiating campaigns against disfranchisement and Jim Crow facilities. "Especially do we want representatives from the so-called 'backward' communities," Weston wrote. "As you know," she continued, "we are living in an era of thought revolution and positive action. The World—even our Glorious Southland—is changing before our eyes whether we realize it or not." Traveling across the state that summer, Weston thought that educational programs for African Americans in these "unprivileged sections" of South Carolina would make them the "citizens of tomorrow."[51] Meanwhile, Modjeska Simkins worked tirelessly to promote the SNYC in Columbia. Simultaneously involved in local campaigns for recreation and for hospital facilities for blacks, Simkins employed "personal 'button-holings'" to get people to join. In late July, Simkins wrote to the SNYC headquarters: "Picture me getting out not less than 10,000 cards and letters in this heat."[52] McKaine, having landed a paid field representative job for the Southern Conference for Human Welfare (SCHW), embarked on a voter registration tour. The SCHW, an interracial organization with liberal and left members, had an overlapping membership and strong alliance with the SNYC. McKaine worked for both groups in his tour of southern states for voter registration.

At the beginning of the tour, McKaine helped lead a SNYC-organized march of veterans in Birmingham. Since the war ended, the SNYC had organized a veterans' committee in Alabama and elected as their leader the twenty-one-year-old Kenneth Kennedy, a Talladega College student who had served with distinction overseas in the Battle of the Bulge. In January 1946, McKaine came to Birmingham to help launch the SNYC voting drive led by veterans. Marching double file through the streets to the Jefferson County Courthouse, a hundred veterans attempted to register. Most were denied, based on their failure to answer the registrar's questions to his satisfaction. But the registrants did not intimidate easily. When the registrar asked one veteran, "What is the government?" he responded defiantly, "The government is the people." Although most of the delegation did not successfully register on that day, they made a powerful gesture by marching in uniform. They demanded the ballot as a human right of citizens and veterans. By the next election, Alabama's black voter registration had doubled. Elsewhere, McKaine registered thousands of new black voters in places like Norfolk, Virginia, and Savannah, Georgia. Simkins applauded McKaine's successful field work but hoped that SCHW leaders would assign McKaine to his home state. In July, Simkins wrote to her allies in South Carolina, asking them to send postcards to SCHW to demand McKaine's return. Simkins called the situation in South Carolina "urgent," and when McKaine returned in the fall he proved instrumental in organizing the Columbia Youth Legislature, the SNYC's upcoming South Carolina conference, which it organized as a mock congressional session.[53]

The SNYC also sought to train a new crop of leaders in South Carolina. For ten days in August, it led a Leadership Training Institute at Harbison Junior College, just outside the small town of Irmo, which included practical training in writing press releases, public speaking, and organizational techniques, along with daily classes in the "History of the Negro in Politics," "Winning

Right-to-vote march, Birmingham, Alabama, 1946. Veterans returned from military service during the Second World War to demand their citizenship rights. O. E. McKaine, black Communists like coal miner Henry Mayfield, and SNYC leaders helped organize militant marches to the local registrar in Birmingham and elsewhere to demand the right to vote. From folder 37, box 2, James E. Jackson and Esther Cooper Jackson Photographs Collection. Courtesy of the Tamiment Library, New York University.

the Ballot," and "World Affairs." The SNYC also benefited from the participation of the Highlander Folk School, the progressive educational institute in Tennessee for labor unions and other activists. Two Highlander teachers, Mary Lawrence and Bill Elkuss, attended the institute, teaching some of the courses, offering critiques to SNYC leaders during the week, and bringing materials from Highlander that the school had gathered over the years. The two dozen participants lived at the college, and when not in class sessions, they spent their leisure time discussing politics, singing spirituals and labor songs, dancing to the radio, and playing sports.[54]

One SNYC goal was to inspire these new leaders to think differently about race. During the 1930s, Franz Boas and other anthropologists had debunked theories of biological determinism based on race. Applying this new anthropology, SNYC teachers challenged race as a biological category and provoked students to rethink notions that they had become accustomed to in the southern United States. A "True-or-False Test" administered to the students at the Leadership Institute illuminates what the SNYC intended. The test asked the students, "What do you know about race?" along with statements to evaluate such as "skin color is the most important physical characteristic," "man's physical appearance is affected by his environment," "American Negroes look to Europe, Africa and America for their ancestry," and "the blood of Negro and white people is the same." Other questions about Germans, Danes, Jews, Africans, and Europeans put race into a world context. Exercises like these, the SNYC educators hoped, would prompt leaders to see their second-class racial status in the United States as historically contingent rather than a fact of nature, thus challenging the underpinnings of Jim Crow ideology, which tied racial "customs" to all daily activities and customs in southern society.[55]

The Highlander teachers who attended the Irmo sessions applauded the SNYC's educational work. They especially approved of the choice of courses and noted that a "lack of group spirit was not a problem at this particular Institute." For the students, whose average age was eighteen and whose professions ranged from teachers to union organizers to college students, the institute sparked further activism. Many of them would participate in discussion sessions during the October SNYC conference and become the local leaders of SNYC councils in Irmo, Moncks Corner, Orangeburg, and other small towns in South Carolina.[56]

Yet an alliance between these new SNYC councils and local Progressive Democrats across the state did not come easily. Since the Chicago Democratic Party Convention, the PDP had splintered between militants like McKaine on the one hand and the NAACP and business professionals on the other, who saw help from outsiders as problematic and internationalism as reckless. In March, A. J. Clement, a leader of the PDP in Charleston and an official of the North Carolina Mutual Life Insurance Company, pressured McCray to oust McKaine from the party. PDP leaders, Clement reported, had been grumbling ever since McKaine had sought alliances with groups outside of South Carolina. These Progressive Democrats imagined their party as a political group within precincts that challenged lily-white Democrats in local elections. Talk of alliances from outside the state, not to mention outside the country, frightened them. Rumors circulated about "outsiders" taking over the PDP, and Clement urged "the leaving of our ranks by McKaine" for the good of the party. During the spring, McCray deliberated over whether to endorse McKaine's plans or to remove him to placate the conservative wing of the PDP. McCray worried about the presence of CIO-PAC members and other outsiders in his state and even began to question Modjeska Simkins, due to her willingness to form alliances with radicals from outside South Carolina. From Nashville, McKaine wrote back a stirring endorsement of Simkins and convinced his ally "Mac" to side with those who sought to push the PDP outside of strict local political boundaries. While sympathetic to his PDP "domestic troubles," McKaine told McCray, "Don't let UNPROVED friends cause you to always become suspicious of those who have never let you down. . . . Stick with Mrs. Simkins." After all, McKaine concluded, taking broad-based action would be a "shot in the arm for the PDP," something the party had desperately needed since the cessation of the tumultuous events of 1944.[57]

McCray did stick with Simkins, and they both began to fuse PDP goals with those of the SNYC. In the spring of 1946, the SNYC joined the state's Progressive Democrats and NAACP chapters to organize "Jim Crow Sunday" to boycott all segregated theaters and local transportation systems on the first Sunday of every month. "In the eyes of God," one pamphlet declared, "ALL men truly, whether Negro or white, are brothers."[58] In August, McCray implored that "Believers in Human Rights for ALL MEN" should boycott every place that segregated white from black in South Carolina. Any person who supported the white primary or used a facility that housed segregated political activities, McCray declared, "is an ENEMY OF AMERICAN DEMOCRACY whether he realizes it or not" and "must be made to pay for his un-Democratic acts." Calling those who continued to support the white primary "traitorous," the PDP committed itself to the SNYC and the SCHW for a human rights struggle.[59]

Nationally, SNYC members participated in an NNC campaign that expressed its internationalism by taking an unprecedented step: petitioning the United Nations "on behalf of 13 million oppressed Negro citizens." Drafted by delegates to its June 1946 Detroit convention (including representatives from the SNYC) and supplemented by eight pages of evidence gathered by the historian Herbert Aptheker, the NNC petition called for an international investigation into "economic, social, and political discrimination resulting from racial oppression" in the United States under Article 71 of the UN Charter. The NNC expressed "profound regret" in a letter to the secretary-general of the United Nations, Trygve Lie, that blacks "having failed to find relief through constitutional appeal, find ourselves forced to bring this vital issue" to the newly created international body. The petition's announcement was followed by a "universal storm of applause" from the 1,000 delegates in Detroit, and it made international headlines after its formal presentation to the secretary of the UN's Commission on Human Rights on June 6 in New York. "It will be interesting how the worthies who run the government," a People's Voice editorial surmised, "will try to squirm off the hot spot they now occupy by virtue of the . . . petition."[60]

Following its submission to the United Nations, Dorothy Burnham brought the petition's spirit to Paris to expose southern forms of fascism in an international forum. As an SNYC delegate to the World Federation Democratic Youth Conference, a group that functioned as a junior United Nations, Burnham appealed to her fellow delegates to condemn the "growing Ku Klux Klan movement and wave of terror against Negroes in the United States." Convinced by her urgent appeal, the delegates, from fifty-three countries, issued a joint statement that cited this terror as "one of the most active fascist forces in the world today," threatening the international cooperative effort for the "consolidation of peace and realization of democracy."[61] Back home, the NNC and the SNYC embarked on a campaign to obtain 5 million endorsement signatures from U.S. citizens, as well as from dozens of international organizations, which included the British Guiana Trade Union Council, the West Indian Negro Association in Trinidad, the Women's International Democratic Federation, and the Barbados Progressive League. While the petitioners waited for a response, they held people's tribunals in several cities but especially looked forward to the upcoming Columbia Youth Legislature, where black and white southerners would formulate their roles against Jim Crow in the coming international freedom movement.[62]

In October 1946, over 800 southern delegates convened at the Township Auditorium in Columbia, South Carolina, to map out a human rights struggle for the Southland.[63] "We do not come together as a mock legislature," the SNYC wrote in the conference program. "We do not intend that the laws which we make here shall end here." For those three days, the delegates felt like the fate of the world was in their hands. They debated resolutions in conference sessions on youth and labor, peace, veterans, and education and held hearings on voting and civil liberties.[64] The sessions "buzzed with excitement," according to North Carolina delegate Junius Scales, who also described Columbia's black community as a "solid bastion of support." Scales, a white University of North Carolina student who had joined the CP, expressed surprise that "grass-roots Negro youth from all over the South" dominated to such an extent that "Party regulars were lost among them." According to a press release, the SNYC chose South Carolina because it represented the only state where blacks legally could not participate in the Democratic primaries, but certainly the choice also came as the result of the PDP formation that so openly challenged black disfranchisement. The mock legislature convened in Columbia to show the world that the next generation of blacks and whites could bring democracy to the southern United States.[65]

The legislature was not just another conference. Three of the most significant African American leaders of the first half of the twentieth century served as the keynote speakers on successive evenings. The SNYC invited Adam Clayton Powell Jr., Paul Robeson, and W. E. B. Du Bois to Columbia. For a weekend at least, this roster of speakers coming southward reversed the flow of the years of the Second World War when civil rights opportunities drew southerners to the North. Now the SNYC would bring New York to Columbia to signal that the postwar battlefront for civil rights would be a southern one. Its leaders billed Powell as the "modern statesman" from New York City who "led the people on the picket lines" before becoming the "clarion voice of justice" in the U.S. House of Representatives.[66] The SNYC deemed Robeson its hero. His call for democracy had been embraced by "the hopeful and striving men and women of all nations and colors." Southern youth also called Robeson their hero because he simultaneously represented a "genius" and an "everyman," a symbolic embodiment of African Americans across class and geographic divides. SNYC saved its highest honor, though, for W. E. B. Du Bois. As an NAACP leader, Pan-African Congress president, historian, and teacher, Du Bois represented the "foremost champion of colonial and oppressed people everywhere." SNYC leaders presented him with an award for past service, reasoning that without him their movement would never have taken root.[67]

The adoration of Du Bois, Robeson, and Powell only represented part of the delegates' employment of the past to draw inspiration. Its organizers had lined the walls of the Township Auditorium with the portraits of southern blacks who had been elected to federal office during Radical Reconstruction in the early 1870s. Seeing these portraits, delegate Jack O'Dell remembered them as "fascinating" because "I did not know that there had been black congressmen."[68] One portrait was of Hiram Revels, a Mississippian who became the first African American elected to the Senate in 1870, and whose grandson, Revels Cayton, went on to serve as executive secretary of the NNC, personifying the connection between southern youth of the 1940s and their ancestors. "The movement of the 'new South'" today, Esther Cooper declared, "was foreshadowed in the glorious achievements of the Reconstruction period, when white men and black men shared political power in true representative state governments." Cooper's vision of Reconstruction echoed a group of black revisionist scholars who since the mid-1930s had sought to undermine the dominant school of professional historians led by Columbia University William Dunning, who depicted blacks as unprepared for citizenship and the era as "tragic."[69] The SNYC saw itself as the vanguard in dismissing the Dun-

Allen University president Samuel Richard Higgins and Esther Cooper Jackson greet
Paul Robeson (left), a longtime NNC ally, upon his arrival in Columbia, South Carolina,
for the SNYC's Southern Youth Legislature, which began on October 17, 1946. From
folder 47, box 2, James E. Jackson and Esther Cooper Jackson Photographs Collection.
Courtesy of the Tamiment Library, New York University.

ning school and validating Radical Reconstruction. African American and
Marxist scholars resurrected this history, but the SNYC made it matter.

SNYC activists especially embraced Howard Fast's 1944 novel *Freedom
Road* because it mixed contemporary leftist politics with the postbellum history of South Carolina. The novel centered on Gideon Jackson, a former plantation slave, who fought in the Union army, served in Congress, and helped
organize a farm for poor whites and freedmen. *Freedom Road* ended, however, when the Ku Klux Klan destroyed the farm and killed Jackson. The novel
forcefully argued that Reconstruction did not fail because of corruption or
poor planning but because white supremacists terrorized its adherents out
of existence. "Not only were the material things wiped out and people slain,"
Fast wrote in the afterword, "but the very memory was expunged."[70]

The use of Fast's novel helped revive the memory of black militancy during the previous Reconstruction after the Civil War. "The post-war world is going to be a Reconstruction era," Adam Clayton Powell Jr. concluded in a review of *Freedom Road* in the NNC's *Congress View*. He believed that "if black and white cannot live together . . . then every sacrifice that the fighting men . . . have made will have been in vain." Fast worked with the NNC's cultural committee to organize events in Harlem, Detroit, and along the West Coast. The SNYC encouraged southern youth to read the book by sponsoring an essay contest in 1944. Paula Robeson (no relation to Paul Robeson) from Talladega College in Alabama won the prize, writing, "In very few, if any history classes would one learn . . . [that] Negroes and whites were meeting together, working together, living together and pledging loyalty for the benefit of all." This interracial cooperation showed that there were "no half-way measures about the supreme matter of living together" and insisted that "it is for us, the youth of today, to find or produce, or to become such men" like Gideon Jackson. *Freedom Road*, as applied by the NNC and SNYC, presented "a promise for the future."[71]

The memory of Reconstruction was never so poignant, however, as when the Columbia Youth Legislature convened. Set in South Carolina like *Freedom Road*, the meeting brought Fast's novel to life inside the Township Auditorium. The white delegates from the University of North Carolina felt as though they had "entered . . . a future we had only dreamed of" and felt the "sheer joy of communication with Negroes as people."[72] Then, on Saturday night Howard Fast appeared in Columbia. Fast recalled speaking with a sharecropper en route to the conference, about thirty miles outside of town. The sharecropper had heard of the coming conference in Columbia and told Fast that while there may have been a lot of talk in New York, there would be "a lot of talk in Columbia too" this weekend. When Fast asked what he meant, the sharecropper replied, "Folks talk and they get to moving, don't they?" Fast concurred. For the "first time since Reconstruction in 1868," he observed, "a thousand Negro and white delegates were meeting together in a youth legislature." The portraits of blacks elected during Reconstruction "were only fitting [in] that they above all others should watch the truth emerging from their gallant and much-traduced struggle for freedom and equality." Although more than seventy years separated their struggles, Fast concluded that the "South is changing" again, and the "counterrevolution" won by elite whites would be overturned.[73]

Following Howard Fast was the personification of Gideon Jackson: Paul Robeson. After singing "Go Down Moses," "Scandalize My Name," and

"Water Boy" to set the mood, Robeson compared the urgent need for action in 1946 with Reconstruction. Robeson thundered, "The history of the Negro people as shown in *Freedom Road*, as shown in the lives of men like Denmark Vesey, has been one of continuous struggle." The previous month, Robeson had led the American Crusade to End Lynching to Washington, a campaign that had demanded that President Truman prosecute those responsible for lynching African Americans. This 3,000-person protest at the Lincoln Memorial, co-chaired by Robeson and Albert Einstein, was composed of people from thirty-eight states, including delegates from the SNYC and the NNC. The United States, Robeson said, had no authority to take the lead in prosecuting Nazis at the Nuremberg War Crimes Trial when southern whites could lynch returning black soldiers with impunity. Rebuffed by Truman when he led a delegation to Washington in September for action against lynching, Robeson hoped to make good on his threat in Columbia that if the president did not do something to stop lynch mobs, "the Negroes will." "Today," he said to the SNYC delegates, "the Negro people refuse to be shot down." The audience responded with tremendous applause.[74]

For all its invocations of the past, the SNYC saw this contemporary reconstruction as international. Robeson told the audience how he had witnessed the destruction of Spain's democracy and worried that the same fate awaited America. Drawing on another international parallel, Robeson explained how in France he had seen how the Vichy government "attacked minorities like the Negro people and the Jewish people. Next, they called everybody a Communist and before you knew it, the jails were filled." The lesson of the war was that people had to stand up for each other when government tried to suppress dissent, freedom of speech, and the rights of its minorities. "It is our great destiny," he concluded, that black southerners act like their grandparents did during Reconstruction and take control of the debate over race and rights so that conservatives do not succeed in "scaring every liberal from fighting for the rights of the oppressed people."[75]

To the SNYC, battles over U.S. citizenship advanced a broader struggle for human rights. At the conference, delegates from Latin America and Africa spoke in person, and telegrams from other youth leaders from abroad were read aloud. Drawing out the historical influence of the Haitian revolution on the United States, Theodore Baker spoke on how the contemporary U.S. government worried that "a country of Negroes, free and independent, desiring to manage its own conditions of life and advancing on the road to progress would be a bad example for the 13 million Negroes who still struggle for their liberty." He urged the southern youth in attendance to see colonialism and disfranchisement as intertwined, saying that the "occupation of the American dollar . . . constitutes another form of slavery." These delegates connected African American struggles to other peoples of color. "May I remind you that in Africa you have a group of your own race who are also struggling to maintain sovereignty," a delegate from Liberia said. "If they fail, the race has failed. If they succeed, the race has succeeded." Less profound but symbolizing America's hypocritical social construction of race, McKaine noted that "the brown skinned Haitian delegate" had "no difficulty procuring a room in a small white hotel" that barred African Americans of lighter skin tones. By taking the struggle of black Americans out of its local context, the delegates exposed Jim Crow as illogical rather than natural and defined resistance as a responsibility to humankind rather than an exercise in futility.[76]

The next day, W. E. B. Du Bois brought the conference to a closing crescendo by declaring South Carolina the "firing line" of the struggle for human rights. This line was not "simply for the emancipation of the American Negro and the Negroes of the West Indies [but for] the emancipation for the colored races; and for the emancipation of the white slaves of modern capitalistic monopoly."[77] No person represented the convergence of these Reconstruction and international ideas better than Du Bois. He published his doctoral thesis in 1896, *The Suppression of the African Slave Trade to the United States of America*; wrote a 1906 essay in *Collier's Weekly* that declared "the Negro problem in America" to be "but a local phase of a world problem"; made a seminal contribution to postbellum historiography with *Black Reconstruction*; and had recently convened the Fifth Pan Africanist Conference in England.[78] Inside the church at Allen University in Columbia, Du Bois tied all of the strands of the conference together.[79] South Carolina stood at the center of the world, Du Bois believed, because it "has led the South for a century" in trying to "build slavery upon freedom" and placing "tyranny upon democracy" and "mob violence on law." In short, South Carolina would become a test of whether the postwar world would become "a reasonable world." Du Bois believed that "reason" would prevail if southern black youth took up the cause of human rights.[80]

While the SNYC discussed the postwar world, Charleston native James Byrnes negotiated its fate. One of President Truman's first decisions after the death of Roosevelt was to appoint Byrnes, an odious figure to many African Americans, as secretary of state.[81] African Americans asked how a man who had defeated a federal antilynching law and denied the right to vote to African

Americans in his home state could lead the United Nations to protect human rights and bring peace. South Carolina activists responded to this appointment by issuing a handbill: "Our Jimmy Byrnes . . . is trying to teach the Bulgarians democracy, [yet] only two out of ten people in his home state take part in elections." The handbill called for the end of the poll tax and for equality of economic opportunity, two issues "our famous son" had overlooked in his mission for world democracy.[82] Despite his busy travel schedule as secretary of state, Byrnes remained aware of the developing movement against him. In the fall of 1946, his politics and those of his critics converged, when Byrnes returned from months of peace negotiations in Paris and the youth legislature convened in Columbia.

The states' rights defense of southern Democrats seemed to contradict Byrnes's role as an international mediator. The U.S. government in the postwar period had much more of a vested interest in the internal political affairs of other nations. Dean Acheson of the State Department declared that "this government is resolved that the rights of religious, political and economic minorities shall be protected" and "is defending the rights of weaker peoples democratically." Would Byrnes, upon his return to the United States, echo Acheson's sentiments? On the same Friday night that the SNYC conference began, Byrnes delivered a national radio address to outline the details of what he had accomplished in Paris and of how the United States and Soviet Union would achieve a lasting peace in the postwar world. He worried about "continued if not increasing tension between us and the Soviet Union" but still expressed confidence in a "people's peace." When it came to local sovereignty, Byrnes's statements seemed less clear. "War is inevitable," he told America, "only if states fail to tolerate and respect the rights of other states to ways of life they cannot and do not share." In future negotiations he hoped for a "reconciliation of difference and not a yielding by one state to the arbitrary will of the other."[83]

Byrnes's rhetoric is open to at least two interpretations. In one sense, his "tolerance" alluded to a "spheres of influence" solution between the Soviet Union and the United States. Surveying the exchanges in Paris between Byrnes and Molotov, a *New York Times* editorial suggested this possibility. "If the stability of [Europe] cannot be restored there may be a kind of stability in each of the ruptured halves." The problem with this stability though, was that "it may be a stability that will impoverish many millions of helpless people."[84] Similarly, the editors of the *Chicago Defender* prophesized that "so long as the 'get tough with Russia' attitude animates our entire foreign policy, just so long will any real action in behalf of the colonial peoples be difficult."[85] In short, this peace would be at the expense of minorities like African Americans in the United States because local tyrants would continue to rule without international interference. Yet the rhetoric of Byrnes and especially of Acheson suggested another interpretation as well. Byrnes's plea for tolerance of difference also implied that peoples should have the freedom to establish their own democracies. Supporting this latter interpretation, Byrnes said, "No state should ignore or veto the aggregate sentiments of mankind."[86] These varied interpretations suggest that Americans did not yet define U.S. foreign policy in Cold War dichotomies; Byrnes's October 1946 speech implied at least two paths for a postwar world.

The delegates and leaders in Columbia, however, did not mince words about Byrnes. They thought they knew him too well. "While Secretary Byrnes was making his nationwide radio address," a snyc press release read, "2,680 citizens of his home state joined with delegates . . . in vigorous condemnation of his hypocritical policy of making speeches about democracy in Europe and denying democracy to millions in the South." The delegates greeted a resolution for his removal from office with "loud applause."[87] Paul Robeson reinforced this resolution on Saturday night. He declared that "one of the weaknesses of Mr. Byrnes' position in Paris" was that "America cannot escape [its] own crimes."[88]

Nobody at the conference, however, worried more about Byrnes's power than Du Bois. The two men had a history of animus dating back to the First World War and the summer of 1919, when race riots had erupted across America, resulting in at least 100 deaths. Du Bois had hoped this racial violence would dissipate with the return of black veterans, who had proven their citizenship through military service. Byrnes also fretted over the postwar violence, which included a riot in Charleston, but for different reasons. He blamed the disturbances on black veterans in general, and on W. E. B. Du Bois specifically. From the floor of the Senate, Byrnes called for the prosecution of Du Bois under the Espionage Act, though his real target may have been blacks in his home state. Soon after his tirade, Byrnes wrote to an editor of a Charleston paper that "if there were a fair registration, [black citizens] would have a slight majority in our state. We cannot idly brush these facts aside. Unfortunate though it may be," he concluded, "our consideration of every question must include this consideration of the race question."[89] With this history in mind, Du Bois told the youth legislature, "Byrnes is the end of a long series of men," including South Carolina's own race-baiter, Ben Tillman, "whose

eternal damnation is the fact he looked truth in the face and did not see it."
Like Jan Smuts, who called for human rights in the United Nations while re-
pressing blacks in South Africa, Byrnes must "yield to the forward march of
civilization."[90]

This SNYC critique of American foreign policy provoked an immediate
response. Governor Ransome J. Williams was among the many white southern Democrats who counterattacked. "It is regrettable," he told the press,
"that 'Communistic elements' came boldly and brazenly into South Carolina in an effort to undermine Secretary of State Byrnes's position."[91] The
local white press also interpreted the SNYC conference as subversive. Ignoring
other components of the proceedings, the *Columbia Record* headline quoted
only one white delegate and headlined its article: "Russia Is Praised at Negro
Meeting." More direct, the *Beaufort Gazette* editorialized that the conference
showed that "there is no place" in the Democratic Party for those who "vilify
the names of such great South Carolinians as John C. Calhoun, Benjamin
Ryan Tillman, and E. D. (Cotton Ed) Smith, whose memories are revered
by all true South Carolinians to say nothing of Secretary James F. Byrnes,
who fortunately in these days of international discord is still in the land of
the living."[92] But most surprising, and portending liberal anti-Communist
policies to come, the *New York Times* reporter proved the most dismissive.
The SNYC's criticisms of Byrnes "revealed the degree to which the Communist Party has been able to guide the actions of the conference," the *Times*
reported. As evidence, the author cited a session at which a debate between
delegates about the labor movement became a "wholesale denouncement of
the AFL." The article omitted the fact that blacks had denounced the AFL's
discriminatory policies for a decade, and even the author admitted that the
attack on Byrnes "was made easy by emphasizing that he is a native of South
Carolina, and for a long time has been a leader of the Democratic party [and]
has persisted in barring Negroes from . . . political affairs."[93]

The real reason for the alarm over the conference, the SNYC surmised,
was the potential effectiveness of its "program of action." In a stern rebuttal to the governor and other state legislators who condemned the meeting,
SNYC leaders argued that his attack was an "obvious attempt to discredit the
highly successful conference." The resolution against Byrnes that "has drawn
your fire," they wrote, "expressed the increasing recognition of the American
people that the foreign and domestic [policies] of our government are inseparable, and that our relations with other powers cannot be entrusted to those
who represent the most backward and undemocratic policies in internal af-

fairs." Importantly, the rebuttal included discussions of American troops in China, the lend-lease policy of Britain that resulted in killings in Indonesia, "bullying" in the Balkans, and the "hysterical 'get tough with Russia' attitude'" of Byrnes's foreign policy.[94]

Criticism from the press aside, the conference made a deep impression on those in attendance. Rose Mae Catchings, a YWCA leader and SNYC member from Tennessee, wrote that "many of the sessions so moved me that tears of joy and satisfaction well-up into my eyes; at times breath became only short-winded gasps. It was great, great, great!" Catchings believed that "[we] now have a rare and extraordinary opportunity," and after the conference she became a lifelong activist for human rights.[95] The conference also convinced W. E. B. Du Bois of the SNYC's promise. Since the early 1940s, Du Bois had singled out Louis Burnham, James Jackson, and Esther Cooper as the "coming young leaders of the South." Thereafter, Du Bois kept apprised of the SNYC and had an especially close friendship with Esther Cooper.[96] After leaving Columbia, Du Bois compared the conference to the 1909 founding of the NAACP, thirty-five years before. It took "rare courage" for the SNYC to host this conference in the South, he wrote, and unlike the "well-to-do 'Leaders'" in the North, SNYC leaders "take their stand on the firing line of race-relations."[97]

The SNYC movement, mapped out at its mock legislature in Columbia, got off to a promising start. In early January, the organization sent a delegation led by Edward Weaver to Washington that represented eleven southern states. The delegates—among them a black veteran from Mississippi, a white housewife from New Orleans, and a black college student from South Carolina—lobbied for the support of legislators on Capitol Hill for the SNYC's eight-point legislative program. Welcomed by progressive legislators like Idaho senator Glenn Taylor, who had supported the "Oust Bilbo" campaign, activists also got commitments from less-sympathetic representatives like Lister Hill of Alabama, who agreed to back the anti–poll tax bill. Meanwhile, the Crusade to End Lynching reconvened in Washington to protest the increased racial violence in the South. Two months earlier, an all-white jury in South Carolina had taken only a half hour to exonerate the police officers from Batesburg of all charges in the beating of Isaac Woodard. Crusade to End Lynching participants blamed President Truman for this injustice and gathered in Washington to implore him and Congress to pass a national anti-lynching statute.[98]

Meanwhile, delegates from the Columbia Youth Legislature returned home

Rose Mae Catchings speaks at the Township Auditorium before the sessions of the SNYC's Columbia Youth Legislature, October 18–20, 1946. Southern Negro Youth Congress Photograph Collection. Courtesy of the Moorland-Spingarn Archives, Howard University, Washington, D.C.

to local councils. In towns like Moncks Corner and Anderson and at schools including Allen University in Columbia and Harbison Junior College, enthusiastic local council presidents reported their membership lists and activities. For example, the three SNYC clubs in Moncks Corner organized a joint conference on labor, health, agriculture, and education. As a guest speaker, the SNYC's Annie Belle Weston held the audience "spellbound" as she discussed her travels to foreign nations and the "Negro's part in his own freedom."

Other councils fought for a local library, registered voters, and conducted busing surveys. "For the first time in the history of little Moncks Corner," one council later reported, "[Negro] school children are riding to school in school buses." The president of one of these councils, Leroy Aiken, a former student at the Leadership Training Institute in Irmo, worked with local SNYC councils and PDP members to achieve this small but significant victory. By the spring of 1947, SNYC reported eleven councils and clubs in South Carolina with a paid membership of over 600.[99]

As the head of the state PDP, McCray believed that the SNYC councils and the PDP could bring the generations into a collaborative movement. Quoting the expression "as South Carolina goes, so goes the South," McCray reported in 1947 how the PDP had elected councilmen in small towns like Conway and come in second in many other local electoral contests during the last election. "Only this last summer," he continued, the PDP idea had spread to cities like Little Rock, Birmingham, Jackson, and Miami. He saw the PDP as both an independent party and a "bludgeon between the major parties" to get African Americans the vote.[100]

The SNYC also secured the services of Herbert Aptheker for a tour of southern colleges. Aptheker, the noted white Communist scholar of African American history, had formed a close relationship with SNYC members the previous year through Du Bois. Organizing for the Columbia Youth Legislature, Modjeska Simkins wrote to SNYC headquarters in Birmingham that she "was particularly happy to hear . . . [that] Mr. Aptheker" would attend. At the conference, Aptheker spoke and led a two-hour discussion on "The Negro and Politics: An Historical Introduction." After the conference, the "innumerable requests" from delegates for his "splendid address" convinced Louis Burnham to hire Aptheker for a monthlong speaking tour of black southern colleges.[101]

In early February, Aptheker set off on a twelve-stop tour of the South to speak on black history and on how scholars and "fighters for the Negro people's liberation . . . have been attempting to rescue this past from oblivion and vilification." He lectured to large gatherings in college chapels, taught as many as six classes in a single day, and discussed the SNYC with students at informal gatherings. Aptheker focused his speeches on how the "United States announced its entry into the world of nations with a flaming manifesto of revolution" in the eighteenth century, yet "twenty percent of [the] country's population was in chains." The contradiction was compounded, Aptheker argued, as the United States took on a larger role in the world through the United Nations while its African American and working-class white populations in the South remained disfranchised. After Aptheker's University of North Carolina visit, SNYC vice president and fellow Communist Junius Scales wrote that he had "never seen an audience so impressed." He specifically mentioned Aptheker's "magnificent" handling of the question-and-answer session and reported that "a Negro preacher in the audience thanked him from the floor for the service he was rendering his people, and the entire audience applauded at length." Aptheker's six pamphlets at this event and others sold out, so the SNYC distributed copies of the newly printed Du Bois "Behold the Land Speech" to recruit new members. The success of Aptheker's tour emboldened young southerners to question their place in the South, past and present. Contrary to the conclusions of the Dunning school of historical thought and even of the contemporary sociologist Gunnar Myrdal that blacks became "enfranchised without their asking for it," Aptheker argued that blacks won the right to vote through their own activism, which now assumed a global dimension.[102]

◈ ◈ ◈ Near the end of his tour, Aptheker spent a weekend at the Columbia home of Mrs. Simkins to assess the SNYC's progress in the four months since the historic conference.[103] Soon thereafter, Simkins wrote to Aptheker expressing feelings of both hope and distress. In early January, Secretary of State James Byrnes resigned due to personal battles with Truman over the president's "Fair Deal" reform policies, which included a civil rights platform. South Carolina activists were vindicated in their assertion that the Jim Crow politician Byrnes had no legitimacy in broadcasting freedom to the world when "forty-three percent of the [state's] electorate" had had the vote stolen from them.[104] On the basis of this disfranchisement, an almost exclusively white voting bloc in South Carolina had elected segregationist Strom Thurmond, a Fifteenth Amendment violation that the federal government brushed aside, choosing instead to intensify a "witch hunt that seems hellbent against all who would want the right thing done about anything." Although she was "still slugging" in Columbia, Simkins reported that "general affairs in the Capital relative to the world picture" made her "all torn up about everything."[105]

The lack of connection with organized labor represented one reason Simkins felt "torn up" about the movement's future direction in South Carolina. At the end of the Second World War, the CIO leadership recognized the largely unorganized South as the Achilles' heel of organized labor. So long as race continued to divide industrial workers below the Mason-Dixon Line, they remained unorganized, with low pay and no protections, and northern industrialists increasingly took advantage of these southern conditions by moving their factories there. With the wartime no-strike clause rescinded, the CIO leadership decided to commit hundreds of organizers and upwards of a million dollars to a campaign they called "Operation Dixie."[106] Yet the program would prove doomed nearly from the start due to the cautious outlook of the CIO in 1945. The hierarchical leadership that Van Bittner had established in the steel industry after NNC organizers helped create a powerful union in the North, as well as the lack of CIO support for the independent SNYC union movement among tobacco workers in Richmond during the late 1930s, revealed that the CIO leadership was less interested in a "culture of unity" than the narrower goals of dues and union recognition.

Osceola McKaine tried to bridge both sides of this coalition, as it seemed to come apart along the seams of race. In a state of shock over the behavior of CIO unionists he encountered as a field organizer for the SCHW in 1946, McKaine wrote to CIO vice president Allan Haywood that "a certain number of white CIO organizers in this region" might "be readily mistaken for AFL . . . if one judged them by racial attitudes." These organizers "should be told," he continued, "that the CIO expects them . . . whenever and wherever possible, to practice what the CIO preaches." CIO organizers, Haywood replied, dealt with race in a "realistic way." Only a month later, McKaine saw the fragmenting results of this policy, as blacks in South Carolina and elsewhere "turn[ed] their backs" on interracialism. Thus, although critical of the CIO for its lack of internal civil rights unionism, McKaine also felt compelled to defend it from the alternative of segregated locals and black nationalism. Blacks and whites won the war "on the basis of unity," he said in one statement, and the postwar CIO represented an "outstanding example in which white and Negro laborers are cooperating."[107]

The CIO's fear of turning off racist white workers, however, had direct implications for the SNYC. The CIO did not want its field workers to engage in political activities, but at the same time it expected to organize laborers in the racially divided South. The SNYC had hoped for strong union representation at its Columbia meeting, noting that its movement needed to be "connected with the CIO drive to organize 1 million underpaid workers in the South."[108] Its leaders invited Philip Murray, the head of the CIO, to the conference, but Murray declined. They instead received a commitment from Mike Quill, the white Communist leader of the Transport Workers Union in New York, to keynote the labor session. But Quill did not show up at the last minute.[109] As

Van Bittner, the head of Operation Dixie, made clear on October 19, 1946 — coincidentally during the same weekend as the Columbia Youth Legislature — the CIO leadership wanted nothing to do with the SNYC or "any other organization living off the CIO."[110] The SNYC's militant and international agenda, most prominently represented in Columbia by Du Bois and the Council on African Affairs, which had forged connections to international trade unions, illuminated a view of unionism that made Bittner queasy. Mid-level CIO organizers, especially black ones, saw the SNYC's goals as parallel to their own. These delegates came from mine, furniture, public, steel, and tobacco unions, all within the left wing of the CIO. The CIO's national leaders, meanwhile, became increasingly antagonistic.[111]

Tobacco unions seemed a promising avenue into southern labor since SNYC members had organized several thousand of these workers in the late 1930s. By the Second World War, the most militant black organizing drive emerged in Winston-Salem, North Carolina.[112] Tobacco organizers there showed that the achievements the SNYC made in 1930s Richmond had similar potential in the 1940s Carolinas. SNYC endorsed the activities with Theodosia Simpson, a key leader in this black-majority union movement who became a board member of the SNYC. The SNYC hoped to spread the union to other tobacco regions like Charleston, and Simpson attempted to organize SNYC councils in Winston-Salem for younger tobacco workers and children of older union members.[113] On his February tour, Aptheker spoke to thousands of workers in the Camel Local in Winston-Salem, a union described by the SNYC as "unique in developing a young Negro working class leadership, specifically among women tobacco workers."[114] But organizers like Simpson were exceptional in the CIO. Soon after the conference, the branch of the Food, Tobacco, Agricultural, and Allied Workers called a strike against American Tobacco in Charleston while launching organizing drives in Columbia and Sumter, as well as at locations in other states. Unlike the previous SNYC organizing role in Richmond against American Tobacco, SNYC members played a much smaller part in this union campaign. Its leaders signed a letter supporting the union's strike but did little else. Black and mostly Communist, the few union leaders who worked with SNYC activists hoped to loosen southern labor from its national CIO straitjacket. With the national CIO becoming hostile to these ideas, this symbiotic connection became less possible. The difference between unionism that reified Jim Crow and an internationalist movement that broke it apart became apparent. "Bittner's policy against outside aid goes a great deal deeper than the announced quarantine on Communists," a *Saturday Eve-*

ning Post reporter observed. "The South has never looked kindly on imported ideas of any character."[115] Yet these outside connections and pressures, SNYC activists realized, represented exactly what local movements needed to break down antidemocratic practices.

The threat of another war, attacks on civil liberties, and the increasing U.S. military role abroad in places like Greece and Turkey forced SNYC leaders into an increasingly anti-American foreign policy position. The Truman Doctrine, announced by the president in March 1947, purported to support free peoples in other parts of the world, but the SNYC, like other organizations on the black left, saw this doctrine as an American takeover of Britain's former colonial role. The commitment, the SNYC wrote in a press release, "to expend *whatever is necessary* to oppose 'communism' in any part of the world . . . is [not] that different from the doctrine [with] which Hitler duped the German people and the people of many other free countries."[116] One month later, the new secretary of state, George Marshall, returned from Moscow convinced that diplomacy would no longer work. Two months later, the Taft-Hartley Act, passed by both houses despite Truman's veto, demanded a purge of Communists in the labor movement if unions wanted to continue to receive government protection. The SNYC saw this new federal turn as disastrous. "Many international governments and individuals look with question at the American program of foreign policy," Edward Weaver of SNYC wrote, "because they wonder if the application of American democracy to their countries (many of whom have colored peoples in them) will mean the same patterns of segregation and discrimination." Seeing the "Negro problem" as primarily "one of economics," Weaver added with pessimism that the "present . . . hysteria and war drive" made him doubt whether "ordinary channels of social change" like a "legislative approach" would work.[117] Even the NNC petition to the United Nations, attributable in part to Eleanor Roosevelt's prioritizing of Cold War imperatives over racial discrimination as chair of the Commission on Human Rights, was dismissed by the UN's General Assembly with little comment.[118] With the SNYC attacked as a "Communist front" organization, previous channels of protest now seemed blocked.

Weaver's pessimism was not shared by Walter White of the NAACP, who saw encouraging signs that the federal government would support racial reforms in exchange for cooperation with new Cold War prerogatives. The near-fatal beating of Isaac Woodard in Batesburg, South Carolina, occurred in February, and it was only through John McCray's muckraking journalism that the national NAACP leadership decided to champion his cause by the summer. The NAACP framed this outrage as an international embarrassment, provoking President Truman to take a tougher stance on civil rights matters. Although the Missouri-born president often employed racial epithets in his speech, Truman nonetheless saw the lynching of Woodard as symbolic of a larger problem. "When a mayor and a City Marshal can take a Negro off a bus in South Carolina, beat him up and put out one of his eyes, and nothing is done by the State Authorities," Truman wrote, "something is radically wrong with the system." This outrage was in part strategic. Truman understood by 1948 that the black vote was becoming crucial to an electoral victory. With the SNYC putting its energy and resources into the campaign of the Progressive Party and Henry Wallace, a third-party effort that criticized U.S. foreign policy and called for a broad array of civil rights reforms, Truman might lose black Democrats. Thus, during the same year of the Truman Doctrine, the president launched a Commission for Civil Rights, presented a platform that condemned lynching and the poll tax, and called for the desegregation of interstate transportation. When in June 1947 Truman said that Americans "cannot wait another decade or another generation to remedy these evils," SNYC leaders must have thought he had quoted one of their own statements.[119]

The Cold War activism climate in the United States, however, was not just the result of the Truman administration's policies. The CP also had detrimental effects on the SNYC, because many of the latter's leaders were CP members or sympathizers, meaning that they were not only susceptible to governmental prosecution but also subject to an increasingly domineering organization. Junius Scales, an SNYC vice president, wrote a memoir that provides a rare glimpse into this side of the domestic Cold War. According to Scales, the SNYC had shown the CP that they "could organize and move the most militant and advanced young Negroes [and] enlist the support of much of the Negro middle class." Yet CP leaders in 1946 and 1947 became dictatorial and divisive as they became isolated from liberals through the sharpened dichotomies of the Cold War. The party jargon that called for "democratic centralism" often seemed like a "pyramid of dictatorships" to Scales. The relationship between the CP and the SNYC was also generational and patriarchal. To SNYC activists and CP members like Esther Cooper, Communist leaders like Sam Hall and Harry Haywood seemed to have a cult of personality about themselves that turned off younger activists, who struggled in the trenches for ethical goals rather than personal ones. The desire to change the CP from within (as well as not link the SNYC directly to it), combined with increasing threats of violence against Cooper and her husband, James Jackson, contributed to their decision to leave the SNYC shortly after the Columbia Youth Legislature in order to join the CP leadership in Detroit.[120] Moreover, with increasing Cold War hostility, local CP leaders became "handcuffed by policies of Stalin's Soviet Party, which cared nothing for the Communist parties of other countries except to the extent to which they were immediately useful to the Soviet Union." The American CP, Scales believed, "narrowed and undercut" many of its ongoing struggles "to make the Bill of Rights a blazing reality" by the way it "glorified all things Soviet" and portrayed the expansion of the Soviet Union into other parts of world as "the advance of social revolution and the well-being of all people everywhere." As Soviet leaders trampled on the human rights of independent peoples abroad, it became harder and harder for SNYC members to see their movement as parallel to Stalin's goals. This separation would "drive wedges between the Negro middle class and the Negro workers," as well as between CP members of the SNYC and the larger grassroots membership.[121]

▨ ▨ ▨ The SNYC's postwar internationalism in South Carolina allowed it to develop and act in ways that went far beyond civil rights reform. By placing their local struggles into international contexts, SNYC activists embraced a broader human rights agenda. This allowed them and their allies to see beyond the fixed racial caste system of South Carolina. As late as 1940, whites controlled the ballot, the benches in the local park, and even southern history. The SNYC urged local blacks to resist this state of physical and mental dominance through a global politics that linked them to other working-class peoples around the world. This link became much more direct when SNYC activists had the opportunity to travel abroad and foster connections to citizens of other nations, and, in the case of the Youth Legislature, bring international delegates to Columbia. Meanwhile, black veterans returning home also experienced circumstances very different from their southern upbringing. These unofficial international diplomats discussed what they had seen with local blacks and formulated plans to put their new ideas into action. This syncretic strategy—combining the international and the local—launched a widespread movement against Jim Crow. The fusion of the SNYC with local activists in the PDP and the NAACP in South Carolina, culminating in the "flash of lightening in Columbia," made the state in 1946 a key front for the struggle for antiracist democracies around the world.

Yet the SNYC movement in South Carolina suffered from the same ties that helped galvanize it. As the United States and the Soviet Union became more antagonistic toward each other, the CP, which had helped provide such a rich array of connections to grassroots democratic movements, also increasingly compromised them. When James Byrnes and Vyacheslav Molotov, the Soviet minister of foreign affairs, discussed the fate of the world in 1946, they ironically had much more in common than SNYC leaders had surmised. SNYC members argued that Byrnes's style of diplomacy stemmed from the way he wielded power in his own state of South Carolina. The disfranchisement, poll taxes, and segregation that served as the backbone of his domestic political career exposed Byrnes's foreign policy as an attempt to create similar dictatorships elsewhere. What SNYC members did not realize or admit was that the Soviet Union had acted with similar intentions. Like Byrnes, Soviet leaders also made deals and advanced on territories at the expense of the democratic rights of the people they affected. Having based so much of their international agenda on CP premises, certain SNYC leaders now had trouble breaking from them because it would mean a refutation of their very identities as activists.

Liberals found this stubborn loyalty to Communism difficult to understand because of its hypocrisy but failed to appreciate the value of SNYC's international political ideology or its accomplishments. While the SNYC and the Wallace campaign suffered defeat at the hands of red-baiters and race-baiters in local towns in the South, as well as suppression by the State Department and the attorney general, they had also helped force a blueprint for civil rights onto the federal agenda. The militant pressure that the South Carolina movement, as elsewhere, placed on the Democratic Party, led President Truman to create a civil rights commission. This commission issued a 1947 report entitled *To Secure These Rights*, which outlined goals very similar to those of the SNYC even as government anti-Communism marginalized it as an organization. The SNYC and other civil rights groups, the report's authors concluded, tried to "prove our democracy an empty fraud," which had made the "mistreatment of any racial, religious, or national group in the United States . . . not only . . . our internal problem." Civil rights action now had an "international reason." One year later, Truman acted on the report by issuing Executive Order 9981, which desegregated America's armed forces.[122]

Federal officials endorsed some of the goals of SNYC while simultaneously isolating its network of activists. The black middle-class and liberal white leaders that had endorsed the SNYC in 1946 now endorsed Truman over Wallace for president in 1948. Suppression of the SNYC would cause its demise in 1949 and push South Carolina far from the center of the next generation's southern freedom struggles. "I went to Charleston," a former PDP leader wrote McCray in 1957, and "there was little imagination, little dash and daring." This lack of action caused him to ask, "Who in South Carolina is traveling about 'talking it up' as we used to do it five and ten years ago? Has every body gotten old and lost heart?" McKaine, at least, became disheartened with the scene there—by August 1947 he was back in Ghent, Belgium, reporting on the freedoms blacks could experience there while continuing to agitate for rights back home. After all, he wrote, "Frederick Douglass fought slavery from this side of the Atlantic." In the Cold War years to come, many other black activists would join McKaine overseas.[123] Back home, Simkins and others in the SNYC continued the fight, but they did so with mixed feelings about a domesticated form of civil rights activism. The SNYC's Rose Mae Withers Catchings would later apply her experience by becoming a leader in the international movement against apartheid in South Africa, but the overall impact on black students and workers in places like Moncks Corner and Anderson seemed less apparent by the 1950s.[124] As one former PDP member wrote to John McCray, "When I think of [Roy] Wilkins, and Martin Luther King . . . I have to laugh" about how their earlier struggles seemed all but forgotten. "Yes, they are getting the front pages now," he concluded, "but I doubt that they had the novel experiences that we had."[125] The South a decade later would again become the "firing line," as activists challenged the lily-white southern Democratic Party at its 1964 Atlantic City convention and struggled to secure the vote for African Americans. Yet, as in the first Reconstruction, the "very memory" of South Carolina's postwar internationalist movement for economic justice had seemingly disappeared from popular memory.[126]

Gone with *What* Wind?

"There's a limit to human endurance," Thelma Dale wrote in 1946, and "I'm afraid I've reached that [limit]." The Cold War had begun to curtail the "Death Blow to Jim Crow" of the National Negro Congress (NNC). Although the postwar era seemed ripe for sustaining a civil rights movement in cities like Detroit, San Francisco, and Columbia, the NNC faced difficulties holding together a coalition that included CIO members, Communists, and liberals in the midst of an unprecedented wave of government repression sponsored by the attorney general, Congress, and the FBI. "Even though [it] doesn't sound very Marxist," Dale wrote, "I'll probably be cutting out" if the "usual intrigue and battle of personalities for power [continues]." The tensions that the NNC had been able to live with in years past became insurmountable by late 1947. In November, the NNC merged its forces with the new Civil Rights Congress, an organization designed to fight (mostly through legal channels) against curtailments of civil liberties and racial violence, and its national office disbanded. Two years later, after a tumultuous confrontation with Police Commissioner Bull Connor in Birmingham, the Southern Negro Youth Congress (SNYC) ceased operation.[1]

The first attack on the NNC came from the organization that it had helped build: the CIO. During its 1946 annual convention in Atlantic City, the CIO created a list of allied organizations. The NNC did not make the list. Attending the convention on behalf of the NNC, Revels Cayton claimed, "I never saw so many guys with the collars turned around in all my life," adding, "though they are Negroes, they have lost all consciousness of that fact."[2] The particular CIO leaders who posed problems for the NNC ironically wielded power within the national CIO's Committee to Abolish Discrimination. This committee had formed during the war to study and eliminate discriminatory practices within CIO locals. Yet, with James Carey as its chairman, George Weaver as its director, and Willard Townsend as its secretary, all liberal anti-Communists, the committee came to be seen by NNC members as a backhanded way to limit its own role within the CIO. In 1946, George Crockett of the United Auto Workers (UAW) demanded that this committee enlarge its membership to represent more unions, increase its frequency of meetings to at least once a quarter, formulate a procedure for handling complaints, and most important, reorganize the committee to "be free from factional alignments." The committee had been ineffectual, its critics in the NNC and the CIO argued, because it more often acted to contain the demands of black unionists than redress them. "We are tired of standing by," Crockett concluded in a letter to Willard Townsend, "while you, Carey, and Weaver play CIO politics with our economic welfare."[3]

Soon thereafter, John Brophy, the CIO director of Industrial Union Councils, sent a letter to all California CIO locals demanding that they cease collaboration with the NNC. Brophy had been with the CIO since its earliest days and had an acute awareness of the importance of NNC organizers in building and sustaining the CIO's unions. Yet by the end of the war, Brophy changed the policy of accepting "any or all workers who were favorable to trade union organization," instead policing the politics of all members who "were in conflict with official C.I.O. program and policy."[4] In response, the NNC compiled its "long record" of work with the CIO to provide "ammunition with which to fight" this new policy of exclusion. A dozen black NNC and CIO labor union leaders wrote to Brophy and accused him of "trying to split the Negro liberation movement." Brophy refused to reconsider his decision, and Weaver responded by writing the NNC out of the CIO's history. "We have never participated in the Congress nor have we endorsed [it]," Weaver wrote. The NNC's advocacy of "lay-offs based on race," which referred to the NNC's adjusted seniority plan, was "completely contrary to the policies of the CIO." More important, Weaver claimed that "there have been widespread and baseless attacks made on the Committee to Abolish Discrimination." Presumably, severing the NNC from the CIO would also quash any criticism of Weaver's own work as director of the committee.[5]

With its CIO members immersed in factional disputes, the NNC relied too much on the Communist Party (CP) to regain its momentum. Revels Cayton declared that the NNC "has to be built" and must "establish a fighting core." Rather than building local councils, Cayton maintained that the NNC had to rely on the CP's "subcommittee of the National Negro Commission" to make a recommendation to the "secretariat, and from there it will be made an important part of the coming national plenum." Only after the CP approved the idea of expanding the NNC through its bureaucratic channels would the NNC "be able to move the top level leadership of all progressive international unions." Cayton believed that black rank-and-file trade unionists could create a mass movement from below, but because the NNC did not yet have a mass following in more than a few cities, he needed the CP to commit its resources to push the organizational campaign. "I personally see," Cayton concluded, "no other way for us to influence or affect . . . this great movement of Negro people."[6] As the Cold War became more repressive, however, the CP became more sectarian. Building the NNC into a mass organization necessitated a flexible Popular Front approach, not the CP's own brand of McCarthyism, which purged members for heresy or simply for a lack of orthodoxy.

As the NNC's allies dispersed, local and federal officials provided powerful backing to the anti-Communist opponents of civil rights and labor. J. Edgar Hoover authorized the FBI to place wiretaps in NNC offices, claiming, despite its own earlier reports to the contrary, that the NNC had always been a front for Communists since its 1936 inception. Meanwhile, local police harassed NNC members. In July 1946, for example, Detroit police raided an NNC event, arresting and jailing thirty-seven members for allegedly selling liquor without a license.[7] Based on FBI reports, Attorney General Tom Clark placed the NNC and the SNYC on a list of forty-seven organizations in 1947 that the government considered "subversive." "The action of the Attorney General in coupling the Southern Negro Youth Congress . . . with the white supremacy bandits of the Ku Klux Klan," the SNYC shot back, "reveals the bankruptcy of the policy of government by hysteria."[8]

Disregarding the SNYC's protests over the infringement of constitutional rights to free speech and association, the newly elected conservative majority in Congress garnered enough votes in June 1947 to override President Truman's veto of the Taft-Hartley Act. This act empowered the CIO leaders—some liberals with long-standing quarrels with leftists and others Machiavellian in their anti-Communism—to expel unionists with leftist influence who did not sign affidavits declaring they were not Communists. In the South, the national CIO sent organizers from the United Transport Service Employees Union (the union of Townsend and Weaver) to take over the leadership of tobacco locals in the Food, Tobacco, Agricultural, and Allied Workers. The locals of this union suffered from these anti-Communist raids, and many of them collapsed when the CIO expelled its most effective black organizers.[9] In the UAW, according to historian Nelson Lichtenstein, the Taft-Hartley Act ensured the victory of Walter Reuther's coalition of Catholics and other anti-Communists, who ousted the left-NNC coalition headed by R. J. Thomas and George Addes. "In 1946 and 1947 the power and influence of Negroes was ascending," African American UAW leader Shelton Tappes recalled, but with the demise of the "Addes-Thomas" coalition, "the Negro issue lost a champion."[10] Following the UAW's shift to anti-Communism, other unions marginalized the NNC's black leaders, and the CIO expelled all unions that refused to comply with Taft-Hartley by 1950. Instead of expanding the interracial unity in the CIO's unions that had most committed themselves to civil rights, CIO leaders and other liberals refashioned their politics to align with the government's growing Cold War policy.

In northern cities like Chicago, the rise of these new black labor leaders proved a bittersweet pill for NNC activists there to swallow. Willoughby Abner, for example, was a law school graduate and anti-Stalinist UAW organizer who rose from a position as a Chicago Studebaker plant employee during the war years to a key union executive after the war. His ascension was in part based on his effectiveness but also stemmed from his loyalty to the leadership of Walter Reuther against the Communist-left within the UAW. In 1947, for example, Abner gave a fiery speech at the UAW convention demanding compliance with Taft-Hartley, which meant that the union would effectively purge Communists from participation. To many UAW leftists and the NNC, this posture smacked of self-serving sectarianism and a betrayal of the Popular Front coalition that had helped make civil rights unionism a reality over the previous decade.[11] Meanwhile, Lucius Love became a Chicago leader of steelworkers. His union work in the Bennett-Wilson plant (which the NNC had helped organize in 1937) led to a career as a black labor leader in Chicago. Love and Abner, along with other black unionists like Charles Hayes of the packinghouse workers, took over the NAACP branch during the 1950s and secured powerful union leadership positions in the Chicago Industrial Union Council. In these roles, they transformed the CIO committee's meetings from narrow discussions on internal business to more expansive activism for NAACP member campaigns to fight against segregated housing and other facilities in Chicago. Nationally, these unionists, backed by the dues and energy of hundreds of thousands of black workers, provided crucial early support for the southern civil rights movement that arose in places like Montgomery, Alabama, in the mid-1950s. While NNC and SNYC activists applauded the emergence of this movement, they remained largely isolated from its strong blue-collar, middle-class base, which they had helped create. James Jackson later described this process as a CIO strategy to "use the left: use their experience, know-how, their crusading commitment to remake the world, but don't let them get voted into power."[12]

Even white leftists in the CIO, who had benefited from the alliance with the NNC and the SNYC, began to show the limits of their interracialism and civil rights advocacy. In 1946, Revels Cayton and Paul Robeson toured the West Coast, giving concerts and political speeches to rally a working-class base for the NNC in California. Although this trip proved successful and its West Coast councils became strong Civil Rights Congress chapters in the years to come, it also revealed the racial attitudes of the white leadership of the unions there. During one such argument about the importance of black leadership and power within the union, Louis Goldblatt of the International Longshore and Warehouse Union physically attacked Cayton and branded him a black nationalist. Additional resentment arose when Cayton, who had become particularly close to Robeson, began to see how "white organizations were using [Robeson]." Cayton later recalled: "Paul was singing concert after concert for white progressive organizations, taking no money," when he should have been "identifying himself with the Black community." At a social affair during this period at which Howard Fast declared that Robeson "isn't black or white but a world citizen," Cayton burst out in anger. "The trouble with you," he retorted, "is that you don't want him to be Black, you want him to be white, and he sure can't pass for white." While these incidents clearly came as the result of frustration that the postwar, black-led movement of the NNC did not come to fruition as expected, it also showed how racial tensions in the left further enervated its possibility.[13]

While leftists argued, other liberals used the economic security they had gained from the CIO's rise in the late 1930s to move away from their black allies. White ethnics, due to the decent wages and stable income protected by unions, rose into the largest middle class in American history in the 1950s. Rather than stay in urban neighborhoods, many whites left urban centers for the suburbs, escaping urban problems rather than confronting them. Even Jews, among the most progressive of these white groups because their leaders had long guarded against threats to civil liberties in America, abandoned these principles when it came to anti-Communism. "Opposition to Communism not only placed American Jews within the larger political framework of Cold War liberalism," one historian argued, "but it served as an important vehicle for Jewish social mobility."[14] By the early 1950s, virtually all liberals defined Communism as a criminal conspiracy rather than as a political ideology, which allowed them to suppress left activists without technically abandoning their principles of free speech and association. Rather than continue to pursue Popular Front advocacy for expansion of the New Deal, progressive whites now settled for a more limited defense of its racially biased form. Blacks too moved from their previous neighborhoods. But this significant black, blue-collar, middle class, not to mention the working class, remained much more urban, segregated, and prone to real estate exploitation.[15]

This rightward turn in American politics destroyed the NNC network and presented its activists with a terrible set of choices. Dorothy Funn bowed to the pressure of McCarthyism by naming as Communists sixty-six people that she had worked alongside as a lobbyist in Washington and as a teacher in New York's public school system.[16] Max Yergan responded by resigning from the NNC and the Council on African Affairs and collaborating with the FBI to inform on his former allies. By the 1960s, he had embraced right-wing politics, which included support for apartheid in South Africa.[17]

Others fought back against their accusers. Ferdinand Smith waged a losing campaign against Joseph Curran, who had formed a coalition of anti-Communists and white racists in the National Maritime Union to oust its progressive leaders. This struggle for control over the union resulted in fights on the docks, the murder of a black union member in South Carolina, and finally the dismissal of organizers like Smith who had helped build the union on charges of "financial irregularities." Two years later, immigration officials, furnished with FBI reports from J. Edgar Hoover, jailed Smith at Ellis Island; soon thereafter a federal judge ordered his deportation to Jamaica.[18] In the South, James Jackson and Ed Strong became key black operatives in an increasingly marginalized and sectarian CP. Jackson went underground to avoid imprisonment and engaged in a campaign to rid the CP of white chauvinism, which mainly served to further divide it. "They were both generals," one CP member recalled of Jackson and Strong in the 1950s, "without much of an army."[19] Still others continued their activism by helping to form new groups like the Harlem Trade Union Council, the Civil Rights Congress, and black caucuses within labor unions.[20] Many of these activists adopted a safer liberalism and buried their NNC pasts in the hope of avoiding persecution. Yet even this strategy did not always work. Marie Richardson, a former D.C. Council leader, went to jail for two years in 1952 for denying Communist membership when she applied for a government job in 1948. Although her accusers provided no proof of her CP membership, her position as the head of the D.C. Council of the NNC was sufficient evidence for her conviction.[21] Even Ralph Bunche, as a UN diplomat in 1954, came under interrogation by a Senate Internal Security Committee for his previous NNC connections. Bunche's security clearance for this distinguished government job came only as the result of John P. Davis's self-incriminating testimony to clear his old Harvard friend. By admitting he had been intimately involved with the CP, Davis confirmed in his testimony that Bunche had no such connection.[22] Thus, the Cold War not only destroyed the NNC as an organization but also scattered its activists and made even discussing its past achievements politically dangerous.

      Even before the onset of the Cold War, Jim Crow, as a national political and cultural ideology, seemed to infest every aspect of American life, seducing whites and many African Americans into complacency. In 1940, Sterling Brown commented at an NNC cultural session about the symbolic power of the movie *Gone with the Wind*, a film that depicted the "good Negro" as "excessively loyal" while the "closer the Negro got his foot to the ballot box the closer he got to the brute." Brown mentioned that the new version of the film in Technicolor only made the film more seductive as a nostalgic glance into the pre-Emancipation South. In the mythical past of the movie, he told the NNC delegates, "no grass was ever so green, no sky so blue, no nature ever so lovely." Inside the Library of Congress the day before his speech, Brown overheard a security guard confirm this seduction. "Wasn't it a terrible thing that the beautiful civilization had to be destroyed," he asked another white person, "in order to set the niggers free?" Even more suggestive of the pervasiveness of Jim Crow, the majority of 500 Howard University students polled during that year voted the motion picture the best they had ever seen. Knowing his NNC audience did not agree with popular opinion, Brown referenced the interracial jazz duo of Count Basie and Benny Goodman, who wrote and recorded a popular jazz song called "Gone with '*What*' Wind?" Like the song, Brown explained, "I have heard many adjectives applied between what and wind, but they cannot bear repetition on a Sunday afternoon."[23]

      Between 1936 and 1947, the NNC and the SNYC applied many of those adjectives in their militant confrontation of Jim Crow in America, past and present. In cities like Chicago and Washington, NNC activists picketed theaters with their own message. In one such protest, pickets read: "The Negroes Were Never Docile Slaves" and "Gone with the Wind Incites Race Hatred."[24] During the Second World War, Langston Hughes also challenged the image of "Negroes, sweet and docile" in the poem "Warning." Perhaps defining the "what wind" as his allies in the NNC, Hughes wrote in the final stanza: "Wind/ In the cotton fields/Gentle breeze:/Beware the hour/It uproots trees!" In 1946, the NNC took aim at Disney's *Song of the South*, a partially animated popular film featuring a character named Uncle Remus, a former slave who lived on a plantation as a servant. Across the country, NNC councils organized boycotts and demonstrations at theaters that showed the film. Pickets at these events featured fiery slogans such as "We fought for Uncle Sam Not Uncle Tom" and "Disney, Creating Cartoons Is Amusing/Discarding History Is Confusing/ Go Back to Mickey Mouse!"[25] This arena of contestation connected the NNC's broader confrontation to decry Jim Crow's pernicious and seductive influence in American life to the government and, increasingly, to the rest of the world.

The demise of the Popular Front in 1947 showed both the efficacy of the NNC and the persistence of old images in new guises. A report found in the papers of California NNC leader Matt Crawford illustrated this new development. It stated that "the struggles of the Negro people for first class citizenship have resulted in . . . a demonstration and achievement—by both outstanding and 'average' Negro men and women—that [black] life itself makes it difficult . . . to maintain the simple, old style white chauvinist stereotype." However, the report also lamented that the media had only "jiggled" stereotypes with "new make-up and hair-do, sprayed [them] with perfume[,] making them alternately acceptable by southern whites, Negroes, and northern liberals." This "new look," the report concluded, had "a striking resemblance to President Truman's 'new look' in the field of civil rights legislation."[26]

During the Cold War, this "new look" also became embedded in civil rights strategy, which one historian termed the "intergroup relations movement."[27] Within this model, white liberals treated racism as a psychological disorder, focusing on education and attitude modification rather than the socioeconomic underpinnings of a Jim Crow society. The foundation for this new model was laid in 1944 when the Swedish sociologist Gunnar Myrdal published *An American Dilemma*. Commissioned to write a study of U.S. race relations by the Carnegie Corporation in late 1935, Myrdal produced a study hailed for the next two decades as the "definitive" and "most important study on the problem of the Negro." Myrdal argued that white Americans believed in a democratic "creed" but often compromised their otherwise egalitarian beliefs when dealing with blacks. Addressing the racial dilemma, he maintained, would bring gradual but "fundamental changes in American race relations." His breakthrough study demonstrated that a transformation in American race relations had occurred during the Second World War, making the "Negro problem" no longer possible to ignore. Yet at the same time Myrdal's study obscured who drove these changes. He saw the nation's white employers and managers as the key agents of change in rectifying this dilemma, paying scant attention to African Americans themselves, let alone wage laborers.[28]

In casting racial discrimination as a moral problem, Myrdal overlooked the NNC's black-led working-class struggle for democracy. Indeed, the earliest critiques of Myrdal came from African American activists and intellectuals who had a firsthand understanding of the movement that propelled social change during the New Deal. Doxey Wilkerson of the NNC argued that by considering discrimination a "moral" problem that would be corrected through the "long, gradual, never-ending process of 'education,'" Myrdal made the "profit seeking foundations of Negro oppression . . . less vulnerable to attack." Ralph Ellison joined the "chorus of 'Yeas'" in 1944 that lauded *American Dilemma* but also registered a "lusty and simultaneous 'Nay'" in his review of the study. Not published until two decades later, the review explained how Myrdal "felt it necessary to carry on a running battle with Marxism" so as to deny the "economic motivation of anti-Negro prejudice" and avoid the "question of power."[29]

In critiquing racial discrimination and economic exploitation as inseparable twinned evils, the NNC and SNYC disagreed sharply with the academic view of Myrdal. "We differ from Gunnar Myrdal," SNYC leader Ed Weaver wrote, because he "holds the problem to be a dilemma and hence incapable of a solution for some years." To the SNYC, "inconsistent practices in the American democracy . . . stem from our profit-driven society, and the necessity for such societies for a cheap labor supply."[30] The NNC's activist-intellectuals agreed that racism in America was less a moral issue than a material one. Applying this American Creed to a nationwide, decade-long, grassroots activist campaign, NNC and SNYC members saw the working class as having the potential power to force U.S. institutions to value human rights above property rights and democracy over Jim Crow.

Moreover, the NNC had shown that African Americans, who had historically played such a vital role in challenging the dominant American culture of exclusion, drove social change. The Swedish sociologist's model of race relations concluded that blacks desired a one-way assimilation. Yet few African Americans agreed. "Can a people . . . live and develop for over three hundred years simply by reacting?" Ellison rhetorically asked Myrdal, and "cannot Negroes have made a life upon the horns of the white man's dilemma?"[31] Myrdal concluded that blacks were "doomed to be introverted and self-consuming" and that their communities were a "pathological form of an American community."[32] In contrast with Myrdal's bleak depiction of black culture, the NNC had shown that blacks represented not America's problem but America's salvation, because of their past and contemporary struggles for freedom. A black-led interracial struggle to destroy Jim Crow, NNC leaders argued, would not only emancipate blacks but also liberate working-class whites from the economic system of oppression that Jim Crow had sustained for the past half century.

Postwar liberals embraced Myrdal's "scientific" study of race relations because it empowered them to manage civil rights while simultaneously destroying troublesome activist networks like the NNC. To be sure, Myrdal's study provided liberals with an important means to push for civil rights reform inside the boundaries of Cold War institutions. President Truman's 1947 Civil Rights Commission report, *To Secure These Rights*, established a blueprint for government reform for the next two decades that implicitly endorsed NNC campaigns for a permanent Fair Employment Practices Committee, federal protection from lynching, and abolition of the poll tax. Yet the committee's report also adopted the heart of Myrdal's argument by deeming racial discrimination an aberration of American liberalism. Charles E. Wilson, the chairman of the committee, considered the report a "rededication of our people to the historical principles which have made us great" by recommending "improvement through the *normal processes* of democracy."[33] Thus, the very network of activists whose creative efforts put civil rights onto the Democratic Party's agenda became extinct after the attorney general labeled the NNC and many of its allies "subversive."

This "subversive" label influenced the opinions of the first intellectuals and activists who studied racial activism during the Popular Front era. Ralph Bunche (the major black contributor to the Myrdal study) and A. Philip Randolph, both disaffected former NNC members who were red-baited themselves, downplayed the organization's relevance. When A. Philip Randolph resigned as president of the NNC in 1940, his published op-ed pieces and articles called the NNC's Washington conference a "miserable failure" because Communists in the organization were a "definite menace and a danger to the

Negro people and labor." Moreover, the opinions of black anti-Communists were adopted wholesale into *An American Dilemma*. In 1944, for example, the SNYC assailed Myrdal's book for its adoption of Ralph Bunche's biased assessment of its organization. Bunche claimed that the SNYC was "lacking competent leadership" and "run by a select group of Negro school boys and girls" who made "no serious effort to reach lower class Negro youth." The perspectives of Bunche and Randolph bolstered the thesis of *An American Dilemma* and helped bury the record of the NNC's activism.[34]

In the two decades that followed, black and white scholars alike, operating under the shadow of the Cold War, disassociated their work from Communism out of political necessity. Meanwhile, many activists remained committed to the NNC's expansive economic vision but downplayed it in favor of the now more viable strategy of demanding that the federal government practice the democratic creed it preached abroad.[35] This new generation of activists used Myrdal's dilemma to advance civil rights during the Cold War, while the narrowed political atmosphere made McCarthyism's victims guarded about revealing past experiences. The trauma inflicted on African Americans during the early Cold War era who considered themselves advocates for justice in America, combined with a desire to protect their children from FBI agents and salacious press reports, led many activists to forget.[36] "An entire generation of political activists," one scholar of McCarthyism concluded, "had been jerked off the stage of history." John P. Davis, for example, omitted all but one reference to the NNC he helped create and lead when he edited the *American Negro Reference Book* in the 1960s.[37] This political climate replaced economic issues with a Myrdalian cultural understanding of civil rights and made the NNC vision disappear from American liberal thought.

By the late 1960s, however, with the confidence of a new mass movement, blacks ventured beyond those Cold War boundaries. Activists and intellectuals of this era criticized Myrdal for ignoring the working class and for defining black culture as pathological. They believed that white Americans' long-standing racism had produced structural economic inequalities that faith in an American Creed alone could not address. "The American dilemma," Kenneth Clark insisted, "is one of power." Others knew of this earlier history from their elders. "My mother was a member of the Southern Negro Youth Congress," radical African American activist Angela Davis recalled, "so I think of racial identification not primarily in terms of the color of one's skin . . . but according to what one does." The activism of her mother's generation, Davis concluded, did not become part of American history because it does not tell a "triumphant narrative" but rather one that "point[s] to unfinished agendas of freedom."[38] Influenced by the movement of the 1960s, scholars began to look back to the 1930s and 1940s as a prelude to their own era's civil rights activity. In more recent years, this scholarship has expanded to analyze cogently particular aspects of the 1930s and 1940s movement, and cumulatively it has enabled a study of the NNC.[39]

▨ ▨ ▨ Studying the history of the activism of the NNC allows us to better understand what historian Jacqueline Dowd Hall called the "decisive first phase" of the long civil rights movement in America. With a focus on the NNC, this study shows that the African American role in the CIO and the Popular Front was vital. Without the NNC's help, neither of these larger networks would have succeeded in implementing and expanding the New Deal to protect labor's right to organize and disperse political power. Moreover, the NNC's activism also suggests a lost opportunity in this era of intertwining economic justice and civil rights through the labor movement. Its advocacy for black tobacco workers in Richmond, for example, predated Operation Dixie by almost a decade. If the CIO's official 1946 Operation Dixie campaign had occurred earlier, or if CIO leaders had provided resources and support to black organizers in the SNYC and NNC, the South's "right to work" labor policy might not have come to dominate the rest of the century. Instead, by 1953, only 17 percent of the South's nonagricultural workforce belonged to unions, the same percentage of organized workers as before Operation Dixie.[40] The demise of the NNC and the SNYC largely decoupled labor organizers from antiracist activists. Although fighting against economic discrimination would remain central to African American activists during the rest of the century, other movements never regained the strong interracial commitments the NNC had sustained in the late 1930s and 1940s.[41]

The NNC also altered American politics through its resurrection, amalgamation, and application of militant forms of protest—including marches, demonstrations, and strikes—which became accepted modes of urban resistance by the 1940s. NNC protests against police brutality and lynching made A. Philip Randolph's threatened March on Washington Movement seem dangerously realistic to President Roosevelt, who issued Executive Order 8802 in June 1941 as a preventative measure. The political support of local and federal candidates by the NNC combined with its mass-based activism to force the Democratic Party in the 1940s to choose between civil rights and white supremacy. Partially to stave off a potential third-party challenge from Henry Wallace, the Democratic Party endorsed a strong civil rights platform in 1948, putting civil rights at the top of the Democratic Party's agenda. During the next two decades, a new generation of activists pressured the federal government to intervene and enforce the Fourteenth and Fifteenth Amendments to the Constitution.

After its 1936 inaugural convention, NNC leaders strategized on how to engage in militant activism while holding together coalitions that crossed traditional class, race, and gender lines. These entangled alliances caused NNC members to have contradictory impulses, especially when dealing with the CP. By the 1940s, the CP had become the most important vehicle for the NNC to traverse racial barriers in its campaign to kill Jim Crow. During a time when many other whites expressed indifference or outright hostility to African Americans, the CP and the wider Popular Front networks provided vehicles and ideological frames for the black-led NNC to think outside of Jim Crow America's seemingly impenetrable barriers in order to sustain its activism. However, due to shifting international alliances, the CP also became the NNC's Achilles' heel. The imagined community of the Soviet Union had allowed some NNC activists to dream of a radical restructuring of American society based on democracy, but others took a more sober view when actual events in the Soviet Union (and specifically news about Stalin's orchestration of antidemocratic and brutal purges from 1936 to 1938) contradicted this vision. Many grassroots allies lost faith in the NNC when the organizational priorities increasingly aligned with the CP, which, in turn, and however indirectly, connected to Stalinism. Anti-Communists, including liberal civil rights and labor activists on the one hand and white supremacists and corporate conservatives on the other, exploited the vulnerabilities of the NNC's alliance with Communists by making it seem conspiratorial and hypocritical. And the CP made this task easier by drastically changing its policies in 1939, 1941, and 1945.

Yet scholars often treat the influence of the CP with a moral condemnation seldom seen in studies of other political parties. Activists understood the situation in more complex terms. "All my life I have been able to hold mutually contradictory views and feelings at the same time," Revels Cayton explained; "could one be a black man living in America and not be torn by ambivalence?"[42] This book has neither dismissed nor celebrated the Communist influence on the NNC but instead has allowed these contradictions to play themselves out in the historical record. In so doing, it takes seriously Jacqueline Hall's call to make civil rights "harder to celebrate as a natural progression of American values."[43] The NNC's work was always fraught with contradictions, and its activist campaigns more often plodded along than caused immediate reform. This approach to the NNC neither condemns it as a "Communist Front" of duplicitous people nor lionizes it as an unambiguously righteous network of activists. By removing the unhelpful moral dichotomies created during the Cold War when dealing with Communism, this study makes civil rights more complicated, and therefore more human.

The story of the NNC also defies the notion of a linear progression from A. Philip Randolph's 1941 March on Washington Movement to the 1963 March on Washington for Jobs and Freedom. Historians have focused on activists like Randolph, Ella Baker, and Bayard Rustin because these figures show the continuity between this earlier phase of civil rights activity and the more famous movement of the 1950s and 1960s. Although Randolph headed the NNC until 1940 and activists like Baker and Rustin interacted with the NNC during the Popular Front era, they did not necessarily always represent the vanguard of the movement. "Insisting that the movement was larger than Dr. King," the scholar Charles Payne has written of the 1960s struggle, "does him no dishonor."[44] This same conclusion should now apply to the earlier generation of black leaders, especially A. Philip Randolph. Recent scholars have largely accomplished their goal of expanding our understanding of who led the 1960s movement; this study makes a similar case for the Popular Front era. The fact that the most dedicated and creative activists of the 1930s and 1940s did not remain at the center of the 1960s movement makes them all the more significant for understanding the long civil rights movement. While the taint of Communism pushed them out of sight, the Cold War did not erase the NNC vision from the minds of these latter-day African American activists. The vision remained largely beneath the surface until the late 1960s, when economic and international issues again came to the forefront of the black freedom struggle. The fact that the Black Power movement raised these economic concerns reinforces that the NNC vision included building power within black America even if it eschewed black separatism and that the late 1960s offered a changed historical context in which the labor movement, due in part to the Cold War, was more of an impediment to black advancement than a vehicle for civil rights.[45] Thus, placing the NNC within the longer civil rights movement shows the pathway of the movement to have been less linear and much more circuitous and tragic than commonly supposed.[46] After all, NNC activists did not believe a later generation would deliver a "Death Blow to Jim Crow"—they saw such an accomplishment as within their own reach.

Looking back on the NNC movement of the past generation, Louis Burnham cautioned blacks in 1960 against the idea of "progress" that produced a "faith that democracy as it unfolds will spread its largess to the Negro, too." The "central lesson of Negro history," Burnham explained, showed that "the advance toward equality has not been a straight path, but a dreary zig-zagged road . . . of fits and starts."[47] Older historians such as W. E. B. Du Bois and Carter Woodson understood this complicated and less romantic version of black history, he concluded, and younger historians like John Hope Franklin have "underscored it in more recent works." Despite all of the forces pressuring Americans to forget the NNC and the SNYC, Burnham wanted future generations to remember it for its accomplishments, tragic errors, and unfinished agenda. The next generation, Burnham demanded, should not allow this past to be blown away by the political winds and technological progress that would otherwise erase it.

The NNC cultivated an oppositional black culture and fostered militant antiracist campaigns that forced American institutions to enact racial and labor reforms for the first time since Reconstruction. Its activists' street-theater tactics also helped remake black culture during this era. They promoted a militant version of black history that made African Americans central to the democratic traditions of America and publicized new understandings of race that contradicted racial hierarchies as natural. Taking inspiration from NNC protest politics, African American artists during this era became more connected to working-class concerns and compared contemporary race rebels to the abolitionists of slavery and leaders during Reconstruction. The cumulative influence of the NNC's political and cultural work made the fate of African Americans central to American democracy. "Jim Crow," Thelma Dale explained, "threatens the existence of every American [and] every freedom loving person in the world over. That is why we [must] DEAL A DEATH BLOW TO JIM CROW."[48] Although the NNC did not accomplish that goal, its forceful activism undermined the ideological premises of white supremacy, reoriented protest politics and black culture, and transformed American politics by making civil rights an urgent and national necessity. The NNC envisioned the vanquishing of Jim Crow not as a moral dilemma but as an economic-based struggle to transform America into the democratic nation it had never been. In 1946, the actor Rex Ingram expressed this vision at an NNC meeting in Washington by reading the words of Langston Hughes:

> O, let America be America again—
> The land that never has been yet—
> And yet must be—the land where *every* man is free.
> The land that's mine—the poor man's, Indian's, Negro's, ME—
> Who made America,
> Whose sweat and blood, whose faith and pain,
> Whose hand at the foundry, whose plow in the rain,
> Must bring back our mighty dream again.[49]

Notes

Abbreviations

ABP   Arna Bontemps Papers, Bird Library, Special Collections Department, Syracuse University, Syracuse, New York.

ACP   Arthur Clement Jr. Papers, South Caroliniana Library, University of South Carolina, Columbia, South Carolina.

BAA   *Baltimore Afro-American*, Washington, D.C., edition.

BSCP   Brotherhood of Sleeping Car Porters

CABP   Claude A. Barnett Papers, Chicago Historical Museum, Chicago, Illinois.

CAP   Chris and Marti Alston Papers, Walter Reuther Archives, Wayne State University, Detroit, Michigan.

CBP   Charlotta Bass Papers, Southern California Library for Social Studies and Research, Los Angeles, California.

CD   *Chicago Defender*. Unless otherwise specified, all references to *CD* refer to the city edition.

CIO   Congress of Industrial Organizations

CP   Communist Party

CPP   Communist Party USA Papers, Manuscript Division, Library of Congress, Washington, D.C., microfilm (cited with delo [file], opis [inventory], and fond numbers in parentheses).

CWP   Charles White Papers, Smithsonian Archives of American Art, Washington, D.C., microfilm.

DONLRB   *Decisions and Orders of the National Labor Relations Board*, vols. 5–62 (Washington, D.C.: Government Publications Office, 1937–45).

ESP   Edward E. Strong Papers, Moorland-Spingarn Research Center, Howard University, Washington, D.C.

FEPCC   Fair Employment Practices Committee Collection, Southern Labor Archives, Georgia State University, Atlanta, Georgia.

FTA	Food, Tobacco, Agricultural, and Allied Workers
GPP	George Patterson Papers, Chicago History Museum, Chicago, Illinois.
HAP	Herbert Aptheker Papers, Department of Special Collections, Stanford University, Palo Alto, California.
ILD	International Labor Defense
ILHS	Illinois Labor Historical Society, Chicago, Illinois.
ILWUP	International Longshore and Warehouse Union Papers, Harry Bridges Library, San Francisco, California.
JBMP	J. B. Matthews Papers, Rare Book, Manuscript, and Special Collections Library, Duke University, Durham, North Carolina.
JJP	James and Esther Jackson Papers, Tamiment Library, New York University, New York, New York.
JMP	John McCray Papers, South Caroliniana Library, Manuscript Collections, University of South Carolina, Columbia, South Carolina, microfilm.
MCP	Matt Crawford and Evelyn Graves Papers, Woodruff Library, Emory University, Atlanta, Georgia.
MOWM	March on Washington Movement
NAACP-DC	Washington, D.C., NAACP Papers, Moorland-Spingarn Research Center, Howard University, Washington, D.C.
NAACPP	*Papers of the NAACP* (Frederick, Md.: University Publications of America, 1990), microfilm, Library of Congress, Washington, D.C.
NLRB	National Labor Relations Board
NLRBT	National Labor Relations Board Transcripts and Exhibits, Record Group 25, National Archives, College Park, Maryland.
NLVC	Negro Labor Victory Committee
NMU	National Maritime Union
NNC	National Negro Congress
NNC-FBI	*The FBI File on the National Negro Congress* (Washington, D.C.: Delaware, Scholarly Resources, 1987), microfilm (cited with frame and reel numbers in parentheses).
NNCP	*Papers of the National Negro Congress* (Frederick, Md.: University Microfilms of America, 1988), microfilm, Schomburg Center for Research in Black Culture, New York Public Library, New York, New York (cited with frame, reel, and series numbers in parentheses).
NRAR	NRA Records, Record Group 9, National Archives, College Park, Maryland.
ODP	*Operation Dixie Papers and the Lucy Randolph Mason Papers* (New York: Microfilming Corporation of America, 1980), microfilm.
PDP	Progressive Democratic Party
PV	*People's Voice* (New York)
PWOC	Packinghouse Workers Organizing Committee

RWP   Richard Wright Papers, Beinecke Rare Book and Manuscript Library,
           Yale University, New Haven, Connecticut.
SNYC   Southern Negro Youth Congress
SNYCP   Southern Negro Youth Congress Papers, Moorland-Spingarn Research
           Center, Howard University, Washington, D.C.
STC   Sheldon Tappes Collection, Walter Reuther Archives, Wayne State
           University, Detroit, Michigan.
SWOC   Steel Workers Organizing Committee
TWIU   Tobacco Workers International Union
TWIUP   Tobacco Workers International Union Papers, Maryland Room,
           Hornbake Library, University of Maryland, College Park, Maryland.
TWUR   Transport Workers Union of America Records, Tamiment Library,
           New York University, New York, New York.
TWUR-L   Transport Workers Union of America, Records of Locals, Tamiment
           Library, New York University, New York, New York.
UAWC   United Auto Workers Local 212 Collection, Walter Reuther Archives,
           Wayne State University, Detroit, Michigan.
UCAPAWA   United Cannery, Agricultural, Packing, and Allied Workers of America
UFWA   United Federal Workers of America
USWAP   United Steelworkers of America District 31 Papers, Chicago Historical
           Museum, Chicago, Illinois.

Introduction

1 "New Deal and Race Discussed at Conference," *CD*, national edition, June 1, 1935;
   speeches at conference reprinted in *Journal of Negro Education* 5, no. 1 (January 1936),
   quotes from 3–4, 11–12, 40, 58.

2 The CP defined the Popular Front in terms of its 1935 ideological shift to seek alliances with democratic forces against fascism. I join recent historians in defining it
   in broader terms as an interracial, labor-based coalition of radicals and liberals. See
   Michael Denning, *The Cultural Front: The Laboring of American Culture in the Twentieth Century* (New York: Verso, 1996), 22–26. See also Martha Biondi, *To Stand and
   Fight: The Struggle for Civil Rights in Postwar New York City* (Cambridge, Mass.: Harvard University Press, 2003).

3 A few prominent examples are Lizabeth Cohen, *Making a New Deal: Industrial Workers
   in Chicago, 1919–1939* (New York: Cambridge University Press, 1990); Irving Bernstein,
   Turbulent Years: A History of the American Worker, 1933–1941 (Boston: Houghton Miff-
   lin, 1970); Robert McElvaine, *The Great Depression in America, 1929–1941* (1984; New
   York: Times Books, 1993); and Nelson Lichtenstein, *Labor's War at Home: The CIO in
   World War II* (New York: Cambridge University Press, 1982).

4 Two popular studies are William Leuchtenburg, *Franklin D. Roosevelt and the New
   Deal, 1932–1940* (New York: Harper and Row, 1963); and Alan Brinkley, *Voices of*

Protest: Huey Long, Father Coughlin, and the Great Depression (New York: Knopf, 1982).

5 See William Chafe, *Unfinished Journey: America since World War II* (New York: Oxford University Press, 2003); Lawrence Wittner, *Cold War America: From Hiroshima to Watergate* (New York: Praeger, 1974); and John Lewis Gaddis, *We Now Know: Rethinking Cold War History* (New York: Oxford University Press, 1997).

6 Recent exceptions that examine civil rights nationally in the 1930s and 1940s include Thomas Sugrue, *Sweet Land of Liberty: The Forgotten Struggles for Civil Rights in the North* (New York: Random House, 2008); and Glenda Gilmore, *Defying Dixie: The Radical Roots of Civil Rights, 1919–1950* (New York: W. W. Norton, 2008).

7 See Howard Zinn et al., *The Cold War and the University: Toward an Intellectual History of the Postwar Years* (New York: New Press, 1997); Ellen Schrecker, *Many Are the Crimes: McCarthyism in America* (Boston: Little, Brown, 1998); and, for an example of an NNC leader who self-censored his past, see John P. Davis, ed., *The American Negro Reference Book* (Englewood Cliffs, N.J.: Prentice-Hall, 1966).

8 Harvard Sitkoff, *A New Deal for Blacks: The Emergence of Civil Rights as a National Issue* (New York: Oxford University Press, 1978); Raymond Wolters, *Negroes and the Great Depression: The Problem of Economic Recovery* (Westport, Ct.: Greenwood Press, 1970); Richard M. Dalfiume, "The 'Forgotten Years' of the Negro Revolution," reprinted in *The Negro in Depression and War: Prelude to Revolution, 1930–1945*, ed. Bernard Sternsher (Chicago: Quadrangle Books, 1969).

9 Robert Korstad and Nelson Lichtenstein, "Opportunities Found and Lost: Labor, Radicals, and the Early Civil Rights Movement," *Journal of American History* 75, 3 (December 1988); Michael K. Honey, *Southern Labor and Black Civil Rights: Organizing Memphis Workers* (Chicago: University of Illinois Press, 1993); August Meier and Elliott Rudwick, *Black Detroit and the Rise of the UAW* (New York: Oxford University Press, 1979); Bruce Nelson, *Divided We Stand: American Workers and the Struggle for Black Equality* (Princeton, N.J.: Princeton University Press, 2001); William P. Jones, *The Tribe of Black Ulysses: African American Lumber Workers in the Jim Crow South* (Chicago: University of Illinois Press, 2005); Ruth Needleman, *Black Freedom Fighters in Steel: The Struggle for Democratic Unionism* (Ithaca, N.Y.: ILR Press, 2003); Robert Korstad, *Civil Rights Unionism: Tobacco Workers and the Struggle for Democracy in the Mid-Twentieth-Century South* (Chapel Hill: University of North Carolina Press, 2003).

10 Biondi, *To Stand and Fight*; Beth Tompkins Bates, *Pullman Porters and the Rise of Protest Politics in Black America* (Chapel Hill: University of North Carolina Press, 2001); Patricia Sullivan, *Days of Hope: Race and Democracy in the New Deal Era* (Chapel Hill: University of North Carolina Press, 1996); John Egerton, *Speak Now against the Day: The Generation before the Civil Rights Movement in the South* (New York: Alfred A. Knopf, 1994); Charles Payne and Adam Green, ed., *Time Longer Than Rope: A Century of African American Activism, 1850–1950* (New York: New York University Press, 2003); Karen Ferguson, *Black Politics in New Deal Atlanta* (Chapel Hill: University of North Carolina Press, 2002); J. Douglas Smith, *Managing White Su-*

premacy: Race, Politics, and Citizenship in Jim Crow Virginia (Chapel Hill: University of North Carolina Press, 2002).

11 Robin D. G. Kelley, *Hammer and Hoe: Alabama Communists during the Great Depression* (Chapel Hill: University of North Carolina Press, 1990); Denning, *The Cultural Front*; Mark Naison, *Communists in Harlem during the Great Depression* (Urbana: University of Illinois Press, 1983); Biondi, *To Stand and Fight*; Korstad, *Civil Rights Unionism*; Honey, *Southern Labor and Black Civil Rights*; Gerald Horne, *Communist Front? The Civil Rights Congress, 1946-1956* (Madison, N.J.: Fairleigh Dickinson University Press, 1988); Jarod Roll, *Spirit of Rebellion: Labor and Religion in the New Cotton South* (Chicago: University of Illinois Press, 2010).

12 Jacquelyn Dowd Hall, "The Long Civil Rights Movement and the Political Uses of the Past," *Journal of American History* 91, no. 4 (March 2005): 1245-46.

13 Few scholars have examined the NNC, and most of these lost interest after the departure of A. Philip Randolph. No historian has written a comprehensive study. Lawrence S. Wittner called on scholars to look at the local councils of the organization in order to reassess its significance. See Lawrence S. Wittner, "The National Negro Congress: A Reassessment," *American Quarterly* 22, no. 4 (Winter 1970). Mark Naison concluded that the NNC existed independently from the CP, which led him to pay only cursory attention to it. See Naison, *Communists in Harlem*. Beth Bates "uses the struggle of the Brotherhood of Sleeping Car Porters to form a union as a vehicle for [how new forms of protest] took root in Chicago." See Bates, *Pullman Porters*. Jonathan Holloway described the NNC's creation at Howard University. See Jonathan Holloway, *Confronting the Veil: Abram Harris Jr., E. Franklin Frazier, and Ralph Bunche, 1919-1941* (Chapel Hill: University of North Carolina Press, 2002). Robin Kelley wrote about the SNYC's activities during the war years in Alabama. See Kelley, *Hammer and Hoe*. Two dissertations provide an organizational overview: John Baxter Streator, "The National Negro Congress, 1936-1947" (Ph.D. diss., University of Cincinnati, 1981); and Cicero Alvin Hughes, "Toward a Black United Front: The National Negro Congress Movement" (Ph.D. diss., Ohio University, 1982). Last, see Hilmar Jensen's biography of John P. Davis, which covers the period up to 1935: Hilmar Ludvig Jensen, "The Rise of the African American Left: John P. Davis and the National Negro Congress" (Ph.D. diss., Cornell University, 1997).

14 Eric Arnesen, "No 'Graver Danger': Black Anticommunism, the Communist Party, and the Race Question," *Labor: Studies in Working-Class History of the Americas* 3 (Winter 2006); Harold Cruse, *The Crisis of the Negro Intellectual* (New York: Morrow, 1967), 172-77, 322, 339.

15 See Leon Fink, *Workingmen's Democracy: The Knights of Labor and American Politics* (Urbana: University of Illinois Press, 1985); Melvin Dubofsky, *We Shall Be All: A History of the Industrial Workers of the World* (Urbana: University of Illinois Press, abridged ed., 2000); Steven Hahn, *A Nation under Our Feet: Black Political Struggles in the Rural South from Slavery to the Great Migration* (Cambridge, Mass.: Harvard University Press, 2005); Judith Stein, *The World of Marcus Garvey: Race and Class*

in Modern Society (Baton Rouge: Louisiana State University Press, 1991); and Roy Rosenzweig, "Organizing the Unemployed: The Early Years of the Great Depression, 1929–1933," *Radical America* 10 (July–August 1976).

16 A. Philip Randolph to John P. Davis, February 15, 1936 (335, 7, 1), *NNCP*.

17 John P. Davis, "Let Us Build a National Negro Congress" (Washington, D.C.: NNC Sponsoring Committee, 1935), 3.

18 A few historians have discussed the NNC in studies of particular urban black communities. See Bates, *Pullman Porters* (Chicago); Kelley, *Hammer and Hoe* (Birmingham); Clarence Lang, *Grassroots at the Gateway: Class Politics and Black Freedom Struggle in St. Louis, 1936–1975* (Ann Arbor: University of Michigan Press, 2009); Kimberley L. Phillips, *AlabamaNorth: African-American Migrants, Community, and Working-Class Activism in Cleveland, 1915–1945* (Chicago: University of Illinois Press, 1999); Naison, *Communists in Harlem*; and Angela Dillard, *Faith in the City: Preaching Radical Social Change in Detroit* (Ann Arbor: University of Michigan Press, 2007). Vibrant NNC chapters also emerged in Philadelphia and in West Coast cities like the San Francisco bay area and Los Angeles. For the SNYC, Miami, New Orleans, and the state of Tennessee stand out.

19 This phrase comes from Leslie Orear, a former CIO packinghouse organizer. See Leslie Orear, *Out of the Jungle: The Packinghouse Workers Fight for Justice and Equality* (Chicago: Hyde Park Press, 1968).

20 See *Richmond Planet*, May 15, 1937.

Prelude

1 Social movement theorists posit that larger socioeconomic shifts create opportunities for activists when the state becomes somewhat vulnerable. If activists exploit this vulnerability through "framing contests," they have potential to then further undermine the system. See the introduction to *Comparative Perspectives on Social Movements: Political Opportunities, Mobilizing Structures, and Cultural Framings*, ed. Doug McAdam, John D. McCarthy, and Mayer N. Zald (New York: Cambridge University Press, 1996), 1–20. Doug McAdam cites these demographic trends to help explain the "historical context of the black insurgency," paralleling the observations of historians who depict the changes of the 1930s and 1940s as the seedbed for the later 1960s "heyday" of the civil rights movement. See Doug McAdam, *Political Process and the Development of the Black Insurgency, 1930–1970* (Chicago: University of Chicago Press, 1982), 65–116.

2 See Paul Stephen Hudson, "A Call for 'Bold Persistent Experimentation': FDR's Oglethorpe University Commencement Address, 1932," *Georgia Historical Quarterly* 78 (Summer 1994).

3 See, especially, "Franklin D. Roosevelt: The Patrician as Opportunist," in Richard Hofstadter, *The American Political Tradition and the Men Who Made It* (New York: Knopf, 1948), 311.

4 See Harvard Sitkoff, *A New Deal for Blacks: The Emergence of Civil Rights as a National Issue* (New York: Oxford University Press, 1978).

5 Patricia Sullivan, *Lift Every Voice: The NAACP and the Making of the Civil Rights Movement* (New York: New Press, 2009), 143, 151; Urban League reports cited in *Labor Fact Book 2* (New York: Oriole Edition, 1934, reissued 1973), 130. The Amenia conference showed that even the younger generation of NAACP leaders embraced new economic-based approaches to racial advancement. In 1935, Abram Harris drafted a report on the future of the NAACP that recommended that it ally itself with organized labor, that it appoint A. C. MacNeal as the director of the branches, and that it hire John P. Davis to research Roosevelt's New Deal policies. Walter White, acting NAACP head, shelved the plan. See Raymond Wolters, *Negroes and the Great Depression: The Problem of Economic Recovery* (Westport, Ct.: Greenwood Press, 1970), 219–27.

6 Beth Tompkins Bates, *Pullman Porters and the Rise of Protest Politics in Black America* (Chapel Hill: University of North Carolina Press, 2001); Manning Marable, "A. Philip Randolph and the Foundations of Black American Socialism," *Radical America* 14, no. 2 (March–April 1980): 19; A. Philip Randolph, "Negro Labor and the Church," in *Labor Speaks for Itself on Religion: A Symposium of Labor Leaders throughout the World*, ed. Jerome Davis (New York: Macmillan, 1929), 74, 76; Walter Galenson, *The CIO Challenge to the AFL: A History of the American Labor Movement, 1935-1941* (Cambridge, Mass.: Harvard University Press, 1960), 626.

7 See Langston Hughes, "Cowards from the Colleges," *Crisis* 41 (August 1934); and Robert Cohen, *When the Old Left Was Young: Student Radicals and America's First Mass Student Movement, 1929-1941* (New York: Oxford University Press, 1993), 135–36, 171–72, 209.

8 Harold Preece, "Ishmael Flory Becomes a Prominent Labor Leader," *CD*, city and national editions, August 26, 1939; Harold Preece, "Fisk and Flory," *Crisis* 41 (April 1934); "Fisk U. Students Decline J.C. Engagement," *BAA*, February 17, 1934.

9 John P. Davis noted on the cusp of the first NNC conference in 1936 that a half million young black men and women were on relief. See John P. Davis, "Let Us Build a National Negro Congress" (Washington, D.C.: NNC Sponsoring Committee, 1935), 19.

10 Revels Cayton, "Appendix," in Richard Hobbs, "The Cayton Legacy: Two Generations of a Black Family, 1859-1976" (Ph.D. diss., University of Washington, 1989), 545–50. Hiram Revels served as a senator from Mississippi during Reconstruction. The family moved to the West Coast after Reconstruction's demise, and his grandsons, Horace and Revels Cayton, grew up in Seattle, Washington.

11 Earl Browder report at General Commission meeting, November 15 and 17, 1935, New York City, 23–24 (3744, 1, 515), and Morris Childs, Illinois report, October 19, 1935 (3750, 1, 515), both CPP; "20,000 Hear Thomas Point Way to Reds," *New York Times*, November 28, 1935; "Hatchet Buried by Communists and Socialists," *Washington Post*, November 28, 1935.

12 FBI report on John Preston Davis, Washington, D.C., June 4, 1951, FBI Records-

100-39058, FOIA request 2010, FBI, Washington, D.C. For a full and brilliant examination of Davis's life before 1935, see Hilmar Ludvig Jensen, "The Rise of the African American Left: John P. Davis and the National Negro Congress" (Ph.D. diss., Cornell University, 1997), 1–307.

13 John P. Davis, FBI interview report, New York, August 11, 1954, FBI Records-100-39058; Jensen, "The Rise of the African American Left," 307–467.

14 Report on the League of Struggle for Negro Rights, February 21, 1935 (3572, 1, 515), and Report by "Dodge," General Commission meeting, November 15 and 17, 1935, 8–9 (3744, 1, 515), both CPP.

15 See Saul Alinsky, *John L. Lewis: An Unauthorized Biography* (New York: Vintage, 1970), 62–85, quotes from 63 and 94; Robert H. Zieger, *The CIO, 1935-1955* (Chapel Hill: University of North Carolina Press, 1995); and J. Joseph Huthmacher, *Senator Robert F. Wagner and the Rise of Urban Liberalism* (New York: Atheneum, 1971), 147–51.

16 John P. Davis to Ralph Bunche, March 14, 1934, folder 8, box 2, Ralph Bunche Papers, Special Collection, Young Research Library, University of California at Los Angeles; see also Sullivan, *Lift Every Voice*, 192–93.

17 "New Deal and Race Discussed at Conference," *CD*, national edition, June 1, 1935. The *Journal of Negro Education* published the major papers from this conference; see *Journal of Negro Education* 5, no. 1 (January 1936). The Howard Conference proved to be "groundbreaking," according to historian Jonathan Holloway. In his study of three prominent Howard professors, Holloway explained the differences in opinion among the participants at this conference. See Jonathan Holloway, *Confronting the Veil: Abram Harris Jr., E. Franklin Frazier, and Ralph Bunche, 1919-1941* (Chapel Hill: University of North Carolina Press, 2002), 69–83. William P. Jones discussed the Howard conference as a means to better understand why these black leaders veered away from a southern labor focus, in *The Tribe of Black Ulysses: African American Lumber Workers in the Jim Crow South* (Urbana: University of Illinois Press, 2005), 139–50.

18 At the AFL convention in May 1935 in Atlantic City, John L. Lewis, head of the United Mine Workers, Sidney Hillman of the Amalgamated Clothing Workers, David Dubinsky of the International Ladies' Garment Workers, and Thomas Brown of the Mine, Mill, and Smelter Workers called for industrial organization. When more conservative craft unions voted against their report, Lewis and his allies left the AFL to form the Committee for Industrial Organization within the AFL framework. By 1937, the CIO had legally separated itself from the AFL and was renamed the Congress of Industrial Organizations. See Zieger, *The CIO, 1935-1955*.

19 Holloway, *Confronting the Veil*, 75.

Chapter One

1 The initial sit-down occurred in December, with a recurrence in March, and by April the strike had been settled. See Oscar Hutton Jr., "The Negro Workers and the Labor

Unions in Chicago" (Ph.D. diss., University of Chicago, 1939), 96–97; "Epidemic of Sit Strikes Becomes a Near Hysteria," *Chicago Daily Tribune*, March 17, 1937; SWOC, Field Workers Meeting, April 15, 1937, folder 6, box 124, USWAP; George Schuyler, "Negro Workers Lead in Great Lakes Steel Drive," *Pittsburgh Courier*, July 31, 1937; "Wilson & Bennett Union in Victory Celebration," advertisement, *CD*, March 9, 1940; William Whyte, *Pattern for Industrial Peace* (New York: Harper and Brothers, 1951), 3–17; James Kollros, "Creating a Steel Workers Union in the Calumet Region, 1933 to 1945" (Ph.D. diss., University of Illinois at Chicago, 1998), 260–61; and *Steel Labor*, March 18, 1938.

2 The authors of this landmark study, St. Clair Drake and Horace Cayton, admitted: "The picture of these chapters is a candid-camera shot of the community in the final stages of the Depression and in the midst of the Second World War." Their camera shots depict the extent of changes that had occurred by 1945 but do not trace the historical causality behind them. Although mentioned in their study only in passing, the NNC's work in Chicago proved pivotal to this movement, according to St. Clair Drake, who served as a member of the NNC Chicago Council through the war years and later explained its significance in an oral history. See St. Clair Drake and Horace Cayton, *Black Metropolis: A Study of Negro Life in a Northern City* (1945; Chicago: University of Chicago Press, 1992), 397, 308, and especially chapters 12 and 23; and St. Clair Drake, interview by Robert E. Martin, July 28, 1969, transcript, 18, 36–37, 56–58, 80, Ralph J. Bunche Oral History Collection, number 462, Moorland-Spingarn Research Center, Howard University, Washington, D.C.

3 Richard Wright, with photos by Edwin Rosskam, *12 Million Black Voices* (1941; New York: Basic Books, 2002), 146–47.

4 The most important account of Black Chicago protest politics during the 1930s is Beth Tompkins Bates, *Pullman Porters and the Rise of Protest Politics in Black America* (Chapel Hill: University of North Carolina Press, 2001), especially 7, 12, 15, 116–25, 135–42. Ruth Needleman's excellent work on steelworkers in northwest Indiana illuminates the Indiana black steelworker leadership in the mills. See Ruth Needleman, *Black Freedom Fighters in Steel* (Ithaca, N.Y.: ILR, 2003), especially 6, 27–35, 188–94. For a general account of the CIO in Chicago during the late 1930s, see the pathbreaking book by Lizabeth Cohen, *Making a New Deal: Industrial Workers in Chicago, 1919–1939* (New York: Cambridge University Press, 1990), 251–368. For packinghouse worker organization in Chicago, see Rick Halpern, *Down on the Killing Floor: Black and White Workers in Chicago's Packinghouses, 1904–1954* (Chicago: University of Illinois Press, 1997), especially 96–166; Rick Halpern and Roger Horowitz, *Meatpackers: An Oral History of Black Packinghouse Workers and Their Struggle for Racial and Economic Equality* (New York: Monthly Review Press, 1999); and Horowitz, *Negro and White, Unite and Fight! A Social History of Industrial Unionism in Meatpacking, 1930–90* (Urbana: University of Illinois Press, 1997). For Chicago's black politics during this era, see Charles Branham, "The Transformation of Black Political Leadership in Chicago, 1864–1942" (Ph.D. diss., University of Chicago, 1981); and William Grimshaw,

Bitter Fruit: Black Politics and the Chicago Machine, 1931-1991 (Chicago: University of Chicago Press, 1992). For black culture, see Robert Bone, "Richard Wright and the Chicago Renaissance," *Callaloo* 28 (Summer 1986). Studies by Davarian Baldwin and Adam Green analyze black cultural and community development before and after the Depression, respectively: Davarian Baldwin, *Chicago's New Negroes: Modernity, the Great Migration, and Black Urban Life* (Chapel Hill: University of North Carolina Press, 2007); Adam Green, *Selling the Race: Culture, Community, and Black Chicago, 1940-1955* (Chicago: University of Chicago Press, 2007).

5 John P. Davis, "Plan Eleven"—Jim-Crow in Steel," *Crisis* 43 (September 1936).

6 Arvarh E. Strickland, *History of the Chicago Urban League* (Urbana: University of Illinois Press, 1966), 106-20.

7 Dennis Bethea, "What the People Say," April 30, 1938, and Lucius Harper, "Dustin' Off the News," April 16, 1938, both *CD*, national edition; Drake and Cayton, *Black Metropolis*, 84-85; Foster quoted in Strickland, *History of the Chicago Urban League*, 123.

8 For more on parallel institutions in the 1920s, see Drake and Cayton, "The Fats Years," in Drake and Cayton, *Black Metropolis*, 78-83.

9 A. C. MacNeal to Frances Perkins, March 29, 1933, MacNeal to Joseph Moss, April 11, 1933, Chicago NAACP, Press Release, June and November [1933], Chicago NAACP petition to President of the United States, n.d. [1933], Chicago NAACP, "A Record of Deeds and Action," n.d. [1933], MacNeal to Sears, Roebuck, and Co., June 16, 19, 1933, MacNeal to White, July 8, 29, 31, September 29, 1933, all reel 3, part 12C, *NAACPP*; Archie Weaver to Walter White, January 14, 1934, with enclosure of 1933 annual branch report, reel 4, part 12C, *NAACPP*; Christopher Reed, *The Chicago NAACP and the Rise of Professional Black Leadership, 1910-1966* (Bloomington: Indiana University Press, 1997), 90-108. On the riot, see James Grossman, *Land of Hope: Chicago, Black Southerners, and the Great Migration* (Chicago: University of Chicago Press, 1989).

10 A. C. MacNeal to Walter White, December 28, 1933, and MacNeal to Roy Wilkins, March 15, 1935, both part 12C, reel 3, *NAACPP*.

11 Roy Wilkins to MacNeal, May 2, 1934, MacNeal to Walter White, April 28, 1934, MacNeal to Mary White Overton, May 12, 1934, and MacNeal to the Board of Directors, NAACP, n.d. [1934], all reel 4, part 12C, *NAACPP*; MacNeal to Houston, March 31, 1936, reel 5, part 12C, *NAACPP*; Patricia Sullivan, *Lift Every Voice: The NAACP and the Making of the Civil Rights Movement* (New York: New Press, 2009), 198-99.

12 MacNeal to White, July 14, 1934, Chicago NAACP, invitation to hear John P. Davis, July 31, 1935, Wabash YMCA, Wilkins to MacNeal, January 23, 1935, Irving Mollison to White, January 28, 1936, and MacNeal to Wilkins, April 4, 1936, all reel 5, part 12C, *NAACPP*; MacNeal to White, January 18, 1936, reel 15, part 10, *NAACPP*.

13 Bates, *Pullman Porters*, 7-14, 45-120, quote from 97.

14 Drake and Cayton, *Black Metropolis*, 87-97, 734-36; Horace Cayton, "The Black Bugs," *Nation*, September 9, 1931; Randi Storch, *Red Chicago: American Communism at Its Grassroots, 1928-1935* (Chicago: University of Illinois Press), 111-15; Harold Lasswell

and Dorothy Blumenstock, *World Revolutionary Propaganda: A Chicago Study* (New York: Knopf, 1939), 196–214.

15 See *CD*, national edition, February 22, 1936; "1936 Delegates to the National Negro Congress," compiled by Lori Husband (Matteson, Ill.: Lori Husband, 1998); and "Race Congress Sidelights," *CD*, February 22, 1936.

16 Dennis A. Bethea, "What the People Say," *CD*, March 7, February 15, 1936; Isaac Mc-Natt, "What the People Say," *CD*, March 21, 1936.

17 "National Negro Congress Which Met in Chicago Acclaimed a Success," *New York Age*, February 22, 1936.

18 The Negro Sanhedrin, a name taken from the Jewish Sanhedrin that Napoleon convened in 1807, was an earlier attempt to unify black organizations into one powerful movement. A. Philip Randolph and Chandler Owen, then copublishers of the *Messenger* in New York City, as well as representatives from the African Blood Brotherhood, represented the radical wing at this meeting. Moderate representatives included Howard University professors and NAACP leaders. It met in Chicago in February 1924, but Kelly Miller, its chief organizer, conceived of it not as a mass organization but as an assembly of leaders. "Conservatism had triumphed," one historian concluded of this meeting, and the movement died after the conference. See "A Negro Sanhedrin: A Call to Conference," reprinted in Charles V. Hamilton, *The Black Experience in American Politics* (New York: G. P. Putnam, 1973); and Alvin Cicero Hughes, "Toward a Black United Front: The National Negro Congress Movement" (Ph.D. diss., Ohio University, 1982), 19–61, quote from 49. For the 1936 NNC conference, estimates ran from 5,000 to 8,000 total attendees. See Richard Wright, "Two Million Black Voices," *New Masses*, February 25, 1936; "Universal Unrest among Black People Revealed at National Congress Here," *CD*, national edition, February 22, 1936; and "Twenty-six States Send Delegates to Congress," *CD*, February 15, 1936.

19 Milton Howard, "Frank X. Martel Will Address National Negro Congress," *Daily Worker*, February 7, 1936; "Race Workers of Nation to Convene Here," *CD*, February 8, 1936; Randolph's speech reprinted in "Randolph Says Hope of Negro People Lies in Unity with Labor," *Daily Worker*, March 1, 1936, and in *CD*, national edition, February 22, 1936; NNC, "The Official Proceedings of the National Negro Congress," February 14, 15, 16, 1936 (Washington, D.C.: NNC, 1936), 7–12.

20 Brascher, "Race Congress Sidelights" and "Congress Opens: Delegates Crowd City for Sessions," both *CD*, February 15, 1936; "Resolutions Adopted by the National Congress," *CD*, February 22, 1936; "As Congress Delegates Argued the Labor Question," photo and caption, *CD*, February 22, 1936; NNC, "Official Proceedings"; "Congress Delegates Urged to Inspect Belmont Grill," *CD*, February 15, 1936.

21 See Brascher, "Race Congress Sidelights." Brascher notes that Langston Hughes complained that "some poets can live three days on a dollar" but that black institutions should nevertheless pay them for their services. See also Wright, "Two Million Black Voices"; "Outline of Program for 4-Day Session of Nat. Negro Congress," *CD*, Febru-

ary 15, 1936; NNC, "Official Proceedings," 32–33; and Hazel Rowley, *Richard Wright: The Life and Times* (New York: Henry Holt, 2001), 115–16.

22 Lester B. Granger, "The National Negro Congress: An Interpretation," *Opportunity* 14 (May 1936).

23 Harry Haywood, for example, had heard that a Colonel Warfield had revealed that machine guns were hidden in the Armory for the use of the Red Squad to close down the conference. However, Earl Browder, the head of the CP USA at the time, did not speak as scheduled, indicating a potential deal between the NNC and the Red Squad. See Harry Haywood, *Black Bolshevik: The Autobiography of a Black Communist* (Chicago: Liberator Press, 1978), 457–62; "National Negro Congress Which Met in Chicago Acclaimed a Success," *New York Age*, February 22, 1936; and Claude M. Lightfoot, *Chicago Slums to World Politics* (New York: New Outlook, 1985), 71.

24 Archibald Carey Jr., pastor of the Woodlawn AME Church in Chicago, led the church session titled "How Can the Negro Church Meet the Problems of the Changing Social Order?" Bishop James Bray, Rev. R. A. Carter, and Rev. W. J. Walls acted as key members of the Chicago sponsoring committee for the NNC but later endorsed the petition of clergy that critiqued the Congress for not having enough religious leadership. The executive committee of the NNC had twelve men of the cloth on it. See Granger, "National Negro Congress"; "Church Leaders Oppose Race Congress Program," *CD*, February 15, 1936; "National Race Congress Says Church Is a Prime Factor in Our Progress," *CD*, February 22, 1936; "Church Session," Saturday, February 15, 10:30 A.M., schedule of NNC reprinted in *CD*, February 11, 1936; "What Local Sponsoring Committees Are Doing," folder "NNC 11/4/35 to 12/24/36," reel 15, part 10, *NAACPP*; and W. J. Walls to John P. Davis, January 24, 1936 (333, 8, 1), *NNCP*.

25 Kelly Miller, "The Leftward Drift of the National Negro Congress," *New York Age*, March 7, 1936.

26 Isaac McNatt, "In Defense of the Congress," letter in "What the People Say," *CD*, March 21, 1936.

27 Granger, "National Negro Congress."

28 A. Philip Randolph, "Randolph Says Race Congress Not Communist," *CD*, February 29, 1936; "Randolph Defends the Negro Congress," *Daily Worker*, March 5, 1936.

29 Granger, "National Negro Congress"; "Red Scare at Race Congress Proves to Be a Colossal Joke," *CD*, national edition, Feb. 22, 1936. For examples of letters, see Dennis Bethea, "My Reaction to the National Negro Congress," *CD*, March 7, 1936; McNatt, "In Defense of the Congress"; and J. Wesley Reed, "Race Congress," *CD*, April 4, 1936.

30 See Heywood [Harry Haywood], 1935 District Conference, Chicago, 89–92 (3853, 1, 515), "Negro Work and the National Negro Congress," 73 (3904, 1, 515), Minutes of Buro Meeting, 1–2 (4022, 1, 515), Special Meeting of the Harlem Commission of C.E.C. and the Section Committee, Harlem Section, June 19, 1935, 19–25 (3775, 1, 515), and Minutes of Negro Commission Meetings, June 22, 23, October 3, 30, November 18, 1935, 26–42 (3775, 1, 515), all CPP.

31 "The Defender Asks a Question," *CD*, February 15, 1936.

32 "Jim Crow Practices Assailed by Miners," *CD*, national edition, February 22, 1936.

33 Wilkins to MacNeal, February 25, 1936, and MacNeal to Wilkins, March 14, 1936, both reel 4, part 12C, *NAACPP*; MacNeal to Wilkins, April 4, 1936, reel 5, part 12C, *NAACPP*; Chicago Council of Negro Organizations, list and memorandum from A. L. Foster and A. C. MacNeal, n.d. [1936–37], reel 4, part 12C, *NAACPP*.

34 Eleanor Rye to John P. Davis, May 13, 1936 (547–48, 7, 1), *NNCP*.

35 Strickland, *History of the Chicago Urban League*, 122, 123; Reed, *Chicago NAACP*, 100–101.

36 Beth Bates explained in her study of the BSCP how, during the 1920s, Milton Webster and other BSCP organizers fought for the allegiance of South Side clergy and other black leaders. Bates concluded, "Perhaps more than any other organizer, Webster understood that the Brotherhood's movement was just as much about organizing middle-class citizens as it was about Pullman porters and maids." See Bates, *Pullman Porters*, 76, 101, 138–42. Ernest Smith of the BSCP and NNC believed that Webster wanted to keep the BSCP out of the NNC because Webster "doesn't have a sufficient Labor Base." See Eleanor Rye to John P. Davis, May 13, 1936 (547–48, 7, 1), and October 3, 1936 (500–502, 7, 1), both *NNCP*.

37 The majority of Chicago Council of Negro Organizations organizational activities during its first two years consisted of benefit dinners and studies of discrimination. See November 30, 1935, June 27, 1936, and May 28, 1938, all *CD*. John P. Davis wrote to Eleanor Rye that "[Hank] Johnson ought to use every possible means . . . to bring about a . . . merger" to "stimulate them into activity." John P. Davis to Henry Johnson, April 23, 1936 (17–18, 6, 1), John P. Davis to Charles Burton, May 20, 1936 (803, 3, 1), and John P. Davis to Eleanor Rye, May 18, 1936 (594–95, 7, 1), all *NNCP*. See also Strickland, *History of the Chicago Urban League*, 130–32.

38 Leonidas McDonald, "McDonald Stirs Federation of Labor on Jim Crow Policies and Rules: 'National Negro Congress Must Live On,'" speech before Chicago Federation of Labor, March 1936 (155–58, 7, 1), and Eleanor Rye to John P. Davis, March 15, 1936 (542, 7, 1), both *NNCP*. McDonald also attended an echo meeting of the NNC conference at the Pilgrim Baptist Church in early March as well as spoke to his own union, the Amalgamated Meat Cutter and Butcher Workmen. See "Meat Workers Hear Congress Reports," *CD*, March 7, 1936.

39 See Interviews for Gary Survey of Steel Situation [summer 1936] and "The Gary Project: Summary and Recommendations" [fall 1936], folder 1, box 280, CABP.

40 Ibid. See also Kim Scipes, "Trade Union Development and Racial Oppression in Chicago's Steel and Meatpacking Industries, 1933–1955" (Ph.D. diss., University of Illinois–Chicago, 2003), 86, 95–96, 155, and Steuben to Jack, May 27, 1935, 166–68 (290, 3750, 1, 515), both CPP.

41 This Marxist revisionist account of the Civil War and Reconstruction illuminated the new economic and working-class focus of the NNC and the emergent CIO during the 1930s. Although Du Bois did not join the NNC, his work reveals as much about the change of black intellectual thought during the New Deal era as it does about the

nineteenth century. See W. E. B. Du Bois, *Black Reconstruction in America: 1860–1880* (1935; New York: Touchstone, 1992), quote from 57.

42 Labor Committee of NNC, "Steel Drive Moves Colored People into Action!" (Philadelphia: NNC, 1936) (948, 20, 1), *NNCP*.

43 Wright, "Two Million Black Voices," 15; Randolph in NNC, "Official Proceedings"; "Randolph Says Hope of Negro People Lies in Unity with Labor."

44 Arna Bontemps, Introduction, *Black Thunder* (1936; Boston: Beacon Press, 1968), xiv–xv; NNC, Fine Arts Committee, Chicago, "Reception in Honor of Arna Bontemps," flyer for April 26, 1936, event, folder "National Negro Congress," box 21, ABP; Waldo Martin, *No Coward Soldiers: Black Cultural Politics in Postwar America* (Cambridge, Mass.: Harvard University Press, 2005), 3–12.

45 Richard Wright, "A Tale of Folk Courage," draft review of *Black Thunder*, item 1018, box 86, RWP; Rowley, *Richard Wright*, 111; Margaret Walker, *Richard Wright, Daemonic Genius: A Portrait of the Man, a Critical Look at His Work* (New York: Amistad, 1988), 78; NNC, "Reception in Honor of Arna Bontemps," ABP.

46 Richard Wright (author of foreword) and other unidentified contributors, "National Negro Congress Issue," *Illinois Labor Notes* 4 (March 1936), copy in *NNCP* vertical file #003–479–480, General Research and Reference Division, Schomburg Center for Research in Black Culture, New York Public Library, New York.

47 John P. Davis to A. Philip Randolph, July 10, 1936 (453–54, 7, 1), John P. Davis to Van Bittner, n.d. [July 14, 1936] (19–20, 4, 1), Bittner to Davis, July 18, 1936 (9, 4, 1), and Davis to Charles Burton, July 22, 1936 (789, 3, 1), all *NNCP*; Dennis Dickerson, *Out of the Crucible: Black Steelworkers in Western Pennsylvania, 1875–1980* (Albany: State University of New York Press, 1986), 136–37.

48 Stephen Brier, "Labor, Politics, and Race: A Black Workers Life" (reprinted 1937 Works Progress Administration interview selection), in *Labor History* 23 (1982): 416–21; John P. Davis to Van Bittner, n.d. [July 14, 1936] (19–20, 4, 1), Bittner to Davis, July 18, 1936 (9, 4, 1), and Davis to Charles Burton, July 22, 1936 (789, 3, 1), all *NNCP*; Halpern, *Down on the Killing Floor*, 121, 137, 160.

49 "Name Gary Negroes as Delegates for Chicago Congress," February 13, 1936, and "Reddix Named an Officer in Negro Group," February 18, 1936, both *Gary Post-Tribune*; "Outline of Program for 4-Day Session of National Negro Congress," *CD*, February 15, 1936.

50 Needleman, *Black Freedom Fighters in Steel*, especially the section on George Kimbley, 13–35, 137, 191–94, quote from 27. See also J. L. Reddix to John P. Davis, April 10, 1936 (339, 7, 1), *NNCP*.

51 Henry Johnson to John P. Davis, September 10, 1936 (73–75, 6, 1), Johnson to Davis, n.d. [summer 1936?] (76–77, 6, 1), Rye to Davis, August 12, 1936 (438–40, 7, 1), and Rye to Davis, October 3, 1936 (542, 7, 1), all *NNCP*.

52 See Schuyler, "Negro Workers Lead in Great Lakes Steel Drive."

53 Henry Johnson to John P. Davis, September 1, 1936 (21–22, 6, 1), *NNCP*; "CIO Suspension Called Joke by Local Director," *CD*, August 8, 1936.

54 "CIO Drives to Organize Race Workers," *CD*, August 1, 1936; Johnson to Davis, September 10, 1936 (73–75, 6, 1), *NNCP*; Clifford Odets, *Waiting for Lefty and Other Plays* (1935; New York: Grove Press, 1993), 30–31.

55 Johnson to Davis, September 1, 1936 (21–22, 6, 1), and September 10, 1936 (73–75, 6, 1), both *NNCP*; SWOC, Field Workers Meeting, November 16, 1936, folder 4, box 124, USWAP; Eleanor Rye to John P. Davis, n.d. [summer 1936] (430, 7, 1), *NNCP*; "Women in Steel," September 12, 1936, and "NNC to Give Cooperation to CIO Drive," August 20, 1936, both *CD*; Eleanor Rye to John P. Davis, August 27, 1936 (461, 7, 1), and Rye to Davis, n.d. [1937] (471, 7, 1), both *NNCP*.

56 Johnson to Davis, n.d. [spring/summer 1936] (76–77, 6, 1), and Johnson to Davis, September 1, 10, 1936, both *NNCP*. In his letter of September 1 to Davis, Johnson (perhaps grudgingly) admitted that Rye had been "of considerable aid" to McDonald in the Indiana Harbor.

57 "CIO Drives to Organize Race Steel Workers," *CD*, August 1, 1936; Eleanor Rye to John P. Davis, October 3, 1936 (500–502, 7, 1), and Rye to Davis, n.d. [fall 1936?] (471, 7, 1), both *NNCP*.

58 Eleanor Rye to John P. Davis, May 13, 1936 (547–48, 7, 1), Rye to Davis, August 27, 1936 (461, 7, 1), Rye to Davis, October 3, 1936 (660–65, 7, 1), and Rye to Davis, October 6, 1936 (660–65, 7, 1), all *NNCP*; "NNC to Give Cooperation to CIO Drive," August 20, 1936, "CIO Endorsed by Labor Mass Meeting Thurs.," October 3, 1936, and "Steel Auxiliary in Local Confab," November 14, 1936, all *CD*.

59 Rye to Davis, n.d. [fall 1936?] (471, 7, 1), October 3, 1936 (471, 7, 1), and August 27, 1936 (461, 7, 1), all *NNCP*; "Workers' Wives Plan Nursery to Aid Steel," September 19, 1936, "Steel Auxiliary in Local Confab," November 14, 1936, and "Women in Steel," September 12, 1936, all *CD*.

60 Frank M. Davis, *Livin' the Blues: Memoirs of a Black Journalist and Poet* (Madison: University of Wisconsin Press, 1992). For McCray, see his columns in *CD* in the 1930s and 1940s. Dewey Jones, former managing editor of the *Defender*, became the head of the Chicago Council in 1939 but passed away suddenly only months later. See "Social Worker Succeeds Late Dewey Jones," *CD*, national edition, May 27, 1939.

61 Rye to Davis, August 27, 1936 (430, 7, 1), and Rye to Davis, n.d. [August/September 1936] (430, 7, 1), both *NNCP*. For articles about race and steelworkers, see *CD*, August 1, 8, 20, 27, September 12, 19, October 3, November 14, 1936. See also Hutton, "Negro Workers and the Labor Unions," 109–12.

62 George Schuyler, "Schuyler Visits Steel Centers in Ohio and Pennsylvania; Finds Race Workers Loyal to Company; Making Big Money," *Pittsburgh Courier*, July 24, 1937. Schuyler noted Chicago, Gary, and Cleveland as major exceptions to the trend of black loyalty to steel companies.

63 See Schuyler, "Negro Workers Lead in Great Lakes Steel Drive."

64 George Powers, "The Legend of Joe Cook: Union and Community Organizer," 1973, file 4, box 3, Samuel C. Evett Papers, Calumet Regional Archives, Indiana University Northwest, Gary.

65 Ibid.

66 Ibid.; NLRB, Case XIII-C-828, May 1, 1939, Testimony of Joe Cook in the Matter of Valley Mould and Iron Corporation and Steel Workers Organization Committee, #1550, p. 15, NLRBT.

67 Powers, "Legend of Joe Cook."

68 "Prominent Negroes Push Steel Drive," *Steel Labor*, February 20, 1937; Ben Carreathers to John Gray, April 22, 1937 (406, 9, 1), John P. Davis to Philip Murray, February 19, 1937 (527–28, 11, 1), Joe Cook to John P. Davis, June 19, 1937 (240, 9, 1), Henry Johnson to Ben Carreathers, February 25, 1937 (635–36, 10, 1), Henry Johnson to John P. Davis, March 5, 1937 (610, 10, 1), and L. McDonald, Report on Mass Meeting, Indiana Harbor, February 19, 1937 (493–94, 11, 1), all *NNCP*. See also Cohen, *Making a New Deal*, 334. On organizing the steel conference, see also John P. Davis to Philip Murray, August 27, 1936 (822–24, 6, 1), John P. Davis to A. Philip Randolph, September 5, 1936 (478, 7, 1), and John P. Davis to Charles Burton, January 14, 1937 (129, 9, 1), all *NNCP*.

69 "More Than 100 Lodges Set Up in Middle West," *Steel Labor*, January 23, 1937; Henry Johnson to Ben Carreathers, February 25, 1937 (635–36, 10, 1), L. McDonald to John P. Davis, n.d. [early 1937] (497, 11, 1), Henry Johnson to John P. Davis, March 5, 1937 (610, 10, 1), and L. McDonald, Report on Mass Meeting, February 19, 1937 (493–94, 11, 1), all *NNCP*; "CIO to Explain Attitude on Race Workers," *CD*, March 13, 1937; Thomas Gugliemo, *White on Arrival: Italians, Race, Color, and Power in Chicago, 1890–1945* (New York: Oxford University Press, 2003), especially 137–40.

70 SWOC, Field Workers Meeting, April 15, 1937, folder 6, box 124, USWAP.

71 Powers, "Legend of Joe Cook"; Cook to Davis, June 19, 1937 (568–69, 11, 1), and John P. Davis to Rev. L. R. Mitchell, April 8, 1937 (568–69, 11, 1), both *NNCP*; "John P. Davis Visits Steel Strike Region," *CD*, July 10, 1937.

72 "Chicago Riot Toll Is 10," *New York Times*, June 20, 1937; "Funeral for Slain Steel Worker Held," *CD*, June 26, 1937; Powers, "Legend of Joe Cook"; Needleman, *Black Freedom Fighters in Steel*, 43; Drake and Cayton, *Black Metropolis*, 320–25.

73 Petrillo and others quoted in "Federation Leaders Loose Attack on 'Mob Movement,'" *Chicago Daily Tribune*, June 10, 1937. See also Barbara Newell, *Chicago and the Labor Movement: Metropolitan Unionism in the 1930's* (Urbana: University of Illinois Press, 1961), 146–47; and "Suppressed Film Reveals Police as Aggressors in Strike Riot," *Washington Post*, June 17, 1937.

74 "Suppressed Film Reveals Police as Aggressors in Strike Riot," *Washington Post*, June 17, 1937; Newell, *Chicago and the Labor Movement*, 147; "Eighth Victim Dies from Chicago Riot," *New York Times*, June 9, 1937; Dr. Lewis Andreas, interview by Studs Terkel in *Hard Times: An Oral History of the Great Depression* (New York: Pantheon, 1970), 144.

75 The union later filed charges with the NLRB, and Cook testified in Washington. Cook "spent two nights in the railroad station, and munched on dry crackers" because neither SWOC nor the NNC had the funds to cover his expenses. See Powers, "Legend of Joe Cook"; and NLRB, May 1, 1939, Testimony of Joe Cook, p. 15, NLRBT.

76 "Workers Vote at Interlake to Test C.I.O.," *CD*, September 11, 1937; Powers, "Legend of Joe Cook"; NLRB, In the Matter of Valley Mould and Iron Corporation and Lodge 1029, Amalgamated Association of Iron, Steel, and Tin Workers of North America, Case No. R-542, decided on February 4, 1938, *DONLRB*, 5:95–99; ibid., Supplemental Decisions, March 23, 1938, 6:133–35; "John P. Davis Visits Steel Strike Region," *CD*, July 10, 1937; "The Fight for a Bonafide Union, Is a Fight for Democracy," n.d. [1937–38] (578, 12, 1), and Joe Cook to John P. Davis, June 19, 1937 (240, 9, 1), both *NNCP*.

77 George Kimbley to John P. Davis, March 18, 1938 (873, 13, 1), *NNCP*; Negro Workers' Councils of the National Urban League, Bulletin #12, August 7, 1936, folder 1, box 280, CABP.

78 NNC, "Excerpts of Speech Delivered by Philip Murray," October 16, 1937, Philadelphia NNC conference proceedings (970–73, 11, 1), *NNCP*; "Delegate," *CD*, national edition, October 23, 1937.

79 NNC, "National Negro Congress Supports the Steel Workers Organizing Committee," n.d. [1936] (947, 20, 1), *NNCP*; Davis, "'Plan Eleven': Jim Crow in Steel."

80 SWOC, Field Workers Meeting report, January 21, 1937, folder 5, box 124, USWAP.

81 See Chicago district SWOC, Field Workers Meeting report, folder 6, box 124, USWAP; Vincent D. Sweeney, "United Steel Workers of America . . . The First Ten Years," *Steel Labor*, August, September, October issues, 1946; Ronald Filippelli, "The History Is Missing, Almost: Philip Murray, the Steelworkers, and the Historians," and David Brody, "The Origins of Modern Steel Unions: The SWOC Era," both in *Forging a Union of Steel: Philip Murray, SWOC, and the United Steelworkers*, ed. Paul F. Clark, Peter Gottlieb, and Donald Kennedy (Ithaca, N.Y.: ILR Press, 1987), quote from 5; and Kollros, "Creating a Steel Workers Union in the Calumet Region," 209–10.

82 Whyte, *Pattern for Industrial Peace*; NLRB, May 1, 1939, Testimony of Joe Cook, pp. 57, 70, and 72, NLRBT.

83 See Newell, *Chicago and the Labor Movement*, 144–45; Mark McColloch, "Consolidating Industrial Citizenship: The USWA at War and Peace, 1939–46," in Clark, Gottlieb, and Kennedy, *Forging a Union of Steel*, 58; and Annette Van Howe to Frank Marshall Davis, January 9, 1946, folder 5, box 280, CABP.

84 Murray and Bittner agreed to speak at several NNC events in 1937 and 1938, but they repeatedly turned down requests for contributions. See Davis to Burton, July 22, 1936 (789, 3, 1), Philip Murray to John P. Davis, November 10, 1936 (797, 6, 1), Davis to Murray, February 19, 1937 (527–28, 11, 1), Murray to Davis, May 14, 1937 (637, 11, 1), Murray to Davis, October 2, 1937 (725, 11, 1), and Regional Director, SWOC [name illegible] to John P. Davis, November 10, 1937 (156–57, 13, 11), all *NNCP*.

85 "Tenants Win 2 Fights in Hi Rent Tilt," *CD*, April 17, 1937; John Gray to John P. Davis, April 12, 1937 (124–25, 10, 1), Davis to John Gray, April 14, 1937 (125, 10, 1), both *NNCP*; Henry Johnson, Assistant National Director, PWOC, Chicago, to John P. Davis, March 16, 1938 (778, 13, 1), B. D. Amis to John P. Davis, May 23, 1938 (25, 12, 1), and John P. Davis to Ethel Clyde, September 7, 1940 (520–23, 12, 1), all *NNCP*; "Housing Paramount Issue on City's South and West Sides," February 28, 1938, "National Negro

Congress Begins Midwest Confab," October 29, 1938, "Labor Pledges Fight on Restrictive Covenants," November 4, 1939, "Picket Buildings in Fight for Lower Rent,"
November 23, 1940, "Pickets Bring Pressure after Tenant's Eviction," November 30,
1940, and "Police 'Keep House' While Tenants Picket," December 7, 1940, all *CD*.

86 E. Pauline Myers and Ishmael Flory to John P. Davis, February 28, 1938 (177, 14, 1),
NNCP; Joint Committee on Labor Education and International Brotherhood of Red
Caps, "The Negro and the Labor Movement Today: A Forum Series," pamphlet of
schedule of events for spring 1938, n.d. [early 1938], folder 8, box 6, GPP; Howard
Lawrence, "Elect Flory as Head of Labor Council," October 28, 1939, "Forum Feb. 12
to Consider Civil Rights," January 28, 1939, "Negro Labor Rallies on South Side Sunday," October 11, 1939, "Labor Council to Make Debut at Conference," October 14,
1939, and "Labor Pledges Fight on Restrictive Covenants," November 4, 1939, all *CD*;
"Negro AFL'ers Push Fight on Discrimination," September 19, 1939, and "Push Drive
to Remove Color Bar in Unions," June 23, 1939, both *Chicago Record*.

87 George Mavigliano and Richard Lawson, *The Federal Art Project in Illinois: 1935–1943*
(Carbondale: Southern Illinois University Press, 1990), 1–16, 24.

88 Ibid., 30–41.

89 Charles White, translation for an article after return to Europe, 4, n.d. [early 1950s], 7,
roll 3189, CWP.

90 Grossman, *Land of Hope*.

91 Herbert Marsh [March], "Stockyards Report on Chicago," July 1935 (3850, 1, 515), CPP;
"squeal" quote by Philip Armour, as cited in Carl Sandburg, "Making the City Effi-
cient," *La Follette's Weekly Magazine* 3, no. 39 (September 30, 1911).

92 Henry Johnson to John P. Davis, September 18, 1937 (686, 10, 1), *NNCP*; Roger Horowitz, "The Path Not Taken: A Social History of Industrial Unionism in Meatpacking"
(Ph.D. diss., University of Wisconsin, Madison, 1990), 241.

93 Harold Preece, "What Goes on in Packingtown?" *CD*, September 23, 1939; Herbert
March, interview by Leslie Orear, December 19, 1979, tape recording, ILHS; Leslie
Orear, interview by author, October 28, 2003, July 27, 2004, Chicago.

94 Orear, interview by author. See also Halpern and Horowitz, *Meatpackers*, 27–64; and
Halpern, *Down on the Killing Floor*.

95 Chicago SWOC, Field Workers Meeting, July 1, 1937, folder 7, box 124, USWAP.

96 Orear, interview by author; March, interview by Orear; Needleman, *Black Freedom
Fighters in Steel*, 28.

97 "Race Man Is Given High Labor Post," January 22, 1938, and "Race Leader Organizes
for Armour Fight," August 13, 1938, both *CD*.

98 Henry Johnson to John P. Davis, March 16, 1938 (778, 13, 1), *NNCP*.

99 E. Pauline Myereres [Myers] to "Friends," February 26, 1938, folder "NNC 1/10/38–
4/1/38," reel 15, part 10, *NAACPP*; "Mass Meet at Du Sable Hits Lynching Evil," *CD*,
March 12, 1938.

100 A Philip Randolph to John P. Davis, February 18, 1938 (672, 14, 1), and March 12,

1938 (675, 14, 1), and Charles Burton to John P. Davis, May 12, 1938 (260, 12, 1), all *NNCP*.

101 Philip Murray to John P. Davis, March 18, 1938 (188, 14, 1), *NNCP*.

102 "Hank Johnson's Advice: 'Organize! Organize! Organize!'" *CIO News*, packinghouse edition, November 14, 1938.

103 The story of PWOC—its black workers, the preachers who allied with them, and the activism that produced work stoppages, strikes, and slowdowns—has been told with eloquence by both the workers themselves and labor historians. See Halpern and Horowitz, *Meatpackers*; Halpern, *Down on the Killing Floor*; and Horowitz, *Negro and White, Unite and Fight!*

104 Chicago Council of the NNC, report, n.d. [1936] (89–90, 7, 1), Eleanor Rye to John P. Davis, May 13, 1936 (547–48, 7, 1), John P. Davis to A. Philip Randolph, June 6, 1936 (618, 7, 1), Chicago NNC, Report on Council at Cleveland NNC Meeting, June 19, 20, 1936, 13–14 (224–25, 2, 1), Davis to Randolph, July 10, 1936 (453–54, 7, 1), and John P. Davis to Philip Murray (822–24, 6, 1), all *NNCP*.

105 See John Gray to John P. Davis, April 14, 1937 (125, 10, 1), John P. Davis to Ishmael Flory, April 22, 1938 (379, 13, 1), Henry Johnson to "Mann" (John P. Davis), n.d. [1936] (76–77, 6, 1), and Eleanor Rye to John P. Davis, August 12, 1936 (438–40, 7, 1), all *NNCP*.

106 The AFL granted the BSCP an international charter in 1936, and the union won its first contract in August 1937. Randolph frequently missed NNC meetings due to AFL conventions and BSCP work. John P. Davis to A. Philip Randolph, September 5, 1936 (478, 7, 1), John P. Davis to A. Philip Randolph, November 4, 1936 (646, 7, 1), Charles Burton to John P. Davis, June 19, 1937 (27, 9, 1), Charles Burton to John P. Davis, October 1, 1938 (149, 12, 1), and Ishmael Flory to John P. Davis, May 31, 1939 (994, 17, 1), all *NNCP*.

107 James Ford, "The United Negro Front in the U.S.A.," March 29, 1937 (4065, 1, 515), "The Negro Movement in the U.S.A.," March 28, 1937 (4065, 1, 515), Bulletin of the Organizational and Educational Commission, "Communist Work for the Second National Negro Congress," August 21, 1937 (4070, 1, 515), and NNC, Minutes of the Meeting of the Executive Board, October 18, 1937, Philadelphia (4074, 1, 515), all CPP. Even the assessments of more conservative black leaders like Claude Barnett of the Associated Negro Press and Roy Wilkins of the NAACP showed that the NNC had Communists within it but that it did not take orders from the CP leadership. In 1937, Barnett wrote: "The National Negro Congress is an organization formed a year ago by groups representing various cities which have local groups. Its projectors are regarded as somewhat radical, a few of them at least being affiliated with the Communist Party." In 1937, Wilkins claimed that rumors of Communist control of the NNC "are wholly without foundation." See Claude Barnett, Memo for John A. Stephens, Manager of Industrial Relations, Chicago district, Carnegie–Illinois Steel Corporation, January 23, 1937, folder 1, box 280, CABP; and Roy Wilkins, Memo to Board of Directors [NAACP], March 9, 1936, part C, folder 383, *NAACPP*.

108 "Communists Meet in 18th Convention," *CD*, April 30, 1938. In addition to these sources, the memoirs of Claude Lightfoot and Harry Haywood, both top black Communists, reveal little work with or knowledge about the NNC. See Lightfoot, *Chicago Slums to World Politics*, 70–83; and Haywood, *Black Bolshevik*, 457–62.

109 The distinction between Communists matters because certain scholars have uncritically romanticized or unreasonably condemned the CP's role in Popular Front networks. See Eric Arnesen, "No 'Graver Danger': Black Anticommunism, the Communist Party, and the Race Question," *Labor: Studies in Working-Class History of the Americas* 3 (Winter 2006): 13–52.

110 John Dorwalksi and George Patterson, SWOC, Sub-District 3, Chicago, to Philip Murray, August 7, 1939, and George Patterson to Philip Murray, August 11, 1939, both folder 1, box 7, GPP.

111 Ben Burns, "Dies, Strikebreaker, Rallies to Packers' Aid," November 18, 1939, "Dies Quiz Flops, Blows Lid off Armour-AFL Tie," November 27, 1939, and "Packing Workers Win Agreements at Armour," January 27, 1940, all *Chicago Record*; "Diversion of CIO Funds for Red Activities Told: Dies Hears Ousted Head of Union," *Chicago Tribune*, November 18, 1939.

112 "Mr. Flory and the A.F. of L.," *CD*, April 6, 1940.

113 Harry W. Deck, Labor's Non-Partisan League, circular letter, March 31, 1939, folder 1, box 7, GPP. This group included Johnson, Cook, and many others from SWOC and PWOC.

114 Herbert March, interview by Leslie Orear, December 19, 1979, ILHS; "Hail CIO Victory in Yards," *Chicago Daily Record*, December 5, 1938; "Union Stock Yards Sign C.I.O. Pact," *CD*, March 11, 1939.

115 Dickerson had participated in a wide array of NNC activities since 1936. See "Prominent Negroes Push Steel Drive," *Steel Labor*, February 20, 1937; "National Negro Congress Begins Midwest Confab," October 29, 1938, "Forum Feb. 12 to Consider Civil Rights," January 28, 1939, "Asks PWOC And Armour to Arbitrate," July 15, 1939, "Labor Council to Make Debut at Conference," October 14, 1939, and "We Need a Man Like Earl Dickerson in Congress," February 10, 1940, all *CD*; "Negro Labor Rallies on South Side Sunday," October 11, 1939, "Map Fight to Guard Civil Rights in State," October 30, 1939, and "South Side Demands State Act on Relief," October 30, 1939, all *Chicago Daily Record*; and Erik S. Gellman, "'Carthage Must Be Destroyed': Race, City Politics, and the Campaign to Integrate Chicago Transportation Work, 1929–1943," *Labor: Studies in Working-Class History of the Americas* 2, no. 2 (Summer 2005): 97–114.

116 Orear, interview by author, October 28, 2003.

117 See Cohen, *Making a New Deal*, 336.

118 Hutton, "Negro Workers and the Labor Unions," 93, 99; interview from November 22, 1937, in Horace Cayton to George Mitchell, *Black Workers in the New Unions* (Chapel Hill: University of North Carolina Press, 1939), 223–24.

119 *Labor Fact Book 5* (New York: Oriole Edition, 1941, reissue 1973), 131, 140. By 1939 in

Chicago, there were 2,000 black members in SWOC (with 7,000 more in Indiana), another 4,000 in PWOC, and 800 porters in Chicago's BSCP. See Hutton, "Negro Workers and the Labor Unions," tables 10 and 11, pp. 118–19. Gary numbers come from *Labor Fact Book 4* (New York: Oriole Edition, 1938, reissue 1973), 138–40, 165.

120 Annette Van Howe to Frank Marshall Davis, January 9, 1946, folder 5, box 280, CABP. After the war, the United Packinghouse Workers remained more immune to red-baiting than most other unions, and with Ralph Helstein as its elected president, it became one of the staunchest antiracist and most democratic unions in the United States. See Sam Parks, interview by Leslie Orear, December 8, 1980, tape recording, ILHS; March, interview by Orear, December 19, 1979; Scipes, "Trade Union Development and Racial Oppression in Chicago's Steel and Meatpacking Industries"; Halpern, *Down on the Killing Floor*; Halpern and Horowitz, *Meatpackers*; and Horowitz, *Negro and White, Unite and Fight!*

121 Margaret Goss Burroughs, "Saga of Chicago's South Side Community Arts Center," 10, copy in author's possession; *American Federation of Arts* 34 (August–September 1941): 370–71; Norman MacLeish, in "Exhibition of Negro Artists of Chicago" catalog, Washington, D.C., 1941, "Material on Other Artists," roll 3195, CWP.

122 Wright, *12 Million Black Voices*, 146–47; Gordon Parks, *A Choice of Weapons* (1965; New York: Berkley Medallion, 1967), 171–72; see also Baldwin, *Chicago's New Negroes*; and Green, *Selling the Race*. Baldwin's book concentrates on the 1920s, and its epilogue signifies the upcoming significance of the NNC. Green analyzes cultural networks after 1940 in Black Chicago.

123 Davis claimed that the votes of 3 million blacks in 1940 could become the deciding factor for 124 congressional races, ten state governor races, and ten senatorial races. See "John P. Davis Predicts New Deal Victory," *CD*, July 29, 1939.

124 Reed, *Chicago NAACP*, 107; Dennis S. Nordin, *A New Deal's Black Congressman: A Life of Arthur Wergs Mitchell* (Columbia: University of Missouri Press, 1997); John P. Davis to Henry Johnson, November 10, 1938 (725, 10, 1), *NNCP*.

125 Christopher Manning, *William L. Dawson and the Limits of Black Electoral Leadership* (DeKalb: Northern Illinois University Press, 2009).

126 "Hold Funeral Service for Slain Labor Leader; Body En Route to Texas for Burial," Associated Negro Press, press release, Chicago, November 1944, folder 3, box 280, CABP; "Labor Leader Slain by Irate Organizer," *Chicago Bee*, October 29, 1944; Drake and Cayton, *Black Metropolis*, 737.

127 "A United Front," editorial, *CD*, September 24, 1938.

128 Cook's community activism included getting black doctors hired at the South Chicago Community Hospital, successfully petitioning for a South Chicago public library, educating students about African American history, integrating the local YMCA, and organizing relief for tenant farmers in Tennessee. See Powers, "Legend of Joe Cook."

129 John P. Davis to Lillian Summers, June 13, 1939 (800, 17, 1), and Chicago NNC Council, Meeting Minutes, March 24, 1942 (376–81, 29, 1), both *NNCP*; "Council Wages War on

Unfair Shift System," December 23, 1939, "Picket Buildings in Fight for Lower Rent," November 23, 1940, "Pickets Bring Pressure after Tenant's Eviction," November 30, 1940, and "Police 'Keep House' While Tenants Picket," December 7, 1940, all *CD*.

130 Frank Marshall Davis, "Negro-White Unity: It Built Unions," *Chicago Star*, August 30, 1947; Gellman, "Carthage Must Be Destroyed"; "Defense Girls' Club Places Job Seekers," September 5, 1942, *CD*, national edition.

Chapter Two

1 Esther Cooper Jackson, "This Is My Husband" (New York: National Committee to Defend Negro Leadership, n.d. [1950s]), 14–22, folder 3, box 4, ESP; James Jackson, interview transcript by Linn Shapiro, October 19, 1992, 1–2, folder 25, box 14, JJP.

2 Esther and James Jackson, "Memories of the Southern Negro Youth Congress," interview by James V. Hatch, April 5, 1992, in *Artist and Influence* 11 (1992): 161–63; Esther Cooper Jackson, "This Is My Husband," 14–22; James Jackson, interview by Shapiro, 9–11; National Student League, flyer and call, Third Convention, December 26–28, 1933, Howard University, folder 36, box 18, and James Jackson, "The World beyond the Campus," part of 1931 Virginia Union University speech, reprinted in *Intercollegian*, October 1932, folder 5, box 2, both JJP.

3 Esther Cooper Jackson, "This Is My Husband," 14–22; *Panther*, newspaper of Virginia Union University, December 2, 1933, Special Collections Library, Virginia Union University, Richmond. For a compelling analysis of Palmer Weber's career, see Patricia Sullivan, *Days of Hope: Race and Democracy in the New Deal Era* (Chapel Hill: University of North Carolina Press, 1996), 70–83, 129–31, 208–17, 260–72.

4 Workers of the Writers' Program of the Work Projects Administration in the State of Virginia and the Hampton Institute, *The Negro in Virginia* (New York: Hastings House, 1940), 309.

5 Megan Shockley, *"We, Too, Are Americans": African American Women in Detroit and Richmond, 1940–54* (Urbana: University of Illinois Press, 2004), 67, 77.

6 Esther Cooper Jackson, "This Is My Husband," ESP.

7 J. Douglas Smith, *Managing White Supremacy: Race, Politics, and Citizenship in Jim Crow Virginia* (Chapel Hill: University of North Carolina Press, 2002); Richard Love, "In Defiance of Custom and Tradition: Black Tobacco Workers and Labor Unions in Richmond, Virginia, 1937–1941," *Labor History* 35 (Winter 1994).

8 Herbert Northrup, *Organized Labor and the Negro* (New York: Harper, 1944), 102–3.

9 Stuart Bruce Kaufman, *Challenge and Change: A History of the Tobacco Workers International Union* (Urbana: University of Illinois Press, 1986), 68–70.

10 Ibid., 69, 70; "Tobacco 'Big Five' Sales Reported," *Richmond Times-Dispatch*, April 14, 1937; Mrs. J. L. [Josephine] Wright, interviewed June 2, 1939, and Kate Beale, interviewed May 12, 1939, in Nancy J. Martin-Perdue, *Talk about Trouble: A New Deal Portrait of Virginians in the Great Depression* (Chapel Hill: University of North Carolina Press, 1996).

11 Northrup, *Organized Labor*, 110–11; James Jackson, interview by Shapiro, 2.

12 Charles S. Johnson, "The Tobacco Worker: A Study of Tobacco Factory Workers and Their Families," 125–34, parts 1, 2, Industrial Studies Section, NRA, entry 39, box 62, Misc. Reports and Documents, 1933–37, NRAR.

13 See Smith, *Managing White Supremacy*, 4, 10; William Chafe, *Civilities and Civil Rights: Greensboro, North Carolina, and the Black Struggle for Freedom* (New York: Oxford University Press, 1980), 8–9; and Arthur Dean, "Problems of Youth," *Richmond News Leader*, February 17, 1937.

14 "Profile: Who Is Ed Strong?" *Cavalcade* (November 1941): 2; "Announcing the Edward E. Strong Memorial Education Trust Fund," n.d. [1950s], folder 15, box 2, ESP; "Sketch: Our National Secretary E. E. Strong," *Congress Vue* 1, no. 2 (May 1943); Lorence Norton, National Negro Youth Movement, to James Jackson, June 9, 1933, folder 3, box 4, and National Student League "Pledge," 1933, folder 36, box 18, both JJP.

15 National Student League "Pledge," 1933, folder 36, box 18, JJP. Protests about quotas and segregation at the YMCA College led to a faculty walkout and formation of Roosevelt College in 1945.

16 "Profile: Who Is Ed Strong?" *Cavalcade* (November 1941).

17 Ed Strong to John P. Davis, June 29, 1936 (724, 7, 1), NNCP; "On to Richmond! For the Southern Negro Youth Conference, February 12–14, 1937," folder 29, box 2, ESP.

18 Louis E. Burnham, "New Attitudes among Youth Pointed Out," *Norfolk Journal and Guide*, February 13, 1937.

19 "Call for a Southern Negro Youth Congress," reel 15, part 10, NAACPP.

20 Burnham, "New Attitudes among Youth."

21 "On to Richmond," January 6, 1937, and editorials, "The Youth's Conference," January 22, 1937, both *Richmond Planet*.

22 *Richmond Times-Dispatch*, February 13, 1937; *Richmond News Leader*, February 12, 1937; James Ford, "The United Negro People's Front in the U.S.A.," March 29, 1937, report, 15 (4065, 1, 515), CPP.

23 *Richmond Planet*, February 20, 1937.

24 *Richmond Times-Dispatch*, February 14, 1937; *Richmond Planet*, February 20, 1937.

25 Cliff MacKay, "Candid Photo Word Personality Study of Negro Youth Session," *Norfolk Journal and Guide*, February 20, 1937; *Richmond Planet*, February 20, 1937.

26 *Richmond Planet*, February 20, 1937. See also *Richmond Times-Dispatch*, February 15, 1937.

27 Jonathan Holloway, *Confronting the Veil: Abram Harris Jr., E. Franklin Frazier, and Ralph Bunche, 1919–1941* (Chapel Hill: University of North Carolina Press, 2002), 155–56, 45–46, 123–56, 202–5. For more on the investigation of Howard University, see folder 3, box 259, JBMP.

28 MacKay, "Candid Photo."

29 "Richmond Inquiring Reporter," *Norfolk Journal and Guide*, February 27, 1937.

30 The headlines of all of the papers included reports of automobile strikes at General Motors in Detroit and steel strikes in places like Chicago and statements about the

strikes and other declarations of John L. Lewis's United Mine Workers. See *Richmond News Leader*, January 14, 27, 1937; *Norfolk Journal and Guide*, March 13, 1937; and *Richmond Times-Dispatch*, February 18, 1937. On the reaction to the Supreme Court's backing of the Wagner Act, see *Richmond News Leader*, April 12, 1937.

31 *Richmond Planet*, February 20, 1937.

32 The Youth Act, backed by the American Youth Congress and SNYC, would have allotted work-study funds and employed the five out of every six jobless youth that the National Youth Act failed to cover. In 1936, three future NNC and SNYC leaders—Ed Strong, Christopher Columbus Alston, and Thelma Dale—testified on behalf of Bill S 3658 during Senate hearings. See *American Youth Act: Hearings before the Committee on Education and Labor, United States Senate, March 19-21, 1936* (Washington, D.C.: Government Printing Office, 1936), 84–87, 187–89, 223–25. See also *Norfolk Journal and Guide*, February 27, 1937; Robert Cohen, *When the Old Left Was Young: Student Radicals and America's First Mass Student Movement, 1929-1941* (New York: Oxford University Press, 1993), 188–95; "Chain Gang Story to F. D.," *BAA*, February 27, 1937.

33 "Judiciary: Black Red Freed," *Time Magazine*, May 3, 1937.

34 *Richmond Times-Dispatch*, April 14, 1937; *Richmond News Leader*, January 27, April 3, 1937; *Richmond Planet*, March 20, 1937. See also *Richmond Times-Dispatch*, February 18, April 13, 1937; and *Norfolk Journal and Guide*, March 13, 1937.

35 *Richmond Times-Dispatch*, April 17, 1937; *Richmond News Leader*, April 17, 19, 1937.

36 "TIWU [*sic*] to Press Tobacco Drive," *Richmond News Leader*, April 16, 1937; *Richmond Times-Dispatch*, April 16, 20, 1937.

37 Mary Schroeder, "'32 Marcher Remembers Friend Who Fell to Guns," *Detroit Free Press*, May 3, 1982, clipping in folder 4, box 1, CAP; Chris Alston, excerpts from 1985 interview, and Alston quotes in "Hunger Marchers Remember," *People's Weekly World*, March 14, 1992, both folder 16, box 1, CP Biography Files, Tamiment Library, New York University, New York.

38 *Richmond Planet*, April 24, 1937; "Richmond Inquiring Reporter," *Norfolk Journal and Guide*, April 24, 1937.

39 *Richmond Planet*, April 24, 1937; *Norfolk Journal and Guide*, April 24, 1937.

40 "CIO Squadron Prepared for Long Battle," *Richmond News Leader*, April 20, 1937; *Richmond Planet*, April 24, 1937; *Norfolk Journal and Guide*, April 24, 1937.

41 *Richmond Planet*, April 24, 1937.

42 *Norfolk Journal and Guide*, May 1, 1937; *Richmond Planet*, May 15, 1937; *Richmond News Leader*, April 27, 1937.

43 *Richmond Times-Dispatch*, May 8, 13, 1937.

44 *Richmond Planet*, May 15, 1937; Augusta Jackson, "A New Deal for Tobacco Workers," *Crisis* 45, no. 10 (October 1938).

45 *Richmond Times-Dispatch*, May 10, 1937; *Richmond News Leader*, May 7, 1937.

46 *Richmond Planet*, May 15, 1937; *Richmond Times-Dispatch*, May 8, 1937; *Norfolk Journal and Guide*, May 22, 1937.

47 "Picket Plant," *Richmond News Leader*, May 7, 1937; Alice Burke, "The World Changes," *Richmond Planet*, May 22, 1937.

48 Alice Burke, "The World Changes"; Edward Strong, "The New Youth Offensive," *Richmond Planet*, May 15, 1937.

49 Hewin quoted in *Richmond Times-Dispatch*, May 13, 1937; Strong, "The New Youth Offensive."

50 *Richmond Times-Dispatch*, May 12, 13, 1937.

51 Lucy Randolph Mason was hired by the CIO to organize clothing workers and was paid a salary of $1,400 in 1937. See Lucy Mason to Sidney Hillman, Textile Workers Organizing Committee, New York, September 11, 1937, "Correspondence 1917–44," reel 62, series 5, *ODP*.

52 Charles Lakey, TWIU, Winston-Salem, to John P. Davis, Washington, D.C., November 4, 1934 (914, 10, 1), "Analysis of Questionnaires in Five Plants in the Tobacco Industry," n.d. [1934–35] (268–72, 15, 1), John P. Davis, "Proposal for Initiation of a National Organizing Campaign for Tobacco Workers," May 18, 1937 (55–58, 9, 1), John P. Davis to John Brophy, CIO, Washington, D.C., May 18, 1937 (55–58, 9, 1), and John P. Davis to E. M. Hutchinson, Winston-Salem, June 15, 1937 (368, 10, 1), all *NNCP*.

53 John P. Davis, "Proposal for Initiation of a National Organizing Campaign for Tobacco Workers," and John P. Davis to John Brophy, CIO, Washington, D.C., May 18, 1937 (55–58, 9, 1), both *NNCP*.

54 In addition to their correspondence with Davis, Alston and Strong went to Washington to meet with Davis and CIO officials. See *Richmond News Leader*, May 17, 1937.

55 Federation Press Release, "CIO TO LAUNCH ORGANIZATION DRIVE IN TOBACCO INDUSTRY," June 11, 1937, and E. Lewis Evans to Messers Blaine and Latta, June 24, 1937, both folder "CIO," box 11, series I, TWIUP.

56 "Virginia's Labor Front," *Richmond News Leader*, April 5, 21, 1937; Evans to Blaine and Latta, June 24, 1937, folder "CIO," box 11, series I, and E. Lewis Evans to J. E. Lentie, Richmond, Va., July 9, 1937, folder "Local 219, 1933–1937," box 31, series III, both TWIUP.

57 *Richmond News Leader*, April 17, 1937; *Richmond Planet*, May 15, 1937.

58 *Richmond Planet*, May 15, 1937.

59 Strong, "The New Youth Offensive."

60 *Norfolk Journal and Guide*, July 3, 1937; *Richmond News Leader*, July 6, 1937; *Richmond Planet*, July 10, 1937.

61 *Norfolk Journal and Guide*, July 10, 1937; *Richmond News Leader*, July 1, 1937.

62 See Contract between Tobacco Stemmers and Laborers Union and Tobacco By-Products & Chemical Corporation, July 8, 1937, in "Tobacco By-Products and Chemical Corp., Richmond, Va." (#228), reel 60, series 4, *ODP*.

63 Workers at the Tobacco By-Products company now earned as much as fourteen dollars per week. See *Richmond News Leader*, July 1, 3, 6, 7, 1937; *Richmond Planet*, July 10, 1937; *Norfolk Journal and Guide*, July 10, 1937.

64 Arts Committee of the Richmond Youth Federation (affiliated with the SNYC), "First Annual Lecture Series on Negro Life and Culture," November 1 to December 6, 1937, Armstrong High School, Richmond, Va., pamphlet and schedule, folder 25, box 3, ESP; *BAA*, Richmond edition, October 29, 1938.

65 Workers of the Writers' Program of the Work Projects Administration, *The Negro in Virginia*, v, 215–46; Arts Committee of the Richmond Youth Federation, "First Annual Lecture Series on Negro Life and Culture."

66 Richardson, a son of a railroad worker from Washington, D.C., attended Virginia Union University, worked with the poet Sterling Brown in organizing a theater in Washington, D.C., and appeared alongside Paul Robeson in a performance of *Emperor Jones* for the Harlem Suitcase Theatre before joining the SNYC in Richmond. See Augusta Strong, "Southern Youth's Proud Heritage," *Freedomways* 4, no. 1 (1964).

67 Edward Strong, "October Youth," *Richmond Planet*, September 25, 1937; *Norfolk Journal and Guide*, October 23, 1937; *Richmond Planet*, February 10, 1938.

68 Alice Burke, "The World Changes"; Donald Burke, "The World Changes," *Richmond Planet*, February 19, 1938; James Jackson, interview by Shapiro, 9.

69 *Richmond Planet*, February 10, 1938; Alice Burke, "The World Changes"; H. Harris, in "Richmond Inquiring Reporter," *Norfolk Journal and Guide*, April 24, 1937.

70 Elsa Barkley Brown, "Negotiating and Transforming the Public Sphere: African American Political Life in the Transition from Slavery to Freedom," *Public Culture* 7 (1994). After the demise of Reconstruction, black female domestic and laundry workers in cities like Atlanta resisted labor exploitation, including engaging in strikes. See Tera W. Hunter, *To 'Joy My Freedom: Southern Black Women's Lives and Labors after the Civil War* (Cambridge, Mass.: Harvard University Press, 1997).

71 L. C. Crump to E. Lewis Evans, May 13, 1937, folder "L. C. Crump, 1934–1937," box 15, series II, and Crump to Evans, August 21, 1937, folder "Local 219, 1933–1937," box 31, series III, both TWIUP.

72 E. Lewis Evans to L. C. Crump, Richmond, August 24, 1937, folder "Local 219, 1933–1937," box 31, series III, TWIUP.

73 NLRB, Case No. R-971, *DONLRB*, 9:579–83.

74 James Jackson, Richmond, to John P. Davis, April 29, 1938 (755, 13, 1), NNCP.

75 John Suttle to John P. Davis, March 5, 1938 (858–59, 14, 1), and James E. Jackson to John P. Davis, April 29, 1938 (755, 13, 1), both NNCP.

76 Details about Grandison's life come from James Jackson, interview by Shapiro, 13.

77 Ibid.; John P. Davis to Francis Grandison and James Jackson, April 30, 1938 (538–39, 13, 1), NNCP.

78 Ed Strong, Francis Grandison, J. M. Tinsley, Henry McDougall, and Thomas Richardson to Harry F. Byrd, U.S. Senate, Washington, D.C., May 17, 1938 (45, 15, 1), NNCP.

79 *Norfolk Journal and Guide*, June 4, 1938. Senator Byrd kept a list of black ministers and other professionals who could be bought. Although no evidence exists placing Arrington on that list, Jackson exposed his collusion with the company. See Lewis Randolph

and Gayle Tate, *Rights for a Season: The Politics of Race, Class, and Gender in Richmond, Virginia* (Knoxville: University of Tennessee Press, 2003).

80 For example, *Richmond News Leader*, June 22, 1938.

81 J. Robert Smith, "Whites Blamed for Rioting" and "Richmond Echoes," BAA, Richmond edition, July 2, 1938; "Negro, White Leaders Decry Fight Disorder," *Richmond News Leader*, June 23, 1938; "Richmond Inquiring Reporter," *Norfolk Journal and Guide*, May 15, 1937. According to Lizabeth Cohen's study of industrial workers in Chicago, the Louis fight broke the record for the largest radio audience (63.7 percent of potential listeners). Cohen linked the battle for industrial unions to Louis, whom she deems "the fighting symbol of the Great Depression." In the South, this symbolism emboldened some while frightening others. See Lizabeth Cohen, *Making a New Deal: Industrial Workers in Chicago, 1919–1939* (New York: Cambridge University Press, 1990), 328, 330.

82 J. R. Smith, "Whites Blamed for Rioting" and "Richmond Echoes," BAA, Richmond edition, July 2, 1938; "Negro, White Leaders Decry Fight Disorder," *Richmond News Leader*, June 23, 1938.

83 Smith, "Whites Blamed for Rioting" and "Richmond Echoes"; "Negro, White Leaders Decry Fight Disorder."

84 John P. Davis and the SNYC had targeted British American Tobacco Company and had informed John Brophy that the CIO should join with them. Davis to John Brophy, May 20, 1937 (23, 9, 1), *NNCP*; *BAA*, Richmond edition, August 6, 1938; *Norfolk Journal and Guide*, August 6, 1938; James Jackson, interview by Shapiro, 1–2.

85 For Corbin background, see *American Tobacco v. United States of America*, U.S. Circuit Court of Appeals, Sixth Circuit, June 30, 1941, 3:1682, from British American Tobacco Documents Archive, digital archive, University of California, San Francisco. Quote from tobacco owner, in Augusta Jackson, "New Deal for Tobacco Workers," 330; James Jackson, interview by Shapiro, 5–6.

86 James Jackson, interview by Shapiro, 13; *Norfolk Journal and Guide*, August 13, 20, 1938; "White Picketers Join Striking Race Workers," *CD*, national edition, August 20, 1938.

87 *Norfolk Journal and Guide*, August 13, 20, 1938; *Richmond News Leader*, August 10, 1938.

88 *Norfolk Journal and Guide*, September 10, 1938; *Richmond News Leader*, August 18, 1938; "Tobacco Workers Win; Dixie Jolted," *Amsterdam News* (New York), September 3, 1938.

89 *Richmond News Leader*, September 27, 1938.

90 *Norfolk Journal and Guide*, October 8, 1938. Later that month, two other black female strikers, Hulda Cox and Mamie Richardson, were arrested for disorderly conduct. See *Richmond News Leader*, September 29, 1938.

91 *Norfolk Journal and Guide*, October 8, 1938; *Richmond News Leader*, September 27, 28, 1938.

92 *BAA*, Richmond edition, October 1, 1938; *Norfolk Journal and Guide*, October 8, 1938.

93 James Jackson, interview by Shapiro, 2–3, 7. See also Eugene Genovese, *Roll, Jordan, Roll: The World the Slaves Made* (New York: Vintage Books, 1972), 109–12.

94 *BAA*, Richmond edition, October 15, 1938; *Richmond News Leader*, October 1, 1938.

95 "Personnel Tobacco Organizing Committee, Richmond, Virginia," August 30, 1938 (436, 17, 1), *NNCP*; *Richmond News Leader*, August 18, 1938.

96 "Personnel Tobacco Organizing Committee, Richmond, Virginia," August 30, 1938 (436, 17, 1), *NNCP*; A. T. White Jr., "Thousands Employed in Carolina," *Norfolk Journal and Guide*, March 26, 1938; Kaufman, *Challenge and Change*, 96, 103–5.

97 *Norfolk Journal and Guide*, October 29, 1938; *Richmond News Leader*, October 20, 1938.

98 Tobacco manufacturing was one of the few industries that did not suffer huge revenue losses during the 1930s, so mechanization explains this decrease. See Northrup, *Organized Labor*, 105.

99 Annual wages in the tobacco industry declined from $870 in 1929 to $705 in 1934. A survey done by the Bureau of Labor Statistics of ten stemmeries in the 1930s shows that not a single company had integrated machines into its production process. See *Richmond News Leader*, August 29, 1938; Northrup, *Organized Labor*, 108, 109; Kaufman, *Challenge and Change*, 76; and *Labor Fact Book 4* (New York: Oriole Edition, 1938, reissue 1973), 72.

100 "New Wage Act May Cost Jobs of 1,000 Here," *Richmond News Leader*, July 2, 1938; "Leaf Labor Policies Hit," *Richmond News Leader*, August 29, 1938.

101 NLRB, Case No. R-971, *DONLRB*, 9:579–83.

102 "If the Fellow on the Ladder Would Just Get Up and Face Forward," political cartoon, *Richmond Leader*, April 9, 1938.

103 Case No. R-971, "Motion of American Tobacco Company, Incorporated, Respondent, Further Hearing," November 7, 1938, folder "American Tobacco Co., 1936–1939," box 6, series I, and E. Lewis Evans to C. H. Farmer, Richmond, May 24, 1938, folder "Local 202, 1937–1944," box 25, series III, both TWIUP; Kaufman, *Challenge and Change*, 90; Northrup, *Organized Labor*, 114.

104 Kaufman, *Challenge and Change*, 90; Northrup, *Organized Labor*, 114.

105 NLRB, Case No. R-971, *DONLRB*, 10:1171–72.

106 E. Lewis Evans to Martha Cosby, Richmond, July 19, 1938, folder "Local 182, 1935–1942," box 11, series III, TWIUP; *Norfolk Journal and Guide*, April 22, 1939; John P. Davis to Francis Grandison and James Jackson, Richmond, April 30, 1938 (538–39, 13, 1), *NNCP*; Kaufman, *Challenge and Change*, 88–89; Northrup, *Organized Labor*.

107 *Norfolk Journal and Guide*, September 16, August 19, 1939; Kaufman, *Challenge and Change*, 91; Northrup, *Organized Labor*, 114, 118; Gunnar Myrdal, *An American Dilemma: The Negro Problem and Modern Democracy* (1944; Evanston: Harper and Row, 1962), 1107; "Total Tobacco Stored Here Sets Record," *Richmond News Leader*, September 23, 1938.

108 Delegates attended the Birmingham SNYC conference in 1939, including a large number of adult community leaders, who "found both leadership and willing aides among the young people." See Augusta Strong, "Southern Youth's Proud Heritage," 42–43.

109 The looming war in Europe became an increasingly important issue for SNYC activists. Applying the CP's newfound policy against intervention in the "imperialist" war abroad (which became the party's dominant policy following the Hitler-Stalin Pact in August 1939) to black youth, the SNYC called for a repeal of the Conscription Act. The *Norfolk Journal and Guide*, October 12, 1939, editorialized against this decision in a column titled "Youth Headed in the Wrong Direction." On behalf of the SNYC, Strong fired back by calling "compulsory military training" the "antithesis of democracy," which had "sold Ethiopia down the river" while promoting a war to "preserve the decadent British empire." See Strong, "To the Editor of the Journal and Guide," n.d. [October 1939], folder 3, box 2, ESP.

110 See Robin D. G. Kelley, *Hammer and Hoe: Alabama Communists during the Great Depression* (Chapel Hill: University of North Carolina Press, 1990), 195–220.

111 Esther Cooper Jackson, "This Is My Husband"; "James Jackson," folder 23, box 3, ESP; "Profile: Who Is Ed Strong?" *Cavalcade* (November 1941); Schroeder, "'32 Marcher Remembers Friend Who Fell to Guns"; C. Columbus Alston to John P. Davis, February 20, 1940 (179, 18, 1), *NNCP*; Robin Kelley, "Christopher Columbus Alston, 1913–1995: Organizer, Fighter, and Historian," clipping from *Against the Current* found in folder 9, box 1, CAP.

112 Contract between Gas, Coke, and Chemical Workers of District #50 and Tobacco By-Products & Chemical Corporation, 1939, and amended on July 22, 1940, in "Tobacco By-Products and Chemical Corp., Richmond, Va." (#228), reel 60, series 4, *ODP*; Robert Korstad, "Food, Tobacco, Agricultural, and Allied Workers (FTA-CIO)," in *Encyclopedia of the American Left*, ed. Paul Buhle, Mari Jo Buhle, and Dan Georgakas (New York: Garland, 1990), 234–35.

113 L. V. Freeman to John P. Davis, NNC, March 14, 1940 (904, 21, 1), and R. E. Himmaugh to John P. Davis, October 2, 1941 (361, 24, 1), both *NNCP*; Shockley, "We, Too, Are Americans," 80. For more on Owen Whitfield and UCAPAWA's organizing during the war, see Erik S. Gellman and Jarod Roll, *The Gospel of the Working Class: Labor's Southern Prophets in New Deal America* (Chicago: University of Illinois Press, 2011).

114 NLRB, In the Matter of American Tobacco Company and Tobacco Workers Organizing Committee, UCAPAWA, Case No. R-5568, decided on July 13, 1943, *DONLRB*, 51:308–13; NLRB, In the Matter of R. J. Reynolds and Tobacco Workers Organizing Committee, UCAPAWA, Case No. 5-R-1356, decided on October 13, 1943, *DONLRB*, 52:1311–23. See also Robert Korstad, *Civil Rights Unionism: Tobacco Workers and the Struggle for Democracy in the Mid-Twentieth-Century South* (Chapel Hill: University of North Carolina Press, 2003); and Michael K. Honey, *Southern Labor and Black Civil Rights: Organizing Memphis Workers* (Chicago: University of Illinois Press, 1993).

115 Theodosia Simpson to Florence Castile, November 16, 1946, folder "North Carolina," box 5, SNYCP. The SNYC also corresponded with Local 15, FTA-CIO, during Operation Dixie. See Reuel Stanfield to "Friends," October 22, 1946, and February 10, 1947, folder "Correspondence, 1946–1947, South Carolina," box 3, SNYCP.

116 Korstad, *Civil Rights Unionism*, 149; Barbara Griffith, *The Crisis of American Labor:*

Operation Dixie and the Defeat of the CIO (Philadelphia: Temple University Press, 1988); Augusta Jackson, "A New Deal for Tobacco Workers," 322–24; Shockley, *"We, Too, Are Americans,"* 150.

117 Allan S. Haywood, Vice President and Director of Organization, CIO, Washington, D.C., to CIO Regional and Sub-Regional Directors, May 24, 1946 (#76), reel 56, series 4, *ODP*; Honey, *Southern Labor and Black Civil Rights*; Griffith, *Crisis of American Labor*, xiii, 26, 42.

118 Kaufman, *Challenge and Change*, 99–105.

119 NLRB, Larus & Brother Company, Inc., and TWIU, Local 219 (AFL), in the Matter of Larus & Brother and UCAPAWA, CIO, Case No. 5-R-1413 and Case No. 5-R-1437, decided on February 16, 1944, *DONLRB*, 54:1345–51; NLRB, In the Matter of Larus & Brother Company, Inc., and TWIU, Local 219 (AFL), Case No. 5-R-1413, decided on June 30, 1945, *DONLRB*, 62:1075–85; Kaufman, *Challenge and Change*, 99–105; Shockley, *"We, Too Are Americans"*, 81.

120 John Egerton's study, for example, focuses on the potentialities of southern liberals during this era. "One of the things I have seen in retrospect," he wrote, "is how favorable the conditions were for substantive social change in the four or five years right after World War II." See John Egerton, *Speak Now against the Day: The Generation before the Civil Rights Movement in the South* (New York: Alfred A. Knopf, 1994), 10.

121 Chafe, *Civilities and Civil Rights*, 238–39.

122 Patricia Sullivan described this period as a hopeful era when the members of this liberal network felt they had the potential to topple Jim Crow, writing further that during the war the network became black-led and southern white liberals either had to come along or become apologists for segregation. The SNYC movement in Richmond confirms this idea, albeit a few years earlier, when during the New Deal its members came out in front of not just the civil rights movement but also the CIO's industrial union movement in the South. See Sullivan, *Days of Hope*, 4–7, 168.

123 "Davis Cites Dangers of Differential," *Norfolk Journal and Guide*, June 26, 1937.

Chapter Three

1 John P. Davis, "Statement . . . before the Sub-Committee of the U.S. Senate on the Wagner-Carter–Van Nuys Anti-Lynching Bill," n.d. [February 1940 hearings] (20–23, 21, 1), *NNCP*; "Lynch Bill Clash Stirs Spectators," *New York Times*, italics added, February 8, 1940.

2 Activists often used this phrase, beginning in 1938, to describe Washington's police brutality. See "Protest Groups to Fight D.C. Cop Brutality," *BAA*, June 11, 1938.

3 Washington Council, NNC, "Wipe Out the Jim-Crow System in Washington!" pamphlet, n.d. [June 1939], folder 1342, box 60, NAACP-DC.

4 See Dan Carter, *Scottsboro: A Tragedy of the American South* (Baton Rouge: Louisiana State University Press, 1979); Harvard Sitkoff, *A New Deal for Blacks: The Emergence of Civil Rights as a National Issue* (New York: Oxford University Press, 1978), 268–97;

Philip Dray, *At the Hands of Persons Unknown: The Lynching of Black America* (New York: Random House, 2002); and Christopher Waldrep, *African Americans Confront Lynching: Strategies of Resistance from the Civil War to the Civil Rights Era* (Latham, Md.: Rowman and Littlefield, 2009). Scholars who have looked broadly at racial violence include Martha Biondi, *To Stand and Fight: The Struggle for Civil Rights in Postwar New York City* (Cambridge, Mass.: Harvard University Press, 2003); Robin D. G. Kelley, *Hammer and Hoe: Alabama Communists during the Great Depression* (Chapel Hill: University of North Carolina Press, 1990); Timothy B. Tyson, *Radio Free Dixie: Robert F. Williams and the Roots of Black Power* (Chapel Hill: University of North Carolina Press, 1999); and Rebecca Hill, *Men, Mobs, and the Law: Anti-Lynching and Labor Defense in U.S. Radical History* (Durham: Duke University Press, 2009).

5 Address of the President of the United States, January 6, 1941, 87, part 1 (Washington, D.C.: Government Printing Office, 1941), 46–47.

6 See Kate Masur, *An Example for All the Land: Emancipation and the Struggle over Equality in Washington, D.C.* (Chapel Hill: University of North Carolina Press, 2010), 8–12, 125, 159, 213.

7 Constance Green, *The Secret City: A History of Race Relations in the Nation's Capital* (Princeton, N.J.: Princeton University Press, 1967), 126–79, quote from 163.

8 Ibid., quotes from 166, 173.

9 For a comparison to Chicago's 1919 riot, see the conclusion of James Grossman, *Land of Hope: Chicago, Black Southerners, and the Great Migration* (Chicago: University of Chicago Press, 1989).

10 Green, *Secret City*, 180–213; Federal Writers' Project, *Washington, City and Capital* (Washington, D.C.: Works Progress Administration, Government Printing Office, 1937), 81–82.

11 Hilmar Ludvig Jensen, "The Rise of the African American Left: John P. Davis and the National Negro Congress" (Ph.D. diss., Cornell University, 1997), 327.

12 Raymond Wolters, *The New Negro on Campus: Black College Rebellions of the 1920s* (Princeton, N.J.: Princeton University Press, 1975).

13 Thelma Dale Perkins, interview by Erik S. Gellman, May 20–24, 2003, Chapel Hill, N.C., transcript, 1.

14 Jonathan Holloway, *Confronting the Veil: Abram Harris Jr., E. Franklin Frazier, and Ralph Bunche, 1919-1941* (Chapel Hill: University of North Carolina Press, 2002), 41.

15 "375 Delegates at Brussels War Enclave," January 16, 1935, and Lyonel Flourant, "In the Vanguard," October 2, 1935, both *Hilltop*, Howard University newspaper, Washington, D.C.; "Ain't Going to Study War No More," May 2, 1936, and "H.U. Students Join National Antiwar Strike," April 25, 1936, both *BAA*; Perkins, interview by Gellman, transcript, 1, 7–8.

16 "New Deal and Race Discussed at Conference," *CD*, national edition, June 1, 1935; *Journal of Negro Education* 5, no. 1 (January 1936): 1–125; Holloway, *Confronting the Veil*, 69–83.

17 "H.U. Students Endorse NNC" and "Youth Committee of N.N.C. Hears Bunche,"

January 20, 1936, and Helen Callis and William Davis, "Howard Sends Delegates to Convention," February 21, 1936, and "Liberal Club Notes," September 30, 1936, all *Hilltop*, Howard University newspaper, Washington, D.C.; "Washington's Social Whirl," *CD*, March 14, 1936.

18 Edward Strong to John P. Davis (870, 7, 1), *NNCP*.

19 The investigation resulted in Ickes dismissing the charges against Johnson as coming largely out of Miller's professional jealousy. See "Kelly Miller Says," *CD*, June 8, 1935; and "Johnson Shielded Dorsey in Howard Communist Probe," June 20, 1936, and "Perry Howard Says His Son Learned Communism at H.U.," July 25, 1936, both *BAA*.

20 Doxey A. Wilkerson, "William Alphaeus Hunton: A Life That Made a Difference," *Freedomways* 10, no. 3 (third quarter, 1970).

21 "Bunche, the future diplomat," historian Jonathan Holloway wrote, "demonstrated astonishingly little sensitivity to a grassroots movement sensibility that was emerging in his own neighborhood." See Holloway, *Confronting the Veil*, quotes from 56, 75. For Dorsey's criticism, see Emmett Dorsey, "The Negro and Social Planning," *Journal of Negro Education* 5, no. 1 (January 1936): especially 107–8.

22 Michele F. Pacifico, "'Don't Buy Where You Can't Work': The New Negro Alliance of Washington," *Washington History* (Spring/Summer 1994): 74, 80, 81; "New Negro Alliance," series on the history of affiliated organizations, *National Negro Congress Washington Council News* 3, no. 5 (June 1939), copy in folder 1342, box 60, NAACP-DC; Paul D. Moreno, *From Direct Action to Affirmative Action: Fair Employment Law and Policy in America, 1933–1972* (Baton Rouge: Louisiana State University Press, 1997).

23 "Legal Lynching Is Deplored at D.C. Scottsboro Meet," *BAA*, April 25, 1936.

24 "Girl, 17, Says Cop Beat Her," *BAA*, May 30, 1936.

25 Charley Cherokee, "National Grapevine," *CD*, national edition, June 14, 1941 (quote); "Roosevelt Attacked on Course in Haiti," *Washington Post*, September 12, 1932; "Races: Elks and Equality," *Time Magazine*, August 12, 1935; "4,000 Groups Contacted for Race Congress," *CD*, national edition, December 28, 1935; "James Finley Wilson," *Journal of Negro History* 37 (1952).

26 Washington Council, NNC, to Ernest Brown, Chief of Police, Washington, D.C., November 5, 1936 (90–92, 4, 1), *NNCP*.

27 Ibid.; see also "10-Year Massacre by Washington Police Takes Forty Race Lives," October 24, 1936, and "Demand Congressional Probe into D.C. Police Massacre," October 31, 1936, both *CD*, national edition.

28 Ernest W. Brown to John P. Davis (10, 9, 1), *NNCP*; "Seek to Authorize Cop Brutality Probe," February 6, 1937, "Washington Group Seeks Member for Police Ct. Bench," March 13, 1937, and "Delegation Seeks Race Judge for District of Columbia," March 27, 1937, all *CD*, national edition.

29 "Murders by Police in Nation's Capital Protested at Meet," May 22, 1937, and "Roosevelt Fails to Name Houston Judge; White Man Nominated by President," August 7, 1937, both *CD*, national edition.

30 John P. Davis, with attached statement by Leroy Scurry to Major Ernest Brown, June 1,

1937 (102–3, 9, 1), *NNCP*; "Shot by Cop, Man Is Fined \$25 at Trial," August 28, 1937, "W. Templeton Is 52nd Victim of D.C. Police," September 4, 1937, and "Officer Exonerated in Death of Youth," September 11, 1937, all *BAA*.

31 Federal Writers' Project, *Washington, City and Capital*, 84.

32 "Shot by Cop, Man Is Fined \$25 at Trial" and "Anti-lynch Bill Set-Back Is Bitter Blow to Father Whose Son, 15, Was Killed in '32," *BAA*, August 28, 1937. See also "FDR Suggests Lynch Probes" and "D.C. Bar Group Raps Police Lawlessness," March 26, 1938, "2nd Cloture Vote Beaten" and "Mother Sues for \$10,000 in Police Slaying," February 19, 1938, all *BAA*.

33 See John P. Davis to Walter White, July 20, 1937, and August 12, 1937, reel 15, part 10, *NAACPP*.

34 Walter White to John P. Davis, February 26, March 8, 14, April 1, 1938, White to Edward P. Lovett, Esq., March 14, 1938, John P. Davis to White, February 2, March 7, 30, 1938, Gertrude B. Stone to White, March 23, 1938, with memorandum, "Anti-Lynching Conference—National Negro Congress," and White to William Pickens, Columbia, S.C., April 19, 1938, all reel 15, part 10, *NAACPP*.

35 Houston quoted in Patricia Sullivan, *Days of Hope: Race and Democracy in the New Deal Era* (Chapel Hill: University of North Carolina Press, 1996), 220, and chapter 6; "Davis Helps Soviets Mark Anniversary," *CD*, national edition, December 4, 1937. Davis's FBI records contain numerous factual errors about his biography and his political views. However, in an interview to have Ralph Bunche cleared of Communist ties in 1954, Davis apparently admitted he did not know if he was a CP member (and never had any evidence like a membership card), but he did for a period consider himself part of the party. See FBI files on Davis and FBI, New York interview with John P. Davis, August 11, 1954, FBI Records-100-39058, FOIA request 2010, FBI, Washington, D.C.

36 Washington Council, NNC, antilynching conference press release (477, 3, 3), and Robert F. Wagner to NNC, March 19, 1938 (613, 15, 1), both *NNCP*; "Push Fight for Anti-lynch Bill, March 19, 1938, "News from the Nation's Capital," March 26, 1938, and "Civic Body to Fight Lynch Bill Baiters" and "N.N.C. Calls It Good Idea," April 2, 1938, all *CD*, national edition. After witnessing the conference, one member of both the NAACP and the NNC in Washington wrote to White asking where the NAACP national executives "now stand" in relation to the "resolutions passed" and also lamented that he "[did] not enjoy seeing friction between such important organizations as the NNC and NAACP." See L. Wray Choate to Walter White, April 1, 1938, reel 15, part 10, *NAACPP*.

37 See Patricia Sullivan, *Lift Every Voice: The NAACP and the Making of the Civil Rights Movement* (New York: New Press, 2009), 228–29; Kenneth R. Janken, *White: The Biography of Walter White, Mr. NAACP* (New York: New Press, 2003), 235–40, 246; and Robert L. Zangrando, *The NAACP Crusade against Lynching, 1909-1950* (Philadelphia: Temple University Press, 1980), 139–65.

38 "Heil Hitler!" editorial, *BAA*, April 9, 1938; James Reese, "Resolution," March 10, 1938

(1064–65, 12, 1), Mavel L. Lockhart to Washington Council, NNC, March 15, 1938 (900, 13, 1), J. M. Harrison Jr. to John P. Davis, March 24, 1938 (590, 13, 1), and Charles Edward Russell to John P. Davis, March 24, 1938 (556, 14, 1), all *NNCP*; "Bar Group Raps Police Lawlessness," *BAA*, March 26, 1938.

39 John P. Davis to Melvin C. Hazen, June 13, 1938 (660–61, 13, 1), and Ernest W. Brown to Senator Robert Bulkley, July 26, 1938 (137–43, 12, 1), both *NNCP*; "Cop Shoots Cabbie," *BAA*, June 4, 1938.

40 "Citizens Protest Police Brutality," *BAA*, June 25, 1938; "Discrimination Scored during Youth Confab," *CD*, national edition, July 15, 1939; L. Wray Choate to "Friends," n.d. [1938] (721, 12, 1), *NNCP*.

41 "D.C. Communists Protest Deaths by Trigger Cops," *BAA*, June 18, 1938.

42 "D.C. Communists Protest Deaths by Trigger Cops," June 18, 1938, "Reds Join War on Police Brutality," July 2, 1938, "How Washington Protests Police Brutality," and "Coffins Barred as Reds March against Police," July 16, 1938, and "Bounce Police Chief, Reds in D.C. Cry Out," July 23, 1938, all *BAA*; "Pickets Protest Police Murders in Washington," *CD*, national edition, July 16, 1938.

43 "Civilization Takes Holiday," *BAA*, July 2, 1938.

44 See Holloway, *Behind the Veil*, 41; and Green, *Secret City*, 199–226, quote from 224.

45 See "Coffins Barred as Reds March against Police," July 16, 1938, and "Cop Killings Must Stop: 59 Killed by Washington Trigger Men—You May Be Next," July 2, 1938, both *BAA*.

46 "Make Washington Safe for Negro Womanhood," press release, August 30, 1938 (71–72, 18, 1), Dorothy Brice and Ruth Clark, Washington, D.C., affidavits, August 11, 1938 (83 and 86, 12, 1), and John P. Davis to Doxey Wilkerson, June 22, 1938 (659, 15, 1), all *NNCP*.

47 Lyonel Flourant, "In the Vanguard," October 2, 1935, *Hilltop*, Howard University newspaper, Washington, D.C.; "H.U. Students Join National Antiwar Strike," April 25, 1936, and "Cop Killings Must Stop: 59 Killed by Washington Trigger Men—You May Be Next," July 2, 1938, both *BAA*.

48 NNC, quotes in support of antilynching conference, n.d. [1938], reel 15, part 10, *NAACPP*; "10,000 Out to Hear Mrs. F. D. Roosevelt," *BAA*, February 19, 1938.

49 "Warn Brutality May Cause Riots," *BAA*, August 6, 1938; Washington Council, NNC, "Stop Police Brutality!" petition, n.d. [1938], folder "Correspondence," reel 1, *John P. Davis Papers* (Wilmington, Del.: Scholarly Resources, 1995), microfilm, Schomburg Center for Research in Black Culture, New York Public Library, New York; Doxey A. Wilkerson to Marvin H. McIntyre, November 23, 1938 (578, 15, 1), *NNCP*; "Aid of President Sought in Drive to Check Brutality of D.C. Police, *CD*, national edition, September 24, 1938.

50 Washington Council, NNC, "8,000 Washington Citizens Add Names to Protest against Police Brutality," press release, n.d. [1938] (538–39, 3, 3), and James A. Thompson to Washington Council, NNC, August 18, 1938 (329, 15, 1), both *NNCP*.

51 "Warn Brutality May Cause Riots," *BAA*, August 6, 1938; John P. Davis to Franklin Delano Roosevelt, August 2, 1938 (533–35, 14, 1), *NNCP*.

52 "Support the National Negro Congress," *Washington Tribune*, June 17, 1939.

53 Arthur D. Gray, President, Washington Council, NNC, to Senator Arthur Capper, Washington, D.C., June 16, 1939 (26–27, 16, 1), *NNCP*.

54 Washington Council, NNC, to Vito Marcantonio, November 29, 1938 (160, 14, 1), and John P. Davis to Doxey A. Wilkerson, Memo, "Campaigns against Police Brutality and for Suffrage," November 28, 1938 (574–76, 15, 1), both *NNCP*.

55 John P. Davis to Thyra Edwards, December 17, 1938 (9, 13, 1), *NNCP*.

56 Miguel Carriga letter quoted by John P. Davis, testimony, Hearing before the Committee on Labor, House of Representatives, in *Proposed Amendments to the National Labor Relations Act*, June 29–30, July 5, 1939 (Washington, D.C.: Government Printing Office, 1939), 4:1461.

57 Davis, testimony, Hearing before the Committee on Labor, House of Representatives, 1466.

58 John P. Davis to Ishmael Flory, May 22, 1939 (496–97, 16, 1), *NNCP*; *National Negro Congress Washington Council News* 2, no. 4 (May 1939), and 3, no. 5 (June 1939), and "Wipe Out the Jim-Crow System in Washington!" all folder 1342, box 60, NAACP-DC.

59 "Mixed Group Pickets 'Sweat Shop' in D.C.," March 13, 1937, and "Cop Brutality Fight May Go to Roosevelt," May 22, 1937 (quote), both *BAA*.

60 "Union Victory for Laundry Work," *National Negro Congress Washington Council News* 2, no. 4 (May 1939), folder 1342, box 60, NAACP-DC.

61 Ibid.; John Lovell Jr. to John P. Davis, June 27, 1939 (270, 17, 1), and John P. Davis to Alain Locke (944, 16, 1), both *NNCP*.

62 Raymond Arsenault, *The Sound of Freedom: Marian Anderson, the Lincoln Memorial, and the Concert That Awakened America* (New York: Bloomsbury, 2009), 117–75, quote from 121; Scott Sandage, "A Marble House Divided: The Lincoln Memorial, the Civil Rights Movement, and the Politics of Memory, 1939–1963," *Journal of American History* (June 1993): quote from 136.

63 "Editorial Summing Up" and "Marion [*sic*] Anderson Reechoes," *National Negro Congress Washington Council News* 2, no. 4 (May 1939), folder 1342, box 60, NAACP-DC.

64 Clyde Robinson to Edward Strong, n.d. [early 1937] (431, 7, 1), Legislative and Civic Affairs and House Committee, NNC, "Report on Public Recreation," July 31, 1939, Washington (183–215, 9, 3), NNC, *National Negro Congress Washington Council News* 1, no. 1 (July–August 1940) (531–34, 2, 1), and Washington Council, NNC, undated report [1940] (421, 7, 3), all *NNCP*; Doxey A. Wilkerson to Joint Committee on Recreation, Washington, D.C., July 26, 1939, folder 1343, box 60, NAACP-DC; "Negro Congress Wins Rights in Gov't Camp in Capital," *Daily Worker*, March 27, 1940; "NNC Wins Fight on Color Bar Tourist Camp," *BAA*, March 30, 1940; "Congress Wins Fight; Cracks Jim-Crow Rule," *CD*, April 6, 1940.

65 See "Howard Head 'Red,' Cobb Tells Probers," November 12, 1938, "Dies Commit-

tee Probes Race Liberals in D.C." and "Denounce Dies Committee as Race Baiter," November 4, 1939, "Dies Committee Unmasked," November 11, 1939, "Dies Committee Reports to Congress," January 13, 1940, and "Prof. Hunton Seeks Hearing before Dies Group on Communist Charges," May 31, 1940, all *CD*, national edition; Congress of the United States, Summons for John P. Davis to testify before the Un-American Activities Committee on September 26, 1939, September 1, 1939 (118, 18, 1), *NNCP*; Wilkerson, "William Alphaeus Hunton: A Life That Made a Difference."

66 "The Defense of American Democracy," *CD*, national edition, November 4, 1939.

67 John P. Davis to William Bankhead, January 17, 1939 (896–906, 23, 1), and Davis to Congressman James P. McGranery, February 1, 1939 (126–27, 17, 1), both *NNCP*; "Negro Congress Leader Assails Dies Committee," *CD*, national edition, February 11, 1939.

68 Richard Randall, "Chicago Starts War on Peonage in Dies' South," *Record Weekly* (Chicago), December 9, 1939; "Two More Oglethorpe Fugitives Arrive in City," *CD*, national edition, April 6, 1940; Affidavits, State of Illinois, County of Cook, by Cleo Fleming, Solomon McCannon, Cora Woods, and Hart E. Baker, February 3, 1940, and Ed Raines, January 5, 1940 (193–209, 15, 1), Affidavit of State of Ohio, of Leonard Woods, Maggie Woods, James Woods, and Addie Woods, November 25, 1939 (193–209, 15, 1), "Peonage—1940 Style of Slavery" (189–91, 16, 1), and Bob Wirtz, Memorandum, February 19, 1940 (231–32, 16, 1), all *NNCP*.

69 John P. Davis to Attorney General Robert H. Jackson, March 11, 1940 (170–73, 16, 1), and O. John Rogge to John P. Davis, November 29, 1940 (565, 17, 1), both *NNCP*. The use of the Thirteenth Amendment to prosecute civil rights violations, according to scholar Risa Goluboff, led the Department of Justice's Civil Rights Division to prosecute cases of peonage during and after the Second World War. See Risa Goluboff, "The Thirteenth Amendment and the Lost Origins Of Civil Rights," *Duke Law Journal* 50, no. 6 (April 2001).

70 "Peonage Fight Received Support of NAACP and National Congress," *CD*, nation edition, March 9, 1940; "STOP TODAY'S SLAVERY TODAY," advertisement by NNC, ILD, and National Council to Aid Agricultural Workers for mass meeting on March 19, 1940 (185, 17, 1), *NNCP*; Tom Connally, extension of remarks, March 9, extension of legislative day of March 4, 1940, p. 4014, *Congressional Record*, copy at (169, 16, 1), *NNCP*.

71 Perkins, interview by Gellman, transcript, 26.

72 See ibid. For mention of the "red-baiting" that forced Thelma Dale from her federal government position, see NNC, "National Executive Committee Meeting," July 11, 1942 (188, 23, 1), *NNCP*.

73 NNC, "Final Report of the Credential Committee," frames 446–47, reel 16, part 18C, *NAACPP*; Ralph Ellison, "A Congress Jim Crow Didn't Attend," *New Masses*, May 14, 1940; L. Newman, "Report of the Third National Negro Congress," folder "correspondence N," box 3, series 1, UAWC.

74 "Davis Decries U.S. Bias at Negro Congress Meet," *CD*, national edition, March 15, 1941.

75 John Breihan, "Between Munich and Pearl Harbor: The Glenn L. Martin Aircraft Company Gears Up for War, 1938–1941," *Maryland Historical Magazine* 88, no. 4 (Winter 1993).

76 Rev. Arthur D. Gray and W. A. Hunton to All Groups Interested in the Welfare of Our Community, April 15, 1941, folder 1343, box 60, NAACP-DC; Breihan, "Between Munich and Pearl Harbor"; FBI, Washington, D.C., report, September 25, 1941 (817–24, 1), *NNC-FBI*.

77 Paul Robeson Jr., *The Undiscovered Paul Robeson* (Hoboken, N.J.: John Wiley, 2010), 26–27.

78 John P. Davis, "Paul Robeson Sings for Negro People," advertising letter, April 15, 1941 (750, 28, 1), *NNCP*; "Robeson to Sing at Uline Arena despite Tiff," *CD*, national edition, April 26, 1941 (quote); "Quits Robeson Benefit," *New York Times*, April 15, 1941; Martin Duberman, *Paul Robeson: A Biography* (New York: Knopf, 1988), 251–52, 653; NNC News, April 4, 1941, 2, folder "Negro Relations, NNC," box "Trade Unions, U.S.," ILWUP; "Mrs. FDR Rebuked for Stand on Defense Bias," *CD*, national edition, April 12, 1941.

79 "6,000 Hail Paul Robeson's Patriotic Song Program," *CD*, national edition, May 3, 1941; "Music Calendar," *Washington Post*, April 20, 1941; Charley Cherokee, "National Grapevine," *CD*, national edition, May 3, 1941 (third quote); "Tickets on Sale Today for Robeson Concert," *Washington Post*, April 3, 1941; Estelie Duke, "Anecdotes from the Capital of the Nation," *CD*, national edition, May 24, 1941 (first and second quotes); Liu Liangmo, "Paul Robeson, the People's Singer," 1950 article, reprinted in *Chinese American Voices: From the Gold Rush to the Present* (Berkeley: University of California Press), 205–7; "Ballad for Americans" (music by Earl Robinson and lyrics by John La Touche), from *Paul Robeson: Songs of Free Men, 1940-1945* (Pearl Gemm 9264 recording).

80 NNC press release, "75,000 Leaflets on Job Drive Distributed by National Negro Congress," May 5, 1941, copy in folder "Negro Relations," box "Trade Unions, U.S.," ILWUP; China Aid Committee to John P. Davis, May 19, 1941 (985, 29, 1), *NNCP*.

81 NNC, Memo, flier for April 27, 1941, jobs conference in Baltimore (480, 1), *NNC-FBI*; NNC flier, "7,000 Jobs for Negroes at Glenn L. Martin's Plant: How?" (897, 26, 1), and "7,000 Jobs for Negroes at Glenn L. Martin!" (354, 8, 3), both *NNCP*; NNC, Press Release, May 2, 1941, folder "Negro Relations," box "Trade Unions, U.S.," ILWUP; FBI, Baltimore report, December 16, 1941 (899–900, 1), *NNC-FBI*.

82 Martin quoted in Breihan, "Between Munich and Pearl Harbor," 408; FBI, Washington, D.C., report, September 25, 1941 (822, 1), and Washington Bureau to J. Edgar Hoover, April 29, 1941 (525, 1), both *NNC-FBI*.

83 J. T. Hartson, Glenn Martin Company, to John P. Davis, August 29, 1941 (886, 26, 1), *NNCP*; "Baltimore Mayor Backs Demand for Plane Jobs," *CD*, national edition,

June 28, 1941; "Resolution of Canton Members," n.d. [1943–44], and report on Martin Plant, untitled and n.d. [1944–45] (304–6, 10, 2), both *NNCP*; Breihan, "Between Munich and Pearl Harbor," 408–9 and n118.

84 "Rap Civil Service 'White Preferred Policy,'" August 17, 1940, and "Typist Denied Federal Jobs; Charged Bias," January 21, 1941, both *CD*, national edition; W. A. Hunton, for the delegation, "Report of Conference with Mr. Edwin Jones, Director of D.C. Employment Center," August 1, 1940, and W. A. Hunton to "Friend," August 2, 1940, both folder 1343, box 60, NAACP-DC.

85 The NNC and its coalition partners probably changed the name so as to not alienate potential allies, who may have hesitated to join the NNC after its 1940 convention split. Citizens Committee against Police Brutality, "Police Brutality Can Be Stopped: Call for an Immediate Program of Action to Stop Police Brutality," pamphlet, 1941 (160–62, 9, 3), "More Facts against Police Brutality," n.d. [1941] (973–76, 23, 1), and Leon A. Ransome and John Lovell Jr. to Major Edward Kelly, August 18, 1941 (366–68, 27, 1), all *NNCP*; Wilkerson, "William Alphaeus Hunton: A Life That Made a Difference."

86 Major Kelly, Speech Delivered at Police Brutality Mass Meeting at Metropolitan Baptist Church, Sunday, September 7, 1941 (964–70, 25, 1), *NNCP*; FBI, Washington, D.C., reports, September 7, 1941 (759–73, 1), *NNC-FBI*.

87 FBI, Washington, D.C., reports, September 7, 1941 (759–73, 1), and October 8, 1941 (827–32, 1), both *NNC-FBI*.

88 FBI, Washington, D.C., report, August 3, 1943 (98–99, 2), *NNC-FBI*; Doxey Wilkerson to Thelma Dale, December 17, 1943 (800, 15, 2), *NNCP*.

89 This paragraph is based on a careful analysis of Davis's FBI file, which contains numerous factual and interpretive errors as well as unsubstantiated claims. See, especially, reports from Washington, D.C., May 14, 1943, June 4, 1951, and August 21, 1953, and from New York, August 9, 1954, and August 11, 1954, all FBI Records-100-39058.

90 John P. Davis, "To My Lord, Jesus Christ," undated poem [1920s], Cambridge, Mass., folder "Writings," reel 2, *John P. Davis Papers*.

91 "The Washington Congress," editorial, *CD*, May 11, 1940; Charles H. Houston to Arthur D. Gray, June 23, 1939 (717, 16, 1), *NNCP*.

92 Election report (447–49, 4, 2), *NNCP*.

93 Davis to Hunton, July 20, 1940 (541, 22, 1), *NNCP*.

94 Adam Clayton Powell, *Adam by Adam: The Autobiography of Adam Clayton Powell, Jr.* (New York: Dial Press, 1971), 74.

95 Thelma Dale to Katherine Hyndmans, August 31, 1945 (558–59, 17, 2), *NNCP*. In 1946, Powell sponsored an amendment to a District of Columbia appropriations bill that outlawed all segregation of public facilities. The amendment lost by a vote of 122 to 49. See "Move to Ban D.C. Jim Crow Lost," *Norfolk New Journal and Guide*, April 13, 1946.

96 NNC, "Black Jim Crow Out of Washington," pamphlet (66–68, 19, 1), Ransome and Lovell to Kelly, August 18, 1941 (366–68, 27, 1), both *NNCP*; John P. Davis to "Friend,"

March 8, 1938, reel 15, part 10, *NAACPP*; "Probe Ordered in Nazi Tactics of D.C. Police," *BAA*, April 20, 1940.

Interlude

1 "F. D. R. Says Nation Should Consider Special Problems of Minorities," April 13, 1940, and "The National Negro Congress," editorial, March 30, 1940, both *CD*, national edition.

2 John P. Davis, "Proposed Plan for Third National Negro Congress," February 23, 1940, reel 16, part 18, series C, *NAACPP*; "C.I.O. Leader to Speak before Negro Congress," *CD*, national edition, March 23, 1940.

3 "Negro Congress and CIO Reach Policy Accord," *BAA*, May 11, 1940; L. Newman, "Report of the Third National Negro Congress," folder "Correspondence 'N,'" box 76, series 1, UAWC; "Lewis Urges Voters to Quit Roosevelt; Party Bid Split N.N.C.," *BAA*, May 4, 1940; "Presentation of Award to John L. Lewis," transcript of Davis's presentation and Lewis's acceptance, April 26, 1940, reel 16, part 18m, series C, *NAACPP*; "Text of Lewis Speech to Negro Congress Delegates at Washington Conference," clipping, n.d. [April 1940], copy in NNC vertical file, Schomburg Center for Research in Black Culture, New York Public Library, New York.

4 Newman, "Report of the Third National Negro Congress"; Ralph Ellison, "A Congress Jim Crow Didn't Attend," *New Masses*, May 14, 1940.

5 John P. Davis, report from Saturday, April 27, 1940, NNC (35–44, 21, 1), *NNCP*.

6 Ibid.; A. Philip Randolph, "Negro Labor and the Church," in *Labor Speaks for Itself on Religion: A Symposium of Labor Leaders throughout the World*, ed. Jerome Davis (New York: Macmillan, 1929), 74, 76. According to the dissertation of Keith Griffler, John P. Davis joined the CP in 1935 and kept his party membership a secret; the FBI file on John P. Davis confirms that Davis considered himself part of the CP in the late 1930s even if his formal status was ambiguous. See Keith Griffler, "The Black Radical Intellectual and the Black Worker: The Emergence of a Program for Black Labor, 1918–1938" (Ph.D. diss., Ohio State University, 1993); and FBI files on John P. Davis, FBI Records-100-39058, FOIA request 2010, FBI, Washington, D.C.

7 Newman, "Report of the Third National Negro Congress"; NNC, "Third National Negro Congress," program (231–51, 21, 1), *NNCP*; "Communism Causes Split in Congress," *CD*, national edition, May 4, 1940; "Lewis Urges Voters to Quit Roosevelt; Party Bid Split N.N.C.," *BAA*, May 4, 1940; A. Philip Randolph, "Why I Would Not Stand for Reelection for President of the National Negro Congress," press release, May 4, 1940, reel 16, part 18, series C, *NAACPP*.

8 NNC, "Final Report of the Credential Committee," n.d. [1940], copy in reel 16, part 18, series C, *NAACPP*. For the financial relationship between the CIO and the NNC, see Davis to John L. Lewis, October 24, 1939 (995–98, 16, 1), *NNCP*. Davis estimated that the total amount of financial support by the CP for the NNC was around 5 percent.

Even if this underestimates the total, the amount was most likely not very significant. See "Randolph Never Opposed Red Money, Says Davis," *BAA*, May 4, 1940.

9 A. Philip Randolph, "Randolph Says Race Congress Not Communist," February 29, 1936, Louis C. Harper, "Dustin' Off the News: Every Black Man a Communist, but Doesn't Know It," May 11, 1940, and A. Philip Randolph, "A Reply to Lucius C. Harper—Randolph Hits Critics in Negro Congress Affair," May 25, 1940, all *CD*, national edition; Randolph, "Why I Would Not Stand for Reelection" and "Whither the National Negro Congress?" May 14, 1940, editorials (italics added to quote), and Alfred Edgar Smith, "Notes to You" and "Reader Takes Issue with AFRO [*Baltimore Afro-American*] on Negro Congress," May 11, 1940, all *BAA*.

10 John P. Davis to A. Philip Randolph, September 5, 1936 (478, 7, 1), John P. Davis to A. Philip Randolph, November 4, 1936 (646, 7, 1), Charles Burton to John P. Davis, June 19, 1937 (27, 9, 1), Charles Burton to John P. Davis, October 1, 1938 (149, 12, 1), and Ishmael Flory to John P. Davis, May 31, 1939 (994, 17, 1), all *NNCP*.

11 Ellison, "A Congress Jim Crow Didn't Attend," 8. Ellison shared criticisms of top black CP leaders but saw the NNC in 1940 as a genuine movement of African American people. See Arnold Rampersad, *Ralph Ellison: A Biography* (New York: Alfred Knopf, 2007), 132–34.

12 The pacifism of black college students at Howard and elsewhere has often been overshadowed in historical accounts by their overwhelming support of the U.S. war effort after Pearl Harbor. For student movement antiwar activism, see Robert Cohen, *When the Old Left Was Young: Student Radicals and America's First Mass Student Movement, 1929–1941* (New York: Oxford University Press, 1993), 135–36, 171–72, 209.

13 Penny Von Eschen, *Race against Empire: Black Americans and Anticolonialism, 1937–1957* (Ithaca, N.Y.: Cornell University Press, 1997), 11; James Meriwether, *Proudly We Can Be Africans: Black Americans and Africa, 1935–1961* (Chapel Hill: University of North Carolina Press, 2002), chapter 1.

14 Randolph, "A Reply to Lucius C. Harper."

15 For example, William Green, the president of the AFL, rejected the request of John P. Davis for cooperation with the NNC on lobbying for the antilynching bill in 1937. See Green to Davis, June 29, 1937 (55, 10, 1), *NNCP*.

16 "Parade Will Open Porters' Conclave," September 8, 1940, and "Defense Program Backed by Porters," September 19, 1940, both *New York Times*; "Green Endorse Plan to Bar Reds from the A.F.L.," *Chicago Daily Tribune*, September 16, 1940; "Porters Rap Reds," September 21, 1940, and "Sees Porters behind F.D.R.," *Amsterdam News* (New York), September 28, 1940.

17 Lester Granger, "The Negro Congress—Its Future," *Opportunity* 18, no. 6 (June 1940); Charley Cherokee, "National Grapevine," November 29, 1941, and "The National Negro Congress," editorial, March 30, 1940, both *CD*, national edition.

18 See Herbert Garfinkel, *When Negroes March* (New York: Macmillan, 1969); Walter White, *A Man Called White: The Autobiography of Walter White* (New York: Viking, 1948), quotes from 189–92.

19 J. Edgar Hoover to Solicitor General, June 20, with enclosed June 18 memorandum, and June 21, 1941, folder 1, box 1506, FEPCC.

20 Ed Strong to John P. Davis, May 26, 1941, and Davis to Strong, May 27, 1941, both (519–23, 29, 1), *NNCP*.

21 Davis to Strong, May 27, 1941 (521–23, 29, 1), and NNC Minutes of Administrative Meeting, May 25, 1940 (11–17, 20, 1), both *NNCP*.

22 Claude Barnett to Henry Wallace, June 20, 1941, folder 5, box 279, CABP; Ed Strong to John P. Davis, May 26, 1941, and Davis to Strong, May 27, 1941, both (519–23, 29, 1), *NNCP*. Certain evidence concerning the early MOWM organization shows that Randolph and the NAACP's Walter White had neither the forces nor the intention to march on Washington in June 1941. "The March on Washington Committee may never have been able to march had its 'bluff' been called," Herbert Garfinkel's study of the MOWM concluded, "because of insufficient organization." See Garfinkel, *When Negroes March*, 45–62, quote from 62. More recent scholarship, however, has confirmed the reports of Strong that the MOWM did have momentum in its organizing campaign by June 1940. See Glenda Gilmore, *Defying Dixie: The Radical Roots of Civil Rights, 1919–1950* (New York: W. W. Norton, 2008), 359–68.

23 Charles Collins quotes in "Job March Must Get Action, Says Negro Leader," *Daily Worker*, June 23, 1941 (1778, 2), *NNC-FBI*.

24 See Merl Reed, "The FBI, MOWM, and CORE, 1941–1946," *Journal of Black Studies* 21, no. 4 (June 1991): 466–67.

25 "The Aircraft Industry," September 7, 1940, "SWOC Workers Foresee CIO Election Victory," September 27, 1941, "Big Business Trembles during FEPC Hearing," November 1, 1941, and "CIO Acts Fast to End Strike against Negro," December 26, 1942, all *CD*, national edition; "FEPC Orders Chicago Firms to Stop Job Discrimination," April 18, 1942, and "Firms Agree to Drop Ban on Negroes," May 23, 1942, both *Pittsburgh Courier*; NNC, "Negro Congress Pledges Full Support to Harvester and Bethlehem Steel Drives," March 28, 1941 (482, 1, 1), *NNCP*; Charles Pearl to Revels Cayton, December 15, 1940, folder "Negro Relations, NNC," box "Trade Unions, U.S., by subject," ILWUP.

26 "Lewis Urges Voters to Quit Roosevelt," May 4, 1940, and "The Inquiring Reporter," June 8, 1940, both *BAA*; "CIO Charged by Green with Blocking Labor Unity," *Los Angeles Times*, September 16, 1940; "Lewis Quits as CIO Head; Assails Dixie Poll Tax," *Amsterdam News* (New York), November 23, 1940; Melvyn Dubofsky and Warren Van Tine, *John L. Lewis: A Biography* (Chicago: University of Illinois Press, 1986); Saul D. Alinsky, *John L. Lewis: An Unauthorized Biography* (1949; New York: Vintage Books, 1970).

27 John P. Davis to John Jones, November 25, 1940 (843–84, 19, 1), *NNCP*.

28 Adam Clayton Powell, "Soapbox," *PV*, December 9, 1944; "Randolph: A.F. of L. or the CIO?" December 16, 1944 (quote), Carl Lawrence, "On the Level," October 24, 1942, "Pullman Porters Stay in AFL," October 24, 1942, and Letter from Union Worker, "A.F. of L. and the Negro," February 8, 1941, all *Amsterdam News* (New York).

29 "The Labor Front," *CD*, national edition, November 7, 1942; "New York Masses Protest for Democracy," June 27, 1942, "12,000 in Chicago Voice Demands for Democracy," July 4, 1942, "FDR Refuses Audience to Negro Race Leaders," September 5, 1942, all *CD*, national edition; Garfinkel, *When Negroes March*, 97–118, 204–5; Ernie Johnson to Claude Barnett, August 5, 1942, folder 5, box 279, CABP; "Town Hall," *PV*, July 24, 1943; MOWM, "Proceedings of Conference Held in Detroit," September 26–27, 1942 (205–27, 3, 2), *NNCP*; FBI reports on MOWM from 1943 to 1946, folder 1, box 1506, FEPCC.

30 See Beth Tompkins Bates, *Pullman Porters and the Rise of Protest Politics in Black America* (Chapel Hill: University of North Carolina Press, 2001); Jervis Anderson, *A. Philip Randolph: A Biographical Portrait* (New York: Harcourt Brace Jovanovich, 1973); and Paula F. Pfeffer, *A. Philip Randolph, Pioneer of the Civil Rights Movement* (Baton Rouge: Louisiana State University Press, 1990).

Chapter Four

1 Hugh Mulzac as told to Louis Burnham and Norval Welch, *A Star to Steer By* (1963; New York: International Publishers, 1972), quotes from 159, 160, 166, 167–68, 176, 237; "Biography of Captain Hugh Mulzac," press release, NMU, September 16, 1944 (723, 6, 3), *NNCP*; "Negro Captain Gets His Ship," *PM*, New York, September 21, 1942; "Honor Captain Mulzac and Crew at Hotel Commodore, January 4," *PV*, January 2, 1943.

2 NNC, "Review: National Negro Congress 1944" (926–29, 20, 2), *NNCP*; "Capt. Mulzac and Crew Honored at Dinner in Hotel Commodore," *PV*, January 16, 1943; Mulzac, *A Star to Steer By*, 138–40, 146.

3 Thelma Dale to Max Yergan, Memorandum, "Congress Strength and Organization," June 29, 1944 (892–94, 20, 2), *NNCP*.

4 Dalfiume made a convincing case against "the majority" of scholars who portrayed the 1950s as the origin of the civil rights movement. But in doing so, he makes the assumption, without giving much evidence, that the Second World War instead marked the origin of the movement. In his own brief survey of wartime activism, Sitkoff discovered that African American loyalty and patriotism (and in the case of many on the left, fealty to the Soviet Union as well) diminished protest against racial discrimination. Sitkoff declared these ideas tentative, however, because the "evidence to prove this . . . argument has yet to appear." See Richard M. Dalfiume, "The 'Forgotten Years' of the Negro Revolution," reprinted in *The Negro in Depression and War: Prelude to Revolution, 1930–1945*, ed. Bernard Sternsher (Chicago: Quadrangle Books, 1969), 299, 301, 319; Harvard Sitkoff, "African American Militancy in the World War II South: Another Perspective," in *Remaking Dixie: The Impact of World War II on the American South*, ed. Neil R. McMillan (Jackson: University of Mississippi Press, 1997), 70, 89, 91, 92; and Leon Litwack, *How Free Is Free? The Long Death of Jim Crow* (Cambridge, Mass.: Harvard University Press, 1999), 90 and chapter 2. More recent work has shown how

black service in the military created a more aggressive outlook after the war. See John Dittmer, *Local People: The Struggle for Civil Rights in Mississippi* (Urbana: University of Illinois Press, 1995), chapter 1; and Timothy B. Tyson, *Radio Free Dixie: Robert F. Williams and the Roots of Black Power* (Chapel Hill: University of North Carolina Press, 1999). See also Maurice Isserman, *Which Side Were You On? The American Communist Party during the Second World War* (Middletown, Ct.: Wesleyan University Press, 1982), 141–43, 169.

5 The "Red Star" designation comes from the poem "Lenin," by Langston Hughes, which he dedicated to Thelma Dale. See Hughes, "Lenin" (901, 8, 2), *NNCP*. The North Star became an important symbol of liberation because escaped slaves used it as a guide on the Underground Railroad.

6 David Henry Anthony III, *Max Yergan: Race Man, Internationalist, Cold Warrior* (New York: New York University Press, 2006), 202, 214–15; Charles V. Hamilton, *Adam Clayton Powell, Jr.: The Political Biography of an American Dilemma* (New York: Atheneum, 1991), 105, 119–20.

7 See "Sketch" biographies, a regular second-page feature in *Congress View*: Thelma Dale, 1, no. 3 (August 1943); Jessie Scott Campbell, 1, no. 5 (October 1943); Dorothy K. Funn, 1, no. 6 (November 1943); Mayme Brown, 1, no. 7 (December 1943); Jeanne Pastor, 1, no. 10 (March 1944); Maude Jett, 2, no. 10 (January 1945); and Ruth Jett, 2, no. 12 (March 1945).

8 NNC, statement on *Vue*, n.d. [1943–44] (32, 5, 2), NNC, "Report *Congress Vue*," September 26, 1943 (167–70, 13, 2), NNC, "*Congress Vue*," n.d. [1943 or 1944] (873, 2, 2), Mayme Brown to Jacob Green, June 16, 1944 (286, 13, 2), Jeanne Pastor to *PV*, June 9, 1945 (229, 17, 2), James Nakamura to Edward Strong, December 17, 1943 (892, 2, 2), Jeanne Pastor, Memorandum, October 30, 1945 (789–93, 20, 2), NNC, "Application for Robert Marshall Foundation," 1943 (319–32, 12, 2), Lloyd Brown to Jeanne Pastor, October 20, 1945 (149, 2, 149), Leonard Osmon to Thelma Dale, July 21, 1944 (648, 13, 2), and Private James L. Watson to NNC, April 8, 1945 (383, 16, 2), all *NNCP*. For more on the "Double V" campaign by the black press, see Lee Finkle, *Forum for Protest: The Black Press during World War II* (Rutherford, N.J.: Fairleigh Dickinson University Press, 1975), and Ernest Perry, "It's Time to Force a Change: The African American Press' Campaign for a True Democracy during World War II," *Journalism History* 28, no. 2 (Summer 2002).

9 George Washington Carver School, "A People's Institute," winter term, January–April 1946 (757–65, 16, 3), and "Breakdown of Student Enrollment," winter term, 1944 (410, 7, 2), both *NNCP*; "Gwen Bennett to Head New Carver School," July 31, 1943, and "Carver School Is Growing in Popularity and Scope," April 29, 1944, both *PV*.

10 Mark Naison, *Communists in Harlem during the Great Depression* (Urbana: University of Illinois Press, 1983), 309; Anthony, *Max Yergan*, 185–87, 200–201.

11 Adam Clayton Powell, "Soapbox," *PV*, January 1, 1944; Gwendolyn Bennett to Thelma Dale, November 19, 1943 (463, 1, 2), *NNCP*.

12 See Marvin Gettleman, "The Lost World of United States Labor Education: Curricula

at East and West Coast Communist Schools, 1944–1957," in *American Labor and the Cold War: Grassroots Politics and Postwar Political Culture*, ed. Robert Cherny, William Issel, and Kieran Taylor (New Brunswick, N.J.: Rutgers University Press, 2004), 205–15.

13 "Announcing . . . George Washington Carver School," advertisement for fall term, October 1943 (408, 2, 2), *NNCP*.

14 "Carver School in Harlem Has Democratic Curriculum," October 23, 1943, "Students Like Carver School's Curriculum," November 27, 1943, "Carver School Festival Stresses World Unity," May 27, 1944, and "Real Democracy in Education," September 23, 1944, all *PV*. See also George Washington Carver School, "Education for All!" spring term 1945 (1100–27, 16, 2), and "Courses," spring 1944 (619–22, 6, 2), both *NNCP*.

15 "Sketch," Charles White, *Congress Vue* 1, no. 9 (February 1944); "Sketch," Elizabeth Catlett, *Congress Vue* 2, no. 2 (June 1944).

16 "Prospectus for the George Washington Carver School," n.d. [1943] (486–89, 1, 2), and Minutes of the Steering Committee for the George Washington Carver School, August 12, 1943 (281, 1, 2), both *NNCP*; "George Washington Carver School Opens in Harlem," *Congress Vue* 1, no. 6 (November 1943).

17 Carl G. Hill, "Of Frederick Douglass," *Congress Vue* 1, no. 1 (April 1943).

18 W. E. B. Du Bois, *Black Reconstruction in America: 1860–1880* (1935; New York: Touchstone, 1992); Herbert Aptheker, *American Negro Slave Revolts* (New York: Columbia University Press, 1943), 236, 374; Herbert Aptheker, "Progress of Lincoln," *New Masses*, February 29, 1944; "Suggested Readings," in "Negro History Week: Eighty-two Years of Freedom," 1945 (345–52, 32, 2), *NNCP*. As a touchstone of the reemergence of this militant black history, Pathway Press reprinted *The Life and Times of Frederick Douglass* in 1941, making the autobiography available for the first time in a half century. See W. Burghardt Turner and Joyce Moore Turner, eds., *Richard B. Moore, Caribbean Militant in Harlem: Collected Writings, 1920–1972*, with biography by Joyce Moore Turner (Bloomington: Indiana University Press, 1988); Frederick Douglass, *Life and Times of Frederick Douglass* (New York: Pathway Press, 1941); and Herbert Aptheker, "Voice of His People," *New Masses*, April 15, 1941. See also *Frederick Douglass: Selections from His Writings*, ed. Philip S. Foner (New York: International Publishers, 1945); and Herbert Aptheker, "Douglass Speaks," *New Masses*, May 7, 1946.

19 Bass specifically mentioned Aptheker, Du Bois, and James Allen. She described the standard history as the following: "Negroes were brought to America as slaves. The climate of the South agreed with them and, in the main, they were content. They were well looked after and enjoyed the love and friendship of their masters. But northern idealists objected to the principal of slavery, and northern industrialists could not abide by the political power of the agricultural south. Thus, the Civil War." See Charlotta Bass, "Discussion for Panel of Writer's Congress," October 2, 1943, folder "Speeches 1940s," box 1 of additions, CBP.

20 Dorothy Funn, "Negro History: What Is Its Value to America," February 2, 1945 (1080–83, 18, 2), *NNCP*.

21 George Murphy, "Town Hall," clipping, *PV*, n.d. [June 1942], copy (684, 29, 1), *NNCP*.

22 Thelma Dale, "Town Hall," *PV*, March 13, 1943.

23 Mayme Brown, "Review: What the Negro Wants, Edited by Rayford Logan," *Congress View* 2, nos. 8 and 9 (November–December 1944). The *PV* also challenged Randolph's decision to ban whites from the MOWM. See "Town Hall," *PV*, July 24, 1943.

24 Ferdinand Smith, "Labor Looks Ahead," *PV*, May 29, 1943.

25 Doxey Wilkerson, "Anniversary of Negro Freedom," *PV*, December 30, 1944; Jessie Scott Campbell, "Military Equality: A Victory Demand," *Congress Vue* 1, no. 5 (October 1943).

26 Nell Dodson, "Screen Workers' Guild Protests Johnson Film," *PV*, January 2, 1943; NNC, "'Tennessee Johnson' Appeases the Southern Poll Taxers, Organization Leaders Protest, after Preview of Metro-Goldwyn-Mayer Film," press release, December 18, 1942 (365, 16, 3), *NNCP*; "'Tennessee Johnson' Race Film Preview Stirs Fans," December 19, 1942, and "Fight to Stop Picture Eulogizing Slave Acts," December 26, 1942, both *CD*, national edition.

27 "A Dangerous Film," editorial, *CD*, national edition, January 2, 1943; Lawrence D. Reddick and George B. Murphy to Howard B. Deitz, Metro-Goldwyn-Mayer, New York, December 15, 1942 (116–17, 28, 1), *NNCP*.

28 "Daily Papers Divided over Picture 'Tennessee Johnson,'" January 23, 1943, and Lucius C. Harper, "'Tennessee Johnson' Libels Good Man, Idolizes Drunkard," September 11, 1943, both *CD*, national edition.

29 W. A. Hunton, "Democratizing Our Films—A Necessary Wartime Measure," *Congress Vue* 1, no. 4 (September 1943).

30 Dorothy K. Funn, "The Negro and the 1944 Elections," speech on radio station WJLB, Detroit (1043, 18, 2), and "Heads Cultural Committee," NNC press release, n.d. [1943–44?] (565, 2, 3), both *NNCP*; "Negro Freedom Rally," *Congress Vue* 1, no. 2 (May 1943); "Detroit Art Exhibit Set for May 29," *CD*, national edition, May 22, 1943.

31 NLVC advertisement, "Pack the Garden, Back the Invasion, Negro Freedom Rally," June 24, 1944, and Llewellyn Ransom, "Freedom Rally Gives Direction to the Negro," July 1, 1944, both *PV*; NLVC, "Read Script of Pageant," press release, New York, May 19, 1944 (513, 13, 2), and "Negro Freedom Rally Program," 1944 (626–47, 7, 4), both *NNCP*.

32 Quoted from CIO Political Action Committee, "For Immediate Release," June 30, 1944 (1001, 9, 1), *NNCP*; see also Owen Dodson, "New World A-Coming," electronic edition (Alexandria, Va.: Alexander Street Press, 2005).

33 Augusta Jackson, "'The Negro Soldier': A Review of the New War Department Film," *Congress Vue* 1, no. 10 (March 1944); W. A. Hunton, "Democratizing Our Films—A Necessary War Measure," *Congress Vue* 1 (September 1943); "'The Negro Soldier' Seen in Detroit" (596, 14, 2), *NNCP*; "A Negro Soldier Writes on 'The Negro Soldier,'" *Congress Vue* 2, no. 4 (July 1944). See also Barbara Savage, *Broadcasting Freedom: Radio, War, and the Politics of Race, 1938-1948* (Chapel Hill: University of North Carolina Press, 1999), especially 142–48.

34 See *Congress Vue* and *Congress View* for this drawing and motto. See also Frederick Douglass, "Men of Color to Arms," reprinted in *Congress Vue* 1 (February 1944).

35 NNC, "Proposal for the Establishment of a Committee for Democratic Culture," n.d. [late 1943] (514–16, 1, 2), "Cultural Meeting," New York, July 28, 1943 (516–17, 1, 2), Jessie Scott Campbell, Minutes to the Cultural Committee Meeting, Harlem, August 10, 1943 (546–47, 1, 2), Virginia Kaye to Ed Strong, June 10, 1944 (583, 7, 2), and Memorandum to Max Yergan and others, n.d. [1943] (550–53, 1, 2), all *NNCP*. See also "Nation-Wide Broadcast Scores Prejudice," *Congress View* 2, no. 3 (June 1944); and "Town Hall," *PV*, April 3, 1943.

36 "The Contribution of the Negro to Democracy in America," invitation to formal presentation of White's mural, Hampton Institute, Virginia, July 25, 1943, subject files, Hampton Institute, roll 3191, CWP; Charles White, interview by Betty Hoag, March 9, 1965, 10, transcript, Smithsonian Archives of American Art, Washington, D.C.

37 Mayme Brown, "Teddy Wilson: A People's Musician," *Congress Vue* 1, no. 7 (December 1943).

38 Louis Burnham, "Review of *New World A-Coming* by Roy Ottley," *Congress Vue* 1, no. 5 (October 1943); Roy Ottley, *New World A-Coming: Inside Black America* (New York: Literary Classics, 1943), 167–85. See also Alain Locke, ed., *The New Negro* (1925; New York: Atheneum, 1992); Arnold Rampersad, introduction to the 1992 edition of *The New Negro*, xviii–xxi; David Levering Lewis, *When Harlem Was in Vogue* (New York: Knopf, 1981); and Sterling Brown, "The New Negro in Literature, 1925–1955," in *The New Negro Thirty Years Afterward: Papers Contributing to the Sixteenth Annual Spring Conference of the Division of Social Sciences*, ed. Rayford Logan, Eugene C. Holmes, and G. Franklin Edwards (Washington, D.C.: Howard University Press, 1955), 62.

39 Richard Wright, "Blueprint for Negro Writing" and "Editorial," *New Challenge* 2, no. 2 (Fall 1937); Richard Wright, with photos by Edwin Rosskam, *12 Million Black Voices* (1941; New York: Basic Books, 2002).

40 "Panel on Cultural Freedom," transcript of NNC conference session, April 28, 1940 (512–53, 21, 1), and Arthur Huff Fauset, "Cultural Contributions of the American Negro," March 1940 (175–213, 19, 1), both *NNCP*; Ralph Ellison to Richard Wright, May 11, 1940, RWP; Arnold Rampersad, *Ralph Ellison: A Biography* (New York: Alfred Knopf, 2007), 132–34, 140–41.

41 Perkins, interview by author, 1; Thelma Dale to Sterling Brown, November 14, 1945 (1082, 16, 2), and George Washington Carver School, "Education for All!" spring term 1945, 12 (1100–27, 16, 2), both *NNCP*.

42 See David Platt, "Nat'l Negro Congress to Present Aubrey Pankey at Carnegie Hall," *Daily Worker*, January 21, 1944; Marvel Cooke, "Aubrey Pankey," *Congress Vue* 1, no. 5 (October 1943); and "Pankey Songs of High Order," *PV*, February 5, 1944.

43 Michael Denning, *The Cultural Front: The Laboring of American Culture in the Twentieth Century* (New York: Verso, 1996), 348–61; Ronald Cohen and Dave Samuelson, *Songs for Political Action* (Hambergen, Germany: Bear Family Records, 1996), 70, 75; CIO Political Action Committee, "For Immediate Release," June 30, 1944 (1001,

9, 1), Dorothy Parker to Thelma Dale, October 24, 1944 (638, 14, 2), and NNC, "Forward through Unity to Full Citizenship for Negro Americans!" pamphlet, Washington Legislative Bureau and Detroit Midwest Office, 1945 (246–47, 17, 2), all *NNCP*; "Negro Freedom Rally Jams Garden," *PV*, June 30, 1945; Robin D. G. Kelley, *Hammer and Hoe: Alabama Communists during the Great Depression* (Chapel Hill: University of North Carolina Press, 1990), 209; Elijah Wald, *Josh White: Society Blues* (Amherst: University of Massachusetts Press, 2000).

44 Edmonia W. Grant, "That All Are One," press release, AMA, n.d. [1942–44], "Race and Science," press release, n.d., and "The Races of Mankind," exhibit prepared by the Cranbrook Institute of Science and circulated by the Race Relations Division of the AMA, n.d. (974–97, 20, 2), all *NNCP*.

45 Adam Clayton Powell Jr., "Soapbox," *PV*, December 26, 1942; see also Sitkoff, "Changing Ideas: Race and Racism," in Harvard Sitkoff, *A New Deal for Blacks: The Emergence of Civil Rights as a National Issue* (New York: Oxford University Press, 1978).

46 Grant, "That All Are One," press release (974–97, 20, 2), *NNCP*.

47 Ruth Jett, "Suggested Bibliography" (846, 23, 2), Dorothy K. Funn to "Brothers," September 1945 (1003, 18, 2), and Dorothy Funn to Friend, March 7, 1945 (1016, 20, 2), all *NNCP*; "'Races of Mankind' Ban Assailed by Writers," *PV*, April 22, 1944; "CIO to Push Race Pamphlet," *Congress Vue* 2, no. 1 (April 1944). For serialized "Races of Mankind," see *PV*, February and March 1943.

48 Augusta Jackson Strong, "Review: The Races of Mankind," *Congress Vue* 2, no. 1 (April 1944).

49 "Mississippi's Rankin Rants on Negro Blood," *PV*, July 4, 1942.

50 "Negro Blood Jim Crowed," *PM*, New York, May 5, 1942; NNC, Memorandum to Colonel Burr Carter, n.d. [spring 1945], with accompanying letter, Adam Clayton Powell Jr., U.S. Congress, to Thelma Dale, April 3, 1945 (109–10, 22, 2), and Dale to Powell, February 28, 1945 (886, 20, 2), both *NNCP*; FBI, Washington, D.C., reports, September 8, 1944 (395, 2), and October 30, 1944 (453–56, 2), both *NNC-FBI*; Howard Ball, *A Defiant Life: Thurgood Marshall and the Persistence of Racism in America* (New York: Crown, 1998), 100.

51 Thelma Dale to Steve [Kingston?], May 11, 1945 (610, 17, 2), *NNCP*; Alphaeus Hunton, "Book Review: 'Color and Democracy' by W. E. B. Du Bois," *Congress View* 3, no. 4 (July 1945). See also John W. Dower, *War without Mercy: Race and Power in the Pacific War* (New York: Pantheon, 1986); and Gerald Horne, *Race War: White Supremacy and the Japanese Attack on the British Empire* (New York: New York University Press, 2004).

52 "NAACP Differs with PV on FDR," Roy Wilkins, letters to the editor, *PV*, February 17, 1945; William Patterson, George S. Schuyler, Ben Davis Jr., Horace Cayton, and James W. Ford, "Round Table: Have the Communists Quit Fighting for Negro Rights?" *Negro Digest* 3, no. 2 (July 1944): quote from 67.

53 Frederick Douglass, "Men of Color to Arms," reprinted in *Congress Vue* 1 (February 1944): 3.

54 Mayme Brown, "Book Review: A Rising Wind by Walter White," *Congress View* 3, no. 1 (April 1945).

55 Naison, *Communists in Harlem*, 299. As David Blight noted, during the Great Depression "an astonishing American appetite reemerged for the nostalgia of the Lost Cause of the Old South." In cities like Chicago, NNC activists contested this portrayal by picketing movie theaters. See David W. Blight, *Race and Reunion: The Civil War in American Memory* (New York: Belknap, 2001), 393; and "Picket 'Gone with the Wind,'" *CD*, February 3, 1940.

56 Thelma Dale to Edwin S. Smith, November 1, 1945 (181–82, 20, 2), *NNCP*.

57 "Stars" from Louis Burnham to Edward [Strong] and Jack [Jackson], n.d., folder 9, box 1, ESP; Ed Strong, Memo, November 1, 1943, "Itinerary of Southern Tour to Be Made by Thelma Dale," James Ford to Ed Strong, October 21, 1943, and Lou Burnham to Ed Strong, all (739–88, 1, 2), *NNCP*. The NAACP had explosive growth in membership during World War II, rising from approximately 50,000 to 300,000 members nationally by summer 1944. See Patricia Sullivan, *Days of Hope: Race and Democracy in the New Deal Era* (Chapel Hill: University of North Carolina Press, 1996), 285–86. Historian Robin Kelley explained: "During the war the NAACP proved a welcome ally to SNYC." See Kelley, *Hammer and Hoe*, 222.

58 SNYC, "Voices for Victory" flyer for November 19, 1943 (827, 1, 2), *NNCP*; "Dorothy Challenor Burnham: From Progressive Movement to Progress Art, Still She Blossoms," *New York Beacon*, December 26, 2001. On Andy Brown, see Kelley, *Hammer and Hoe*, 222; "Sketch: Oscar Bryant," *Congress View* 2, no. 1 (April 1944); and Esther Cooper to James Jackson, November 16 and 17, 1943, folder 4, box 7, JJP.

59 See Esther and James Jackson, interview by Hatch, 158–59, 164; Erik S. McDuffie, "Long Journeys: Four Black Women in the Communist Party, USA, 1930–1956" (Ph.D. diss., New York University, 2003), 284–303; and folder "Town Hall Meetings, Birmingham," box 2, and Southern Youth Legislature Program, Columbia, S.C., October 1946, 8, folders "Columbia Conference," box 6, both SNYCP.

60 Esther Cooper, "The Negro Woman Domestic Worker in Relation to Trade Unionism" (master's thesis, Fisk University, 1940), 28–30, 105, quote from 27.

61 Esther Cooper to Peter [Price], June 5, 1941, folder 18, box 167-2, ESP; Esther Jackson, interview by Hatch, 159, 164. Cooper did interview soldiers for the Rosenwald Grant but never completed the study due to her full-time activist work with the SNYC.

62 SNYC, "Negro Youth Building a New South," Official Proceedings, Third All-Southern Negro Youth Conference, Birmingham, April 28–30, 1939, folder 1, box 3, and SNYC, "Agenda," December 30, 1939, meeting, Nashville, folder 29, box 167-2, both ESP; "Nora Wilson Breakfast," June 22, 1941, and other documents, in folder "Nora Wilson breakfast," box 2, SNYCP; "Nora Wilson: Youth in Chains" and "Summer Activities Hit New Peak," *SNYC News*, October 1940, folder 14, box 2, ESP; Kelley, *Hammer and Hoe*, 216.

63 Joe Gelders to Augusta Strong, March 16, 1940, folder 3, box 167-1, and "All Out . . . to Protect Pratt City Youths Intimidated by Police Department," folder 23, box 3, both

ESP; Kelley, *Hammer and Hoe*, 217; "Birmingham Organizes to Discourage Recurrences," *Pittsburgh Courier*, May 25, 1940; Burnham to Strong and Jackson, n.d., folder 9, box 167-1, ESP.

64 Jefferson County Committee against Police Brutality, "Police Brutality Must Stop," folder "National Anti-Poll Tax Campaign," box 2, SNYCP; Esther Cooper to Peter [Price], June 5, 1941, folder 18, box 2, ESP; "How Much More Police Tyranny in Jefferson County" (747, 22, 1), *NNCP*; SNYC, press release, June 2, 1941, folder "National Anti-Poll Tax Campaign," box 2, SNYCP; "Citizens Carry Right-to-Vote to Court," *CD*, national edition, March 2, 1940.

65 "November Fifth Demonstrations!!!" *SNYC News*, November 1940, folder 26, box 3, and Augusta Jackson Strong, "3,000 Ignore Rebuffs of Alabama Poll Bosses; Register for Primaries," undated clipping, folder 5, box 4, both ESP; "Youth in Southern Town Demonstrate for the Ballot," *Amsterdam News* (New York), November 24, 1940.

66 SNYC, report of Executive Secretary, December 13, 1943 (707–8, 4, 2), *NNCP*; Esther Cooper to James Jackson, August 9 and November 16, 1943, folder 4, box 7, JJP.

67 Esther Cooper to James Jackson, October 23, 1943, folder 4, box 7, and March 3, 1945, folder 8, box 7, both JJP.

68 SNYC, report of Executive Secretary, December 13, 1943 (707–8, 4, 2), *NNCP*.

69 Thelma [Dale] to Ed [Strong], Monday [November 1943] (789–90, 1, 2), *NNCP*; Esther Cooper to James Jackson, November 16 and 17, 1943, folder 4, box 7, JJP.

70 Esther Cooper to James Jackson, November 25, 1944, folder 6, box 7, JJP; Esther Jackson, interview by Hatch, 170–71.

71 Thelma [Dale] to Ed [Strong], Monday [November 1943] (789–90, 1, 2), Dale to John Dixon (996, 14, 2), and Dale to "Coke," February 4, 1944 (141, 13, 2), all *NNCP*; Thelma Dale, "New Currents in the South," *Congress Vue* 1, no. 7 (December 1943): 6; Esther Cooper to James Jackson, Sunday afternoon [November 1943], folder 4, box 5, JJP.

72 Mayme Brown to Deacon William Anderson, n.d. (34, 15, 2), "Members of Victory Club, NNC, Montgomery," February 25, 1944 (313–14, 19, 2), Deacon Anderson to Mayme Brown, n.d. (313–14, 19, 2), Deacon Anderson to Mayme Brown, December 28, 1944 (315–16, 19, 2), and Oscar Bryant to Mayme Brown, September 27, 1944 (925, 16, 2), all *NNCP*; "Leader of Youth Accuse Police of Jailing and Slugging Her," December 26, 1942, *Black Dispatch*, folder 6, box 4, ESP; Esther Cooper to James Jackson, July 22 [1945], folder 10, box 7, and E. D. Nixon to Esther Cooper, September 8, 1944, folder 6, box 14, both JJP; Kelley, *Hammer and Hoe*, 223. E. D. Nixon and P. M. Blair were among those who had a role in the 1955–56 bus boycott in Montgomery. The 1950s historical context included Supreme Court decisions against segregation—including *Morgan v. Virginia* in 1946, about interstate transportation, and *Brown v. Board of Education* in 1954, concerning schools—and Cold War propaganda that had the potential to embarrass the United States. See Jo Ann Gibson Robinson, *The Montgomery Bus Boycott and the Women Who Started It* (Knoxville: University of Tennessee Press, 1987), 85–87, 181.

73 "Welcomed by White Workers Say Negroes," *Daily Worker*, May 28, 1941; "Democracy

at Sperry Gyroscope," *PV*, September 30, 1944; Martha Biondi, *To Stand and Fight: The Struggle for Civil Rights in Postwar New York City* (Cambridge, Mass.: Harvard University Press, 2003), 7–8.

74 Rupert S. M. Bath, Porters' Section No. 23, to Frank R. Crosswaith, Negro Labor Committee, April 12, 1937, folder 23, box 33, TWUR; Minutes of the Negro Labor Assembly, Harlem Labor Center, May 10, 1938, folder 5, box 71, and TWU Executive Board Meeting Minutes, July 25, 1938, folder 30, box 1, both TWUR-L; August Meier and Elliott Rudwick, "Communist Unions and the Black Community: The Case of the Transport Workers Union, 1934–1944," *Labor History* 23, no. 2 (1982).

75 "National Negro Congress Urges Harlem to Support Transit Labor," May 1941 handbill, folder 36, box 17, TWUR; Naison, *Communists in Harlem*, 305–8; "Negro Congress Asks Lehman End Jim Crow on Jobs," *Daily Worker*, January 13, 1941; Meier and Rudwick, "Communist Unions," 176–78; Erik S. Gellman, "'Carthage Must Be Destroyed': Race, City Politics, and the Campaign to Integrate Chicago Transportation Work, 1929–1943," *Labor: Studies in Working-Class History of the Americas* 2, no. 2 (Summer 2005).

76 John P. Davis to Max Yergan, April 8, 1942 (228–31, 30, 1), *NNCP*; Minutes of Meeting at NMU, New York, April 15, 1942 (840–42, 28, 1), *NNCP*.

77 See Bay Area Council of the NNC and Publicity Committee of the Joint Strike Committee, "Negroes and the Maritime Strike," pamphlet, n.d. [1936–37], folder "Minorities—Blacks—through 1959," ILWUP.

78 Richard Hart, "This Man Smith" (Kingstown, Jamaica: People's Educational Association, 1953), University of Florida Library, Miami; NMU, "Equality for All: The Stand of the NMU on Discrimination" (New York: NMU Education Department, 1947); Gerald Horne, "Black Thinkers at Sea: Ferdinand Smith and the Decline of African American Proletarian Intellectuals," *Souls* 4, no. 2 (Spring 2002); "Thumbnail Sketches," *Pilot*, September 2, 1938.

79 "Whalen Attacks Negro Discrimination, Says Shipping Must Rotate," January 7, 1938, "Colored Member Charges NMU Discriminates" and "Opposes Resolution on Mixed Crews," April 7, 1939, "Report of the Negro Committee," April 18, 1940, and "Save Jobs of Colored Deck Crew on M&M Ship," January 3, 1941, all *Pilot*. For other letters and articles in the *Pilot* on race in the NMU, see February 4, June 3, July 22, August 5, August 26, September 23, 1938, March 31, 1939, and February 2, June 27, August 15, September 26, 1941.

80 See Ferdinand Smith, "Freedom Not a Gift, Must Be Fought For," and Llewellyn Ransom, "They All Face Death to 'Keep 'Em Sailing," September 26, 1942, Yvonne Gregory, "National Maritime Union Is Beacon to Men of All Nations Who Sail Seas," April 3, 1943, and "Victory Rally Attracts 10,000," July 4, 1942, all *PV*.

81 Gerald Horne, *Red Seas: Ferdinand Smith and Radical Black Sailors in the United States and Jamaica* (New York: New York University Press, 2005), 96; "Schedule of Contributions Received," January to March 1944 (1042, 15, 2), and Joseph Curran to Ed Strong, April 7, 1943 (757, 5, 2), both *NNCP*.

82 See Mulzac, *A Star to Steer By*, 156; "Captain Mulzac Honored at Pre-Voyage Birthday," *PV*, April 1, 1944; and "Capt. Mulzac Answers Poll-Taxer Smith," *Congress Vue* 2, no. 1 (April 1944).

83 "Maritime Union Pledges No-Discrimination Policy," *CD*, national edition, December 26, 1942; Horne, *Red Seas*, 74, 98; Ferdinand Smith, "Labor Looks Ahead," *PV*, undated clipping (13, 2, 2), *NNCP*; NMU, "Equality for All."

84 The *Negro Champion* was the short-lived publication of the Manhattan Council of the NNC in 1941. See "Rally Calls for End to Jim Crow," *Negro Champion* 1, no. 1 (September 1941) (1087–94, 1), *NNC-FBI*.

85 Eben Miller, "Born along the Color Line: The Second Generation of Talented Tenth and the 'Problem of the Twentieth Century'" (Ph.D. diss., Brandeis University, 2004), 320–48.

86 See "Union Seeking Pact with Navy," *PV*, August 12, 1944; "Notable Achievements of 1944," *Congress View* 2, no. 10 (January 1945); "UFWA: Out in Front," *Congress View* 3, no. 9 (December 1945); and "Charlie" Collins to St. Clair Bourne, July 21, 1943 (415–19, 3, 4), NLVC, "50,000 Freedom Fighters by Frederick Douglass' Birthday," February 14, 1944 (336–37, 8, 4), and NLVC, "What We Have Done" (15–18, 6, 4), all *NNCP*.

87 See "Dixie Labor Head Raps John Davis," *CD*, national edition, June 27, 1942; "20,000 Negro Miners in Pay Increase Fight," *PV*, May 8, 1943; and Nelson Lichtenstein, *Labor's War at Home: The CIO in World War II* (New York: Cambridge University Press, 1982), 161–71.

88 "The Gains," December 12, 1942, and "Democracy at Sperry Gyroscope," September 30, 1944, both *PV*; Biondi, *To Stand and Fight*, 7–8.

89 "NNC Survey Indicates High Proportion of Negroes Will Lose Jobs in Post War Unless Special Steps Are Taken," news release, November 16, 1944 (922–24, 29, 1), and "Negro Workers after the War" (New York: NNC, 1945) (466–77, 17, 2), both *NNCP*; William Patterson, "Negro Jobs in Postwar Will Gauge Democracy," *Daily Worker*, July 18, 1945.

90 Florence Murray, "Shall Seniority Rules Be Modified to Forestall Discharge of Negroes?" September 30, 1944, Thelma Dale, "Labor Looks Ahead," October 28, 1944, and "Negro Congress Calls for Seniority Changes," December 2, 1944, all *PV*; "Revision of Seniority Rules Urged by NNC," *CD*, national edition, November 25, 1944; Thelma Dale to Louis Goldblatt, November 28, 1944, with enclosed statement on adjustment, folder "Minorities — Blacks — through 1959," ILWUP.

91 UFWA, "From the Proceedings of the Third Constitutional Convention," October 25, 1944, New York (451–56, 21, 2), *NNCP*; "UFWA: Out in Front," *Congress View* 3, no. 9 (December 1945). After 1940, Fauset changed the name of the Philadelphia NNC to the United People's Action Committee, but it remained an NNC affiliate. See "Sketch: Arthur Huff Fauset," *Congress View* 3, no. 2 (May 1945).

92 "Weaver Names to CIO Post," May 1, 1943, "CIO Conference Opens Political Action Campaign," January 15, 1944, and "Debate CIO Stand on Negro Job Seniority," all *CD*, national edition; George L.P. Weaver to Editor, *Amsterdam News* (New York), October 5, 1944, and Report of the CIO National Committee to Abolish Racial Discrimi-

nation, August 16, 1944 (2–18, 10, 2), and Thelma Dale, draft of a review for *PV* on Weaver's "Seniority and the Negro Worker" (649–60, 17, 2), all *NNCP*; Thelma Dale, published review, "Seniority Works Both Ways," *PV*, September 29, 1945.

93 Biondi, *To Stand and Fight*, 23; "Seniority for Negroes Weighed by Parley," *Daily Worker*, January 15, 1945; "Negro Congress Acts to Preserve War Gains," *PV*, January 20, 1945; NNC, "Conference on Post-War Employment," January 13, 1945, New York (536, 21, 2), *NNCP*; NNC, "Proceedings: Conference on Postwar Employment," January 13, 1945, at the Institute for International Democracy (New York: NNC, 1945).

94 This undermining of the NNC role in the CIO would become more apparent in the postwar period. See FBI, New York report, January 30, 1946 (832, 2), *NNC-FBI*; and Davis's denouncement of Weaver and Townsend in Gerald Horne, *Black Liberation/ Red Scare: Ben Davis and the Communist Party* (Newark: University of Delaware Press, 1994), 182.

95 "A Sane Approach to Job Seniority," editorial, *CD*, national edition, December 16, 1944. For the CIO's plan for full employment, see Philip Murray, "To Help Put 'Full' before Employment," copy at (281, 18, 2), *NNCP*.

96 "245,000 Workers Laid Off in State, 23,000 to Be Recalled in 60 Days," *New York Times*, September 12, 1945; "U.E.'s Plan," *Congress Vue* 1, no. 10 (March 1944); Thelma Dale, "Post-War Job Rights for Negroes," *Congress View* 2, nos. 8 and 9 (November–December 1944); "Union Sets Farseeing Plan for Negro Jobs," December 29, 1945, "Local 450 UE," political cartoon, January 19, 1946, "Negro Losing 400,000 Jobs," August 25, 1945, and "2,000,000 Jobs Lost under Reconversion," September 22, 1945, all *PV*; Biondi, *To Stand and Fight*, 24.

97 "NNC Exposes Governor Dewey for Killing FEPC Bills in NY," *Congress View* 2, no. 1 (April 1944); "N.Y.'s Busiest Assemblyman: An Interview with Hulan Jack," *Congress View* 3, no. 1 (April 1945); "Now, Let's Fight It Through!" editorial, *PV*, March 17, 1945.

98 Louis Colman, "It Is against the Law," review, June 2, 1945, "Electrical Workers, FEPC Sign Pact," July 7, 1945, and "Save FEPC Demonstration," December 22, 1945, all *PV*.

99 FBI, Washington, D.C., report, January 30, 1946 (834–57, 2), *NNC-FBI*.

100 See Florence Murray, "Will Women Keep Gains Made in Industry during the War?" *PV*, September 22, 1945; Yvonne Gregory, "Negro Women in Industry," *Congress Vue* 1, no. 1 (April 1943).

101 "First Negro Nurses Reach Europe," *Congress View* 2, no. 6 (September 1944); "Hold Conference on Post War" and "Postwar Employment for Women in Industry," *Congress View* 2, no. 11 (February 1945); NNC, Executive Committee Minutes, March 28, 1945 (358–60, 18, 2), and Thelma Dale, "The Status of Negro Women in the United States of America," report, New York, February 3, 1947 (486–92, 34, 3), both *NNCP*; "Miss Negro War Worker to Be Picked for Negro Freedom Rally at Garden," May 1, 1943, Ferdinand Smith, "Labor Looks Ahead," July 22, 1944, and "Freedom Rally Star Studded," June 23, 1945, all *PV*.

102 Naomi Kornacker, "Town Hall," *PV*, June 13, 1942; Dale, "The Status of Negro Women in the United States of America."

103 Portland Branch, Women's International League for Peace and Freedom, "Women Uniting for One World," February 1946 (781, 22, 2), Thelma Dale, draft of "Guest Editorial" for *New York Age*, November 1945 (785–88, 17, 2), "Draft Resolution to Be Submitted to the American Delegation" (757, 17, 2), and Manuscript #44 newsletter, January 15, 1946 (12, 17, 3), all *NNCP*; Thelma Dale, "The Paris Conference," *Christian Unitarian Register* 125, no. 4 (April 1946); John Robert Badger, "World View: Problems of Negro Women," *CD*, December 8, 1945. See also Amy Swerdlow, "The Congress of American Women: Left-Feminist Peace Politics in the Cold War," in *U.S. History as Women's History*, ed. Linda K. Kerber, Alice Kessler-Harris, and Kathryn Kish Sklar (Chapel Hill: University of North Carolina Press, 1995).

104 Dale, "The Status of Negro Women in the United States of America," quotes from 3, 5.

105 Thelma Dale to Jeanne Pastor, February 24, 1944 (467–68, 7, 2), *NNCP*; "Sketch: Thelma Dale," *Congress Vue* 1, no. 3 (August 1943); "Executive at Paris Women's Meet," *Congress View* 3, no. 9 (December 1945).

106 Ben Davis, *Communist Councilman from Harlem* (New York: International Publishers, 1969), 107–13; Horne, *Black Liberation/Red Scare*, 90, 161; Ferdinand Smith, "Labor Looks Ahead," *PV*, October 23, 1942; Non-Partisan Registration Committee, "Register to Vote This Week," pamphlet (62, 6, 4), NLVC, "For Immediate Release," 1943 (163–64, 4, 2), and [October 1944] (19, 6, 4), all *NNCP*.

107 "Dorothy Funn Named NY Representative for PAC," *CD*, national edition, August 26, 1944; "Rally Echoes Still Heard," June 19, 1943, and "Victory Committee Works for Powell" and "Trade Unions Issue Call for Powell Campaign," July 29, 1944, all *PV*; Thelma Dale to Ben Davis Jr., July 28, 1944 (225, 7, 2), and Manhattan Council of the NNC, "Harlem's People's Candidate for Congress: Adam Clayton Powell, Jr.," campaign flyer, 1944 (548, 9, 3), both *NNCP*; "Clergy and Labor Endorse Powell for Congress," *Congress Vue* 2, no. 1 (April 1944); "Powell Campaign Aided by Dorothy Funn," *Congress View* 2, no. 5 (August 1944); Hamilton, *Adam Clayton Powell*, 103, 115–17, 156–57.

108 NMU, "Ferdinand Smith and Capt. Hugh Mulzac to Make Six-Week Tour for Truman-Roosevelt Ticket," press release, September 20, 1944 (724, 6, 3), and CIO PAC, "For Immediate Release," September 7, 1944 (79–80, 7, 2), both *NNCP*; "Negroes Join Drive for 1944 Election," *Daily Worker*, July 29, 1945; Max Yergan, Adam Powell, Hope Stevens, Charles Buchanan, and Ferdinand Smith, "Elect Roosevelt for a Fourth Term for President," *PV*, July 15, 1944.

109 Charles A. Collins, "Town Hall," March 23, 1943, Doxey Wilkerson, "Why We Must Elect Roosevelt and Truman," November 4, 1944, and Thelma Dale, "Town Hall," July 29, 1944, all *PV*.

110 "Labor, Negroes Hail 4th Term; Want Wallace," *PV*, July 22, 1944; Non-Partisan Statement, "Reelect Roosevelt — For the Freedom and Security of the Negro People and All America," September 21, 1944 (392–95, 13, 2), *NNCP*.

111 Earl Browder, "A Great Ordeal," speech at Madison Square Garden, *PV*, July 8, 1944;

Horne, *Black Liberation/Red Scare*, 119–46; Isserman, *Which Side Were You On?* 187–213.

112 Horne, *Black Liberation/Red Scare*, 130, 134, 136; NNC, "Review: 1944" (492–95, 10, 2), *NNCP*.

113 Executive Committee Memo, "NNC Organization," December 1944 (132, 7, 2), and NNC, partial transcript of January 1945 executive board meeting, January 1945 (640–64, 16, 2), both *NNCP*.

114 "NNC Councils at Work," *Congress Vue* 2, no. 1 (April 1944); "Negroes and National Defense," April 8–9, 1941, Detroit NNC proceedings, folder 73, box 1, STC; Christopher Alston, "Henry Ford and the Negro People," Michigan NNC pamphlet, NNC Vertical File, Tamiment Library, New York University, New York; Thelma Dale to Mayme Brown, February 29, 1944 (472–73, 7, 2), and "Join the National Negro Congress in the Battle of 1945," Detroit pamphlet, spring 1945 (202–4, 18, 2), both *NNCP*. See also August Meier and Elliott Rudwick, *Black Detroit and the Rise of the UAW* (New York: Oxford University Press, 1979); Thomas Sugrue, *The Origins of the Urban Crisis: Race and Inequality in Postwar Detroit* (Princeton, N.J.: Princeton University Press, 2005); Angela Dillard, *Faith in the City: Preaching Radical Social Change in Detroit* (Ann Arbor: University of Michigan Press, 2007); David Lewis-Colman, *Race against Liberalism: Black Workers and the UAW in Detroit* (Chicago: University of Illinois Press, 2008), 7–14; and Erik S. Gellman and Jarod Roll, *The Gospel of the Working Class: Labor's Southern Prophets in New Deal America* (Chicago: University of Illinois Press, 2011).

115 FBI, Chicago report, May 17, 1945 (699, 2), June 16, 1945 (714, 2), and August 23, 1944 (377–79, 2), all *NNC-FBI*.

116 Fraser M. Ottanelli, *The Communist Party of the United States: From Depression to World War II* (New Brunswick, N.J.: Rutgers University Press, 1991), 197, 211–12.

117 Wilkerson quoted in Horne, *Black Liberation/Red Scare*, 131, 140; Ruth Jett to "Bill," September 19, 1945 (439–40, 19, 2), and Dorothy Funn to Ed Strong, July 23, 1945 (899–900, 18, 2), both *NNCP*.

118 Thelma Dale to "Dick," January 31, 1943 (302, 4, 2), *NNCP*.

119 Ed Strong to Thelma Dale, New York, June 24, 1945 (453–58, 16, 2), *NNCP*.

120 James Jackson to Esther Cooper, January 12, 1944, folder 15, box 7, Cooper to Jackson, May 28, 1945, folder 9, box 7, and Jackson to Cooper, June 18, 1945, folder 26, box 7, all JJP.

121 See, for example, Ben Davis, "Let the Jimcroers Beware!" guest editorial, *PV*, June 23, 1945.

122 "Revels Cayton Gets Negro Congress Job," *CD*, national edition, December 22, 1945; Mason Roberson, "New Negro Congress Exec, Long a Fighter," *PV*, January 5, 1946. See also Martin Duberman, *Paul Robeson: A Biography* (New York: Knopf, 1988), 310.

123 Cayton quoted in FBI, Chicago report, January 1, 1946 (810–11, 2), *NNC-FBI*. Further FBI reports show how the NNC continued to have ambivalent feelings about too much direct CP involvement from the top leadership in New York. An October 1945 report

from New York quoted an NNC member who complained that "the Party was wrong in not appreciating the role . . . the NNC . . . could play in the liberation of the negro people." See FBI, New York report, October 1, 1945 (746–47, 2), and January 16, 1947 (1173–74, 2), both *NNC-FBI*.

124 See FBI, Washington, D.C., report, January 30, 1946 (845–57, 2), *NNC-FBI*; "Drive to Send Bilbo Back to Dixie," August 11, 1945, and Venice Spraggs, "Bilbo Defends Self in Congress," September 15, 1945, both *CD*, national edition; "Bilbo Must Go" and "7,000 Persons Demand Jobs, 'Oust Bilbo,'" October 27, 1945, and "1,000 March on D.C." and "Huge FEPC Delegation Startles Congressmen," January 26, 1946, all *PV*.

125 Max Yergan, in NNC, Executive Committee Minutes, November 8, 1945 (329–31, 18, 2), *NNCP*.

126 Dalfiume, "The 'Forgotten Years,'" 299, 301, 319; Sitkoff, "African American Militancy," 70, 89, 91, 92; Isserman, *Which Side Were You On?* 141–43, 169.

127 Labor Research Association, *Labor Fact Book 8* (New York: Oriole Edition, 1947, re-issued 1973), 85–86.

128 Mulzac, *A Star to Steer By*, 237–38, 244.

129 Esther Cooper to James Jackson, October 27, 1944, folder 6, box 7, JJP.

Chapter Five

1 W. E. B. Du Bois, "Behold the Land," address at the Southern Youth Legislature, October 20, 1946, typescript and pamphlet produced by the Southern Negro Youth Congress, boxes 6–7, SNYCP, quoting Deuteronomy 1:18 and 1:21, reprinted in *Freedomways* 1, no. 4 (Winter 1964).

2 Peter Lau delineated the broad terrain of domestic civil rights efforts in South Carolina, including a short treatment of the SNYC there. See Peter Lau, *Democracy Rising: South Carolina and the Fight for Black Equality since 1865* (Lexington: University of Kentucky Press, 2006), especially chapter 5. See also Barbara Woods Aba-Mecha, "Black Woman Activist in Twentieth Century South Carolina: Modjeska M. Simkins" (Ph.D. diss., Emory University, 1978); and Miles S. Richards, "Osceola E. McKaine and the Struggle for Black Civil Rights, 1917–1946" (Ph.D. diss., University of South Carolina, 1994). Two works that cover the entire South during this era discuss South Carolina as an important site of activism. See Patricia Sullivan, *Days of Hope: Race and Democracy in the New Deal Era* (Chapel Hill: University of North Carolina Press, 1996), quote from 143; and John Egerton, *Speak Now against the Day: The Generation before the Civil Rights Movement in the South* (New York: Alfred A. Knopf, 1994). Last, a few articles have focused on this local movement. See Wim Roefs, "Leading the Civil Rights Vanguard in South Carolina: John McCray and the *Lighthouse and Informer*, 1939–1954," in *Time Longer Than Rope: A Century of African American Activism, 1850–1950*, ed. Charles M. Payne and Adam Green (New York: New York University Press, 2003), 462–91; Bryant Simon, "Race Reactions: African American Organizing, Liberalism, and White Working-Class Politics in Postwar South Carolina," in *Jumpin' Jim*

Crow: South Politics from the Civil War to Civil Rights, ed. Jane Dailey, Glenda Gilmore, and Bryant Simon (Princeton, N.J.: Princeton University Press, 2000); and Miles S. Richards, "The Progressive Democrats in Chicago, July 1944," *South Carolina Historical Magazine* 102, no. 3 (July 2001).

3 W. E. B. Du Bois, Carter Woodson, and C. L. R. James all considered global circumstances vital to African American politics and history. Yet during the Cold War, historians did not focus on their international work because this framework had been largely marginalized from consideration as civil rights. Over the last decade, however, a new strain of scholarship has placed African American freedom struggles into an international context, making this context essential to understanding domestic civil rights. But the question of how African Americans at the grassroots, especially southerners, thought and acted in terms of civil rights internationalism remains largely unaddressed. See Penny Von Eschen, *Race against Empire: Black Americans and Anticolonialism, 1937–1957* (Ithaca, N.Y.: Cornell University Press, 1997); Carol Anderson, *Eyes Off the Prize: The United Nations and the African American Struggle for Human Rights, 1944–1955* (Cambridge: Cambridge University Press, 2003); Mary L. Dudziak, *Cold War Civil Rights: Race and the Image of American Democracy* (Princeton, N.J.: Princeton University Press, 2000); Thomas Borstelmann, *The Cold War and the Color Line: American Race Relations in the Global Arena* (Cambridge, Mass.: Harvard University Press, 2001); and Brenda Gayle Plummer, ed., *Window on Freedom: Race, Civil Rights, and Foreign Affairs, 1945–1988* (Chapel Hill: University of North Carolina Press, 2003).

4 See Wilhelmina Jackson, "Greenville Notes," "Charleston Memorandum," "Columbia Memorandum," and "Report on the Sea Islands," 1940, for Gunnar Myrdal study (*An American Dilemma*), folders 1 and 2, box 36, Ralph Bunche Papers, Schomburg Center for Research in Black Culture, New York Public Library, New York; and John Bolt Culbertson to John P. Davis, May 30, 1940 (1, 16, 135–36), NNCP.

5 Jackson, "Charleston Memorandum" and "Columbia Memorandum."

6 Ibid.

7 Ibid.

8 See Turner Catledge, "Negro Issue Raised in South at 'Purge,'" *New York Times*, August 23, 1938; David Robertson, *Sly and Able: A Political Biography of James F. Byrnes* (New York: W. W. Norton, 1994), 190–94; Egerton, *Speak Now against the Day*, 86–87; and William Leuchtenburg, *Franklin D. Roosevelt and the New Deal, 1932–1940* (New York: Harper and Row, 1963), 267–68.

9 Simkins, Civil Rights Studies conference, session I, 1989, audio recording, Tamiment Library, New York University, New York; Barbara A. Woods, "Modjeska Simkins and the South Carolina Conference of the NAACP, 1939–1957," in *Women in the Civil Rights Movement: Trailblazers and Torchbearers, 1941–1965*, ed. Vicki Crawford, Jacqueline Rouse, and Barbara Woods (Bloomington: Indiana University Press, 1993), 99–107, quote from 101.

10 Simon, "Race Reactions," 240–41.

11 The *Lighthouse and Informer* (Columbia, S.C.) was a consolidation of two smaller papers. See "John Henry McCray," introduction to the JMP, roll 1, JMP; "Immediate Release," PDP, n.d. [probably 1945], folder "McKaine," roll 9, JMP; and Jackson, "Columbia Memorandum."

12 See Osceola McKaine vertical file folder, African-American Biography, Reference Department, South Caroliniana Library, Columbia, S.C.; Miles S. Richards, "The Eminent Lieutenant McKaine," *Carologue: A Publication of the South Carolina Historical Society* (Autumn 1991); Richards, "Osceola E. McKaine and the Struggle for Black Civil Rights, 1917–1946," 1–93; and Osceola McKaine, candidate for U.S. Senate, PDP, radio address, October 18, 1944, folder "McKaine," roll 9, JMP.

13 See "Syboney, Battered by Gale, Brings 384," *New York Times*, January 30, 1941.

14 Lieutenant Osceola E. McKaine, "A Negro in Nazi-Europe," *Palmetto Leader* (Columbia, S.C.), May 10, 1941.

15 O. E. McKaine, letter to editor, "Sumter Negro Finds Town Better Than North," *Columbia State*, May 18, 1941, in Osceola McKaine vertical file folder, African-American Biography, Reference Department, South Caroliniana Library, Columbia, S.C.

16 O. E. McKaine to SNYC, October 7, 1942, folder "Charleston, SC," box 3, SNYCP; Richards, "Osceola E. McKaine and the Struggle for Black Civil Rights, 1917–1946," 107–30.

17 J. M. Hinton and Mrs. Andrew W. Simkins, in Herbert Aptheker, "Listen to the Rumble: South Carolina: 'They Are Still Battling,'" *New Masses*, March 16, 1947, HAP.

18 Quoted in Richards, "The Progressive Democrats," 223.

19 Ibid.; draft of Osceola McKaine speech, May 24, 1944, box 4, ACP.

20 Osceola McKaine, letter to editor, "Progressive Keynoter Made No Threats," *Columbia Record*, June 2, 1944.

21 Quoted in Richards, "The Progressive Democrats," 228. "Maybank Says Negro Move Is Doomed," *Columbia Record*, May 27, 1944; "Negro Group May Seek to Replace White Delegates," *Charleston Evening Post*, April 28, 1944.

22 Richards, "The Progressive Democrats," 231–34; "Progressives Not Seated," *Pittsburgh Courier*, July 22, 1944; "McCray Group Denied Seats at Convention," *BAA*, July 22, 1944; "Dem Convention Refuses to Seat Negro Delegates," *Michigan Chronicle*, July 22, 1944.

23 Robertson, *Sly and Able*, 312–15, 343–44; David McCullough, *Truman* (New York: Simon and Schuster, 1992), 307.

24 John McCray, "The Way It Was," *Charleston Chronicle*, November 9, 1985, roll 16, JMP; Richards, "The Progressive Democrats"; Doris E. Saunders, "1944 Pre-Convention Maneuverings: The Day Dawson Saved America from a Racist President," *Ebony* (July 1972): quote from 50; McCullough, *Truman*, 297, 302–3, 311.

25 Richards, "The Progressive Democrats"; Saunders, "1944 Pre-Convention Maneuverings," 42–50; McCullough, *Truman*, 297–311.

26 PDP, "County Campaign Schedule of Osceola E. McKaine, Candidate for the United States Senate from the Progressive Democratic Party," n.d. [1944], folder "McKaine," roll 9, JMP.

27 Osceola McKaine, candidate for U.S. Senate, PDP, transcript of radio address, October 18, 1944, folder "McKaine," roll 9, JMP; "Negro Party Picks McKaine as Nominee," *Columbia Record*, August 30, 1944; Richards, "Osceola E. McKaine and the Struggle for Black Civil Rights, 1917–1946," 193–204.

28 "Constituting No Threat," *Columbia Record*, December 11, 1944.

29 John McCray to Thurgood Marshall, November 9, 1944, folder "McKaine," roll 9, JMP.

30 Ibid.; "Protest Threat Voiced by Two Parties in SC," *Columbia State*, November 7, 1944; C. P. Trussell, "Dies Group Is Put on Permanent Basis in House," *New York Times*, January 4, 1945.

31 Paul Robeson, notes from informal talk delivered at the cultural session of the Fifth All-Southern Negro Youth Conference, Tuskegee, Ala., April 18, 1942, printed in the *Waco Messenger*, June 19, 1942, clipping in folders 5–8, box 4, ESP; SNYC, "Negro Youth Fighting for America: 5th All-Southern Negro Youth Conference program," April 17–19, 1942 (256–59, 30, 1), NNCP.

32 O. E. McKaine to SNYC, October 7, 1942, and Louis Burnham to Osceola McKaine, October 20, 1942, both folder "Charleston, South Carolina," box 3, SNYCP.

33 Louis Burnham to "Jack," February 2, 1942, folder 19, box 2, ESP.

34 John P. Davis to Louis Burnham, November 28, 1942, folders "Correspondence 1943," box 3, SNYCP.

35 Esther Cooper, "Negro Youth Organizing for Victory," April 18, 1942, speech at Fifth All-Southern Negro Youth Conference, Tuskegee, Ala., April 18, 1942, folder 3, box 3, ESP.

36 See Maurice Isserman, *Which Side Were You On? The American Communist Party during the Second World War* (Middletown, Ct.: Wesleyan University Press, 1982), 141–43, 169.

37 O. E. McKaine to Louis Burnham, April 6, 1945, folder "Correspondence 1944–1945, South Carolina," box 3, SNYCP.

38 O. E. McKaine, "For Victory at the Ballot Box," speech delivered at May 1, 1945, SNYC voting rally, Birmingham (6–11, 15, 3), NNCP.

39 Ibid.

40 See issues of *Cavalcade: The March of Southern Youth*, Birmingham, from 1941 and 1942, in folder 26, box 3, SNYCP.

41 Executive Secretary, report on SNYC, December 13, 1943 (706–15, 4, 2), NNCP.

42 "International Student Assembly Draws SNYC Members," *SNYC News*, October 1942, Birmingham, folder 26, box 3, ESP.

43 "Detour the Roosevelt Road to War!" *SNYC News*, January 1941, Birmingham (489–93, 29, 1), NNCP.

44 "Negro Youth Congress Issues July 4th Declaration," *Arkansas Baptist Flashlight* reprint of declaration, June 6, 1942, copy in folders 5–8, box 4, ESP; SNYC, "Youth

Congress Leaders Present Petitions to End Jim-Crow Army to War Department Officials," news release, May 31, 1944 (318–19, 16, 2), *NNCP*; "On the Conduct of the War:
Wanted: A Second Front," *SNYC News*, October 1942, Birmingham, copy in folder 26,
box 3, ESP.

45 James E. Jackson Jr. to Sherman William, September 17, 1942, folder "Correspondence
1943," box 3, SNYCP; Esther Cooper, "Negro Youth Organizing for Victory," April 18,
1942, speech at Fifth All-Southern Negro Youth Conference, Tuskegee, Ala., April 18,
1942, folder 3, box 3, and "Home Making and Greater Participation in the War Effort to
Be Discussed," *Pittsburgh Courier*, March 28, 1942, clipping in folders 5–8, box 4, both
ESP; Erik S. McDuffie, "Long Journeys: Four Black Women in the Communist Party,
USA, 1930–1956" (Ph.D. diss., New York University, 2003), 366; contents of folder
"Town Hall Meetings, Birmingham," box 2, SNYCP.

46 Esther Cooper Jackson, "This Is My Husband" (New York: National Committee to
Defend Negro Leadership, n.d. [1950s]), 14–22, folder 3, box 4, ESP.

47 Esther Cooper Jackson, "Historic London Conference Unites Youth of the World,"
n.d. [1946], folder 18, box 7, ESP; Louis Burnham, Memorandum to Southern and
Gulf Port Agents of the National Maritime Union, December 4, 1945, folder "Finances
NMU," box 4, SNYCP; "Esther V. Cooper to Be Youth Congress Delegate to London,"
SNYC news release, 9, no. 9 (September 10, 1945) (23, 15, 3), *NNCP*; Chatwood Hall,
"Youth Parley Delegate Guest of Russ," *CD*, national edition, January 26, 1946; McDuf-
fie, "Long Journeys," 386–91.

48 SNYC, "The Southern Negro Youth Congress Presents Esther Cooper Jackson and
James E. Jackson Jr. in a Vital, Provocative Series of Lectures," leaflet advertising tour,
n.d. [March 1946], folder 23, box 3, ESP; Louis Burnham to Rose Mae Catchings, Nashville, March 2, 1946, folder "Executive Board," box 1, and Louis Burnham to Annie
Belle Weston, March 5, 1946, folder "Columbia, SC," box 5, both SNYCP; McDuffie, "Long Journeys," 393. For CP criticism, see James Jackson to "Jim," July 7, 1945,
folder 8, box 4, JJP.

49 Mrs. Andrew W. Simkins to SNYC, January 14, 1946, Louis Burnham, Memorandum
on 7th All-Southern Youth Congress to Members of Conference Planning Committee,
n.d. [early 1946], Louis Burnham to A. B. Weston, January 16, 1946, and A. B. Weston,
O. E. McKaine, Mrs. Andrew W. Simkins, and Rev. Robert H. Wilson to "Fellow-
Citizens," February 8, 1946, all folders "Columbia Conference," boxes 6–7, SNYCP;
Annie Bell Weston to Louis Burnham, March 3, 1946, and Louis Burnham, Organizational Secretary, SNYC, to A. B. Weston, March 6, 1946, both folder "Columbia, SC,"
box 5, SNYCP.

50 Kari Frederickson, "'The Slowest State' and 'Most Backward Community': Racial Violence in South Carolina and Federal Civil-Rights Legislation, 1946–1948," *South Carolina Historical Magazine* 98, no. 2 (April 1997); Egerton, *Speak Now against the Day*,
362–63, 408, 414; Sullivan, *Days of Hope*, 219.

51 A. B. Weston to "Fellow Citizen and Friend," February 25, 1946, folders "Columbia
Conference," boxes 6–7, SNYCP.

52 The Modjeska Simkins correspondence suggests that she and Weston had prob-
lems working together on behalf of the SNYC campaign. Yet she never doubted her
competence in working hard and getting results. "We are good friends but impos-
sible stablemates," she wrote in confidence to Louis Burnham. See Mrs. Andrew W.
Simkins to Louis Burnham, July 23, 1946, Mrs. Andrew W. Simkins to Louis Burnham,
July 25, 1946 (quote), Mrs. Andrew W. Simkins to James Jackson, July 19, 1946, and "S"
[Mrs. Andrew W. Simkins] to Louis Burnham, "confidential," July 25, 1946, all folder
"Columbia, SC," box 5, SNYCP.

53 "Alabama Veterans Form Organization," *Norfolk Journal and Guide*, March 30, 1946;
"Battle for Vote Unites Negroes," *CD*, national edition, June 26, 1946; SNYC, "Bir-
mingham Negro Veterans Denied Registration," press release, January 23, 1946 (39–
40, 15, 3), *NNCP*; Mrs. Andrew W. Simkins to "Fellow Citizen," July 25, 1946, folder
"Columbia, SC," box 5, SNYCP. For more about McKaine's activities as a Southern
Conference for Human Welfare field worker, see Egerton, *Speak Now against the Day*,
441, 444; Sullivan, *Days of Hope*, 195–97, 201–2, 217; and Richards, "Osceola E. Mc-
Kaine and the Struggle for Black Civil Rights, 1917–1946," 230, 242–43.

54 SNYC, "The SNYC Third Leadership Training School," Harbison Junior College, near
Irmo, S.C., August 8–18, 1946, schedule and application, folder 23, box 3, ESP; O. E.
McKaine, "The Palmetto State," *Norfolk Journal and Guide*, August 17, 1946; Dorothy
Burnham to Mike Ross, June 27, 1946, and Ross reply to Burnham, July 22, 1946, both
folder 19, box 2, ESP; James E. Jackson to William Elkuss, July 24, 1946, and Mary Law-
rence and Bill Elkuss, Memo for Southern Negro Youth Congress Leadership Institute,
August 1946, near Irmo, SC, August 1946, both folder "3rd Leadership Training Insti-
tute," box 2, SNYCP; Louis Burnham to Esther Cooper Jackson, July 6, 1946, folders
"Columbia Conference," boxes 6–7, SNYCP.

55 Edmonia W. Grant, American Missionary Society, "What Do You Know about Race?
A True-or-False Test," folder "3rd Leadership Training School," box 2, SNYCP.

56 Mary Lawrence and Bill Elkuss, Memo, August 1946, folder "3rd Leadership Training Institute," box 2, SNYCP. For evidence of participants becoming SNYC council
leaders, see Ida E. Scott and Miss Constance Hammond, "Membership Report," January 6, 1947, and W. J. Nelson to Louis Burnham, November 8, 1946, both folder "Harbison A&I," box 5, SNYCP; Leroy Aiken to Louis Burnham, December 9, 1946, folder
"Moncks Corner," box 5, SNYCP; Esther V. Cooper to Miriam L. McTear, August 21,
1946, and Florence Valentine to Esther Cooper Jackson, September 16, 1946, folders
"Columbia Conference," boxes 6–7, SNYCP; and Julian Dargan and Herman Alston
to Esther Cooper Jackson, folder "Orangeburg," box 5, SNYCP.

57 A. J. Clement Jr. to John McCray, May 12, July 21, November 5, 1945, March 6, July 16,
1946, folder "Clement, A. J.," roll 9, and O. E. McKaine to "Mac" [John McCray],
April 10, 1946, folder "McKaine," roll 9, all JMP.

58 "Columbia Committee against Jim Crow Urges You to Join Jim Crow Sunday," post-
card mailing to Kenneth Kennedy, February 1946, and Anti-Jim Crow Committee,
Columbia, S.C., "The Lord's Word: The Bible Says 'Of One Blood All Nations,'" pam-

phlet, n.d. [1946], folder "Columbia, SC," box 5, SNYCP; Paul B. Newman to Esther Cooper Jackson, January 21, 1946, folder "Correspondence, 1946–1947, SC," box 3, SNYCP.

59 John H. McCray, Chairman, PDP, Columbia, to "Party Members and All Other Believers," n.d. [August 1946], Osceola McKaine vertical file folder, African-American Biography, Reference Department, South Caroliniana Library, Columbia, S.C.

60 NNC, "A Petition on Behalf of 13 Million Oppressed Negro Citizens of the United States of America" (New York: NNC, 1946); NNC, "A Petition" (501, 15, 2), *NNCP*. See also "U.S. Bias May Get UN Hearing," *Norfolk Journal and Guide*, June 8, 1946; "Urges United Nations to Find Relief from Racial Oppression," *Pittsburgh Courier*, June 8, 1946; "NNC Petitions U.S. to Stop U.S. Jimcro," June 8, 1946, and "U.N. and the Negro," June 8, 1946, both *PV*; "U.N. Silent on Appeal by Negro Group It Probe Jimcrow Oppression," *California Eagle*, June 13, 1946; "Nat'l. Negro Congress Petitions UNO to End Nat'l Bias," *New York Age*, June 8, 1946.

61 "U.S. Fascism Hit in Paris," *Pittsburgh Courier*, August 17, 1946; "World Groups Hit Lynchings," *Amsterdam News* (New York), August 10, 1946.

62 H. J. M. Hubbard to Max Yergan, September 19, 1946 (177–78, 28, 2), E. Cris Le Maitre and Rolley T. Lashley to H. Aptheker, July 16, 1946 (175, 28, 2), G. Herbert Adams to Max Yergan, October 21, 1946 (475, 28, 2), Thelma Dale to Will Brown, July 26, 1946 (336, 23, 2), Max Yergan to Trygve Lie, June 1, 1946 (258, 26, 2), M. E. Jeffries to Ewart Guinier, July 24, 1946 (185, 28, 2), NNC, "Summary Record of Presentation of a Petition . . ." (295, 26, 2), NNC memo, "Tasks," n.d. [1946] (305–6, 26, 2), Andrew Cordier to Max Yergan, June 11, 1946 (172, 28, 2), NNC, Meeting Minutes of NNC Conference on U.N. Petition, February 8, 1947 (199–202, 28, 2), and Women's International Democratic Federation to Mr. Secretary General, United Nations, New York, November 26, 1946 (481, 28, 2), all *NNCP*. See also Anderson, *Eyes Off the Prize*.

63 The *Lighthouse and Informer* listed delegates from Allen University, Benedict College, South Carolina State, Avery Institute, Burke Industrial School, Morris Brown AME Church, and the CIO Tobacco Workers local in Charleston. See "5,000 Visitors Expected for Weekend SNYC Meeting," *Lighthouse and Informer* (Columbia, S.C.), October 20, 1946.

64 SNYC, "Southern Youth Legislature" and "Program," 3, 6, in folders "Columbia Conference," box 6, SNYCP.

65 Junius Scales and Richard Nickson, *Cause at Heart: A Former Communist Remembers* (Athens: University of Georgia Press, 1987), 162–63; "Youth Congress Takes Militant Stand on Race Oppression," *CD*, national edition, October 26, 1946.

66 Due to a last-minute illness, Powell did not attend the conference but did send the speech he had written for the event. John McCray replaced Powell as the keynote speaker on Friday evening. See Adam Clayton Powell Jr., "Excerpts of Speech to Southern Negro Youth Congress," and John H. McCray, "Speech at Southern Youth Legislature," October 18, 1946, both folders "Columbia Conference," boxes 6–7, SNYCP. Miles Richards asserted that a rumor spread during the conference that Powell did

not attend because the anti-Communist feelings of other black Democrats pressured him to bow out. See Richards, "Osceola E. McKaine and the Struggle for Black Civil Rights, 1917–1946," 248.

67 See SNYC, Columbia Conference Program, 2–4, 7, folders "Columbia Conference," box 6, SNYCP.

68 Jack O'Dell, "I Wasn't Interested in Living in the United States If I Wasn't Going to Be in the Movement," interview by Sam Sills, August 5, 1993, transcript and audio at http://historymatters.gmu.edu/d/6926 (August 5, 2005). O'Dell, in part because of his experience with the NMU and SNYC, became a lifelong activist. See Jack O'Dell, *Climbin' Jacob's Ladder: The Black Freedom Movement Writings of Jack O'Dell*, ed. Nikhil Singh (Berkeley: University of California Press, 2010).

69 See also Bruce Baker, *What Reconstruction Meant: Historical Memory in the American South* (Charlottesville: University of Virginia Press, 2007).

70 Howard Fast, *Freedom Road* (New York: Duell, Sloan, and Pierce, 1944), 261–63.

71 NNC, Draft of Minutes Taken by Elsie Jackson at Cultural Meeting, November 28 [1945 or 1946], and Max Yergan, Howard Fast, Herman Shumlin, and Fredi Washington, draft of letter, November 1943 (570–76, 1, 2), *NNCP*; Revels Cayton to Matt Crawford, November 25, 1946, folder 7, box 2, MCP; "Howard Fast in Harlem," *Congress View* 2 (October 1944); Adam Clayton Powell Jr., "Freedom Road by Howard Fast," *Congress View* 2 (September 1944); Betty White to Revels Cayton, May 30, 1946 (146, 26, 2), *NNCP*; Paula Robeson, essay for Association of Young Writers and Artists Contest, 1944, folder "Assoc. of Young Writers and Artists Contest, 1944," box 1, SNYCP.

72 See Scales and Nickson, *Cause at Heart*, 163.

73 Howard Fast, "They're Marching Up Freedom Road," *New Masses*, November 5, 1946; "Southern Youth Group Holds Legislature," *Events and Trends in Race Relations* (Nashville: Fisk University, October 1946), 115 (1198, 16, 3), *NNCP*; Esther V. Cooper to Howard Fast, July 2, 1946, and Howard Fast to Louis Burnham, October 10, 1946, folders "Columbia Conference," boxes 6–7, SNYCP; SNYC, "Final Call to the Conference!" Pre-Conference News Bulletin, Southern Youth Legislature, Columbia, S.C., October 18, 19, 20, 1946 (105–8, 11, 3), *NNCP*.

74 Paul Robeson, "Address Delivered at the Southern Youth Legislature," October 19, 1946, folders "Columbia Conference," boxes 6–7, SNYCP. For more on Robeson and the American Crusade to End Lynching, see Associated Press, "Robeson to President Truman — 'Government Must Act against Lynching or the Negroes Will,'" September 24, 1946, and other reports reprinted in Philip S. Foner, ed., *Paul Robeson Speaks* (New York: Citadel, 1978), 173–78. For NNC involvement, see Ewart Guinier and Vicki Best to "Friend," August 2, 1946 (131, 12, 2), Thelma Dale to William Anderson, September 19, 1946 (327, 23, 2), newspaper clippings (262–74, 24, 2), and Washington Council, NNC, "Stop Lynching!" pamphlet, n.d. [1946] (621–23, 30, 2), all *NNCP*.

75 Robeson, "Address Delivered at the Southern Youth Legislature."

76 A. Romeo Horton and Theodore Baker, speeches at Southern Youth Legislature, October 19, 1946, folders "Columbia Conference," boxes 6–7, SNYCP; Southern Youth

Legislature Program, Columbia, S.C., October 1946, 6, in folders "Columbia Conference," box 6, SNYCP; O. E. McKaine, "Europeans Shocked at U.S. Race Problems," *Norfolk New Journal and Guide*, August 23, 1947.

77 Du Bois, "Behold the Land," 8–9, reprinted in *Freedomways* 1, no. 4 (Winter 1964).

78 W. E. B. Du Bois, *The Suppression of the African Slave Trade to the United States of America, 1638–1870* (1896; Millwood, N.Y.: Kraus-Thomson Organization, 1973); W. E. B. Du Bois, "The Color Line Belts the World," in *W. E. B. Du Bois: A Reader*, ed. David L. Lewis (New York: H. Holt, 1995), 42; W. E. B. Du Bois, *Black Reconstruction in America: 1860–1880* (1935; New York: Touchstone, 1992). See also Kelley, "'But a Local Phase of World Problem': Black History's Global Vision, 1883–1950," *Journal of American History* 86 no. 3 (December 1999).

79 SNYC, Columbia Conference program, 7, in folders "Columbia Conference," box 6, SNYCP.

80 Du Bois, "Behold the Land," 12, reprinted in *Freedomways* 1, no. 4 (Winter 1964).

81 "The President Leaves a Legacy," editorial, *CD*, national edition, April 21, 1945.

82 Having received a copy of this handbill from a friend, Byrnes attributed the letter to "some of our CIO friends." See Colonel Lawrence Pickney to James Byrnes, March 5, 1946, with attached handbill by Committee for Charleston, Southern Conference for Human Welfare, and Byrnes to Pinckney, March 8, 1946, both folder 2, correspondence P, 1945–46, box 6, series 5, State Department, James Francis Byrnes Papers (Mss 90), Clemson University Libraries, Special Collections Unit, Clemson, S.C.

83 Bertram D. Hulen, "Byrnes Bids Russia Aid U.S. to Uphold World Charter 'With Force if Necessary,'" *New York Times*, October 19, 1946; "Mr. Byrnes Reports," editorial, *New York Times*, October 19, 1946.

84 "Paris to Flushing Meadows," editorial, *New York Times*, October 17, 1946.

85 "Big Three Unity Vital to Colonial Advancement," editorial, *CD*, October 12, 1946.

86 "United Nations to See the American Picture," *New York Times*, October 20, 1946.

87 SNYC, draft of press release, October 18, 1946, folder "Correspondence, 1946–1947, SC," box 3, SNYCP; "Negroes Urge That Byrnes Be Ousted from Cabinet," *Columbia State*, October 21, 1946, folders 5–8, box 4, ESP.

88 Robeson, "Address Delivered at the Southern Youth Legislature."

89 Robertson, *Sly and Able*, 85–86, 282; John McCray, "Why James F. Byrnes Is Being Opposed," *Atlanta Daily World*, November 5, 1946.

90 Du Bois, "Behold the Land," 11, reprinted in *Freedomways* 1, no. 4 (Winter 1964); George Streator, "Negro Youth Told Future Is in South," *New York Times*, October 21, 1946.

91 Edward K. Weaver, Louis Burnham, Mrs. Andrew W. Simkins, O. E. McKaine, and John H. McCray to Honorable Ransome J. Williams, October 21, 1946, folder "SNYC," roll 14, JMP; "Youth Congress Ends in Wrangle with Governor," *Atlanta Daily World*, October 26, 1946.

92 "Russia Is Praised at Negro Meeting," *Columbia Record*, October 19, 1946, and Alderman Duncan, "Negroes Urge That Byrnes Be Ousted from Cabinet," *Columbia State*,

October 21, 1946, both folders 5–8, box 4, ESP; "Beaufort White Paper Hits Lighthouse Editor," *Atlanta Daily World*, November 5, 1946.

93 George Streator, "Byrnes Is Scored by Young Negroes," *New York Times*, October 20, 1946.

94 Weaver, Burnham, Simkins, McKaine, and McCray to Honorable Ransome J. Williams, October 21, 1946, folder "SNYC," roll 14, JMP.

95 "Mae" [Rose Mae Catchings] to Louis Burnham, November 2, 1946, folder "Advisory Board, 1947," box 1, SNYCP.

96 John P. Davis to Louis Burnham, November 28, 1942, folder "Correspondence 1943," box 3, SNYCP; McDuffie, "Long Journeys," 390; Esther V. Cooper to W. E. B. Du Bois, September 11, 1946, folders "Columbia Conference," boxes 6–7, SNYCP.

97 W. E. B. Du Bois, "The Winds of Time" column, *CD*, national edition, November 11, 1946.

98 SNYC, "News Release," January 13, 1947 (577, 16, 3), *NNCP*; Grace Tillman, Minutes of Executive Board, December 7–8, 1946, folder 13, box 3, ESP; "Anti-Lynch Crusade Studies Candidates' Records," *CD*, national edition, October 19, 1946; Edward Weaver to President Harry Truman, folder "1947 Delegation to Washington D.C.," box 2, SNYCP; James L. Hicks, "Youth Ask Square Deal from Senators," *Pittsburgh Courier*, January 18, 1947.

99 Miss L. M. Patterson, "SNYC Institute Held in Berkeley County, SC," n.d. [early 1947], Leroy Aiken to Louis Burnham, December 9, 1946, and February 18, 1947, L. H. Lindsay to Louis Burnham, January 13, 1947, Elizabeth McCants to Florence Castile, April 3, 1947, all folder "Moncks Corner, SC," box 5, SNYCP; Miss N. L. Herd, Secretary, and Mr. Alvin Rucker to SNYC, January 1, 1947, folder "Anderson," box 5, SNYCP; SNYC, Clubs and Councils of the SNYC, n.d. [1946–47], and Abie Wilson, President, Report on Bus Transportation in South Carolina for School Pupils, n.d. [1947], both folder "Allen University," box 5, SNYCP.

100 John H. McCray, editor and publisher, *Lighthouse and Informer* (Columbia, S.C.), "The Voteless Are a Helpless People," speech given at A&T College, Greensboro, N.C., March 30, 1947, roll 1, JMP; "Columbia Ready for 'Jim Crow' Demonstration," *Charleston News and Courier*, November 3, 1946; O. E. McKaine, "Negro Vote Highlight in South Carolina," *Norfolk Journal and Guide*, November 11, 1946, in Osceola McKaine vertical file folder, African-American Biography, Reference Department, South Caroliniana Library, Columbia, S.C.

101 Esther Cooper Jackson to Herbert Aptheker, June 26, July 25, September 26, 1946, folder 2, box 2, HAP; Esther Cooper Jackson to Herbert Aptheker, September 11, 1946, folders "Columbia Conference," boxes 6–7, SNYCP; Louis Burnham to Herbert Aptheker, September 29, 1946, folder 2, box 2, HAP; SNYC [probably Louis Burnham], "A Word about Each Place," n.d. [early 1947], folder "Aptheker tour," box 2, SNYCP.

102 Louis Burnham to Theodosia Simpson, folder "North Carolina," box 5, SNYCP; SNYC, handwritten itinerary for Aptheker tour, and SNYC, "Number of Aptheker Pamphlets

Sent," February 1, 1947, both folder "Aptheker tour," box 2, SNYCP; Dorothy Burnham to Herbert Aptheker, February 12, 1947, and Aptheker to Burnham, February 15, 1947, both folder 7, box 2, HAP; Junius Scales to Dorothy Burnham, February 7, 1947, folder "Executive Board Meeting, 1947," box 1, Nancy L. Pinkard to Louis Burnham, SNYC, February 12, 1947, folder "Correspondence, 1947," box 3, and Abie Wilson to SNYC, March 27, 1947, folder "Allen University," box 5, all SNYCP. See also "Dr. Herbert Aptheker: Noted Authority of the American Negro People Speaks," March 25, 26, 1947, Ann Arbor, Mich., with excerpt from *New Masses* article from February 11, 1947, folder 9, box 2, HAP.

103 Herbert Aptheker to Dorothy Burnham, February 15, 1947, folder 7, box 2, HAP; SNYC [probably Louis Burnham], "A Word about Each Place," n.d. [early 1947], folder "Aptheker tour," box 2, SNYCP.

104 J. M. Hinton and Mrs. Andrew W. Simkins, statement in Herbert Aptheker, "Listen to the Rumble: South Carolina: 'They Are Still Battling,'" *New Masses*, March 16, 1947.

105 Modjeska Simkins to Herbert Aptheker, March 24, 1947, folder 2, box 2, HAP.

106 Barbara Griffith, *The Crisis of American Labor: Operation Dixie and the Defeat of the CIO* (Philadelphia: Temple University Press, 1988); Michael Goldfield, "The Failure of Operation Dixie: A Critical Turning Point in American Political Development?" in *Race, Class, and Community in Southern Labor History*, ed. Gary Fink and Merl Reed (Tuscaloosa: University of Alabama Press, 1994); Natalie Saba, "Alive, Kicking, and Carryin' On: The Mine Mill Union, Civil Rights, and the Red Scare in Tennessee, 1940–1955" (history undergraduate honors thesis, Northwestern University, 2005), copy in author's possession.

107 Osceola McKaine to Allan S. Haywood, April 14, 1946, and Haywood to McKaine, April 18, 1946, box 3, Southern Conference for Human Welfare records, cited in Thomas Krueger, *And Promises to Keep: The Southern Conference for Human Welfare, 1938–1948* (Nashville: Vanderbilt University Press, 1967), 140; O. E. McKaine, "What the People Say," *CD*, national edition, May 4, 1946.

108 Louis Burnham, Memorandum on 7th All-Southern Youth Congress to Members of Conference Planning Committee and All Officers, n.d. [early 1946], folders "Columbia Conference," boxes 6–7, SNYCP.

109 Philip Murray to Esther V. Cooper, "Greetings," SNYC, "Mike Quill, Other Prominent C.I.O. Leaders to Address Youth," press release, September 26, 1946, and Councilman Michael Quill to Esther V. Cooper, October 20, 1946, all folders "Columbia Conference," boxes 6–7, SNYCP.

110 "CIO Stands Alone Organizing South," *New York Times*, October 19, 1946.

111 "Russia Is Praised at Negro Meeting," *Columbia Record*, October 19, 1946; SNYC, "Final Call to Conference!" October 1946, 3 (105–8, 11, 3), NNCP.

112 For Winston-Salem, see Robert Korstad, *Civil Rights Unionism: Tobacco Workers and the Struggle for Democracy in the Mid-Twentieth-Century South* (Chapel Hill: University of North Carolina Press, 2003), 273–74.

113 SNYC, "Columbia Conference Pledges," October 1946, folders "Columbia Conference," box 7, and SNYC, Executive Board Meeting Minutes, January 3, 1948, folder "Minutes, Executive Board Meeting, 1/3/48," box 1, both SNYCP.

114 Louis Burnham to Theodosia Simpson, folders "North Carolina," box 5, SNYC, Executive Board Meeting Minutes, March 29, 1947, folder "Minutes, Executive Board Meeting, 1947," box 1, and SNYC [probably Louis Burnham], "A Word about Each Place," n.d. [early 1947], folder "Aptheker tour," box 2 (quote), all SNYCP.

115 Milton MacKaye, "The CIO Invades Dixie," *Saturday Evening Post*, July 20, 1946. On the Charleston strike, see Karl Korstad, "Negro, White Workers United in Dixie Strike," *PV*, January 12, 1946.

116 SNYC, Executive Board Meeting Minutes, March 29–30, 1947, folder "Minutes Executive Board Meeting, 1947," box 1, SNYCP; SNYC, "Youth's Stake in the Fight for Economic Security," press release, April 10, 1947, folder "SNYC," roll 14, JMP; McCullough, *Truman*, 547–82.

117 Edward K. Weaver to Harold E. Murray, Antioch College, Ohio, February 11, 1948, folder "Correspondence 1945–1948," box 3, SNYCP.

118 Anderson, *Eyes Off the Prize*; Eleanor Roosevelt correspondence from November and December 1946, frames 810–925, reel 3, part 1: United Nations Correspondence, Eleanor Roosevelt Papers (Bethesda, Md.: LexisNexis, 2003).

119 Frederickson, "The Slowest State," 177–202, quote from 178; McCullough, *Truman*, 586–93.

120 Esther Cooper Jackson, interview by Erik S. McDuffie, August 19, 2001, folder 25, box 1, transcript p. 2, JJP; Marjorie McKenzie, "Pursuit of Democracy," *Pittsburgh Courier*, January 25, 1947; Daniel J. Leab, preface, in *Red Activists and Black Freedom: James and Esther Jackson and the Long Civil Rights Revolution*, ed. David L. Lewis, Michael H. Nash, and Daniel J. Leab (New York: Routledge, 2010), xi.

121 See Scales and Nickson, *Cause at Heart*, especially 165, 167, 172, 177–80, 203–7. The SNYC's listing as a subversive organization by the attorney general became hard to counteract. In early 1948, for example, its Nashville Council wrote to the Birmingham leaders asking: "On what grounds was the SNYC branded Communistic?" See Vivian T. Hampton to SNYC, January 1, 1948, folder "Executive Board Meeting, 1948," box 1, SNYCP.

122 "Excerpt from To Secure These Rights: The Report of the President's Committee on Civil Rights (1947)," reprinted in Steven F. Lawson and Charles Payne, *Debating the Civil Rights Movement: 1945–1968* (New York: Rowman and Littlefield, 1998), 51–53; McCullough, *Truman*.

123 McKaine, "Europeans Shocked at U.S. Race Problems," *Norfolk New Journal and Guide*, August 23, 1947.

124 James Jackson on Rose Mae Withers, in "Memories of the Southern Negro Youth Congress," interview by James V. Hatch, April 5, 1992, in *Artist and Influence* 11 (1992): 175.

125 A. J. Clement Jr. to John McCray, folder "Clement, A. J.," roll 9, and Mrs. Andrew W.

Simkins, "The 'Lighthouse' Is Alive and Slugging!!" circular letter, March 27, 1954, roll 13, both JMP.

126 See John H. McCray, "South Carolina—The Way It Was," *Charleston Chronicle*, May 4, 1985; Paul S. Lofton Jr., "Calm and Exemplary: Desegregation in Columbia, South Carolina," in *Southern Businessmen and Desegregation*, ed. Elizabeth Jacoway and David R. Colburn (Baton Rouge: Louisiana State University Press, 1982), 70–81; Jack Bass and Jack Nelson, *The Orangeburg Massacre* (Macon, Ga.: Mercer, 1984, second rev. ed.).

Conclusion

1 Thelma Dale to Matt Crawford, n.d. [January–February 1946], item 60, box 2, MCP. For a compelling account of the SNYC's last convention in Birmingham and Henry Wallace's 1948 campaign, see Patricia Sullivan, *Days of Hope: Race and Democracy in the New Deal Era* (Chapel Hill: University of North Carolina Press, 1996). See also Gerald Horne, *Communist Front? The Civil Rights Congress, 1946-1956* (Rutherford, N.J.: Fairleigh Dickinson University Press, 1988).

2 Revels Cayton to Matt Crawford, November 25, 1946, item 55, box 2, MCP.

3 See Revels Cayton to Mervyn Rathborne, December 28, 1945, "Cayton, Revels," and George W. Crockett Jr. to Willard Townsend, November 21, 1946, "NNC/NLVC" organizations, all ILWU correspondence files, ILWUP; Dorothy Funn to Revels Cayton, January 8, 1946 (484–85, 33, 2), *NNCP*.

4 "CIO Council Leader Bars Negro Congress Support," December 14, 1946, and "Four Race Groups among 36 Officially Sanctioned by CIO," February 1, 1947, both *CD*, national edition; John Brophy, "Chapter XI: Union Building and Communist Intrigue," unpublished memoir, folder 5, box 38, John Brophy Papers, American Catholic History Research Center and University Archives, Catholic University of America, Washington, D.C.; John Brophy, interviews by Dean Albertson, "The Reminiscences of John Brophy," oral history collection, Columbia University, N.Y. (on microfilm), 672–945, quotes from 773, 944.

5 Revels Cayton to Matt Crawford, December 9, 1946, item 56, box 2, MCP; Al George to Ed Strong, December 19, 1946 (342–43, 32, 2), Naola Mae Smith to John Brophy, January 4, 1947 (375–77, 32, 2), Hugh Bryson to John Brophy, December 9, 1946 (766–67, 34, 2), and NNC, Executive Board Meeting Minutes, February 12, 1947 (660–61, 35, 2), all *NNCP*; George L-P Weaver to Louis Goldblatt, March 13, 1947, item 25, box 1, MCP.

6 Revels Cayton to Matt Crawford, January 14, 1946, item 49, box 2, and Cayton to Crawford, November 25, 1946, item 55, box 2, both MCP.

7 John Edgar Hoover, Memorandum for the Attorney General, February 11, 1946 (872, 2), and "Detroit Cops Raid Negro Congress Affair, Arrest 37," *Daily Worker* clipping, n.d. [early July 1946] (1579, 2), both *NNC-FBI*.

8 Ed Weaver and Louis Burnham, "Statement of Southern Negro Youth Congress Offi-

cials Concerning Attorney General Clark's Listing of 'Subversive' Organizations,"
December 8, 1947, box 7, SNYCP; "Groups Called Disloyal," *New York Times*, December 5, 1947.

9 See Ellen Schrecker, *Many Are the Crimes: McCarthyism in America* (Boston: Little, Brown, 1998); Michael Honey, "Operation Dixie, the Red Scare, and the Defeat of Southern Labor Organizing," in *American Labor and the Cold War: Grassroots Politics and Postwar Political Culture*, ed. Robert Cherny, William Issel, and Kieran Taylor (New Brunswick, N.J.: Rutgers University Press, 2004); and Korstad, *Civil Rights Unionism*.

10 Nelson Lichtenstein's biography of Walter Reuther explains how Reuther, after becoming president of the UAW in March 1946, waged a twenty-month battle inside the UAW to consolidate his power. See Nelson Lichtenstein, *The Most Dangerous Man in Detroit: Walter Reuther and the Fate of American Labor* (New York: Basic Books, 1995), 248–70, quote from 261. See also Herbert Hill, interviews with Joseph Billups, Shelton Tappes, and R. McBride, October 27, 1967, 10–11, 19–21, and Shelton Tappes, February 10, 1968, transcript pp. 7–8, Walter P. Reuther Library, Wayne State University, Detroit.

11 Lichtenstein, *Most Dangerous Man*, 377–78, 534; Tony Griggs, "Willoughby Abner Dies," *CD*, national edition, December 4, 1972.

12 CIO Cook County Industrial Union Council, Meeting Minutes, folder 2, box 42, Chicago Federation of Labor Papers, Chicago History Museum, Chicago; Christopher Reed, *The Chicago NAACP and the Rise of Professional Black Leadership, 1910–1966* (Bloomington: Indiana University Press, 1997); Erik S. Gellman, "'Armed Arbiters and Scrupulous Pioneers': The Chicago NAACP's Quest for Status, Welfare, and Dignity, 1933–1957," paper delivered at NAACP: A Centenary Appraisal Conference, University of Sussex, UK, September 24–25, 2009; James Jackson, interview transcript by Linn Shapiro, October 19, 1992, 1–2, folder 25, box 14, JJP.

13 Revels Cayton, interview transcripts by Richard Hobbs, August 1978, 19, May 1978, 22, 36, and July 1985, 40, Richard S. Hobbs oral history interviews with Revels Cayton, box 1, Special Collections, University of Washington, Seattle; Sydney Roger, "A Liberal Journalist on the Air and on the Waterfront: Labor and Political Issues, 1932–1990," interviews by Julie Shearer, 1989–90, pp. 541–43, Bancroft Library, University of California, Berkeley; Horne, *Communist Front*, 40.

14 See Stuart Svonkin, *Jews against Prejudice: American Jews and the Fight for Civil Liberties* (New York: Columbia University Press, 1999), 7, 132, 162, 177; and Marc Dollinger, *Quest for Inclusion: Jews and Liberalism in Modern America* (Princeton, N.J.: Princeton University Press, 2000), 6, 8, 129, quote from 130.

15 Mary Pattillo, *Black Picket Fences: Privilege and Peril among the Black Middle Class* (Chicago: University of Chicago Press, 1999); Beryl Satter, *Family Properties: Race, Real Estate, and the Exploitation of Black Urban America* (New York: Metropolitan, 2009).

16 "Teacher Threatened after Naming 23 Reds at U.S. Probe," folder 7, box 342, CABP;

"Communist Plot to Disrupt Red Inequality Bared," *Chicago Tribune*, May 9, 1953; "Stander Lectures House Red Inquiry," *New York Times*, May 7, 1953.

17 "Dr. Max Yergan Is Dead at 82," *New York Times*, April 13, 1975; David Henry Anthony III, *Max Yergan: Race Man, Internationalist, Cold Warrior* (New York: New York University Press, 2006), 228–70; Glenda Gilmore, *Defying Dixie: The Radical Roots of Civil Rights, 1919-1950* (New York: W. W. Norton, 2008).

18 "Negro Labor Leader Ferdinand Smith Deported," August 22, 1951, folder 3, box 343, CABP; "Smith, CIO Leader, Held as Alien Red," *New York Times*, February 17, 1948; "Ferdinand Smith, Labor Leader, 67," *New York Times*, August 16, 1961; Gerald Horne, *Red Seas: Ferdinand Smith and Radical Black Sailors in the United States and Jamaica* (New York: New York University Press, 2005), 152, 157–58, 167–77, 182, 196–202.

19 Esther Cooper Jackson, "This Is My Husband" (New York: National Committee to Defend Negro Leadership, n.d. [1950s]), 27–29, folder 3, box 4, ESP; Junius Scales and Richard Nickson, *Cause at Heart: A Former Communist Remembers* (Athens: University of Georgia Press, 1987), 209, 225–27, 248–50, quote from 249. See also Randi Storch, "The United Packinghouse Workers of America, Civil Rights, and the Communist Party in Chicago," in *American Labor and the Cold War: Grassroots Politics and Postwar Political Culture*, ed. Robert Cherny, William Issel, and Kieran Taylor (New Brunswick, N.J.: Rutgers University Press, 2004).

20 Revels Cayton, "Challenge to Labor," *March of Labor* (New York) (March 1951): 14–15, 28; Horne, *Communist Front*.

21 "Woman Faces 40 Years Jail, Fine for Perjury," March 8, 1952, and "Jail Woman Who Denies Red Ties," March 15, 1952, both *CD*, national edition.

22 See *Ralph Bunche: An American Odyssey*, a film by William Greaves (New York: Schomburg Center for Research in Black Culture, 2001).

23 "Sterling Brown, "Panel on Cultural Freedom," transcript of NNC conference session, April 28, 1940 (512–53, 21, 1), *NNCP*; "Howard Students Air Their Views," *CD*, national edition, June 8, 1940.

24 "Picket 'Gone with the Wind,'" *CD*, February 3, 1940; "Crowd Pass 'Wind' Picket," *Amsterdam News* (New York), March 16, 1940.

25 "Slogans for National Negro Congress Demonstration" (307, 34, 2), "Why We Protest" and "Why Picket Uncle Remus?" (8–9, 32, 2), Kenneth Spencer to Benjamin Fielding, January 31, 1947 (205, 34, 2), and "Wipe Out Jim Crow," NNC Cultural Conference, March 16, 1947 (291–306, 34, 2), all *NNCP*; "WHY WE PICKET," NNC, Los Angeles, NNC Vertical File, Southern California Library for Social Studies and Research, Los Angeles; Charlotta Bass to Matt Crawford, February 7, 1947, folder 23, box 3, R. F. Kemp to San Francisco NNC, April 15, 1947, folder 1, box 2, "Do Not Patronize the Coliseum Theatre" and "Don't See Song of the South," folder 16, box 3, and "Resolution against 'Song of the South,'" folder 1, box 2, all MCP; Langston Hughes, "Warning" (1942), in Langston Hughes, *Poems* (New York: Knopf, 1999). See also Leon Litwack, *How Free Is Free? The Long Death of Jim Crow* (Cambridge, Mass.: Harvard University Press, 1999), 51; "The Arts vs. Bias," *New York Times*, March 16, 1947; and James

Snead, "Trimming Uncle Remus's Tales: Narrative Revisions in Walt Disney's *Song of the South*," in *White Screens/Black Images: Hollywood from the Dark Side* (New York: Routledge, 1994).

26 Undated report, folder 26, box 10, MCP.

27 Svonkin, *Jews against Prejudice*.

28 "Generally speaking," Myrdal concluded, "the lower classes in America have been inarticulate and powerless." See Gunnar Myrdal, *An American Dilemma* (New York: Carnegie Corporation, 1944), xix, 669, 713–17, quote from 715; Herbert Aptheker, *The Negro People in American History: A Critique of Gunnar Myrdal's "An American Dilemma"* (New York: International Publishers, 1946), 17; and David W. Southern, *Gunnar Myrdal and Black-White Relations: The Use and Abuse of "An American Dilemma," 1944–1969* (Baton Rouge: Louisiana State University Press, 1987).

29 Wilkerson introduction to Aptheker, *Negro People in American History*, 9; Ralph Ellison, "An American Dilemma: A Review," in *Shadow and Act* (1964; New York: Quality Paperback Club Edition, 1994), 303, 314; see also Myrdal, *An American Dilemma*, 676, 713–17, 750, 789–91.

30 Edward K. Weaver to Harold E. Murray, February 11, 1948, folder "Correspondence 1945–1948," box 3, SNYCP.

31 Ellison, "An American Dilemma."

32 Myrdal, *An American Dilemma*, 757, 927.

33 See *To Secure These Rights: The Report of the U.S. President's Committee on Civil Rights* (New York: Simon and Schuster, 1947), iii, ix, 24, 88–92, 101, 139, 160–67, italics added; and Svonkin, *Jews against Prejudice*, 7, 197.

34 For the NNC and the SNYC in *American Dilemma*, see Myrdal, *An American Dilemma*, 817–18 and the citations on 1400–1402. See also Ralph Bunche, "The Programs, Ideologies, Tactics, and Achievements of Negro Betterment and Interracial Organizations: A Brief and Tentative Analysis of Negro Leadership," in Carnegie-Myrdal Study, *The Negro in America: Research Memoranda for Use in the Preparation of Dr. Gunnar Myrdal's An American Dilemma* (New York: 3M International Microfilm, 1970), original 1940 typescripts, Schomburg Center for Research in Black Culture, New York Public Library, New York; SNYC, "Youth Congress Statement Calls Bunche Evaluation in *An American Dilemma* False," February 24, 1944, press release (876, 6, 3), *NNCP*; Wilson Record, *The Negro and the Communist Party* (Chapel Hill: University of North Carolina Press, 1951); and A. Philip Randolph, "Why I Would Not Stand for Reelection as President of the National Negro Congress," *American Federationist*, July 1940, folder 2, box 279, CABP. For attempts to red-bait Bunche and Randolph, see folder 1, box 419, and folders "United Nations," box 538, both JBMP.

35 See Penny Von Eschen, *Race against Empire: Black Americans and Anticolonialism, 1937–1957* (Ithaca, N.Y.: Cornell University Press, 1997); Mary L. Dudziak, *Cold War Civil Rights: Race and the Image of American Democracy* (Princeton, N.J.: Princeton University Press, 2000); and Thomas Borstelmann, *The Cold War and the Color Line:*

American Race Relations in the Global Arena (Cambridge, Mass.: Harvard University Press, 2001).

36 Howard Zinn et al., *The Cold War and the University: Toward an Intellectual History of the Postwar Years* (New York: New Press, 1997).

37 Schrecker, *Many Are the Crimes*, 369; John P. Davis, ed., *The American Negro Reference Book* (Englewood Cliffs, N.J.: Prentice-Hall, 1966).

38 Southern, *Gunnar Myrdal and Black-White Relations*, 264, 268, 273, 283; Angela Davis quoted in *The Black List, Volume 2* (Indican Pictures, DVD, 2010); Angela Davis, "James and Esther Jackson: Connecting the Past to the Present," in *Red Activists and Black Freedom: James and Esther Jackson and the Long Civil Rights Revolution*, ed. David L. Lewis, Michael H. Nash, and Daniel J. Leab (New York: Routledge, 2010), 102.

39 See introduction, notes 9–15, 18.

40 Honey, "Operation Dixie," 225, 237.

41 Jacquelyn Dowd Hall, "The Long Civil Rights Movement and the Political Uses of the Past," *Journal of American History* 91, no. 4 (March 2005): 1245; Nancy K. MacLean, *Freedom Isn't Enough: The Opening of the American Workplace* (Boston: Harvard University Press/Russell Sage Foundation, 2006); Thomas Sugrue, *Sweet Land of Liberty: The Forgotten Struggles for Civil Rights in the North* (New York: Random House, 2008).

42 See Revels Cayton, appendix, in Richard Hobbs, "The Cayton Legacy: Two Generations of a Black Family, 1859–1976" (Ph.D. diss., University of Washington, 1989), 545–50.

43 Hall, "The Long Civil Rights Movement," quotes from 1235, 1245–46.

44 See Charles Payne, "The View from the Trenches," in Steven F. Lawson and Charles Payne, *Debating the Civil Rights Movement: 1945–1968* (New York: Rowman and Littlefield, 1998), 155; Charles Payne, *I've Got the Light of Freedom: The Organizing Tradition and the Mississippi Freedom Struggle* (Berkeley: University of California Press, 1995), 427–30; and Gilmore, *Defying Dixie*, 8. See also Barbara Ransby's brilliant biographical approach to Ella Baker, *Ella Baker and the Black Radical Tradition* (Chapel Hill: University of North Carolina Press, 2003).

45 Harold Cruse blasted the NNC as "the working-class sellout of the black ghettoes—by the Negro left." See Harold Cruse, *The Crisis of the Negro Intellectual* (New York: Morrow, 1967), 177. Since the publication of Cruse's 1967 account, historians have analyzed the complex connections between the 1930s–40s period and the late 1960s and have treated them as having more of a complementary trajectory. See Davarian Baldwin, *Chicago's New Negroes: Modernity, the Great Migration, and Black Urban Life* (Chapel Hill: University of North Carolina Press, 2007); Sugrue, *Sweet Land of Liberty*; Peniel Joseph, *Waiting 'Til the Midnight Hour: A Narrative History of Black Power in America* (New York: Henry Holt, 2006); Robert Self, *American Babylon: Race and the Struggle for Postwar Oakland* (Princeton, N.J.: Princeton University Press, 2003); Komozi Woodard, *A Nation within a Nation: Amiri Baraka and Black Power Politics in Newark* (Chapel Hill: University of North Carolina Press, 1999); Michael

Dawson, *Black Visions: The Roots of Contemporary African-American Political Ideologies* (Chicago: University of Chicago Press, 2001); Erik S. Gellman, "'The Stone Wall Behind': Chicago's Coalition for United Community Action and Labor's Overseers, 1968–1973"; and chapters in Trevor Griffey and David Goldberg, eds., *Black Power at Work: Community Control, Affirmative Action, and the Construction Industry* (Ithaca, N.Y.: Cornell University Press, 2010), 112–33.

46 For example, see Merl Reed, *Seedtime for the Modern Civil Rights Movement: The President's Committee on Fair Employment Practice, 1941–1946* (Baton Rouge: Louisiana State University Press, 1991); Harvard Sitkoff, *A New Deal for Blacks: The Emergence of Civil Rights as a National Issue* (New York: Oxford University Press, 1978); and Bernard Sternsher, ed., *The Negro in Depression and War: Prelude to Revolution, 1930–1945* (Chicago: Quadrangle Books, 1969).

47 Louis Burnham, "The Cry Is How Long, O Lord, How Long?" *National Guardian* (New York), February 13, 1961.

48 Thelma Dale, "Minority Opinion," May 6, 1946, radio program, Cleveland (723–27, 22, 2), *NNCP*.

49 Langston Hughes, "Let America Be America Again" (381–82, 17, 2), NNC; Staff Meeting Minutes, January 8, 1946 (198–99, 25, 2), *NNCP*.

Index

Note: Page numbers in italics refer to illustrations.

Committee, 130, 131; and Eleanor Roosevelt, 137; resignation from NNC, 143, 144, 146, 163; and Randolph, 156, 160; and MOWM, 161

Davis, Peter, 61

Davis, Robert, 81

Davis, Sallye Belle, 189

Davis, "Sister," 64, 87

Dawson, William, 60, 61, 204, 220, 221, 222

Dean, Arthur, 68–69

Defense Committee for Civil Rights, 36

De Mond, Marguerite, 14

Denmark Vesey Forum, 11

Denning, Michael, 181

Department of Justice, 131, 132, 133, 145, 202

Derieux, Florence, 215

Detroit, Michigan, 25, 77, 103, 120, 162, 163, 176, 209, 210, 233, 237, 251, 255, 257; and NNC, 135, 206, 207

Dewey, Thomas, 204

Dickerson, Earl, 57, 58, 60, 61

Dies, Martin, 5, 56, 130. *See also* Dies Committee

Dies Committee, 5, 56, 57, 60, 130, 131, 133, 149, 151

Diggs, Charles, 206

Dining Car Cooks and Waiters, 50, 57

Dining Car Employees Union, 50, 57, 126, 127

Dixiecrats, 29, 183

Dixon, Lessie, 97, 98

Dodson, Owen, 175, 177. *See also* "New World A-Coming"

Domestic workers, 24, 127, 128

Dorsey, Emmett, 16, 113, 114, 115–16

Doty, Ed, 50

"Double V" campaign, 171, 172

Douglas, Paul, 45

Douglass, Frederick, 71, 150, 173, 174, 176, 225, 253

Drake, St. Clair, 20, 24, 61

Du Bois, W. E. B., 182; and talented tenth, 11, 113; and 1935 Howard University conference, 16, 114; and integration, 22–23; *Black Reconstruction*, 33; and Davis, 121; and NNC, 121; *Color and Democracy*, 183–84; and SNYC, 213, 235, 243; Niagara Movement, 216; and World War II, 227, 228; and Pan-Africanist Conference, 228, 239; and Byrnes, 241; "Behold the Land," 246; and Council on African Affairs, 248; and Reconstruction, 239

Duclos, Jacques, 207, 208

Dunning, William: and school of historians, 235, 236, 246

Du Sable High School (Chicago), 50–51

Edwards, Thyra, 34

Einstein, Albert, 238

Elks (Improved Benevolent Protective Order of Elks of the World), 14, 42, 117, 118, 119, 139, 142–43

Elkuss, Bill, 231

Ellison, Ralph, 134, 153, 157, 180, 263, 264

Emancipation Proclamation, 173–74

Ennes, Howard, 123

Ethiopia: Italian invasion of, 113, 157

Evans, E. Lewis, 76–77, 83, 84, 88, 101, 102, 105, 106

Even the Dead Arise, 53

Executive Order 8802, 135, 139, 162, 174, 199, 266. *See also* Fair Employment Practices Committee

Executive Order 9981, 252

Export Leaf, 93, 94, 95, 96, 97

Fair Employment Practices Committee (FEPC), 65, 135, 169, 204, 208, 264; creation of, 162; in New York, 201

Fairfield, Alabama, 186, 188, 189

Fascism: fight against at home and abroad, 92, 93, 97, 106, 113, 122, 155, 160, 185, 188, 198, 214, 218, 226, 227, 233, 246

Fast, Howard, 236, 237, 259

Fauset, Arthur Huff, 198–99

FBI: and NNC, 137, 139, 142, 143, 209, 255; and J. Finley Wilson, 142; and Davis, 143; and MOWM, 160, 161; and *People's Voice*, 168; and CP, 209

Federal Writers' Project, 27

Federated Hotel Workers Union, 50

Fellowship of Reconciliation, 186

Fields, A. M., 29

Fifth Street Baptist Church, 72

Fisk University, 11, 187

Fitzhugh, Howard Naylor, 115

Flory, Ishmael, 11, 50, 55, 57, 61

Flourant, Lyonel, 11, 113

Folkes, Elben C., 98

Fontecchio, Nicholas, 43

Food, Tobacco, Agricultural, and Allied Workers (FTA), 104, 248, 257

Ford, Henry, 206

Ford, James, 16, 24, 25, 28, 55, 114, 143, 160, 207

Ford Motor Company factories, 77, 206

"The 'Forgotten Years' of the Negro Revolution" (essay), 167

Foster, A. L., 21, 22, 31, 40

Foster, William Z., 207, 208

Hughes, Langston, 11, 22, 25, 26, 71, 166, 209, 261–62, 270

Hunton, William Alphaeus, 115, 130, 143, 146, 172, 183, 184

Hutcheson, William, 15

I. N. Vaughan and Company, 80, 81, 84, 89, 94, 97, 98, 99

Ickes, Harold, 114, 129, 130

Ida B. Wells Club, 23

Ida B. Wells Homes, 50

Illinois Arts Project, 50–51

Illinois Labor Notes, 34

Indiana Harbor, 36, 38, 39, 40, 43, 44, 45, 47

Industrial Union Council, 143, 256, 258

Ingersol, Minneola, 39

Ingram, Rex, 209, 270

Interborough Rapid Transit (IRT), 193, 194

Interdenominational Ministers Alliance, 117, 119, 125

International Labor Defense (ILD), 12, 13, 131, 201

International Ladies Garment Workers Union, 50

International Longshore and Warehouse Union, 259

International Student Congress against War and Fascism, 113

International Union of Mine, Mill, and Smelter Workers, 188

International Workers of the World, 4, 35

International Youth Council, 227

Irmo, South Carolina, 230, 232, 245

Ives-Quinn Law, 200–201

Jack, Hulan, 200

Jackson, Augusta, 86, 189, 212

Jackson, C. E., 104

Jackson, Gideon, 236, 237

Jackson, Howard, 139

Jackson, James E., 64, 69, 103, 115, 243; and SNYC, 72, 212, 250; and TSLU, 82, 89, 94, 95, 97, 98; and NNC, 87; and militancy, 91; and Tobacco Organizing Committee, 98; and Cooper, 187, 227; in army, 208, 227; and internationalism, 226; and CP, 228; southern tour of, 228; departure from SNYC, 251

Jackson, Robert H., 131

Jackson, Wilhelmina, 127, 214, 215, 219

Jefferson, Joseph, 49

Jefferson School, 171, 198

Jernagin, W. H., 117, 149

Jett, Jenny, 169

Jett, Maude, 169

Jett, Ruth, 169, 191, 207

Jim Crow: as status quo, 9, 63, 65, 66, 86, 93, 105, 110, 113, 134, 146, 191; fight against, 65, 73, 75, 85, 94, 96, 98, 146, 155, 156, 158, 214; rise of, 174; as economic system of oppression, 264, 269

"Jim Crow Sunday" boycotts, 233

Johnson, Andrew, 174

Johnson, Charles S., 68

Johnson, Clarence, 127

Johnson, Henry "Hank," 25, 35, 39, 40, 41, 43, 45, 50, 52–58, 61, 157

Johnson, James P., 172

Johnson, Mordecai, 73, 113, 114

Johnson, W. T., 74

Johnston, Olin D., 219, 222

Joint Committee on Civil Rights, 119

Joint Committee on Employment, 193

Joint Committee on National Recovery (JCNR), 12–13, 23, 113, 121

Jordan, Rufus, 30

Kelly, Edward, 28, 45, 49, 57, 142, 221, 222

Kennedy, Kenneth, 230

Kentucky Federation of Labor, 105

Keys, Leroy, 122, 123; and coalition, 124

Kimbley, George, 36, 38, 39, 46

King, Martin Luther, Jr., 268

King, William, 119

Kingston, Steve, 166

Knights of Labor, 4

Kornacker, Naomi, 201–2

Korstad, Robert, 104–5

Kruck, Frank, 78, 86, 91

Krupa, Gene, 177

Ku Klux Klan, 28, 45, 56, 203; in Richmond, 96; in D.C., 110, 133, 257; and peonage statutes, 132; and violence, 214, 236; in South Carolina, 215, 219, 227, 234

Kyles, L. W., 122

Labor's Non-Partisan League, 57, 122, 151, 153, 155, 162

Labor unions: as means for economic and racial equality, 1, 11, 46, 47, 48, 50, 99, 104, 105, 113, 115, 150, 151, 155, 195; racism and antilabor movements, 125. *See also* American Federation of Labor; Congress of Industrial Organizations

La Guardia, Fiorello, 158, 194